On the Run

With greeting and
Good wishes to Dave
from Philip Ayre
1991

On the Run

by Philip Agee

Lyle Stuart Inc.   *Secaucus, New Jersey*

Published by Lyle Stuart Inc.
120 Enterprise Ave., Secaucus, N.J. 07094
In Canada: Musson Book Company
A division of General Publishing Co. Limited
Don Mills, Ontario

Queries regarding rights and permissions should be
addressed to: Lyle Stuart, 120 Enterprise Avenue,
Secaucus, N.J. 07094

Manufactured in the United States of America

Library of Congress Cataloging-in-Publication Data

Agee, Philip.
  On the run.

  Includes index.
  1. Agee, Philip.   2. Intelligence officers—
United States—Biography.   3. United States.
Central Intelligence Agency.   I. Title.
UB271.U52A34   1987   327.1′2′0924   [B]   87-10057
ISBN 0-8184-0419-1

To my father,
Who taught me never to give up,
and,
To my sons,
That they will learn the same.

Contents

On the Run

I

S.S. *Bahía de Santiago de Cuba*

"Why did I leave the CIA? I fell in love with a woman who thought Che Guevara was the most wonderful man in the world."

I couldn't believe I'd said it—in ten years of interviews and public meetings I never had before—but the crowd loved it. Applause, cheers, all sorts of commotion. I laughed too, but inside I was embarrassed. If I told the story it might sound frivolous, or at least diminish the political reasons I always gave in answer to that question. But I'd hooked myself and they were all waiting for more.

Maybe it was fatigue, maybe the *gemütlich* surroundings. I was in Munich, nearing the end of a ten-country speaking tour to raise money for the Maurice Bishop Foundation which had been set up in Grenada a few months after his assassination and the U.S. invasion.

It was the kind of meeting I like best: not in a formal auditorium where people are locked into chairs facing a stage, but in a "movement" center with tables, chairs, beer and wine, hot food, and no artificial separation from the audience. It was called the *Manege*, or

Circus Arena, the walls decorated with paintings of circus acts and animals. About half of the 250 people who came had to stand along the sides and in the back. "Go ahead," I thought to myself, "tell them how it happened."

And so I did, answering the same questions that have been asked at every public meeting, and in almost every interview, since I "came into the cold" in 1974. Why did you go into the CIA? Why did you leave? Why did you decide to expose their operations and work against them? Why haven't they killed you? In one variation or another these questions always come up, reminding me again and again that most people are as interested in the "personality factor" as they are in how the CIA operates—probably even more. At the beginning, when *Inside the Company: CIA Diary* came out, people asked, "But where are *you*?" I answered that I wanted to write about the CIA and not about myself. It didn't matter if I came out one-dimensional. Yet in Munich, as everywhere, they wanted to know more about the personal side.

For a young man of my background, I began, going into the CIA in the 1950's was nothing unusual. I'd had a privileged upbringing in a big white house bordering an exclusive golf club. I'd been an altar boy, educated by Jesuits in secondary school, then attended a leading Catholic university. I had even seriously considered becoming a priest at one time. My entire background and education were conservative, during the height of the cold war and McCarthyism. That meant conformity and acceptance of authority. Nothing could have been more natural than to go into the CIA to fight the holy war against Communism.

But there was also another side. I didn't want to go into my father's business, even though, barring unforeseen disaster, I could have been a wealthy man. Part of the reason, I think, was the racism I saw all around as I was growing up. One of my earliest memories—I must have been three or four at the time—is my parents' admonition not to kiss my nanny when she went away for a weekend. Anna Lily was what was then called a "live-in" maid, and since both my father and mother worked, she was the closest adult human contact I had. She dressed me in the morning, fixed my meals, played with me, bathed me, and put me to bed at night. "You don't kiss colored people," my mother said, she might have something—we can never know. Still, I loved Anna dearly and the acute sense of loss when she went away just didn't reconcile with not being able to kiss her goodbye.

A couple of years later I used to visit the laundry and dry cleaning plant owned by my father and grandfather. Eventually, thanks in part to military contracts, it expanded into one of Florida's biggest linen and uniform rental companies. But when I was a boy it still occupied the old wooden building where the steam pipes and presses made the heat almost unbearable. Most of the plant employees were black, and a lot of these were women who operated presses or worked on the mangles. Often in bare feet and skimpy torn dresses, they sang gospel songs in rhythm with the machines. When I'd walk in they would shower me with attention. "How you doin' today, Mr. Philip?" "You doin' all right in school, Mr. Philip?" "You sure growin' up, Mr. Philip." "My, how handsome you gettin', Mr. Philip." Their concern was honest and genuine, but it made me so uncomfortable. They were practically in rags, lived in shacks in "colored town"—while we lived in a big white house on the golf course.

As the business grew and improved, so did wages and working conditions for the "good darkies." Of course, racism was part and parcel of growing up in the South in the forties and fifties, but I think it may have been an unthought and unspoken factor in my reluctance to go into the family business. At the same time I never felt comfortable with the prospect of commerce, wherein one's achievement would be measured largely in dollars and cents. At university I switched from business administration to philosophy, then decided to study law. A couple of months before finishing undergraduate studies a message came from the university placement bureau—it's the office where big companies like General Motors and IBM come looking for junior executive trainees. The message was from a company all right: one I would later learn called itself internally *the* company. Someone from Washington wanted to see me the following week.

His name was Gus. He said I had been recommended for the CIA's most important training program, the one through which they recruited the future executive leadership of the Agency. He couldn't tell me much about it, or about what the Agency did, but that was all right because I told him I had other plans. I was going on to law school—which I did, but didn't stay long. Less than a year after the visit from Gus I had quit law school and would soon be drafted into military service.

I decided to write to the CIA and ask to be reconsidered for their training program. Why now? I didn't want to spend two years washing dishes and peeling potatoes on some army base. Gus had told me that I could do my compulsory military service as part of the Agency's program. I would spend a year in military training, receive an officer's commission, spend a year with a military unit in intelligence work, then be transferred back to Washington for the CIA's year-long training program. Eventually, if I wanted, I could receive an assignment overseas.

I had just turned twenty-two when I wrote for reconsideration, but my motives went beyond simple opportunism. My imagination was full of romantic fantasies of secret encounters in the dark alleyways of Vienna or Hong Kong. And I loved travelling. I had already spent a summer working in a sawmill in Alaska, and had driven twice from coast to coast. Just recently I visited Cuba where I'd seen the Presidential Palace surrounded by sandbags and machine guns. I wanted a life of adventure and intellectual challenge. If I wasn't going to be a lawyer, and possibly go into politics, I would be an intelligence officer, preferably in secret overseas operations. Intrigue and mystery: those were strong attractions. Besides, it would be a patriotic thing to do, and at the same time provide a good excuse for not entering the family business.

So that's how it happened. Six months after that letter I was in the CIA, and three years later, in 1960, I was in South America working under cover as an American Embassy diplomat. I was all of twenty-five years old.

"Yeah. I read your book. But why did you quit?"

I'll get to that. First I want to stress how normal, even prestigious, it was to go into the CIA in the 1950's. That was long before the world knew they were into political assassinations, torture and overthrowing governments. After you're in, the revelations and experiences come little by little as you work, and it's very easy to become career-minded. By that I mean an attitude of getting ahead, of promotions, of increasing responsibility. Most CIA officers, like people everywhere, also develop family responsibilities that demand a reasonable income and job stability. You almost never reflect on the morality of your work: it's a job that has to be done in the fight against the enemy.

So it was with me, in part. I spent six years in South America, about half the time in Ecuador and half in Uruguay, with temporary assignments in other countries. I learned the language, read histories of the countries where I worked, and spent most of my time with local people. I also worked in almost every kind of operation: recruitment of Communist Party members, liaison with Ministers of Interior and police, telephone tapping and bugging, falsification of documents and other types of propaganda, penetrations of Soviet, Cuban and other enemy diplomatic missions—you name it, I probably did it at one time or another. And all the while my chiefs wrote glowing reports on my work which brought me regular promotions. Prospects for a long and successful career were bright.

But there was another side. My work immersed me totally in the life of the countries where I lived. I knew them inside and out, and I spent almost every waking hour assembling information and using it to manipulate events. We justified this secret intervention in several ways. First, from 1959 on, we were fighting to arrest the influence of the Cuban Revolution which had an enormous impact throughout Latin America. The Cuban alliance with the Soviet Union then brought the principal adversary onto the scene. Second, we sought to divide, weaken and destroy our local "enemies" (every group from left social democrats to legal communist parties to armed revolutionaries) in order to buy time for our "friends" to make political and economic reforms.

As a counterpart to U.S. assistance, the Latin American governments were expected to enact reform programs such as redistribution of land and income to ease the extreme imbalances of wealth and opportunity. The combination of economic growth and internal reform would improve life for everyone, supposedly, and at the same time diminish the appeal of the Cuban Revolution. When John Kennedy became President in 1961 he greatly expanded the aid programs under the so-called *Alliance for Progress.*

During those six years in South America, even as I was working in the CIA, I changed. I started out in 1960 with all the idealism you could imagine, thinking that my work to prop up America's "friends" and to suppress its "enemies" was an integral part of the reform process. The early sixties was also a period, not unlike the mid-1980s, in which various Latin American countries were returning to liberal democratic electoral processes after years of military dictatorships. I felt very much a part of a new dawn in Latin America and of the defense of American interests against Soviet Bloc and Cuban encroachment.

We did our job, but what about the reform programs? By the time I returned to Washington in 1966 I had no more illusions about internal reforms. They hadn't happened. In fact, the more successful we were in our operations to promote repression of the left, the further away any possibilities for reform moved. Why? Because the pressures for reforms got correspondingly weaker. The result? The same old oligarchies, the large land owners and commercial interests, in other words our best "friends," continued enjoyment of their power, prestige and privilege as they always had.

I kept thinking about Brazil and the Dominican Republic. I knew the Agency had been working overtime in the early 1960's to undermine the reformist Goulart government and had played a key role in the 1964 Brazilian military coup. The following year Johnson sent in the Marines to prevent another well-known reformist, Juan Bosch, from returning to power. I wondered why we were so afraid of governments that put priorities on helping peasants and other poor people?

Gradually I began to understand that all the preaching about reform was nothing more than rhetoric, both in Washington and in Latin America, where it came from the very people and groups who most benefitted from my work. I saw them as no more than the current generation of a system of greed and corruption going back centuries. They weren't about to install reforms that might threaten their wealth and power. I asked myself: why should I spend a lifetime helping them? We might have the same "enemies," but without internal reforms those "enemies" would always have a cause—and not a bad one at that.

For me these were more feelings than articulated thought. Besides that, the work had become less interesting. It could, in fact, be a deadly bore to sit at a desk writing reports and shuffling papers. Back in Washington I considered resigning. I was only thirty-one and surely could find another way to earn a living. I even mentioned this to a friend, another CIA officer with whom I'd gone through the training program. Trouble was my marriage had fallen apart. I was living separately from my wife, and divorce was coming up. I needed to keep an income to provide for her and for two young sons born during my South American tour.

My new assignment was to the Mexico Branch of the Western Hemisphere Division—one of the regional divisions of the Directorate of Operations. I was put in charge of Headquarters support for operations against the Soviet mission in Mexico City. Only a few weeks into the job, and before I even started looking into other job possibilities, a secret cable arrived from Mexico City that would keep me in the Agency for two more years. It required an answer, and in this case the responsibility was mine.

Our Ambassador to Mexico, according to the CIA Chief of Station, had said that he wanted a Special Assistant for the 1968 Olympic Games. The person would be called the Embassy Olympic Attaché, and he would be responsible for official U.S. participation in the preparations and in the Games themselves. Although the Games were still two years away, the Ambassador wanted someone assigned as soon as possible, since already there were various preparatory activities going on. The Ambassador and the Chief of Station had discussed the fact that the Soviets and other communist missions were using intelligence officers in Olympic-related duties. Would the CIA, asked the Ambassador, be interested in providing an officer for Olympic Attaché duties?

The Chief of Station recommended that Headquarters consider the suggestion, adding that he believed assignment of a CIA officer under Olympic Games cover could help the Station's programs in many ways. For one thing the officer would be in a good position to monitor the activities of the Soviet Bloc intelligence officers working with the Organizing Committee, including the development of personal relationships with those officers.

Also, and perhaps of greater importance, the CIA officer would have direct access to the entire Organizing Committee which already numbered hundreds of people and would grow to several thousand by the time the Games arrived. This organizing milieu was filled with people of interest to the Station, but to whom direct contact by officers under Embassy cover was severely limited. Our man in the Olympics, wrote the Chief, could meet these people, make direct assessments of operational potential, and eventually some recruitments. Of special interest in this respect were the Station's continuing priorities for agent penetrations of the Mexican Foreign Ministry and the ruling Institutional Revolutionary Party, the PRI.

By the time I'd finished reading the cable I knew how I'd try to get it answered. I would propose myself. I had the qualifications: plenty of experience behind me, including development of personal contacts with KGB officers; fluent Spanish; a knowledge of sports; and the ability to meet and cultivate people. If I went to Mexico, I thought, I might meet people through whom I could find new work after the Games. Mexico also was a fascinating country, and I might even want to remain there after I left the Agency.

My plan worked, although not without some delay. The Department of State eventually decided to assign someone of their own—a former university basketball coach who had been working in the Peace Corps. By mid-1967 we were both in Mexico City and had set up our Olympics office in the Embassy. From then until the Games I did meet many people of interest to the CIA. But in the end I re-

cruited no one. I resigned in late 1968, following the Games, and
hoped to start a new life in Mexico City—leaving the CIA and all
those years far behind.

"What about the woman who was in love with Che Guevara?"

That's the good part. Muriel wasn't in love with Che or anybody
else when I first met her. She just thought he was wonderful. What
happened was this. The Organizing Committee planned a vast cultural program intended to rival the sports competitions in importance. There would be nineteen cultural events, with broad international participation, corresponding with the nineteen sports events.
The Organizing Committee assigned Muriel to work with the U.S.
Embassy in arranging for U.S. participation in the cultural program.
Within the Embassy, it fell to me to deal with her.

Muriel had grown up in New York City in a prominent family with
roots going back to the *Mayflower*. She'd gone to Bennington College
where she studied drama, but then she quit and married a Mexican
who worked in the Institute of Fine Arts. They had three daughters,
but the marriage failed; she'd been divorced about six years when we
met. She was seven years older than I, but that didn't seem to matter.
I liked her instantly, probably because her life, interests and outlook
were so different from mine. In contrast to the disciplined, security
conscious and often humorless life of an intelligence officer, Muriel
was a free spirit with an open mind, loved a laugh, and spurned convention. I'd already come part of the way to leaving the Agency and
she was the stimulus, without knowing it, that I needed to take the
final steps out.

All the political factors I mentioned earlier, especially my disillusion with liberal reformism, found a catalyst in Muriel. And the better
I knew her, the more nervous it made me about the Agency. The key
event was her reaction to the capture and execution of Che Guevara
in October 1967, just a few months after I'd met her. I had kept my
cover with her, pretending to be no more than a Foreign Service
Officer working as the Ambassador's aide in Olympic matters. But
one night—we were at dinner, I think—she remarked with strong
emotion how despicable it was that the CIA had murdered Che, one
of the great hopes of Latin America.

I didn't exactly choke on my food, but I knew one thing: I could
never tell her the truth about my real work, not for a long time anyway. If I told her, any number of disasters would follow. First, she
wouldn't see me anymore, and second, she might tell someone, a rumor would start, my cover would be blown, and the Ambassador

would order me back to Washington. It so happened that her closest friends had just returned from a couple of years in Cuba where the wife had taught modern dance and the husband had worked as a theater director. Muriel and I had been together a number of times with these friends, and there was no doubting where their political sympathies pointed—certainly not in the CIA's direction. So I just kept quiet, knowing full well that my involvement with her was incompatible with my work as a CIA officer.

After about six months our relationship had come to the point where we were seriously talking of marriage. But the question arose: how could I consider that kind of commitment to someone I couldn't even tell who I really was? There was no clear answer to that. Over the years you get so used to living a cover it becomes second nature. It's like having two lives, one the true one within the CIA, and the other a cover to everyone else. But the lie, or cover, becomes so natural, so normal, that it seemed okay to keep the facts hidden from Muriel. To tell her might have ended our relationship, and I'd already made my choice. I'd keep the CIA happy doing the Olympic work, and at an appropriate time I would tell them I was quitting for *personal reasons.*

Even so, it wasn't easy during those months keeping up a dual deception toward both Muriel and the Agency. With her I wasn't so worried because I was doing only the Olympic work and had no intention of using it for the Station's operational purposes. By the end of the year I'd be out, and the past would be past. But I was worried that Muriel's politics might somehow surface in the Station. It was no secret that we were together, and on one occasion—I think it was a diplomatic reception—we chatted with the Chief of Station, Winston Scott. Muriel disliked him instinctively—wondering aloud if he was a CIA man.

And so it came as a relief when, in early April 1968, I had the right opportunity to tell the Agency I was quitting. Scott told me that Headquarters had sent a cable informing him that I was to receive another promotion. He also said that arrangements had been made, including approval by the Ambassador, that following the Olympics I would move into the Station offices on the top floor and continue developing the contacts I was then making.

I told him the truth, in part. I said I planned to resign following the Olympics and also to marry Muriel, once my divorce was final. I kept my reasons strictly on the personal level with no mention of political disenchantment. I was sending about half my salary to the U.S. for support of my children and could hardly take on new responsibilities with my Agency income. In fact I was so weary by then of anything involving politics—including the CIA—that my only conscious concern was simply to get out and start a new life. But I had to be very careful with Scott. He had close personal relationships with the Mexican President and other top government officials. If he had the slightest fear that I might become a political problem, or a security risk, he could have had me out of Mexico in a day—whether before or after my resignation. I just had to be careful for the six months remaining until the Games were over.

Both Scott and Headquarters were surprised and disappointed when I said I was quitting. The promotion would have been my fifth in eight years—to the rough equivalent of lieutenant colonel in the military—which was fast by any standard. Then Headquarters started getting difficult about Muriel. They wrote that if I wanted to marry her I would have to fill out a seven-page biographic history on her, have her sign it, and send it to Headquarters. Obviously it would require my telling her I was a CIA officer.

With the biography I would have to request Headquarters' permission to marry her and at the same time submit my resignation from the Agency. Headquarters would then make a security investigation on which they would approve or disapprove the marriage. If they refused approval my resignation would be accepted. If they approved I could go ahead, but I could expect a transfer from Mexico either before the actual marriage or immediately thereafter.

It was dumb and ridiculous. She had no intention of leaving Mexico and neither did I. I told Scott quite frankly that I couldn't do it—that Muriel was so anti-CIA she would never marry me if I told her about my Agency affiliation, and that furthermore I doubted Headquarters would grant the security clearance. I said I'd simply wait until after my resignation when the Games were over. That was only six months away.

Years later, when I wrote *Inside the Company*, I had forgotten these problems with Headquarters over Muriel. I even wrote that I had "taken a chance" and told her that I had worked for the Agency. That was misleading because the most I might have mentioned was having had vague dealings with Agency people years earlier. The slip-up must have caused her problems. But I know the details now thanks to CIA documents on my resignation that I got in the late 1970's under the Freedom of Information Act (FOIA). From examining those documents I'm sure I didn't tell her, and I don't know why I wrote that I did.

But then I was faced with another decision, this one a dilemma involving my sons, who were then six and three. They had remained with their mother, Janet, in the Washington area when I went to Mexico. I started divorce proceedings, but she succeeded in delaying a final decree on property settlement and custody of the children. During the summer of 1968 I went to Washington for discussions at the State Department on U.S. participation in the Olympic Cultural Program. I then planned to take two weeks off to be with my sons, whom I had not seen for a year.

At this point a thoroughly unhappy custody dispute began, one that would remain unresolved for years. Domestic quarrels are seldom interesting to others, but this one developed into a serious threat to my cover in Mexico as well as a lasting family problem. What happened was that Janet rejected my plan to take the children to the mountains or to my parents' home in Florida. She insisted that I see them only at home—in her environment. I couldn't accept this. My lawyer told me that it was within my rights to take them to Mexico if I wanted. I did, and my wife's reaction was stronger than I expected.

She contacted the Agency in Washington, threatening to expose me as a CIA officer. Then she initiated proceedings for a court order demanding their return. Lawyers and Congressmen were involved, and the Agency was understandably upset. Scott told me to send them back after he got a secret "informal" letter from Headquarters instructing him to make clear to me "the facts of life," adding, "You will appreciate that this could well affect all of us if allowed to go too far." I hadn't known of this letter—it was another little gem I got under FOIA.

I stood on my rights and refused to be pressured, especially after the children said they wanted to remain in Mexico. Meanwhile I got a Mexican court order allowing them to stay, even though my original intention was for them to stay just two weeks, then until the Olympics were over, and finally permanently. It was one of those personal conflicts. I didn't want to exclude my wife from their upbringing, but I didn't want to be excluded—or restricted to seeing them during school vacations. During the three months to the end of the Olympics my wife didn't go through with her threat, and I kept the Agency at bay on legal grounds.

As soon as the Games were over, I went with my sons to Muriel's country house in the valley of Morelos below Cuernavaca. We spent almost every weekend there, and I was nursing a severe cold. I called the Embassy to report sick, but was told Scott wanted to speak to me immediately. So I drove back to Mexico City to read a most surprising cable. Headquarters said I was to return on permanent transfer back to Washington within two weeks, with my children. Otherwise I could resign. I told Scott how odd it seemed, when months before I had written that I would resign following the Games. So I did, and my departure from the CIA was final at last.

Again with Scott's influence in mind, I wrote a conciliatory letter of resignation expressing appreciation of the agency's understanding of my personal situation. I ended with an upbeat paragraph I hoped would eliminate any possible doubts that I might be a security threat:

> I will continue to hold in high regard the importance of the Agency's activities in the interest of the security of the United States. I am hopeful that as my personal crisis subsides I can be of use to Agency programs in years to come.

Under FOIA I received additional documents in which the Mexico City Station reported, at the time of my resignation, that I had done "practically nothing of value." The last official evaluation of my Mexican assignment was equally pleasing in that my work was "definitely less than satisfactory," and that I had made "little or no effort to fulfill [my] obligations to the organization. The result was an unfortunate situation in which little or nothing was accomplished for the benefit of the organization."

Also under FOIA I received the psychological assessment written on me during the training program in 1959–60. It was prophetic. While allowing that I was capable of the work required of a CIA officer, the assessment concluded: "The chances of his remaining with the Agency on a career basis are poor."

Of course, there was nothing deceptive in my efforts to preclude fears that I might be a security risk in Mexico. I may have had political reasons for rejecting the CIA, but I hadn't the wildest notion of taking any action: not of writing a book, or of speaking out, or of joining the growing anti-war movement in the United States. I simply wanted to start a new life with Muriel and forget all about politics, the Cold War, the Soviet Threat and the CIA. And I succeeded. From the day I signed the receipt for my retirement refund payment, I never returned to the Station and never met with any Station personnel. That was no change because I never saw any of them socially anyway. I wasn't giving up any friendships, since now my whole life was wrapped up in Muriel, my sons and her daughters, and our Mexican friends.

People sometimes wonder whether it's really possible to leave the CIA. There's a belief that, like the Mafia, once you're in you can never get out. Not so. Employees are entering and leaving every day. Operations also end for many different reasons, and the foreign agents working in them are released if not transferred to other operations. Besides, the CIA doesn't want unhappy employees who might become security risks, and like any business they fire employees who are unproductive or unneeded.

During the months following my resignation, I looked for new work in Mexico. At one point I wrote up a public relations youth project involving sports clinics, but in the end I went to work in a new company just formed by a friend I met in Olympic work. It had the perfect name for an ex-CIA officer: SPECTRA. We manufactured and sold mirrors, plastic mirrors of the kind you might install in a dance studio, or as a ceiling in a nightclub, or in commercial displays. For about a year I worked in this company, but in the meantime other things were happening.

For one, Muriel and I did not marry. It was her decision to split; a bitter disappointment for me. As I recall, even after leaving the CIA I didn't tell her about my Agency work, so that wasn't a factor. She had a number of problems, saw me as one of them, and decided to cool it.

We drifted in different directions, I toward a circle of Mexico City artists and writers who had progressive political ideas. I began to think about the possibility of writing a book on how the CIA operates. It could be a treatise on methodology, showing parallels between the Agency's operations in Latin America and in Vietnam.

Everybody I knew was against the war, and their influence on me was pretty strong. I had some idea of how the CIA had tried in Vietnam in the 1950's the same kinds of anti-communist operations that I had done in Latin America. And I knew it was the failure of these operations in Vietnam that brought on the introduction of combat advisers and eventually an army of half a million. Maybe, I thought, such a book would help the anti-war movement in the United States and elsewhere—maybe even help prevent other Vietnams by showing its roots in support by the CIA and other government agencies for corrupt oligarchies.

For months I only thought about it. After all, I had agreed in writing never to reveal anything I had done or learned in the CIA. There would be no way for me to write anything meaningful without describing the operations. More difficult was the continuing fear I'd always had about the Agency's influence in Mexico. How could I

write a book that would undoubtedly hurt the CIA while remaining in
Mexico? Maybe I could write it in secret, but what would happen
when it was published? I could submit it to the Agency for censorship, but what they might approve would be worthless. Then too, I
had to think about my sons, who had years of school ahead of them.

I can't recall a "moment of decision" or any event that led me to say
inside: "I'm going to do it." I had, of course, the same political reasons for writing a book as I had for leaving the Agency. But the decision was something else. Looking back, I think that the longer I had
the idea in the back of my mind, the more it changed from fantasy to
reality or from a possibility to something I would actually try. The
transformation wasn't a conscious process. It was almost like meeting
someone interesting, thinking over whether to call or invite her out,
then deciding and doing it.

Years later after being asked many times why I decided to write a
book, I wondered if the Jesuits had something to do with it. Perhaps
it was something from those early formative years. I remembered
how they drilled into you the moral dimension, i.e., the need always
to perceive and act on the difference between how things are and how
they *ought* to be, how I as an individual am, and how I should or
could be. My duty was to try to close the gap. I'd like to blame the
Jesuits, they're an easy target, both for my decision to enter the CIA
and for my decision to speak out. Activists, that's what they make of
their kids.

In early 1970, a little more than a year after I'd left the Agency, I
began to put my first ideas for a book on paper. These were mostly in
the form of chapter outlines and general ideas like the generic divisions of operations, i.e., political action vs. propaganda vs. parami-li-
tary. In fact it was much more like putting reflections on paper than
beginning a book. As months went by I doodled alone with notes and
outlines.

At the same time I began thinking the unthinkable: revealing secrets without CIA authorization. I didn't realize it at the time, but
something quite drastic had happened. The pressures of discipline,
secrecy and security consciousness that so straitjacketed my life as a
CIA officer had gradually faded away. Still, I was fearful enough to
discuss the book idea only with Veronica, as I now recall. She was an
artist and art dealer of Catalan origin whom I had started seeing after
my breakup with Muriel. She encouraged me to continue, and I
refined the chapter outlines, even wrote a little text.

In mid-1970 I was in Tampa visiting my father and Nancy. Her sons had been my childhood friends, and she and my father had married after my mother died. I discussed my idea for a book with them, and they did nothing to dissuade me. At that time Salvador Allende was running for President of Chile, and I was certain the Nixon Administration would use the CIA to defeat him—I had participated in operations against Allende in the last Chilean elections in 1964. I suppose that if one event encouraged me on the book idea it was the Allende campaign. Everyone I knew in Mexico was for Allende, and his program for nationalizing the copper mines and improving conditions for workers and peasants seemed appropriate.

I decided to go from Tampa to New York to speak with publishers about my book project. I knew it was a risk, that the Agency might now learn of my plans, but I thought a publisher's advance would allow me to quit SPECTRA and use the additional time for the book. The editors at Random House and Viking seemed to think I was a little crazy—I suppose because I really was nervous. The one editor who was interested, and who encouraged me, was a man named Barney Rosset at Grove Press. But he wanted me to write more before he could make a decision.

On my return to Mexico I began thinking of other possibilities for the future in addition to writing a book. Teaching was one that seemed promising, but I would need a graduate degree. So I looked into the programs offered by the National Autonomous University of Mexico (UNAM) which was just a few blocks from my apartment in Coyoacan. I settled on a masters and doctoral program in Latin American history and culture, enrolling in the fall of 1970. At the same time I tried all the documentation centers in Mexico City for research materials I needed for my book, but with scant success. The information I needed to reconstruct events, and to show the CIA's participation in those events, just wasn't around.

The studies at UNAM were the most stimulating experience I'd had in years. Time and again I thought to myself, if only I had known this, from this point of view, before I went into the CIA. In one of my seminars, on the history of Latin American thought, I met a Brazilian woman who had been ransomed from prison in the kidnapping of the American Ambassador in Rio de Janeiro. As she told the horror story of her ordeal as a political prisoner, torture and all, I kept quiet. But inside I was thinking of the CIA's successful campaign to subvert the elected government of Brazil and install the military dictatorship that had tormented her.

The university studies strengthened my belief in the importance of a book about the CIA. I discussed the idea with a Spanish writer whom I knew well enough to trust. He thought I was foolish to attempt to write the book in Mexico, and he promised to discuss my project with Francois Maspero, a French publisher, whom he planned to see in Paris in a couple of months. Maspero had published Che Guevara's Bolivian diary and might be interested.

The one factor keeping me in Mexico at that time was my children. If I left the university, and Mexico, should I take them with me to Europe? Would I have enough money to support them there while writing a book? The decision was taken out of my hands. I sent them to spend Christmas with their mother in Virginia, and she refused to send them back despite her promise to them, and to me, that they would return. There was nothing I could do, since my court order granting custody was valid only in Mexico. Another sad development, but like the split with Muriel it eliminated any further need to stay in Mexico. The book would now come first, and I could go anywhere to get it done.

In early 1971 I got word from Maspero that he was interested. But where could I find two things: the research facilities I needed and protection from the CIA? Paris might be a good location and so might Brussels or London. Cuba might be a possibility—Maspero had publishing connections there. But would the Cubans, against whom I had worked before, trust me enough to let me in? And could I find there the information I needed?

If the Cubans would give me a visa I would go and see. Only one condition: I did not want to be treated as a defector, in the sense of sitting for endless debriefings on CIA operations and personnel. I wanted to write a book, but did not want to risk violation of U.S. espionage laws.

From Maspero I received word that the Cubans would give me a visa. I didn't want to fly from Mexico City because passengers bound for Cuba in those days had to report to the airport three hours ahead of flight time, and their names were routinely checked with the CIA Station. The Agency even took photographs of all the passengers. The Mexicans would no more have let me on a flight to Havana than the CIA itself. The last thing I wanted was for the CIA to learn I intended to visit Cuba.

In April the UNAM student body went on indefinite strike. I think it was in solidarity with pay demands of administrative personnel. I would have several weeks free. Without telling anyone of my destination, I went to Montreal, got a visa at the Cuban Consulate, and took the train to St. John, New Brunswick. I would have a berth on the *Bahía de Santiago de Cuba*, a Cuban freighter that was to sail in a few days for Havana.

I took a taxi to the port and almost didn't get out. My ship was a rusty old tub, a World War II Liberty Ship built to last no more than ten years. It was now over twenty-five and showing every year. The bow had no rake, neither did the smokestack. Decrepitude and corrosion were everywhere. Still, the momentum of my trip from Mexico and my strong curiosity to visit Cuba led me to pay the taxi and report on board.

As I waited to see the Captain I observed that the ship was being filled from stem to stern with sacks of powdered milk. But my vision of the moment, and the days ahead, were from my favorite books of boyhood, the sea novels of Howard Pease. It was as though I had just stepped onto one of the tramp steamers of *Shanghai Passage*, *Wind in the Rigging*, or *The Tattooed Man*. For a former CIA officer embarking for Havana in 1971 the spirit of adventure could not have been more real.

The purser assigned me to a bunk in the very stern of the ship in a small cabin with one leaky porthole. My cabinmate was Pedro, an oiler who spent most of his time in the engine room or somewhere down in the ship where I wasn't supposed to go. For the first forty-eight hours, the sea was extremely rough and each time the stern lifted out of the water the turn of the propeller threatened to shake the ship apart. A steam engine, mounted right at my cabin door, drove the tiller, and each time the helmsman altered course, which was constantly those first days, the steam engine hissed and pounded like a half-speed jack hammer.

A week or so after leaving Canada we passed Miami—so close that with binoculars I could watch people sunning on the beach. By now it was quite hot, and I spent my last days on board painting superstructure and reading in the sun. During the traditional last-night-at-sea party I couldn't help regretting it was over. I just hoped the atmosphere after arrival would be as pleasant.

It was late afternoon when we passed through the narrow entrance to Havana harbor on the west side of Morro Castle. On our right a lovely palm-fringed park fronted on the channel, and there, in large numbers, were the families of the crew waving and shouting a noisy welcome home. By the time we moored it was already dark, and I went ashore with two young men who came to meet me on behalf of the Cuban Friendship Institute.

As we drove away from the port, through the oldest part of Havana, I noticed how different things looked from 1957. There was the Prado, formerly the center of town and bustling with people in the evenings. Now it was dark and almost deserted. And there was the Presidential Palace where Batista had lived, now closed and abandoned. We entered the Malecon, Havana's long seafront boulevard, for the drive out to 23rd, better known as La Rampa and now the center of Havana's night life. We turned in just as we came to the Hotel Nacional up on a bluff overlooking the sea, and a couple of minutes later we were in the Habana Libre, formerly the Hilton and easily the biggest hotel in town.

During the next few weeks I made lists of books and other background materials I needed, then visited the national library and other places where they might be found. The results were mixed, but I was determined to find everything I could there, and to write as much as possible before leaving. Nothing I was looking for involved secret information. What I needed most was information on political, economic and social conditions in countries where I had worked, along with current events from that period. I could fill in the details on our operations later, putting them into a context of local realities.

As the weeks went by my interest in Cuba and the revolution grew. I'd finished all the books I brought with me, was reading everything I could get my hands on, while battering the Cubans I met with non-stop questions. As my fascination and curiosity about Cuba grew, the importance and desirability of returning to Mexico waned. Still, I had my apartment and belongings there, together with personal affairs and other pending matters, not to mention my studies and possible future in teaching.

All the while what impressed me most was the friendliness and spontaneity of the Cubans I met—a total of perhaps fifteen from different documentation centers, from the party bureaucracy and from the Foreign Ministry. Were any of these intelligence or security officers? Considering my background some of them had to be. Yet there seemed to be no crisis of confidence. The first night in Havana I warned that for my book to be effective I must avoid any compromise that might suggest I had written it under their influence.

This meant I wanted to be treated as an author writing something of value for the people of Latin America and the United States. I did not want to go through the kind of "processing" that an intelligence service would arrange for a "defector." Additionally I knew that my ability to get the book written would be jeopardized if information on specific CIA operations began filtering back to counter-intelligence analysts at Headquarters because the finger could eventually point to me. The same might happen if the Cubans or other services began taking counter-measures against CIA operations that I knew about.

These were practical matters having nothing to do with loyalty to the CIA. I simply didn't want to get caught giving secrets on CIA operations to the Cuban intelligence service. They would come out in my book soon enough, I hoped, and in any case I was writing for another audience.

Looking back, almost fifteen years later, I admit that was a stupid and contradictory attitude: quite shallow and *petit bourgeois*. So many individuals and organizations in Latin America needed every bit of information I could have told them. But CIA officers can be so contemptuous of defectors from the Soviet Union and other communist countries that I had an insurmountable psychological block at putting myself in the defector category. Yet defector I was—not *to* any other country but certainly *from* the CIA and American foreign policy.

After a month or perhaps six weeks I was getting nervous about returning to Mexico. I worried that people would wonder where I'd been, that my rent was overdue, that I'd miss examinations. On the other hand there seemed to be a lot more I could do in Havana. After much reflection and discussions with the Cubans who were helping me, I decided to return to Mexico only to arrange personal affairs. I would withdraw from the university and return to Havana to continue on my book. Then I would go to Paris.

My decision to leave Mexico completely, and to drop everything else to get the book done, was in large part a result of what I had seen and read of the Cuban revolution. Such a contrast with the other Latin America that I knew, where Kennedy's grandiose Alliance for Progress had been a near-total failure. In Cuba they had all but wiped out illiteracy and started enormous investments in educational programs of all kinds. Radical agrarian and urban reforms had changed forever the lot of peasants and renters. The Cubans were trying, at least, to build a new society free of corruption and exploitation. No question that they were still far from their goals, and they were quick to admit it. On balance, though, revolutionary Cuba made the rest of Latin America look like it was in a political and social stone age.

Before leaving I toured from one end of the island to the other, visiting all kinds of development projects in education, public health and the economy. With the Cubans I left lists of the materials I had

located, or that I still needed to find, and they promised to bring it all
together by the time I returned—at most, I figured, a month later.
Yet I sensed something odd, a kind of resignation on their part that
suggested they thought I wouldn't be coming back. Not that anyone
thought I didn't want to, but that something, most likely the CIA,
would prevent my return.

In order to avoid the controls at the Mexico City airport, I decided
to return to Mexico via Europe and the U.S. That would be less risky
and would also give me a couple of weeks with my sons. I took an
Aeroflot flight to Morocco, then Air France to Paris. When I telephoned Phil and Chris I discovered that I had indeed been missed—a
number of people in fact thought I was dead. Janet came on the
phone to say that friends in Mexico had already turned my apartment
back to the owner and divided my furniture and other belongings.

I lied that I had been in Paris all that time, from where I sent several letters that must have gone astray. I assured Philip and
Christopher that I would see them in a couple of days, then called my
father in Florida to relieve him. I would take the children for a couple
weeks' visit with him and Nancy and forget returning to Mexico—
there was no need for that now.

On the flight to Washington I thought over all the ways I could get
out of the mess I'd made by staying so long in Cuba. There was really
only one. I'd have to stick with the lame "lost letters" ruse and try to
make it look as if I'd been in Paris all that time. And what if the CIA
had learned I was in Cuba? After all, they had computer lists of all the
travelers to and from Havana, including names from flight manifests.
Well, I thought, if they approached me about the Cuba trip I'd just
tell them I was sight-seeing. I had as much right to visit Cuba as Canada or Mexico, and if they didn't like it, too bad. There was no visit
from the Agency. They must not have known. To this day I don't
know how I slipped through the controls. I was as lucky as I was reck-
less.

While in Washington I mended fences with Janet over the children. We agreed that they would live with her during the coming two
school years but would spend Christmas and summer vacations with
me. Then they would come to live with me, wherever I happened to
be. I gave the details to my lawyer and asked him to draw up the papers. What a relief to have an amiable agreement after all the earlier
troubles.

At the end of August I was in Madrid boarding a flight back to Havana. During the months ahead I lived in a beach house in Santa Ma-

ria, making the twenty-minute trip to Havana whenever necessary by motorcycle. The hippie look was not in style in Cuba then, never was in fact, so when people saw this guy roaring along on a motorcycle in jeans and Mexican sandals, with long hair and a Zapata moustache, they looked like they were seeing a man from Mars. Nobody told me I should "go straight," but I got the point when a barber showed up at my house. Oh well, "when in Rome . . .," I thought, as he cut my hair.

Gradually I accumulated a pile of books, press clippings and publications of all kinds that I needed to refresh my memory and get the facts straight. Yet all the while I had a growing feeling of uneasiness that I wasn't making progress fast enough. What I had found was valuable all right, but it wasn't enough. When Maspero visited in November we agreed that I should return to Paris and continue there.

Before leaving I decided to take two steps that for me meant joining forces with progressive and socialist movements in Latin America, in particular the Allende government in Chile that was just ending its first year in office, and the Broad Front in Uruguay, a coalition similar to Allende's Popular Unity. In Uruguay elections were due in just a few weeks, and I was certain the Agency would be much involved to prevent another socialist electoral victory, or even a good showing.

First I wrote a long memorandum for the Allende government in which I described the ways I thought the CIA would be working to undermine them. These included financing and directing opposition front organizations among workers, students, peasants and women, fomenting strikes and street violence, propaganda, rumors, sabotage and paramilitary actions. I gave examples from my own experience in all these areas, in the hope that I could contribute to the Chileans' understanding of, and defense against, Agency subversion.

Then I wrote a letter to the editor of *Marcha,* the leading left-wing political weekly in Uruguay. I used Maspero's office in Paris as a return address. In the letter I said I was a former CIA officer who had worked in American embassies in Ecuador, Uruguay and Mexico. I described some of the ways the CIA intervened in electoral campaigns to favor certain parties and defeat others, giving past examples from Chile and Brazil. I said the elections in Uruguay were a logical and traditional target for Agency intervention, and I outlined some of the visible signs that would create a pattern. At the end I said I was writing a book on my work in the CIA and that I would be glad to provide additional details that might apply to Uruguay. I signed my name.

I gave the documents to one of the Cubans who were helping me
and asked him to pass them along to people who could judge their
usefulness better than I could. If they were considered worth
sending, fine. If not, that was okay too. He came back saying they
thought it was risky, with me about to go to Paris to continue my
book. The risk didn't matter to me, I said. Do with them whatever
you want.

I never forgot the last words of Alejandro, the person I had come to
know best in Havana, when we said farewell at the airport. "Felipe, if
you are ever able to get your book written, it will be an important
work for us, for millions of other Latin Americans, and for North
Americans too. But the CIA will never forgive. They will never leave
you in peace."

Years later in Munich, or in other public meetings, I could only
give the bare outlines of how I changed. Even now I'm sure there
were people whose influence I've forgotten. In many ways I was lucky
to meet the right people at the right time. These were human factors,
like Muriel and Veronica, who helped turn a set of intellectual conclusions into actions. But there was no sudden conversion in a religious sense. Instead I experienced a gradual, step-by-step progres-
sion, with both human and political influences constantly at work
until I reached the point, when I decided to visit Cuba, that I would
do whatever was required to put my knowledge and experience at the
service of those who needed it to defend themselves and their ideals.
I never thought I was unique in that sense—people are changing every day, and politically I was a late arrival. What made me different,
of course, was my CIA background.

"And why hasn't the CIA *done something* to you?"

Aah, but they have. Through the years they've constantly used
their agents and contacts in the media to plant articles discrediting
me. They've tried to make me look like everything from a traitor to a
drunk to a womanizer to a mental case. They, and their friends, have
had me expelled from country to country like a human pinball. But
these were political attacks that began after I had finished my book.
By then I was a public figure, notorious to some, and it was too late
for them to resort to physical violence like assassination. Besides, you
can't go around always looking back over your shoulder. If I were to
let fear dominate my life, I'd be paralyzed.

It was different during the years following my return to Paris while
I was researching and writing the book, and when I was still publicly
unknown. I was vulnerable to almost anything they wanted to do.

Again by luck and instinct, I escaped most of the plots they hatched—not always by much. Years later, in Munich, I didn't mention the danger that some nut or fanatic might come to one of my public meetings. But when people started crowding around my table at the end, as they always do, with more questions, I was ready to move pretty fast—kind of second nature I guess.

I went on with the tour. Thirty meetings in thirty-three days, each in a different city, from Vienna to Helsinki. Altogether people gave about $10,000 for the Maurice Bishop Foundation. No attacks, no hostility. Just universal condemnation of the U.S. invasion and its continued occupation of that small Caribbean island.

II

10, Passage des Eaux

Maspero warned me that the Latin Quarter was full of police and other undesirables, but some of the cheapest hotels in Paris were there, as well as cheap restaurants catering to students and North Africans. I rented a $5 a night room a few blocks from the Sorbonne. My sons Philip and Christopher, now ten and seven, would be flying over for the Christmas-New Years vacations, and I couldn't wait to show them around Paris. After they returned in January I would resume work on my book in earnest.

Like most foreigners just settling in, I was captivated by the beauty and elegance of Paris—then enhanced by the seasonal decorations, especially the white lights in the trees along the Champs Elysées. After first taking the Cityrama bus tour we went back by Metro to the most attractive places, like the Etoile, Pantheon, Hotel des Invalides and Montmartre.

Every bit the American tourists, and loving it, we had our portraits done at the Place du Tertre, went up the Tour Eiffel, roamed around the Contrescarpe, and went to an organ concert at Notre Dame on Christmas Eve. Each night we played the electronic games along

Boulevard Saint Michel, eating roasted chestnuts or, in my case, indulging my passion for fresh oysters. All in all it couldn't have been a happier, more carefree time.

One evening, after the marionette show at the Jardin du Luxembourg, we were resting in the hotel before going to Chris's favorite pizzeria, the one on Rue Saint Jacques with the yellow sign. There was a knock on the door, and Chris and Phil rushed to open it. Who should be standing there but Keith Gardiner, an old friend from the CIA. We had gone through the training program together, and he had become a specialist on Brazil. The last I had heard of him was that he bought a house not far from where Phil and Chris lived with their mother in Virginia. They knew Keith because his children went to the same school, and he helped coach the soccer team.

If Phil and Chris were happy to see him, I was not. He must have been sent by the Agency. Why didn't he ring from reception instead of coming straight up? And how did he know the room number? If he had asked down below the clerk would have rung. For that matter how did he know what hotel we were in? These and other questions rolled through my mind even before we shook hands. Something was up and I didn't like it.

"Hi, Phil. I was in London and thought I'd stop in to say hello. Janet gave me the name of your hotel before I left."

Bullshit, I thought. Janet doesn't know which hotel we're in. But I was stuck, just the way they planned it. In front of Phil and Chris I couldn't make an ugly scene, couldn't even ask him to leave. Before I could say much he invited us all to dinner which my sons thought was a wonderful idea—we would show him that great pizzeria with the yellow sign. I offered him a drink while I finished mine. He accepted, and we began an inane conversation about Holmes Run Acres, Falls Church, Virginia, the schools, his kids, and the soccer team.

I let him do the talking.

Okay, okay, let's go eat. As we walked through the lobby Keith said he'd be just a minute and would catch up with us on the corner. First he wanted to tell "a friend" who was waiting across the street not to wait any longer. He had come accompanied, he said, because he didn't know what kind of reception I would give him, obviously meaning friendly or hostile. I acted dumb but understood.

He rejoined us and we walked over to the pizzeria. More inane conversation. After dinner, as we were walking back toward Boulevard Saint Michel and the games, Keith said to me, out of the boys' earshot, that as I could suppose, he had come to discuss something with me. Would I speak with him alone? Sure, I said. I was curious and a little worried, but not especially intimidated.

I left Phil and Chris in the hotel to go to bed. Then Keith and I found a dark bar around the corner and took a table.

"What's up," I asked. "How'd you find my hotel?"

"The Paris Station got it through the police," he answered. Just as I suspected. Without hesitation Keith took out a sheet of paper, and while handing it to me said, "Helms sent me to ask what this is all about."

Umm, the Director no less.

It was a faint Xerox copy of something I could hardly read in the dim light. But there it was: shit, my letter to *Marcha* in Montevideo. I'll be damned, I thought, they got it and published it.

"Yeah, I wrote it. I'm also writing a book about the Agency, with Francois Maspero, that return address is his office." Surely they already knew this, but I decided to play it as relaxed and open as possible.

"Headquarters wants to know why you wrote that letter and why you included the stuff on election operations in Brazil and Chile."

"Look, Keith," I said, "I'm not the same person you knew in the Agency. I've changed. I think the Agency's operations in Latin America are wrong—wrong from every point of view except that of the rich minorities they help. I thought the letter might help the *Frente Amplio*, but I didn't know whether or not *Marcha* would publish it. Chances are ten-to-one that the Montevideo Station was up to its neck in those elections. The *Frente* didn't do so bad either—got almost twenty per cent of the vote."

Gardiner also wanted to know how I got hooked up with a guy like Maspero and what the book was all about. "The book? Well, it's about the Agency. So far I've been doing research on social and economic conditions in the countries where I worked, and some others. Against that background I want to relate political events and show how we influenced them. The point of the book is to make clear that we in the CIA, along with State, USIA, AID and the military missions, work to shore up the traditional power structures of those countries against the people who stand for change.

"You remember the Alliance for Progress and how miserably it failed? All that talk about fiscal reforms for redistribution of income and land reform to eliminate the *latifundia-minifundia* problems? The only place that really changed was Cuba and there it took a revolution to do it."

I reminded him that in our propaganda operations, for years we peddled the tired slogan, "Evolution not revolution," and the only thing that evolved were bigger bank accounts for our friends.

"You see, Keith," I went on, "our operations in Latin America went far beyond the mere collection of information. You know that as well as I do. We *used* the intelligence to influence events, and this included political repression through our friends in police and military services.

"Let's take Brazil, the country you know best. You know perfectly well how the Agency set up bases all over to funnel money and instructions out to the political opposition. Goulart was President as a result of democratic elections. Did we care? Hell no. The Agency organized and financed so much turmoil the country seemed ungovernable, and that's just what the military needed."

Keith listened without comment and I continued. "At the right moment they sent Goulart packing and set up their own government. And what's happening there today, after eight years of military rule? Institutionalized torture by security services the Agency trained. My guess is they're doing the same right now in Chile that they did in Brazil, and again against a democratically elected government."

He finally spoke. "At Headquarters they want to know how much you've written about operations and given to Maspero. He's no friend of the United States, and people are worried he might pass on your manuscript to the enemy?"

Oh, oh, I thought. What if they try to stop me. I'd better make them think I've done a first draft and that it's in safe hands. "I've written a 700-page draft. It still has to be edited, and some details added, but it should be ready in a couple of months. Maspero likes it. What's this about enemies? Who are you talking about?"

"The KGB," Keith answered, "the Cubans. You know who."

"I don't know about Maspero and the Sovs," I said, "but as for the Cubans they're no enemies of mine. I just came from there—spent almost six months in Cuba this year working on my book. It's a fantastic place. You ought to go and see for yourself what they've done." Shit. I shouldn't have said that.

"You were in Cuba? You're joking. How did you get in?" I was watching his reaction for some sign that he already knew, but his surprise seemed genuine.

"I got there. Maspero got me in. I thought I could locate research materials there that I couldn't find in Mexico. I found some stuff though not as much as I'd hoped. But I did have a great time. I lived at the beach, had a motorcycle and travelled all over."

Keith shook his head disapprovingly. His tone got graver as he went on. "Phil, Headquarters is upset enough about your letter to *Marcha* and your writing a book. When they find out you spent six months in Cuba they're gonna flip out. How the Christ did you get into that?"

"I just told you. I'm doing a book and I wanted to get background materials. You can tell them at Headquarters not to worry, I didn't tell the Cubans a thing."

"Who's going to believe *that*? Nobody. They're gonna think you defected. Do you want to be the first defector in the Agency's history? You must be crazy!"

"Look Keith. I told you I've changed. But I'm not a defector, not in that sense. And frankly I don't care what they believe or don't believe in Headquarters. So don't go on about Cuba. Forget it."

"They told me to remind you that you have to submit any writings on the Agency for approval before it's published—before anybody else, including Maspero, sees it."

"Tell those people to relax," I said, thinking of all the wild imaginings in the Office of Security and the Counter-Intelligence Staff. Those offices were peopled by paranoids who spent their whole careers trying to figure out the *true* loyalties of the Agency's staff employees and foreign agents. "Tell them I'm going to submit it all, and if they want anything changed I'll change it."

This was a lie, but I thought I should reassure them, for what it was worth. After all, I had a long way still to go, and didn't need problems from the Agency.

Keith and I continued talking. I evaded his questions on the specifics I had written about. He wanted to know if he would be in the book because if so he might have problems. The Deputy Directorate of Operations had just assigned him to a course in Latin American studies at the University of Wisconsin. He would be starting next September, the first DDO operations officer in living memory to be sent for graduate study. He would have to keep up his State Department cover while there, and obviously it would be blown if I mentioned him.

I told him truthfully not to worry—he didn't figure in the book.

"Too bad you can't study in Cuba, or even in Mexico," I said. "I thought I knew a lot about Latin America, but after I got going at UNAM it seemed like a whole world was opening up."

A couple of times I took the conversation back to Cuba, insisting that he study the revolution and, like me, go there and see for himself. We both knew the only way he could go was as a spy, but I'd taken the attitude that my trip was nothing unusual and nothing to cause alarm. I also told him that they should see my effort to write a book as a political question, not as evidence of personal animosity or a vendetta.

My argument was with the policymakers who used the CIA to manipulate and support reactionary political forces. As we both knew, the Agency was simply a bureaucracy—one more instrument of the President.

I decided to go back to the hotel, but before we parted he said he'd have to send a cable to Headquarters on our meeting. They would probably have some more questions for me, so would I be around the next few days and willing to see him again? Sure, I said. Come over to the hotel anytime. We'll probably go out to Versailles, maybe to Fontainebleau, but we'll be around. As we parted he said, "Phil, you shouldn't have gone to Cuba."

Back at the hotel I lay awake wondering what Keith's visit really meant. How much trouble was I in? What would their next move be? What about Phil and Chris? We still had a week before they were to fly back. Should I see Keith again? Should I answer more dumb questions from Headquarters?

I remembered Keith said they found me through the police. What else, I wondered, would the French services do to help them. Would they arrest me and send me to the States? Would the Agency just sit back and let me continue on the book without trying to bring me under their control? Not likely. The more these thoughts rolled through my head, the more I worried.

I began to feel closed in and panicky.

I decided not to see Keith again, even if that made them think I was afraid or had something to hide.

We would get out of Paris so they couldn't find us again. But where to? Where to? Spain, maybe? Spain, that's it. We could take a train to Spain, and Phil and Chris could fly back to Washington from Madrid. They'd love it there.

My mind kept racing. How do we get out of this hotel? They may have a surveillance team outside. Maybe the police asked the manager to call if we check out. We'll have to move fast, but we have all these bags. How do I do it without scaring Phil and Chris, or having them think I'm running away from Gardiner? I need help, somebody with a car, but not Maspero. I don't want to bother him with this.

I remembered a woman we'd met in the cafe on Boulevard Saint Germain. She spoke good English and had started up a conversation when she saw we were Americans. Said her name was Nicole, gave me her telephone number, wanted to meet again. What if she's part of the Gardiner operation? I doubt it. I'll call her and see if she'll help. I'll have to tell her the whole story, and I don't even know her, and she'll think I'm crazy, and she probably never heard of the CIA. But she's the only person I know in Paris besides Maspero.

Just after six I got up and was about to call Nicole when I thought: no, no, can't call from the hotel. They might keep a record and give her number to the police. Besides, if I go out now, there won't be many people on the streets and I can see if there's any surveillance. I walked a few blocks up toward the Pantheon. Nobody following. Then I doubled back to Boulevard Saint Germain, found a telephone and woke up Nicole. I said I was in trouble. Could I talk with her right now. She gave me her address, near the Port d'Auteuil, and I took a taxi over. Nobody followed.

She was half-asleep when I told her of my work in the CIA which I had to explain was the American secret service. I told her I had quit for political reasons and was writing a book to be published by Maspero. His name impressed her because besides publishing, he owned the Joie d' Lire, the biggest bookstore in the Latin Quarter.

She didn't really understand the significance of Gardiner's visit. She actually seemed amused, but agreed to help anyway. We could come to her flat and stay until we could catch a train to Spain. She thought there was one every night to Barcelona.

How to get out of the hotel? Gardiner wouldn't be back this morning, but maybe they'd put on a surveillance team about eight or nine. We had to get our bags over to Nicole's. We could be followed too easily in the Metro, same for a taxi. We needed a car to drive around a little and be sure, before coming to Nicole's. She didn't have a car, but she agreed to rent one and pick us up at ten just around the corner from the hotel.

I took another taxi back, packed our things, and woke up Phil and Chris. Over breakfast in the room I told them we were going to visit the pretty blond lady we'd met in the cafe. Then I asked if they wanted to take a train to Spain. A train? Spain? Sure!

At ten we carried the bags down, paid the bill as quickly as possible and left. Nothing suspicious outside, but maybe the manager is calling the police right now. Around the corner to the pick-up spot—and no Nicole. Shit! If the manager's calling the police somebody's going to be over here quick, and I don't want them to catch us standing on the street like this. Where is she?

About five long minutes later she pulled up in a little Citroen. We piled in, and she started off in the direction of her flat. I asked her to make a few turns and watched for cars following. Nothing, it seemed. Nicole was not taking my concerns very seriously. She kept laughing and pretending she was in a movie. Chris and Phil didn't know what to think. But once in her flat I felt certain we were safe.

I was dead tired from no sleep but I had two more things to do. I took the Metro to the Gare d'Austerlitz, bought tickets for that night's train to Barcelona, then another Metro to Maspero's office. He wasn't in, but I talked to his wife. I told her about Gardiner's visit, the *Marcha* letter, and the conversation. I didn't have to explain that I was worried. It showed. Then I told her we were going to Spain, and I would be back in about a week.

After a couple of days in Barcelona, and a few more in Madrid, the vacation was over. At one point Phil said he knew why we left Paris. It was Mr. Gardiner, wasn't it? "Yes it was," I told him. "You know I'm writing a book about the CIA. They sent him over to talk to me. They don't like the idea, and I decided it would be better not to talk about it anymore. Keith's okay. They sent him because he's an old friend who knows you and your mother. There's nothing to worry about."

At the airport I was grim. How many times have I had to say goodbye to my sons, not knowing when I'd see them again? Was I wrong to take them to Mexico, away from Janet? Will that Washington suburb environment spoil them forever? Will it make them nice, conformist, middle class sheep?

"Why can't we stay with you, Dad?"

"Well, you have school and I have this book to write . . . but let's hope you can come over during the summer."

Then that old, gripping sadness again. Bye, kids. Study hard. Big kiss. I'll miss you. God I hate to choke like that.

Another night train. Paris was cold and rainy, and now lonely and threatening.

What to do about a place to live? How could I avoid being found again? Maspero offered me his house in the south of France, but the documentation centers I needed were in Paris. I could change hotels every day, since police receipt of the registry slips must be a day or so late. I tried it for a few days, but sometimes I'd have to go to four or five hotels to get a room. And moving all my papers and books was too much. I decided to stay on indefinitely at the Minerve, one of the cheaper hotels on Rue des Ecoles not far from Maspero's office.

I was resigned to the fact that they could find me, but I took one precaution: I rented a safe deposit box at a bank near the Sorbonne for the text I'd written so far and other papers I didn't need each day. Then I rented a typewriter, began daily research in the Bibliotheque Nationale, and wondered what the Agency would do next.

Years later I learned that two courses of action were taken, one to restructure operations in Latin America, and the other to stop me from writing my book.

In 1976, Joseph Smith, a CIA officer I had known in Latin America, published his memoirs, *Portrait of a Cold Warrior*. He described how the Agency, after Gardiner's visit to Paris, reacted in near panic. "A defensive operation was started immediately and every activity, agent, and officer was scrutinized to determine if Agee had already blow them or if he could write about them in his book."

They must have thought I knew a lot because they decided to terminate "most of" the Latin American operations. All the Stations and many officers were involved. Smith spent the last year of his career issuing summary dismissals to agents in Mexico, which so upset him he decided to retire. Another CIA man later revealed the shut-down cost millions of dollars. Of course, for every operation they terminated, they would try to start another for the same purposes, but they certainly were put on the defensive—and I was still two-and-a-half years from finishing my book.

In the early 1980's, in my FOIA case, a Federal court forced the Agency to turn over some of their documents relating to this period. Most were heavily censored but not all. As soon as the Montevideo Station cabled Headquarters about the *Marcha* letter, a cable went to Paris asking for information on the return address (Maspero's). A four-page "Action Memorandum" was prepared for the Deputy Director for Operations giving background on the letter, my work in the Agency, and my resignation.

Strangely, the memorandum said that an item in my security file dated 19 December 1969, over a year after I'd resigned, indicated that I had married a Mexican woman. It had to be a reference to Muriel, but we had already split by then. The "Action Memorandum" said that "attempts to date to pinpoint the present whereabouts of Agee have been unsuccessful," but that the Paris Station was trying. After speculating on whether I had in fact written the letter, or whether it may have been a forgery, the memorandum went on to recommend certain actions, all of which were censored but no doubt outlined the Gardiner visit if I could be found.

Other memoranda flowed to the DDO. The Director of Personnel wrote of my performance in training: "He was particularly adept at interviewing and demonstrated an excellent grasp of tradecraft principles. His is industrious, intelligent, enthusiastic, persistent, and likeable. Probably due to his youth he is inclined toward impulsiveness and impatience. . . ."

Another memorandum reviewed the reasons for my resignation in Mexico, erroneously stating that Muriel and I had been living together. Still another showed that the Office of Security was analyzing my file, including the lie detector test I took when I first went in, and coordinating its work with the Counter-Intelligence Staff. Additionally, a memorandum was prepared on how the government regulations allowed for cancellation of passports.

None of that was surprising, but one document from that period was interesting, more for what it didn't say than what it did. It was a memorandum written by a psychiatrist or psychologist, whose name was censored, on a meeting in which various unidentified CIA men, including no doubt analysts from the Counter-Intelligence Staff and the Office of Security, discussed my motivations and what to do about me.

In part, their assessment was based on the psychological tests given me in the 1950's with the conclusion in 1972 that I joined the CIA for "largely opportunistic" reasons. Using those tests and information supplied by officers who knew me, the Agency shrink wrote:

> Thus, we would seem to be dealing with an individual who was especially driven to achieve success and recognition, who had overblown estimates of his own worth, and saw himself as superior to other individuals. There was a significant gap between his own self-estimate of his abilities and his actual abilities, so that he likely would feel he was not succeeding to the degree to which he was entitled. There was no particular evidence early in his career of significant ideological conviction. Rather, the impression is of a man whose primary loyalty was to himself.
>
> Although Subject, on several occasions, indicated he had no animosity toward the Agency at the time of his resignation, it is felt he protests too much. This would seem to be the type of individual who has difficulty accepting responsibility for his own feelings and probably has a need to blame others for his lack of success. A residue of resentful feelings toward the Agency for interfering with his career seems probable.

The mid-life period is particularly critical for individuals with especially high needs for achievement and recognition who are blocked in their careers and have unrewarding marriages. Emotional pressure built up during this age period to achieve success and recognition can often lead individuals to try new ventures.

The ideological conversion of which Subject speaks would seem to rest on a rather shallow base. It is probably his rationalization for this self-aggrandizing act. Yet, we do need to take note of the zeal and Messianic fervor of which several observers speak. Feelings of personal inadequacy lead some individuals to overcompensate by developing a Messiah complex, feelings of being a world savior.

If these speculations are correct it would seem that he would probably find nothing more delightful than engaging in warfare through the headlines. Indeed, he may even use his righteous indignation over attempts to squelch him as justification for further disclosures. The question has been raised whether his appetite for recognition could be satisfied. Our hunch is that Subject's appetite is insatiable, and would not be easily appeased.

Most individuals who behave in treasonous ways do not see themselves as traitors, but rather as serving a larger cause. To the extent that Subject has some fragile strands of loyalty remaining, it may be this would deter him from being too specific. It could be that a senior official could influence Subject in terms of protecting colleagues' and friends' identities, but such a contact may only whet his appetite, and, considering the lack of scruples and opportunism in other regards, I am rather pessimistic about the outcome of such a meeting.

There is a suggestion of decisiveness and determination in Subject's signing over his house to his wife. Patients about to commit suicide often plan in a decisive way for the future. This careful planning concerning the disposition of his property and the attempt to protect himself from suit or other action suggests that Subject means business.

Although Subject is apparently strongly driven to achieve recognition, and has many self and other destructive qualities, none of the material reviewed suggests that he is out of contact with reality in the sense of being psychotic. However misguided he may be, there is no suggestion in the data reviewed that Subject is suffering from a major mental illness or is legally incompetent.

In general, it is my impression that Subject is waiting with some relish to do battle, and that the more actively we confront him, the more counterproductive it is likely to be.

Waiting with relish to do battle? I wanted nothing less than trouble from them. Suicide? I had only signed as purchaser of that house when Janet and I separated so that she and our sons would have a

place to live. I'd never lived there. Not succeeding in my career? I
could hardly have been promoted faster or been given more responsibility. Messiah complex? At that time I couldn't have been less
confident or more doubtful of my future.

But those were small errors, it seemed to me, when I saw how little
consideration they'd given to the truth. In this and other documents
on "why is he doing it?", they came back time and again to a supposed
hostility that I must have had toward the Agency, toward *them*. Yet I
had told Gardiner truthfully that I considered the Agency only an instrument of policy, and that the policy of successive administrations
since World War II was the real issue.

It seemed they simply could not believe that a person can change
his ideals, values and goals and that intellectual growth was possible.
That there was a whole world "out there" inhabited by perfectly honest people who opposed American reactionary policies from political
or moral convictions and who would welcome and encourage me. I
suppose they could be forgiven their clinical, myopic approach—
they'd never had a case like this before. But they went ahead laying
plans to stop me, as I would soon enough see.

Evenings I began hanging out in Le Yam's, a corner cafe next to the
Minerve. Gradually I came to know most of the regulars, by face if
not by name. One was a woman of French Canadian origin named
Therese Roberge. She had married an American, divorced early on,
and raised her two children in New York. The previous summer she'd
decided to emigrate to France and was working temporary jobs as a
secretary.

Therese had a keen interest in politics and no small scorn for then-
President Nixon, so we spent long hours in Yam's talking politics over
beer and wine. As with everyone else I met I was careful to be vague
about the book I was writing—saying only that it was about American
foreign policy and Latin America.

As the weeks went by I felt safer. No more visits from the CIA,
thank god. And I met other people. At Yam's, I became friendly with
an American, a journalist in his twenties named Sal Ferrera. He
wrote for "underground" publications in the U.S. and had recently
published an interview with Le Duc Tho, head of the North Vietnamese delegation to the Paris peace negotiations. Another American
friend was Thea, a folk singer from Boston who lived in the room next
to mine. Through her I met a young French woman, Catherine, a
dropout from the University of Paris who was a cartoonist. During the
rebellion of May 1968 she had lived behind the barricades at Beaux

Arts designing posters. But she didn't like the Latin Quarter, so I usually saw her over in the Passy area where she lived.

In my research I branched out to other documentation centers where I found much of what I'd been searching for earlier in Mexico and Cuba. This was information on the distribution of income and land in countries where I'd worked, the political situation when I arrived, and other objective data I wanted in order to place our operations in context. What I couldn't find was specific information on the current events in those countries during the years I was there. Without this I couldn't describe our operations and their effects very well.

There was one possible solution, though, and that was in London. I'd been calling around looking for publications of the North American Congress on Latin America (NACLA), the progressive collective in New York that did excellent reporting. Someone gave me the Paris telephone number of John Gerassi, the American author who was also an expert on Latin America. He told me that the British Museum had a newspaper library where I might find some of the publications I needed. I called London and, sure enough, they had microfilm of all the major daily newspapers from the countries where I'd worked and the years I was there. I decided to finish getting what I could in Paris, then go to London for current events.

In the spring I went back to Havana on a short trip to check on research I'd left pending in the belief that it would be done in my absence. It wasn't, and worse, I noted a distinct lack of interest in my book. It seemed I was the only person who understood the kind of book I wanted, and the steps needed to get it done.

In Paris, Maspero also had his doubts. "Now you want to go to London? And you haven't even started the operational episodes? Your book was going to be on the CIA, not an encyclopedic treatise on Latin America."

I wondered if he was right—that I'd never get it done. We also had differences over a contract amendment and decided to cool it. I was on my own.

It was not a good time to fall out. By June my money was running low. I knew I had several more months of work in Paris, and had no idea how long the British Museum research would take. I wondered how I could get the money I needed to continue. Just enough to eat, pay the hotel, and get over to London. And another bitter pill: I wouldn't have enough money to bring Chris and Phil over in the summer.

Sure, I talked to them once in a while by telephone, but it wasn't the same. And it was dangerous "stealing" that professor's telephone in the university where people stand in line to make calls all over the world. Somebody's going to get arrested there, and it could be me.

I settled on the possible solutions to the money problem. First, I wrote Barney Rosset at Grove Press in New York telling him I was still at work and asking if he'd like to see what I'd written. I added that I was afraid to send it over by post lest it fall into the CIA's hands. He wrote back that he would stop in Paris to see me following the Frankfurt Book Fair in October. Great! I had all summer to get a presentable version read, and I knew he'd like it. The only thing lacking was the descriptions of operations that I'd write as I worked at the British Museum.

Meanwhile I needed money to get to October. I decided to take a chance and tell Sal Ferrera who I was and what I was doing. Then I'd propose that he do an interview with me, in which we would discuss some of the more interesting operations, and he could try to sell it to a major magazine like *Playboy*. If successful we would split the fee.

It worked. Just as I thought, he grabbed the interview idea and mentioned three or four publications that would probably be interested. Also thought my book was a great idea and would make a big impact in the States, especially in the anti-war movement. Next week we would do the first recordings.

It was late May then, and in less than a day my situation changed from relative calm to sudden fear. Sal came over to my hotel room to record the interview. After a couple of hours we decided to get some lunch, and I suggested the pizzeria with the yellow sign. We were walking along Rue Saint Jacques when Sal said, "Hey, don't look now, but we're being followed."

I stopped and looked in a shop window. "What do you mean? Where are they?"

"Just up the street," Sal said. "They went in a doorway. I think I saw three of them."

"Let's keep walking and be really sure. We can go to the pizzeria and see along the way."

Sal was right. It looked like three or four of them, an everyday surveillance team of the kind I'd run in both Ecuador and Uruguay. I didn't like it but thought we should try not to let them know we'd noticed.

Over lunch Sal suggested a way to shake them discreetly. We'd go back to my hotel where he could get his recorder, cameras and notes. Then we could walk down to the Sciences Faculty at Jussieu. The buildings are huge, and there are lots of them. We could go up an elevator, walk down a couple of floors, then take another elevator to the underground garage. From the garage we could walk out the other side, the river side, and they'd never know where we went.

We got Sal's stuff. At the university Sal suggested we go out on the roof—one of the low ones only two or three stories up. From there we saw the team below. They hadn't followed us onto the university grounds but were waiting by a *crêperie* on the other side of the street. Sal took five or six shots of them with his cameras, then we went to the garage and out the river side. Sal went off to develop the film, and I headed toward my hotel. I'd drop by his room the next day.

I walked roundabout, taking an odd turn here or there, wondering what the surveillance meant. Instead of going directly to my hotel I went to a cafe for coffee. As I sat there thinking, I got the same feeling of unease and alarm that I'd had after Keith's visit. I felt I had to do something to avoid more surveillance. I could change hotels each day, but that took so much time. Then I thought of Catherine. Maybe I could stay at her place for a few days while deciding what to do.

Catherine had no telephone, so I took the Metro over to the Passy station and walked the three or four minutes to her room. The building where she lived, 10 Passage des Eaux, was in an odd location— down a long walkway with steps that descended from Rue Raynouard to the Seine embankment.

Catherine's room was two flights up and halfway down a narrow corridor. Happily, she was in. Till now I hadn't told her the whole story, just that my book was on American policy in Latin America. When I told her I was a former CIA officer writing an expose she, like Sal before, thought it was a great idea. But then I told her of the Gardiner visit and of the surveillance a few hours earlier when I was with Sal.

I told her I needed a place to stay for a couple of days, and she agreed immediately. Only a couple of days, I said, because it's really too crowded here for two people. Her cramped room had barely enough space for the bed and a small round table with two chairs at the window. Off to one side was another, much smaller room where Catherine had a mini-refrigerator and a hot plate.

Catherine agreed that no one should know I was there, Sal included. Nobody!

After dark I returned to the hotel, packed, and left as quickly as possible. I took a taxi to a train station, was pretty sure I was clean, then took another to Catherine's room. It would be my secret refuge for the next five months.

At Catherine's I felt safe, but early on I developed the habit of peeking around the curtain at the walkway down below. A couple of days after the surveillance I called Sal to continue recording the interview. We set a time for the following morning at his place. When I arrived he was excited and worried because he had called me at the hotel. Thought my disappearance might mean the police picked me up.

No, no. I went to live somewhere else. Where? Can't tell anybody—can't get anybody else involved. I'll have to keep contact by calling you. He agreed I could use his address for my mail and give his telephone number for any emergency call. Then he protested that he might have to get in touch with me quickly. I promised to call him regularly.

I looked at the pictures of the surveillance team. Not bad. Only one print each? Sal, I want copies. He was evasive. Sal, I'll take the negatives to the darkroom and make prints myself. Finally he relented, and agreed we'd go together one night. We recorded another hour of interview and went to lunch.

On leaving the cafe we both saw the surveillance team again. How the Christ did they find us? Was Sal's telephone tapped? Did they get my call for the meeting? Better not call him anymore from the cafe near Catherine's. Better not call at all. Just show up. Or leave a note. We made arrangements to meet in a couple of days. Sal was going back to the Sciences Faculty to shake them, but I decided to go in a different direction. I couldn't be sure how many there were, but at least three stayed with me.

Then I started a procedure I would follow at least a dozen times in coming weeks to shake surveillance teams that picked me up on visits to the Latin Quarter. I went down the nearest Metro station, took a train to a station where two lines crossed, then walked to the platform of the other line. They had to stay pretty close to avoid getting caught behind the automatic gates, which nevertheless sometimes happened. Normally, though, I would stand near the door of the next train, let others get on, and then fade into the last passengers getting off. If any of the surveillants hadn't gotten on, I'd walk to a bench and sit down. It would be too obvious if the surveillant did the same, so he was forced to exit the platform. Usually I could get away on the next train or repeat the maneuver at another station.

At night, just to be sure, I would get off the Metro at the Bir Hakeim station, walk around outside, then across the bridge to the Passy station, and from there to Catherine's. Or, I would get off at Trocadero, about ten minutes' walk from Catherine's, and wander around the gardens and fountains of the Palais de Chaillot until I was sure.

One day my maneuver didn't work at the La Motte-Picquet station, so I walked out to the taxi stand and told the driver I wanted to go to the Etoile. They followed in another taxi. Mine stopped by the curb, theirs also about thirty meters behind. I purposely couldn't find my money. I turned around and saw they had quickly paid, their taxi was gone, and they were taking up positions. Then I gave my driver another destination. As we pulled away I couldn't resist giving them a finger through the rear window.

I usually wasn't so bold. Each time they picked me up I'd either been at Sal's or at Yam's talking with Therese and her Brazilian friends. It made me extremely nervous trying to get away and then to be sure before going to Catherine's. I wondered who they were and what exactly they were after. They looked French but could be Americans. Were they a team from the States? From one of the French security services doing a favor for the Agency? Did they just want to discover where I was living? If they did, then what? Could they be planning to kidnap me? Or worse? More and more I peered down at Passage des Eaux for suspicious-looking people.

I continued my research and typing. Catherine, meanwhile, had moved her drawing board and paints into the tiny kitchen and was spending almost all her time on her comic strip. It came out in a magazine six months of the year, but these were the off six months, so she had almost no money either. One day I had to take my rented typewriter back to the shop to get the deposit back. With this money we could eat for at least a couple of weeks.

Sal was transcribing the interview. When he finished, we would go over it together, make additions and corrections, then he would write it and send it in. But he seemed to be taking so long getting it transcribed. No, I was just impatient to get the money. But when I told him I'd turned in my typewriter, he loaned me money—not much, but it helped—and then got another typewriter for me. This one belonged to a friend of his who would be away for the summer. The friend had loaned it to Sal, and he was uneasy about lending it to me, but I could use it if I returned it quickly. Wonderful.

A couple days after the Watergate break-in, I picked up my *Herald Tribune* and got a shock. The address book of one of the burglars carried the name and telephone numbers of E. Howard Hunt, a consultant at the White House and former CIA officer. He was also employed at the Robert R. Mullen public relations firm. I rushed over to Sal's, thinking this would really get him going.

"Sal! Get out your tape recorder! I've got something to add that will tie the interview to the Watergate scandal. You can formulate the question later, but here's the answer. They say E. Howard Hunt isn't with the Agency any longer. Maybe, maybe not. But his employer, the Robert R. Mullen public relations company, has provided cover for the CIA in several countries.

"In 1966 while I was at Headquarters, I helped set up an office of the Mullen company in Mexico City as cover for Jack Kindschi, a CIA officer who'd worked under the same cover in Stockholm. I think the Mullen company was also used as cover in Singapore and Amsterdam. Could be that Hunt is still with the Agency, using Mullen cover in Washington. The person who would know all about it is Marty Lukasky, the Headquarters officer in Central Cover Division who handles the Mullen cover. Be sure and get his name in the interview so the press can find him. Great news, right?"

"Yeah," Sal answered, "but do you think we should put in the names of Mullen and Lukasky? It might cause a lot of problems."

"Don't be a dope, Sal. That's the idea. Now please, get those tapes transcribed so we can edit a final version and get it off. I've got to get some money in."

As I was leaving. Sal said he wanted to invite me out for dinner, a couple of nights later. It seemed odd, so formal when we'd always had meals together more or less spontaneously. But I didn't mind a free meal, and the Italian restaurant he suggested was a good one.

I came as planned, and as we were walking up to the Contrescarpe we passed the Mayflower, an English-style pub, where Sal said we should stop for a real British beer after dinner. Fine with me. From Marcel's we ambled back to the Mayflower and took stools at one end of the bar. I was hardly into my Double Diamond when a tall, attractive young woman took the stool on my left. Hmm. About twenty-three and what some would call well endowed. I noticed the *Time* magazine she was carrying and thought, well, she speaks English, see who she is.

"What's in *Time* this week?" My brilliant opener worked. We struck up a three-way conversation. She was American, name Leslie Donegan, graduate of Boston University, studied French at the Uni-

versity of Geneva the past year, spending the summer in Paris prac-
ticing the language. What was I doing in Paris? Writing a book. Ah,
the great American novel? No, it's on American foreign policy in
Latin America—I was a Foreign Service Officer there. Then you
speak Spanish. Sure. Me, too. I grew up in Caracas. My father was an
American businessman, my mother Venezuelan. They're both dead
now, but they left me enough so I can continue studies—at least I
don't have to find a job. And what do you think about our government
in Latin America? Stinks, that's why I quit. Me too, it stinks.

After a while I decided I'd better start my trek back to Catherine's.
Leslie suggested we all meet again sometime. She'd only just arrived
and didn't know anyone yet. Sure, I said. Give me your number. Sal
and I left the Mayflower, then went in different directions. No surveillance this time, I thought.

A few days later I went by Sal's to pick up a letter. He was still
struggling with the transcription. I asked him again to hurry it up and
told him that I was really hurting for money. He loaned me some
more.

"By the way," he said, "did you call the girl we met the other
night?"

"No, Sal, I'm not interested. Here, you take the number and call
her."

"Phil, don't you remember what she said? She's an heiress. She's
got money. Maybe she would help."

I thought it over for a week or so, then called. Oh, hi! Thought you
wouldn't call. Sure. Tomorrow night. Dinner on me. 15, Rue
Georges-Pitard, just below the Montparnasse train station. Eighth
floor. Right. See you then.

Leslie's studio apartment was in a modern building of twenty-odd
stories—a truly ugly monolith about ten minutes' walk from the
Plaisance Metro station. She'd fixed herself up real nice: faded designer jeans a trifle snug, a tight designer T-shirt, and the latest platform shoes. At dinner we talked mostly about ourselves, and I was
careful to maintain my cover as a former State Department diplomat.

For days afterwards I pondered whether to tell her of my project
and ask her help. Every instinct said "no." I hardly knew her. But I
was so desperate for money, I decided to tell her. Her first reaction
was to say she'd suspected I worked for CIA rather than the State Department. Then she agreed to help, gave me two five hundred franc
notes "for now," and asked to read during the coming weekend all
that I had written so far.

I agreed. What the hell, I thought. I hadn't written very much on operations, and what she'll get is only the beginning of a first draft. She'll see how important it is for me to reorganize the materials and get a typist, so that when Barney Rosset comes, it'll look good.

At the safe deposit box I got the draft and other papers, then stood with Leslie for two hours at the copying machine in the Sorbonne. The following Monday I went to her place to get the copy back, and to my relief she said she would finance my needs and the cost of a typist.

Within days Leslie said she was bored with Paris and was going to Barcelona to see her boyfriend. If I wanted, I could use her studio for the remaining two months—she would come back in September to turn it back to the owner. She gave me two thousand additional francs and said I could call her whenever I needed more.

So. My luck was changing. I had a perfect place to get the manuscript typed. I had money, and time enough to finish my Paris research, reorganize what I'd already done, and write it all up. Plenty of time till October.

Now who to type? Maybe Therese Roberge. Her politics were right, and she was a professional typist. But she already had a full-time job. And would she keep quiet? I'd take the chance and ask her. She accepted, said she could use a little extra money, and agreed to work at night. She also agreed to tell no one what she was doing for me, including Sal and the rest of the Yam's crowd.

During the weeks ahead I continued to live at Catherine's. I still evaded all queries, including those from Sal, Leslie and even Therese, about where I was living. With no one but Catherine knowing, it was the one place I felt really safe.

Days I continued research, nights I met Therese at Leslie's secret apartment where she typed for a few hours and I worked on my notes. Usually we took time off for dinner at a little cafe around the corner. We were making progress and my spirits were high, although going through my counter-surveillance routine every night left me weary and haggard.

Therese and I talked a lot about our children in the States. She worried about her son, who was in his early twenties and worked in carnivals—a tough scene she thought. Her daughter, Giselle, was a dancer with the New York City Ballet and having a fine career. One night we decided to stop by an "express telephone" we'd heard about. This was one of several in Paris where someone had drilled a small hole in the plastic over the counter. With a paper clip you could stop the counter and call anywhere for twenty centimes.

I talked to Phil and Chris for awhile, they were okay, and then
Therese called her daughter. After a while Therese gave me the
phone and I asked Giselle if she would deliver a letter to a journalist
at the *Village Voice* for me. I didn't have the address. Sure. No problem. Later I sent her a letter for Paul Cowan, whose book on the
Peace Corps I'd read, asking for advice on where to find certain information. He didn't answer.

Leslie called several times, each time inviting me to go to Majorca.
It was so much fun, she said. I needed a rest and would love it. Just a
weekend, she insisted. I told her I had to keep working, but I needed
more money. "Could you send some?" She did.

One night in September as we were finishing, Therese asked me if
I wanted to go to a party. It was the birthday of one of her Brazilian
friends. We took a Metro over. At the party I met Angela Seixas, a
Brazilian who had just arrived in Paris. She was in her early twenties
and had come to study mathematics at the University of Paris. I liked
her and we arranged to meet again.

On a subsequent visit with Angela she told me her story. She had
just been released after three years in a Brazilian prison. In 1968,
while studying at the Catholic University in Rio de Janeiro, she
joined the student movement against the military dictatorship. From
there she went into a revolutionary political party, then into the
urban guerrilla struggle. She was only nineteen.

One night when she and a comrade were entering a "safe" apartment, shots came from the inside. Her friend was killed immediately,
and she was wounded in the stomach. It was a trap by security forces.
They turned off the electricity, and in the darkness and confusion she
was able to walk a couple of floors up, get adhesive tape from someone, and patch her wound. Then she got to the ground floor and outside. A block away a patrol spotted her, saw the blood on her clothing, and took her away.

At the Villa Militar, a Rio security installation, they put her in a
torture chamber. She was stripped, strapped to a table, and wired.
Then the electricity started, along with questions. She refused to talk.
The shocks continued, made worse when they threw water on her.
Several times she fainted and thought she was dying. But a doctor was
there, and they revived her. They moved the electrodes to more sensitive areas. She passed out again and eventually awoke in a hospital
cell. They had cleaned and dressed her wound which was small in
front but left a gaping hole in the back. The torture sessions continued day and night.

After a week or so, convulsions caused her wound to split open. They didn't only use electricity—but every kind of beating and torment to inflict pain. In the end she admitted belonging to the party, but she had held out long enough to protect others. The trap, in fact, had been set after the capture the night before of a comrade who couldn't resist the torture. Eventually she was sent to prison, and when released got a passport through a family connection and left. Political prisoners who were released had to report weekly to the police, and often were re-arrested and again put through the torture chambers. A kind of terror she didn't want to endure. She felt she could serve more effectively from exile.

As I listened I thought about the Agency and its role in bringing the military to power. Then their training and other support for the Brazilian security services. God, what a horror story. Should I tell her who I am and what my book is about? I did, along with the Gardiner visit, the interview with Sal, the surveillance, Leslie and her money, and Therese's work. Several times Angela came over to the secret apartment, met Therese, and looked over the manuscript. I described many of the operations I was going to reveal, along with the true names of all the participants, both the CIA officers involved and their local agents. Trouble was, Angela spoke only Portuguese and French, while I spoke only English and Spanish. Therese was our interpreter, although other times we managed without her.

With Leslie's money coming there wasn't so much urgency for Sal to get our interview published. On thinking it over I was glad he was so slow. Another provocation like the *Marcha* letter wouldn't help matters. So I didn't mention it again, and Sal didn't either. In late September Sal received a letter for me, from my father about a visit he'd had from a lawyer in the CIA's Office of the General Counsel, a Mr. John Greaney. He'd come on behalf of Helms, the CIA Director, who was concerned about what I was writing. He gave my father a copy of the secrecy agreement I had signed, along with a copy of the most recent court decision in the Victor Marchetti case.

Marchetti had also worked for the CIA and was writing a book. I didn't know him but had read that the Agency went to court demanding that he submit his book for censorship before publication. The decision Greaney gave my father upheld the Agency's right to censor former employees' writings. Well, I thought, neither the Agency nor the court can touch me legally outside the States. Under no circumstances will I go back before publication. My book isn't going to be censored if I can help it.

Much later under FOIA I got Greaney's five-page memorandum on
his meeting with my father. He wrote of my father's hostility toward
the Agency and his defense of my right to write a book. He also concluded "from the home surroundings" that my father could support
me financially if I asked him. Then he wrote:

> I also explained that the Agency would like to talk to Philip about his
> trip to Cuba and in a very low key stated that the Agency did not make
> any decisions about criminal prosecution but this was entirely up to the
> Department of Justice. It should be noted that Mr. Agee did not react
> to the mention of criminal action, but I think he fully comprehended
> the impact of the statement.

Following the Greaney visit, and without doubt at the Agency's request, the Internal Revenue Service started harassing my father with
audits that lasted several years. They were looking for anything they
could use against him, such as evidence that he was financing my
book, in order to put pressure on us both. It didn't work. His accounts were in order.

Greaney also visited my ex-wife Janet. I learned of this through another letter sent in care of Sal. It was from Philip, my older son, just
turned eleven. He wrote:

> Hi,
> I wanted to tell you that a man from the government came to talk to
> Mom about you, but she did not say anything except your address.
> What they told her is that they wanted to pay you money to stop and
> that they would offer another job (the job I'm not certain about).

Money to stop, eh? Another job? Fuck you people.

Janet also wrote of Greaney's visit and quoted him as saying that I'd
had an outstanding career and that they were very disappointed when
I resigned. He'd said the same to my father, and with Janet he also
went through the Marchetti case. I should submit the book for approval, she wrote, as a "good American."

Leslie came back at the end of September to turn over the apartment to the owner, and just in time, because I needed money again.
But then she started some new problems. Against my advice she
moved into a hotel just down Rue du Cardinal Lemoine from Sal's,
and started hanging out in Yam's. Before I knew it she had told Sal,
whom she seemed to be sleeping with, all about her financing me,
leaving me the apartment, and Therese's work. That destroyed my

efforts to keep Sal from knowing of my support from Therese and Leslie. Oh, well. We've got over five hundred pages neatly typed, all ready for Rosset. He'll be impressed.

The next week I called on Rosset at his hotel. I didn't want to leave my manuscript with him, didn't know him well enough to trust him, so I got him to agree to read it with me at his side—just in case he had any questions. In a meeting with Sal, Leslie and Therese, we discussed the security situation. Somebody else should be with me just in case there's trouble while Rosset is reading the manuscript. Leslie volunteered. The next morning we sat with Rosset at a sidewalk cafe as he leafed through page after page. I was holding my breath and trying not to show it, while watching all the while for surveillance. It must have taken him two hours. In the end he handed it back to me, without great enthusiasm, and said he'd have to think it over. I should call him tomorrow at the hotel.

It can't be. I was so sure he'd take it, right then and there. What went wrong? Almost three years I'd been working on this. Had the CIA gotten to him? I was pretty shattered. But wait. He's thinking it over. When he does, he'll take it.

The next day he put me off, but suggested we meet the following day at a cafe on his way to the airport. Rosset told me the book had too much background on Latin America, and the tone was too academic. Besides, the last two sections were the crucial ones: the descriptions of operations, which I hadn't written. The part on the training course was good, also the theory and types of operations. But he wanted to see the rest before making a decision. And he wanted me to write it more as an adventure story.

Back at Catherine's I sunk into a chair, deeply depressed. After all this time and work I still didn't have an acceptable manuscript. All these months running away from surveillance teams. All those days peering out the window thinking they might catch me. All the worry about money. All that for nothing.

Catherine encouraged me not to give up. She said I had to go on. She brought a portrait of me that she'd done as a surprise. It was an ink silhouette done from a heroic angle accenting my shoulder-length hair and handle-bar moustache. I liked it but I felt even worse. I had been such a bad companion during these months, and a terrible lover. In response to her affection I was either evasive or just didn't notice. She had put up with all my troubles and tantrums, and had lived all the stress and pressures too. I felt down and out about everything.

III

Down and Up in Paris and London

Rosset's rejection was more than a severe disappointment. It left me completely dependent on Leslie for financial support, a situation I'd wanted so much to end. It wasn't only her occasional frivolity and silliness. She was so superficial politically. No real commitment.

I couldn't help wondering why Leslie was helping me. Was it for kicks? Adventure? Maybe. Certainly not for political reasons. Other things about her also worried me. One little item stuck in my head. When I saw her the first time after she'd read my manuscript, that weekend her Spanish friend was in town, she remarked with disapproval that I had written about Jim Noland, my Chief of Station in Ecuador. She thought it was wrong for me to name him, blow his cover, cause all sorts of problems. I agreed, falsely, and said it was only a draft. Later I would substitute aliases for any true names in the draft.

And why had she been so insistent that I visit her in Spain, even offering to send me a ticket, when she knew I had so much work to do in preparation for Rosset's visit? And after his rejection, when I felt so badly about not having money to bring my sons over for Christmas, she offered to help me go to the States, both to see them and to discuss the book with other publishers. How could she suggest that? She knew it was impossible. Yet another irritant: she kept complaining that I wouldn't tell her where I lived, as if I didn't trust her. In that she was right.

I also had problems with Sal. He hadn't wanted to give me photographs of the surveillance team. He was also evasive about the owner of the typewriter he loaned me. He had never finished transcribing the interview, and it could well have meant money for him. And he, too, still found reasons for needing a way to contact me. Why had I picked up surveillance so often after seeing him?

I discussed these doubts with Angela Seixas, thinking that her experience might be valuable in judging those two. She came over to Yam's a few times to meet them, and her gut feeling was negative. Neither, she felt, had political or ideological levels consistent with their professed interest in and support for me. She and I both agreed that I should break away from them.

Yet, Leslie had the only money available, and I still needed to get to London. I made a plan with Leslie and Sal. We would go to London together and work as a team. Leslie and I would research the Latin American newspapers, record our findings, and Sal would type out transcripts. That way it would all be finished quickly. Anything to keep the money coming. In London, if I could find financial support, I would break with them.

I wanted to stay another couple of weeks in Paris in order to see Dad and Nancy, who would be passing through Brussels on a tour. I hadn't seen them for more than a year, and I also wanted to discuss Greaney's visit with them. I would use this time to record what I could remember about a series of CIA operations—about forty in all—along with reminders of what to look for in London in order to fill out the picture. I worried about going to Britain because the Agency and the British services were so close. Just in case, I would leave copies of the tapes with Angela. If anything happened to me someone else could use them to finish the book.

One afternoon a couple of days after Rosset's visit, I took time off from my tapes for a meeting with Sal. I'd stopped going to his place to avoid picking up surveillance, so I set it for five at a cafe in the Latin Quarter called Choppe Monge. It was close to the Arenes de Lutece, a Roman ruin where it would be easy to spot and elude any surveillance. After seeing Sal I'd go through my park routine.

It was cold, rainy and getting dark when Leslie walked in carrying what looked like an old typewriter case. She had a bad cold but spoke with a sense of urgency. "Sal couldn't come because he had to go to a photo exhibit. But a guy came to his room, said he wanted his typewriter. He got very upset when it wasn't there. We said we'd get it back to him tonight. Can you get it and bring it right away?"

"Sure, sure. I can get it."

"Look. I got you another one. It's a little old—I just found it at a typewriter repair shop—but it works fine. At least you'll have something."

"Thanks Leslie. I'll take it and meet you back here in two hours."

"Can you make it quicker? Take a taxi home and back? I'll pay."

"I don't know. Two hours just to be sure."

I walked to the ruins, hurrying because I knew the gates would be closed any minute. Some men were standing around in doorways, and I couldn't tell if they were the surveillance agents. I ran through the ruins and out to a back street, then down a block to the Jussieu metro station.

Leslie's typewriter was getting heavy. I was only two blocks from Therese's flat and decided to leave it there. She never locked her place, and I could pick it up some other time.

She wasn't in but the door was open. As I placed the typewriter against a wall, I noticed an unsealed envelope with a letter inside on Therese's little table. It was addressed to her daughter, Giselle, in New York. Should I read it? I'd wondered about Therese too. Had she really come to Paris because she just couldn't stand New York and the United States any longer? That letter might tell me more about her. She's typed everything I wrote and knows a lot that could hurt me. Go on, I thought, read it.

I slipped out the letter, and as I began to read I was stunned. She was telling her daughter about all the tricks she turned during lunchtime near the Bois de Boulogne—along a street called "Baguette Boulevard." And she sold heroin hidden inside *baguettes*, those long loaves of bread.

Oh, no. It can't be. I couldn't have picked a hooker to type my manuscript. And a dope peddler? But there it was, with vivid descriptions of other prostitutes who worked the "B.B." "Baguette Boulevard?" I never heard of that street. Maybe there's a bakery there. Well, it's too late now. But I must talk with her about the absolute need to keep my stuff secret. She'd be vulnerable if the police knew she'd typed my manuscript. I'd have never believed it.

I made my circuitous way back to Catherine's, got the typewriter

Sal had lent me, then went back to Choppe Monge where this time
Sal showed up. He was in a hurry, had to get it to the owner, so we
agreed to meet for lunch two days later.

Over pizza, Sal, Leslie and I discussed our plans for London.
Leslie, still with a bad cold, asked how I liked the typewriter she
bought.

"I haven't used it yet," I said, "don't really need it right now because I'm doing tapes. I left it at Therese's flat for the time being."

She looked irritated so I changed the subject. "Leslie, I need
money for Brussels and London, enough to get there and live until
you and Sal arrive." How much? Oh, I'd say . . . thanks, thanks a lot.
That'll do fine. Ha! Got it. That's a load off my mind.

Next day I met Sal. He was worried. "Phil, Leslie is really hurt
about that typewriter. With that bad cold she went out in the rain to
buy it, then you left it at Therese's. Everybody knows she never locks
the door; she's already had her radio stolen. If somebody steals that
typewriter Leslie's really gonna be pissed off. Might just quit the
whole project. And then where would we be?"

Sal was right. I couldn't afford to lose Leslie's financial support at
this point, not with all the uncertainties facing me in London. On the
way to Therese's I decided to tell her I read her letter. She'd probably be offended, and I didn't want to lose her friendship, but I had to
warn her to be careful. Chances were that with all the surveillance
she's been a target too. Luckily she was in.

"Therese, the other day, when I left the typewriter here, ah, I saw
a letter you wrote to your daughter. I . . ."

She broke out laughing. "Philip, you don't know me very well, do
you? Even after all we've worked together. You know, Giselle's had a
very bad experience. Her brother was in trouble. She went to Texas
to help him, missed a couple of weeks' rehearsals for her Russian
tour. It was Balanchine's first trip back after fifty years. He dropped
her from the tour and she quit City Ballet. She's very depressed and I
was just trying to write something funny to cheer her up. You didn't
really believe that, did you?"

I felt like a fool and wondered how stupid could I be. Was I getting
paranoid or something? I took Leslie's typewriter to Catherine's,
thinking, "Baguette Boulevard"! If the Agency knew I was that dumb
they wouldn't have anything to worry about.

Saturday afternoon about five I finished the last of four tapes and
decided to buy some beer. I took my usual look out the window.
Nothing suspicious. On my return, when the elevator stopped on

Catherine's floor, I noticed two people standing down the hallway. It was dark, but I could see they were at Catherine's door as if they'd just knocked. They were a man and a woman wearing trench coats. Huh, I didn't know Catherine was expecting visitors.

Then something strange. As I approached the door, they backed off a little and embraced. Mmm. What does that mean? Are they friends of hers or not? I knocked, and Catherine opened the door. The moment I stepped inside my heart sank. I knew I'd been found. That man and woman had discovered my hideout. Oh my god, what now?

Catherine laughed when she saw them embracing in the dark. I closed the door quickly and said, almost whispering, "I think they've found me. I think those two are monitors of some electronic device in here."

"Yes," Catherine said, "the man had something like a hearing aid in his ear."

"And those coats. They both had something bulky under their coats. Catherine, listen, they're walking to the steps, now they're going down."

"Yes, I hear them. I'll see where they go. Maybe I can get a good look at them." She left quietly.

I know, I kept thinking. I know they've got me. Shit. That beeping sound in the hallway just as I reached the door. It was the same beeping sound I'd been hearing on my cassette-radio. That irritating sound when we played the FM. For a second in the hallway I wondered how the beeping could be so strong. But when Catherine opened the door I saw the radio was off.

What I heard was the listening device of those two people. There had to be a transmitter in the room. I turned on the radio. There it was, the beeping sound again. I got it in different places up and down the dial. But one place was strongest. Real strong. Could it be the radio itself? No. They would have found me months ago. What could it be? What the hell could it be? The typewriter? Oh my god, the typewriter! Leslie's typewriter!

It was sitting under the table. If there was a transmitter inside it would probably be directional, strong down one axis and weak on the other so they could get fixes. I picked it up by the handle, turning it slowly. There it was. The beeping on the radio got stronger and weaker as I turned it. The bug was in the typewriter. That fuckin' Leslie.

Catherine came back, breathless. "They went down the steps. All the way down. Either forgot the entrance was halfway down, or thought they could get out the service entrance. But they didn't have the key. They tried the door and couldn't open it.

"I walked over to the garbage containers, tried to look like I was looking for something. They embraced again but I think they were talking. Then they started up the steps. I let them get ahead, but when I got to the entrance they were gone. I think they went down the walk."

"Catherine, look, it's in here, in this typewriter Leslie gave me. See? As I turn it the signal gets weaker, then stronger, then weaker again. All depends on the angle to the radio."

I looked at the typewriter wondering where the transmitter was. Could it be in the roller? I didn't have tools to take it apart. I detached the lid of the case from the base and looked underneath the typewriter. Nothing there. I started to hook the lid back to the base and noticed something odd. The cloth covering on the inside of the lid looked different, right at the top. I peeled back the cloth a little. It was glued to a thin piece of cardboard which came way with the cloth.

Then I saw it. "Shit! Catherine, look at this! The whole inside roof is covered with little transistors, and batteries, and look at that: must be some kind of directional antenna."

How neat, I thought. Every little piece was set in its own notch cut out of a piece of plywood the exact size of the inside of the lid.

I opened a beer, took a long swallow from the bottle, and stared at the transmitter. I had that feeling of fear and desperation, like after Gardiner's visit and the first time I saw the surveillance. Catherine poured a glass of wine. "What do we do now?" she asked.

"Well," I said, "one thing's certain. I have to get out of here. Go somewhere. Hotels, moving every day. Somewhere up toward Montmartre."

I thought a minute, then said, "Catherine, I think I should stay here until later, say around ten, then go out, look around, and if nobody's there I'll go to a hotel."

But what to do with all my papers? I couldn't possibly take everything with me, then move it every day. And there was a lot I had to get rid of before going to London: stuff I'd brought from Cuba and all my notes for the tapes on operations. I couldn't let the operational notes fall into the Agency's hands.

Catherine had an idea. Tomorrow night, Sunday, everybody in her area would put out their garbage pails for collection on Monday morn-

ing. We could go around putting the papers in different pails, and in
the morning it would all be gone. Meanwhile she wouldn't leave her
room.

Good idea. I would also leave the typewriter and hope they would
think we hadn't discovered it. That way they wouldn't be sure I was
on to Leslie. Thank god I had already gotten the money for London.

About eleven I walked out and around a couple of blocks. Nobody
there. Then back to Catherine's for my suitcase, then a taxi over to
Montmartre. On the way I had the driver stop at a small hotel that
looked about right. Nobody followed the taxi. I'd be safe for the night.

I lay awake reviewing in my mind what the Agency had learned
through Leslie and Sal. Sal. Is he with them too? She gave me the
bugged typewriter, not Sal. He gave me the first one. Was that to set
the stage for the switch? I don't know. I don't know. What else about
Sal? All those things I always wondered about. Why wouldn't he tell
me about the owner of the first typewriter? Would they let Leslie
sleep with Sal if he wasn't part of it all? Don't know.

But one thing's certain. The "secret apartment" where Therese did
the typing was theirs. Some secret. They got everything on tape. All
the conversations with Therese, everything I said to Angela about my
plans and the operations I'm going to blow. All about how I'm going
to name all the names. Shit. They know practically everything. But I
got the money. CIA money got me through the whole summer and
fall and on to London. Ha!

Sunday morning I was clean. I checked into another hotel, then
took the Metro to Trocadero, walked through the gardens and down
to the Seine. Just to see if there was a stakeout around—I was pretty
close to Catherine's—I crossed over the river drive to the sidewalk
along the water. Looking down I noticed a small beach, sand and all.
That's it, I thought. That's where I can make a bonfire with all that
paper. Then we won't have to do the *clochard* number with the garbage cans.

Everything was okay at Catherine's. No stake-out that I could see.
I separated the papers I needed to keep from those I would burn. I
put these in Catherine's suitcase and carried it down to the river. I
jumped over the wall onto the beach where I crumpled enough papers to get the fire going, then started feeding the rest onto the blaze.
I only hoped nobody would call the fire department.

I looked at the smoke going over the wall toward the road, and suddenly I noticed a man filming with a small movie camera pointed in
my direction. He was standing at the wall not ten meters away. I

looked down in near panic wondering how they'd found me. Then I noticed the Eiffel Tower behind me. Was he filming me or the Eiffel Tower? I thought he had the camera on me and decided to get out of there.

I put the fire out, and when I looked again the guy had disappeared. What, I wondered, are they going to do with a movie of me making a bonfire with my papers?

When I got back up on the sidewalk with the papers in the suitcase, I thought of another solution. I would take the papers across the bridge to the Allee des Cynges, the long narrow island in the middle of the river. I had often taken walks there. I could tear the pages into little pieces and drop them in the river.

That didn't work either. There were too many people around staring as if I was polluting the river. And the little pieces wouldn't float away. No current. They stayed right where I threw them without sinking. Back to Catherine's.

After midnight we walked around, opening thirty or forty garbage cans, slinking along like thieves, hoping police didn't see us, stuffing in a little here, a little there. Got rid of it, anyway. Catherine and I said our goodbyes. To avoid any trouble she was going to her parents' house in the countryside for a week. We'd get back in touch after I got to London.

Now to Brussels and London. I wondered if the Agency would try to use my visit with Dad and Nancy to contact me. Maybe they would get the British to post an immigration lookout control on the boats from Belgium to England. I changed plans. I left all my stuff with Angela in Paris, including Leslie's typewriter. I would return to Paris after Brussels, then take the train from Paris. Maybe they wouldn't be watching for me on the Calais-Dover route.

The CIA left me alone in Brussels, but my meeting with my father was difficult in any case. He'd certainly gotten Greaney's point about criminal prosecution. Did I really know what I was doing? Was I going to submit the book for censorship? Why, of all places, did I go to Cuba? The Agency was pretty worried about that.

"Dad, have you been following all the troubles in Chile? Right now the whole trucking industry has gone on strike. It's a political strike, in fact a lockout, to bring down the government. A government elected by the people of Chile.

"I'm as sure as I am of my own name that the CIA is promoting and financing that strike. We did that kind of thing when I was in the Agency. No problem, because the Agency has paid agents in unions all over Latin America and in the international labor organizations. They're trying to sow chaos and provoke a military coup.

"Allende's no communist. He's a socialist and a nationalist who finally took back Chile's biggest natural resource, its copper. In my book I want to expose all this, showing exactly how the CIA is used to undermine democratically elected governments. I'll take whatever chances I have to in order to get that done. I'm sorry the CIA involved you."

I paused. "Don't worry. Those people are thugs and hoodlums who just happen to work for our so-called government."

My speech didn't help much. Dad was worried and nothing I could say would change that.

Nancy was different. "You show them, Phil," she said. "Don't let them get you down!"

My father gave me some money and suggested I buy some clothes. He was right. I really looked shabby. But I saved it for London.

Back in Paris I got my stuff from Angela: the big suitcase full of papers, a smaller bag with my tapes and other papers, and Leslie's typewriter. Even though it was bugged I wasn't going to leave it behind. It was a museum piece and my best proof yet of the Agency's work to stop me. Maybe it would impress a publisher in London.

I spent that night in a cheap hotel near the Gare du Nord where I'd take the train in the morning. As I was approaching the ticket control I saw Angela waiting. She was excited. The police had arrested Therese. Picked her up at Yams. Kept her four hours, asking questions about me. Then let her go. She seemed okay, but maybe I should call her from London. Yeah. Damn. I wonder what that means.

Carrying all that stuff in the rain from the train to the ramp to the ferry was a struggle, but I made it. Now, what's going to happen. Ah, that sign says they check passports at sea. After a long wait in line I gave my passport to the British immigration officer. The minute he saw my name he set it aside, told me to take a seat, and wait to be called over the p.a. system. Oh, god, what does this mean. Are they going to arrest me? Refuse entry? Send me back to France? To the States? Read my papers? Take them away from me? Take the typewriter away? Turn me over to the CIA?

The tapes! They might take those. Those tapes have all the details on operations I'm going to blow. It's what they *don't* know. Dammit. I didn't make copies for Angela. What about those joint CIA-British operations I mentioned on the tapes? How would the British react to that?

What to do? What to do? Gotta get rid of them. How? In a waste can? Somebody might see me. Somebody in this crowd is probably watching me right now. Can't flush them down a toilet. Maybe I could throw them overboard. Nobody will be on deck with all this rain. I'll go up those steps to the top deck. But what about my stuff? Maybe someone will take the typewriter. Or my papers. I'll have to take the chance. Ask this woman next to me to watch my stuff for a minute. O.K.? Thanks. I'll be right back. Up the steps, then another flight. There's the door. Not locked. Don't see anybody out here. Damn, it's cold. Throw them over, quick. Ah, look at them sail in that wind. Down to the bottom. That's it.

"Will Mr. Philip Agee come to the immigration counter?" I walked over.

"Why are you coming to Britain?"

"To do research at the British Museum in London."

"How long do you plan to stay?"

"About a month, maybe two."

"How much money do you have? May I see it please? That's not enough for a month in Britain."

"I know. My publisher in Paris will send me more as I need it. I'm just coming now to see if what I need is in the Museum."

"Where do you plan to stay?"

"One of these hotels here, in *Europe on $5 a Day*. This one at Sussex Gardens."

He made a note. "Mr. Agee, I'm going to give you leave to enter the United Kingdom for six months. Within one week of your arrival you must report to the Metropolitan Police at 10 Lamb's Conduit St. to register as a temporary alien resident. Here is your passport."

Shit. I'm in! Didn't even ask what I'm bringing. Didn't have to show Leslie's typewriter either. Damn! I didn't have to throw the tapes away. Oh, well. Two weeks' work. I can do them again.

I made three calls that night. First to Angela to tell her I arrived okay. Then to Therese. She didn't seem too alarmed. The police knew about my background in the CIA and my work on a book. They told Therese the U.S. considered me "an enemy of the state." Strong words. What was I writing about? Where was I living? They should have known this already from the typewriter.

Therese played dumb, and eventually they let her go. Her arrest

didn't make sense. The CIA and the French were surely working together. Both knew everything except what I recorded on the tapes.
They didn't have to ask what I was writing about or where I lived.
Why Therese, and not Angela or Catherine? Or Sal or Leslie just to
confuse me?

Then I called Sal. He was nervous about Therese's arrest, feared he
would be next. Leslie had already bugged out, went to Madrid the
same day as Therese's arrest. Sal was going too. Madrid? Why there?
You and she are supposed to come here. What about our plan? Things
are too hot right now. Maybe the British would give us trouble.

"Sal, come on over here. There's no problem. Can you call Leslie
and ask her to come to London? We have to get going right away."

My number here? Think quick.

"Sal, I'm changing hotels every day. Look. Take this number. It's a
public telephone. I'll be standing here tomorrow night at eight sharp.
If we miss tomorrow, the next night, same time."

Now it was clear why Therese was arrested: to give Leslie and Sal
an excuse not to come to London—too hot, eh? Two nights later Sal
called—from Madrid. He was just too nervous to come.

"Leslie's all right," Sal said. "She just wants to let things cool off for
now. Wants to talk to you, but she's in Granada at some house where
there's no phone. She wants you to come here."

"Sal, I can't take time off to go there. You both should come here
like we planned. Tell Leslie I'll need more money in a week or so."

In the next two weeks Sal and I spoke several times again. Leslie
wanted me to go there to talk things over. She would give me more
money there. She would send me a prepaid ticket to Madrid. No, I
couldn't fly to Madrid. I'd have to fly to France, then take a train or
bus. Go indirectly and hope I wouldn't have trouble from the Spanish
police. Leslie should send me the money and I'll buy the ticket. No,
she would only send a prepaid ticket.

The more they tried to get me to Spain, the more suspicious I was.
I knew the Agency and the Franco services were thick as thieves.
They could plan anything. Maybe a drug plant, then arrest, prison,
years on ice. Lots of Americans were in Spanish prisons for drug running out of North Africa. They won't get me that way.

In my FOIA case I later received documents showing that CIA
officers committed crimes against me during this period. These "illegal acts," according to the documents, came to light in the Justice Department when they were considering a CIA request to bring criminal prosecution against me in 1975.

The Justice lawyers found that the CIA actions against me were serious enough to prompt an investigation of whether Justice should prosecute the CIA people. If I had been prosecuted I would have had access to the details of these crimes through court discovery procedures. The CIA told Justice that the activities could not be revealed, so Justice could not prosecute me—then and in the years ahead when possible prosecution came up again. For reasons not revealed, the Justice Department also decided not to prosecute the CIA officers for what they did to me.

What were those crimes? Gerhard Gesell, the Federal Judge in charge of the FOIA case, acknowledged that the details were contained in some twenty-five documents that Justice and the CIA said I could not have because the information was classified. We asked him to release the documents, but he refused, saying that would cause serious injury to the national security. So I never learned the details. But all the indications suggest that the crimes were conspiracy at the very least—that they were planning something very serious for me, probably both in France and in Spain, with cooperation of the security services of those countries. Participation of the liaison services was the reason why the information could not be revealed.

It is ironic that the CIA's efforts to stop me precluded prosecution later when they asked for it. What were they planning? I would think anything from the drug plant I suspected to kidnapping to assassination. The documents make one thing clear: what they were doing was not routine or marginal.

London was depressing. All those old red brick buildings. And the rain and yellow street lights. After Paris it seemed so ugly. I didn't know a soul, and nights I had nowhere to go except that little dimly lit room in the "Bed and Breakfast."

No more *croissants* and *café au lait* for breakfast. Now it was watery coffee, greasy eggs, uncooked bacon, or those awful sausages they called "bangers." The bright spot was that the newspaper library was a gold mine. I did a new outline of the operations I had recorded, using Leslie's typewriter that actually worked pretty well. Then I started a routine, going each day to read the microfilm, and making notes on stenographic pads.

When I went to register with the police, I decided to tell them the name of the hotel where I was staying. I didn't want to give them any pretext for expulsion. I needed that library. I also needed money. What Leslie and my father gave me would last only a few weeks, and then I'd be really destitute—not even enough for the Underground out to Colindale at the end of the Northern Line. The newspaper library was way out there, not at the main building of the British Museum in Bloomsbury. I just had to get a publishing contract and an advance.

Someone told me that a certain peace group called the International Commission for Peace and Disarmament had an excellent documentation center. I went there and asked for some materials. They wanted to know who I was and why I wanted the publications. I was so desperate I decided to tell the truth, even though they would probably think I was crazy. After I told my story, a young man, a Cambodian, suggested that I speak with Robin Blackburn, one of the editors of the magazine *New Left Review.* I found the office just off Soho Square, but Blackburn wasn't there. The secretary asked who I was and what I wanted. Oh, no, not the whole story again. I decided to leave a short note saying I was a former CIA officer, trying to write a book about the Agency, and in need of advice on a possible publisher.

The next day Blackburn called me, and we arranged to meet late that afternoon. He listened quietly to my story and seemed duly impressed with the evidence of Leslie's typewriter. He thought my book had big possibilities. He offered to speak to Neil Middleton, his own editor at Penguin Books, about me. Within a few days I had a meeting with Middleton, gave him all I'd written so far, and explained what I still had to do. I could probably complete the manuscript within six to eight months.

The following week Middleton offered me a contract with a two thousand pounds advance. I couldn't believe it. Relief. Saved at last. I had hardly enough breath to say yes. Plenty of money to get to the end. And no more games with Leslie and Sal. They could stay in Spain waiting for me forever.

The first thing I did was call Phil and Chris and tell them I had the money for them to fly over for the Christmas vacation. I was so anxious to see them.

I spoke to Janet to give her the good news. "Sorry," she said, "they can't go. You come here if you want to see them."

"What? You know I'm writing this book and don't dare go back to the States now. You promised me last year that they could visit me during vacations no matter where I was."

She was adamant. "I won't send them. If you want to see them, come here."

As I walked away from the telephone I was furious. How could she be that way? I hadn't seen them for a year. She let them come last Christmas, why not now? And they so want to come. It just isn't fair to them, let alone me. Why her insistence that I go there? Could it be that she's cooperating with the Agency to get me back? Using our sons as pawns? No, it couldn't be. But it could. Janet later admitted that the Agency had asked her not to let Chris and Phil visit in the hope that I would be so desperate to see them that I'd return to the States. And she agreed.

Goddamned lawyer. Over a year ago I sent him money and the details of our agreement. Janet was ready to sign then, before the *Marcha* letter, before any problems with the Agency. But he didn't prepare the document. Twice in the last six months I'd written him anticipating this very problem. No answer. So now she didn't have a legal obligation to send them. I wondered if he was cooperating with the Agency too.

As my anger turned to resignation and depression, I remembered what Alejandro said in Havana the year before. He was trying to convince me of the danger of going to the States after I had been in Cuba. I told I couldn't wait. I wanted to see my sons no matter what the risk.

"Felipe," he said, "they're your Achilles Heel. The CIA knows that. They'll use it against you whenever they can."

In November Sal returned to Paris and sent a message through Angela that he was coming to London. I called him, and we arranged to meet at a pub after his arrival. I still had a lingering idea that Sal just *might* be clean. Maybe a meeting would help resolve the question. The key was the first typewriter he gave me. He had evaded telling me the owner's name even though I'd been somewhat insistent. Would he tell me now? I would start by telling him that Leslie is a spy. Then I would say I also have some problems with him, but would like to resolve them by asking him some questions.

Sal was offended when I said that, but agreed to discuss the matter. Name: Salvatore John Ferrera. Born: Chicago, 5 January 1945. Grew up Chicago North Side. Graduate of Loyola University (Chicago) 1966. Master's Degree in International Relations, same school, 1968. Studied for Ph.D. at Georgetown University, Washington, D.C., from 1968 to end 1970. While at Georgetown joined anti-war movement and helped found underground paper called *Quicksilver Times*. In August 1969 *QT* published names of some two hundred CIA employees. Participated in 1971 May Day anti-war demonstrations. Came to London June 1971, went to Paris in September. Received

French Foreign Ministry journalist's card January 1972. Began writing for Denver-based College Press Service and Berkeley-based Alternative Features Service.

"Sal, you remember that typewriter you lent me last summer, the one someone had left with you? What was the owner's name?"

"I can't tell you. He's someone I met, and have cultivated as a source on the French student movement. I won't tell you my sources."

"Sal, what do you mean source? I'm talking about a typewriter, not information. I don't want to know your sources, just who owned that typewriter."

We went on about the typewriter for about five more minutes. Then I said, "If you can't tell me the name of that person, I can't see you anymore. I won't tell you why, and I won't see you again."

Sal was clearly upset. He protested and said he was offering to continue helping me on the book. I said, "Goodbye, Sal," and left the pub. I was convinced that the Agency had given Sal the typewriter so they could arrange the switch with the bugged one later, when they had it ready. After meeting me Sal had made a trip to Frankfurt, where the Agency has a large technical support center—just the place where they could make the installation in the second typewriter—but Sal wouldn't talk about that trip either. They hadn't given him a backup for ownership of the first one. "Source." What a lame excuse.

London was dreadfully lonely as the end of the year approached. I didn't dare start meeting people at a pub like Yam's. But I remembered Wolf and Shirley Rilla, a couple from London whom I'd met in Mexico. He was a writer and film director who made a movie on the Olympics. Muriel and I had spent some time with them. I found them in the telephone book, and they invited me over. They were sympathetic—a relief to have someone to talk with—and my visits became fairly regular. They also agreed that I could use their address for correspondence and their telephone for any emergency call from the States.

But then I noticed surveillance again. They started picking me up at the Colindale tube station, or the next one toward town, about six in the afternoon when the library closed. I began a routine, as in Paris, to escape from them in the Underground stations. But they were more persistent and even less discreet than the Paris teams. What do they want? I kept asking myself. I'm here legally and registered with the police. Are they part of a kidnapping plan, to bundle me in a car and deliver me to a U.S. military base in Britain? Or worse?

I decided to move from the hotel to a "bed sitter," a British institution that means a room with mini-fridge, hotplate and sink. Toilet and shower down the hall. I got one at Belsize Square near the Belsize Park tube station and much closer to the library. Now the journey would take only twenty to thirty minutes.

I didn't change my police registry because of the surveillance. The effect was just the opposite from what I wanted. They followed me with even greater determination. One night I thought I'd shaken them a few blocks from my room. I sat down on a low wall bordering a churchyard, behind a parked moving van. Suddenly I could hear footsteps approaching—someone was running—and through the darkness one of them emerged. He wasn't more than ten steps away when he saw me. Instinctively, I supposed, he tried to slow, slipped on gravel, almost fell at my feet, then managed to keep going.

They soon discovered my room. After all day reading microfilm I was simply too tired to spend an hour shaking them. From the coin telephone at the entrance to the house where I lived, I called Wolf and Shirley one night. We agreed I would go over to their place in an hour. As I walked the last block to their flat I noticed a car parked across the street with three, maybe four, men in it. Inside I told Wolf and Shirley. We could see the car from their flat.

Wolf suggested that we take a walk. We headed down toward Belsize Village, a little shopping area, and both the car and two men on foot followed us. We kept walking and they kept following, the car circling continuously around the block. Wolf got angry. At one point he ran into the street shaking his fist at the car and shouting for them to disappear. We didn't see them again.

Despite Wolf and Shirley the loneliness and worries over the constant surveillance were having an effect. I felt extremely vulnerable. I was getting fearful when I went walking. Sometimes at a stop light I was almost afraid to cross when it turned green.

The same with restaurants. I was afraid to go in and order a meal. Not that the food might be poisoned—just the act of walking in. Then I started envisioning weird scenes and couldn't be sure if they were from a dream or from reality. Once while walking down a sidewalk a man was approaching from the opposite direction. I looked at him and saw that his left eye was shining, like a star, like he had a blue sapphire for an eye. Were they putting drugs in my food while I was reading the microfilm at Colindale? How could I know?

Angela saved me from going under completely. I talked to her by telephone almost every night. When she came over to visit for a few days I felt normal again. Then I went to Paris for Christmas and New

Year's, an enormous relief from the surreal situation in London. I had already spoken with Catherine about Angela, and also written, and with difficulty she accepted the changed situation. For a while she was living in Corsica, and then, regrettably, we lost contact altogether.

In Paris I asked Angela to come to London. She couldn't. She had her studies at the university and her work in the Brazilian exile community. Back in London the surveillance continued, and my state of mind got no better. At Colindale the microfilm reading room was small and dark. I wondered constantly about the others in there. Were they part of the surveillance, watching what I was reading? Might I be attacked in that dark room? Read. Concentrate.

In mid-January Angela visited again. This time she agreed to come and stay. She returned to Paris to settle her affairs, and by the end of the month she was back. Almost overnight my fears and paranoia disappeared. I felt like a normal person again, albeit bent on writing a most unusual book. Had Angela not come over the chances are I would have ended up in a hospital.

She began studying English, working with me at Colindale, and collecting documentation from other libraries. In time, the surveillance teams disappeared.

At Penguin Books, Neil Middleton gave me all the support I needed. He provided a dictaphone with which each night I recorded what I had found on the microfilm that day. And he assigned two stenographers to transcribe my tapes. When I needed more money, he got it for me. And he agreed that I could take the time to read all the daily newspapers from the places I had worked, even though this meant an additional year to finish the book. I gave him Leslie's typewriter for safekeeping, and he gave me another. He also made available the Penguin Xerox machines so that I could make several copies of everything for security's sake.

As the summer of 1973 approached I could see that I would finish my research at Colindale just about the time Chris and Phil would be starting their summer vacation. In my letters, tapes and telephone conversations with them I'd had no choice but to tell them that they would have to convince their mother if they wanted to come for the summer. This time she said they could come, probably because they'd been so insistent.

I wrote to my lawyer again, asking why he hadn't taken action. But when he answered he was evasive and said I should return for a hearing.

Before Phil and Chris arrived, Angela and I rented a two-bedroom flat. In making the arrangement, we tried to conceal our plans. On the morning of our move, however, Angela called a taxi from the coin telephone in our building. We were only moving eight blocks away, but at least three cars followed our taxi from Primrose Gardens to Eton Avenue.

When Chris and Phil came, we saw all the sights in London. Then we made excursions by rail: Windsor Castle, Salisbury Cathedral, Stonehenge, Stratford-upon-Avon, Oxford, and Hampton Court. A day with nothing to do? Back to the British Museum to see the Egyptian mummies, the Rosetta stone, or the Elgin marbles. Or back to the London zoo, a fifteen-minute walk from our flat, to see the snakes, the tarantulas or the elephants.

We were a happy family. I wasn't surprised when my sons started talking about staying with us. Angela and I both would have liked it.

Though I had promised Janet they would return, I offered to write telling her they wanted to stay. I told them of my hope to return to the States in the coming spring after publication of my book. If they stayed, they would have to switch schools twice in two years. They decided on their own to continue with their mother for the coming school term, visit again during the year-end vacation, then come to live with us in June 1974.

During that summer I began writing a "final" manuscript. I had accumulated a couple thousand pages of preliminary notes and research materials, but lacked a book outline. Since so many of the Agency operations progressed in different places at different times, it would be no easy matter to present them coherently.

One day I happened to think that a diary format might work. I discussed the idea with Middleton, and he agreed. Then I filled several hundred 5 x 7 cards with references to the "raw" materials, each of which would be a diary entry, and I started to write. I would explain in an introduction that the diary format was merely a literary device, not something written at the time of the events.

I didn't realize it at the time, but the three-and-a-half years I'd spent in research was a kind of re-education program. First I had studied Latin American social and economic conditions using documentation from institutions like the U.N. Economic Commission for Latin America and the Inter-American Development Bank. Then I had re-lived the political events where I'd worked, and our participation in them, and I saw things quite differently now.

In hindsight our operations were far from just a holy war against communism, but part of a larger international conflict based on social and economic class. And I became more convinced than ever that no real structural changes in Latin America were possible without popular revolution, and almost everywhere this meant armed struggle sooner or later. The question was timing.

I would try to show how our operations help sustain favorable operating conditions for U.S.-based multi-national corporations. These conditions, together with political hegemony, were our real goals. So-called liberal democracy and pluralism were only means to those ends. "Free elections" really meant freedom for us to intervene with secret funds for *our* candidates. "Free trade unions" meant freedom for us to establish *our* unions. "Freedom of the press" meant freedom for us to pay journalists to publish *our* material as if it were the journalists' own. When an elected government threatened U.S. economic and political interests, it had to go. Social and economic justice were fine concepts for public relations, but only for that.

I would not take the line that our manipulation and secret interventions were aberrations or abuses that could be eliminated by more responsible or effective controls such as Congressional oversight. The Agency's operations in Latin America, as in other Third World regions, were a necessary element for the maintenance of corporate prosperity at home—as important to sustaining the U.S. power structure as, say, the police, the media, or the educational system.

Mine would not be a liberal approach holding out reforms as solutions. Rather, I hoped my book would be a contribution to socialism and to revolution in Latin America and in the United States, however improbable that might seem. I knew I was putting myself outside the pale of "respectable" or "realistic" critics, but I had no interest in that kind of respectability.

That was not to say I failed to see value in reforms. Every progressive political step that improved the lot of ordinary people and curbed corporate power was valuable. But reform would not eliminate the fundamental unfairness and corruption of a society in which greed was the motivating force, power and prestige depended upon accumulated wealth, and a person's labor was a marketplace commodity.

Strange things happened with such intensive study. In Paris, sometimes lying awake at night, sometimes riding on the Metro, I started remembering operations and agents I'd long since forgotten. I carried a little notebook so I wouldn't forget. Same in London. By the time my research ended I thought I had what I'd set out to find: the objective realities in Latin America and the operational details of my experience. Rather than simply describing what the CIA did and who did it, I could show how the operations affected the people of those countries: in prolonging social and economic injustices and in promoting political repression. Now the question was to make it all fit together in a readable, coherent fashion.

I had hardly begun writing when another nasty episode with Janet began, and again the CIA was involved. The boys hadn't been back with Janet a week when Phil called in tears asking to come back to London. Janet said he could come. Then Chris wanted to come. Then Janet said neither could come. I sent airline tickets. Janet sent them back. Numerous distressing telephone calls. During one of these Janet admitted cooperation with the Agency, but said she had refused their request not to send the boys for the past summer.

I contacted my sleeping lawyer. He would talk to Janet. She said she was still in contact with the Agency. Wouldn't let them come. He said Phil and Chris could appear before a judge. They said they wanted to. Our only chance was for me to appear in court to make our case. But I couldn't. I wrote an 18-page history of the conflict for the judge. Chris and Phil wrote letters to the judge.

Janet contended my book was about to come out, which was not the case, and she didn't want the boys exposed to all the publicity and controversy that would follow. Besides, Angela and I were not married. At the hearing in November, I wasn't present. The judged ruled for Janet. Then she refused to let the boys visit at Christmas.

Because of the Agency's interference with Janet, I contacted an American lawyer in Cambridge, Tom Culver, who had connections with the American Civil Liberties Union (ACLU). He was a former U.S. Air Force lawyer who was drummed out of the service. They didn't like it when, in uniform and before thousands of people, he presented a petition against the Vietnam war on the steps of the U.S. Embassy in London. He'd stayed to continue studies at Cambridge University and often helped defend deserters and other G.I.'s in court martial proceedings. He put me in contact with Melvin Wulf, the Legal Director of the ACLU in New York.

Wulf offered to help in any problems arising from publication of my book—he was already litigating the CIA's censorship of *The CIA and the Cult of Intelligence* by Victor Marchetti and John Marks. Marchetti had also worked in the Agency, although not in overseas operations, while Marks had worked in the State Department's intelligence bureau. Before a court hearing on that book, Wulf confronted his CIA opposite number, the same John Greaney who had visited my father and was dealing with Janet.

Wulf asked Greaney what he was doing, trying to prevent Philip

Agee's wife from letting him see his children. Wulf wrote me that Greaney's eyes almost popped out. In Greaney's memorandum on Wulf's remarks, which I got in my FOIA suit, he did not deny Wulf's accusation. But he didn't interfere with Janet anymore, and she finally agreed that the boys could come to live with us beginning in June 1974.

As Angela and I watched the news from Chile on television that summer, I told her again and again that the Agency was fomenting the civil disorder: the strikes by shopkeepers, professionals, and again the truckers, as well as the middle class "pots and pans" marches. The whole operation looked so classic—all the elements of political subversion I knew so well.

I wondered what had happened to the memorandum for Chile I'd written in 1971 outlining the CIA's methods of subversion and listing U.S. and international organizations, such as trade unions, used as fronts. Why, I wondered, had the American Institute for Free Labor Development been allowed to continue operating in Chile?

When the coup finally came, we watched in horror. Then the scenes of soldiers rounding up hundreds, then thousands in the national football stadium. Then the disappearances, executions and bodies floating in the river. The more I watched, the harder I worked. With each new section of ten or fifteen pages either I or Angela would go to the Penguin copy room to make extra copies for safekeeping. No matter what they might try, they couldn't destroy that.

By January I had a first draft completed. It was far too long for publication, but Middleton arranged for a special editor, a Dominican priest named Laurence Bright, to go over it with me. Together we would eliminate the more marginal operations and agents, improve the style, and get a "final" version ready.

One night in early 1974 someone rang from the main entrance of our apartment house. It was Sal. I decided not to buzz him in but to go down. He had a couple of presents for Angela: a Vietcong postage stamp and a bracelet supposedly made from the 2,000th American plane shot down in Vietnam. He also wanted to talk with me.

I agreed and suggested we take a walk. As we strolled, Sal seemingly poured his heart out. He said he knew I thought he was a spy, that I'd said that to Therese and others, and it simply wasn't so. He was going back to the States soon, and would be ruined as a journalist if his name appeared in my book. He wanted to try one last time to convince me I was wrong.

I went back to the typewriter. "Do you want to tell me now who owned that typewriter?" He would. I wanted to take notes so I suggested we go into the Swiss Cottage pub. It was crowded, but we found a table and ordered two pints of beer.

For about fifteen minutes Sal tried to explain the typewriter he had loaned me, but he couldn't remember for sure the name of the owner. I asked Sal how he'd used that person as a "source," but he couldn't name an article he wrote based on his information.

As the conversation went on, Sal's voice began to crack. When at last I told him I didn't believe him, he suddenly jumped to his feet. He picked up his pint of beer, which was about half full, and threw it on the table. Glass and beer went everywhere. The pub went silent as everyone turned in our direction.

Better get out of here, I thought. No brawls, no police. I rose, brushing the beer and glass off my coat, walked to the door and straight to the flat. I never saw Sal again.

Through the spring of 1974 I worked with Laurence Bright, shortening the draft and integrating last-minute research findings. By late May I was finished. Finished! Well, not quite. I still had several organizational charts and indices to do, but the text was ready. It was more than four years after I began. The sense of relief was dizzying, what a mountain climber must feel at the top, after a long and stormy climb. Now it was a matter for Penguin to get it set, printed and published. That would take six to nine months, which seemed like a long time to me, but Middleton had his reflex explanation on the time publishers require for programming, manufacturing and marketing books.

Still, I couldn't help wondering, as I had so often before, why the British government let me in, why they let me do the research, and then why they left me in peace to write the book. The surveillance had stopped. And if my mail was crudely opened, that didn't matter. They let me do it, and now the book was coming out. Why?

At last we would have time to relax. Phil and Chris would be flying over in mid-June to stay with us permanently—unless Janet changed her mind yet again. No. That wouldn't be possible. Let's get out of London. Maybe to the countryside or the coast for the summer. I'd been reading the *Sunday Times* ads for summer cottages all spring, dreaming of the day I'd be finished. Now it was real.

I called a number in Truro, on the south coast of Cornwall, where they had advertised a two-bedroom cabin on the edge of a renowned bird-watching sanctuary. Yes, it was available for the whole summer. And cheap. On the edge of a river, across from Lord Falmouth's estate. I sent a check for the first month. Then I bought a second-hand Land Rover, a big safari wagon with five doors, roof rack, four-wheel drive and extra tires.

Angela and I arrived at Penmoor, a small country estate in Saint Clement, late one afternoon after the long drive from London. The van was overloaded with all our possessions. What a quaint little hamlet. No more than ten houses, maybe twelve. And look at that old stone church, must be centuries old. Sally and Robert Moor, a good-looking, amiable couple with an infant, showed us to Trebilly, our little cabin under the trees on a perch overlooking the river. They lived in the big house about a hundred meters up the hill. Damn. This is going to be nice.

And that it was. Idyllic. Just a few steps from our entrance a wide path started along the river in the upstream direction. It was lined with enormous old trees and shrubbery so thick that at places it formed a canopy over the path. You could walk for thirty minutes down that path and never see a house, usually not another soul. At low tide all the water disappeared, leaving mud flats exposed for herons and other birds searching out cockles and mussels. At high tide the river was often mirror still, about two hundred meters across to the woods and pastures on the other side. Everything seemed overgrown with greenery.

IV

Penmoor

During the weeks before Phil and Chris were due, Angela and I scraped and painted a sailing dinghy that belonged to the village eccentric. He was a tall, stout man about sixty whose main pleasure, it seemed, was to dress up in his Venetian gondolier's costume and oar his gondola around at high tide. If we wanted to refurbish the dinghy, he'd said, we could use it all summer.

Just as we began sailing, Tom Culver, the Cambridge lawyer who put me in contact with the ACLU, and his wife, Anne, arrived. We had become friends, and they had pedaled their tandem tricycle from Cambridge to Cornwall for a short vacation. They were staying in a flat in the big house.

The boys finally arrived. They loved Penmoor, as Angela and I did, especially the dogs and other animals, but also the birds. There was one spindly robin that Chris could coax just inside the cabin door with cheese—he named it "Fatty" and composed a song to it on his guitar. We moored the dinghy at Tolverne on the River Fal, a twenty-minute drive from St. Clement, where a half-timbered, thatch-roofed inn served scones with Cornish cream tea. The sailing was better there, no mud flats and only a half-hour downriver past King Harry's Ferry to Carrick Roads. In the Land Rover we explored the north coast as well, small picture-postcard fishing villages and high cliffs overlooking pounding seas.

We explored still more: the lighthouse at St. Anthony's Head and the cliffs across from Falmouth, the tiny port at Mevagissey, and the Helford River where they still dredged oysters under sail. Evenings we played cards and listened to Phil and Chris on guitar. No telephone, no television, no newspapers, nothing to interrupt our tranquility.

One Sunday morning, before anybody was up, Sally called from in front of the cabin. The post had rung at two A.M. with a long, urgent telegram for me. Said it was from America, from a person named Marchetti. It was 250 words, too long to copy at that hour, but they promised to deliver it at about ten this morning.

That had to be Victor Marchetti. We'd exchanged several letters and I'd just read a pre-publication copy of his book, *The CIA and the Cult of Intelligence*. The book was terrific, due out next month, and sure to be a hit. So much in it I'd never known. But a 250-word telegram? What could that be about?

Tom and Anne, Phil and Chris, and Angela and I were sitting on the terrace in front of Trebilly when a little red truck of Her Majesty's Post rolled up. I signed, and then read it out loud for the others:

"Urgent.
"Dear Philip: A friend of mine, Larry Stern of the *Washington Post*, has learned of your existence and would urgently like to talk to you. I vouch for Larry and I also strongly recommend that you speak with him for I am picking up information that the Agency is now trying to discredit you. Also I have doubts whether the book will ever be published by Penguin. I recommend you speak in total candor with Larry because he will get your story out even if the Agency uses its connections in England to delay or squelch your book. Larry will be standing by in Washington for word from you that you will see him. If you have any questions you can call me collect at 703-938-1380 in Vienna, Virginia. Or you can signify your willingness to see Larry by calling the *Washington Post*'s London correspondent, Bernard Nossiter, at 730-9012. I will be reachable at home all day Sunday until the evening. Larry is prepared to leave Washington immediately on receiving word from you. He too can be called collect in Washington at 202-387-4111. Best regards. Victor Marchetti."

I read it a second and a third time. Everybody else read it. What does he mean, "I am picking up information that the Agency is now trying to discredit you." And, "I have doubts that the book will ever be published by Penguin."

That's impossible! Neil Middleton and I had only to go through it together one more time, looking for ways to shorten it. Then to the printers, and then out. They couldn't stop it now. Or could they? I couldn't call now. It's the middle of the night in America. I'd have to wait until three or four in the afternoon.

We walked over to the Heron Inn for fish and chips and St. Austell ale, speculating all the while about what could be up. What's this about a *Washington Post* reporter? How did he hear of me and why's he so interested in talking? I don't want to talk to any reporter. At least not until my book is published. Let them read it and then we can talk. Why all the urgency?

About three we headed back across the pastures to St. Clement. At the old church we walked through the wooded graveyard, 18th-century tombstones overgrown with bushes, and up through the carriage entrance under the rectory annex. Out back stood the red phone booth—the only public telephone around.

"Phil, you got the telegram," said Marchetti. "You've been on the front pages here the last few days. You've seen the stories, right?"

"No. I don't get papers out here. We're completely isolated. What are you talking about?" My breathing quickened as I strained to hear.

Marchetti's story was incredible, weird, shocking. Thursday the *New York Times* had published a story about an unnamed former CIA officer who told everything he knew to the KGB. The officer had worked in Latin America, and Victor was certain they meant me. The Agency's plan obviously was to plant the story, then leak my name as the CIA man. They tied it in with the Senate investigation of Watergate. Their way of discrediting me even before my book was published.

Victor wanted to help, so he decided to talk to Larry Stern, told him of me and my book, and said the *Times* story was bullshit. Stern had a long article in this morning's *Post* quoting "informed sources," i.e., Marchetti, as saying the KGB story was "nonsense." But Stern's article identified me by name as the subject of the *Times* article. Victor thought Stern could help if I'd tell him my story. Would I see him?

I was stunned, couldn't think. "I don't know, Victor. That's a lot to take in. I don't know what to do. KGB. Christ, that's so typical. Look, let me talk it over here and call you back. Thanks for your help. Call you back in less than an hour."

We walked back to Trebilly as I told the others what Marchetti

said. What to do? What to do? A man was standing at the cabin door.
Who's he?

"Hi, Mr. Agee, I'm John Raines from the *Daily Telegraph*,
Plymouth correspondent. London phoned and asked me to drive
down to talk to you. Got a minute?"

"What about?" I was nervous and so thankful we were all together.
Thank god Phil and Chris are already here.

"London wants an interview on your work in the CIA, your book,
the report on your connection with the KGB. Got a minute? Any
other press been out here? Got the book here?"

Pushy prick. I decided not to talk to him. "Look, this is Sunday.
I'm with my family and friends. Leave me your name and telephone
number. I'll call you next week."

"Next week? I need the story today. London can't wait."

I asked him to leave. He protested in disbelief. Finally I got him on
his way.

We discussed what I should tell Marchetti. My feeling was to refuse all statements, all contacts with the press until the book was out.
Angela disagreed. Publication was months away. Press was already on
the story. I had to answer the attack now. Expose it as a CIA plant.
Defend. Never let the enemy monopolize the media. Tom and Anne
agreed. I should see the *Washington Post* reporter first. Get the background on the *Times* story and anything else that's come out. Then
make my denial and counter-attack. Okay, okay. My mind was in
such turmoil I'd have agreed to anything. KGB, eh? Those dirty,
fucking bastards.

Up the hill, around the pond, and back through the cemetery to
the telephone. Called Marchetti, said I'd meet Stern. He had a reservation that night. Would arrive Heathrow Monday morning and drive
straight to Cornwall. Could he bring the *Times* article, his own from
this morning's *Post* and anything else? Thanks, Victor, thanks so
much.

Then I called Dad and Nancy—something I would do many times
in years ahead to forewarn them of some impending press story on
me. They didn't need any warning.

"Well, Phil," my father said, "looks like they're going after you.
The *Tampa Times* headline story on Thursday—that was the 4th of
July—told about a CIA man who was talking to the Russians. Apparently told them everything. The article didn't say who it was, but I
figured they meant you. This morning's *Tribune* identifies you as that
person."

"Dad, I want you and Nancy to know that it's not true. The Agency planted that story. It was *The New York Times,* right?"

"No, the one on the 4th was Associated Press, by a man named Michael Sniffen. The one this morning is from the *Washington Post.*"

"Well, that means they planted it with AP as well as the *Times.* The *Post* man who wrote that story identifying me is flying over tonight. Victor Marchetti gave him my name, and Victor just told me by phone that he'll help get the truth out. I'm awfully sorry it started this way. Must be embarrassing for you."

"Don't worry about that, Phil, we can take care of ourselves, and I hope you do the same."

"I hope the papers there publish what I tell the *Post.* And I hope it doesn't cause any more trouble. Sorry again. Bye, Dad."

Stern arrived at the Truro hotel Monday evening completely exhausted. We agreed to meet the next morning, but meanwhile I could see the articles and look over the "Baker Report" on possible CIA involvement in Watergate. This was a follow-up investigation, Stern explained, by Senator Howard Baker who was the ranking Republican member of the Senate Watergate Committee. Baker had decided to continue investigation of several tantalizing leads that emerged during the main Watergate investigation. One of these, a reference in CIA documents to a "W.H. flap," led to me.

Back at Trebilly we read the articles and the report. Practically in a daze, I saw the Agency's Machiavellian plots all come together. The *Times* article was front page, with two-column headlines at the top: "CIA Agent Said to Give Secrets to Russian in 1972." The patsy they picked to surface the story was a reporter named John M. Crewdson, whose opening line set the perfect stage: "A tale of a drunken and despondent CIA agent who apparently sat down with a Soviet KGB operative somewhere in Latin America and told him what he knew has emerged as a result of a Senate Watergate committee inquiry into the activities of the Central Intelligence Agency."

Citing unnamed "sources," Crewdson wrote: "The CIA man, believed to have been stationed somewhere in Latin America, was described as 'despondent,' 'disgruntled' with the Agency and 'in his cups' at the time of his contact with the Russians a little more than two years ago." The CIA man, who later retired, "clearly provided information of value to the Russians" because the CIA's Deputy Director told the Watergate Committee that the affair "threatened to compromise Western Hemisphere operations."

"It could not be learned what specific information the American imparted, but the sources said today that the matter was still considered extremely sensitive. One of the lesser Agency secrets compromised in the conversation, however, was the fact that a Washington public relations concern, Robert R. Mullen and Co., had for years been providing 'cover' for CIA agents stationed abroad."

Crewdson went on to describe how the "Baker Report," made public a day earlier, mentioned a CIA memorandum written by Martin Lukasky on 10 July 1972. Lukasky, the CIA man in charge of the Mullen cover, had written of a mysterious "W.H. flap," W.H. meaning Western Hemisphere Division of the CIA's Clandestine Services. At that time, according to the report, Mullen was providing cover for CIA officers in Amsterdam and Singapore. Referring to the "W.H. flap," Lukasky wrote that if the Mullen cover were terminated, Watergate could not be used as an excuse. The "W.H. flap," obviously, was the CIA man's conversation with the KGB.

Yet, Crewdson wrote, the "Baker Report" said a later Lukasky memo showed that the Agency had convinced the Mullen company to terminate the Singapore cover "through an agreed upon scenario which included a falsified Watergate publicity crisis."

The second memo said the Agency told the Mullen company that shortly after Watergate someone in Singapore had approached a CIA officer under Mullen cover with a copy of the *International Herald Tribune* in hand. It had the article showing E. Howard Hunt's employment with the CIA and the Mullen Company and his connection with the break-in. The person said that was proof that the officer in Singapore was in the CIA. Mullen was then told the office would have to be closed. But later, Crewdson's "source" said, "it was established that the entire incident in Singapore never took place."

Of course. It didn't happen in Singapore but in Paris. That was my meeting with Sal, when I went running over to record the stuff about Hunt, Mullen and the Agency. And they'd converted Sal into a KGB man. What a convoluted irony. I'd helped set up the Mullen cover in Mexico, then blew it to a CIA spy.

The Mexico office had already been closed, but Sal's report back to the CIA was the reason Lukasky wrote of closing down the remaining offices. The Agency then used my meeting with Sal, abundantly falsified, to justify closing the Amsterdam and Singapore offices. Two years later, knowing the "Baker Report" was coming out with the "W.H. flap" reference, they again converted my meeting with Sal, this time into the KGB story, but juicing it up with the "drunk" and "despondent" nonsense. Even the timing was perfect: my meeting with Sal had in fact been "a little more than two years ago," but in Paris, not "somewhere in Latin America."

Stern's *Post* article from the day before was a relief. Besides citing the KGB story as "nonsense," he outlined my Agency career and included details that could only have come from my letters to Marchetti. "'He's obviously become quite radicalized,' said Agee's correspondent, 'a good Catholic boy who was finally fed up to the teeth with hypocrisy and deception. Like some Catholic priests who have gone down there, he became freaked out with poverty and repression and what our government was doing. . . . But this guy was an operative for fourteen years and he knows names and places. There are people in Washington who are scared shitless of this guy.' "

Stern also wrote at some length of an unresolved and intriguing possibility that my planned book was the pretext behind President Nixon's instruction, just days after the Watergate arrests, that the CIA should have the FBI call off its investigation in Mexico where the burglars' money had been laundered.

Nixon's Chief of Staff, H. R. Haldeman, had sent General Vernon Walters, the recently appointed Deputy CIA Director, to the FBI Director to say the investigation of the money might expose an unrelated CIA covert operation in Mexico. The ploy worked for a few weeks, but eventually the Agency told the FBI that no operations were endangered. Whether the "W.H. flap" was connected with Nixon's instruction was unclear to the Senate Watergate investigators because, according to the "Baker Report," the Agency's explanation "is clouded by conflicting evidence."

About dark, the little red postal truck arrived with another telegram—this one from Sniffen of the AP asking me to telephone him collect in Washington. Bastard. Like Crewdson, he'd put out that first story. Probably published all over the world. Should I call him? Angela said yes, but to demand they publish my denial before giving an interview. Then everyone agreed that with Stern I shouldn't talk about the details of my book, just generalities.

I spent most of the next day with Larry Stern. I told him I wouldn't let him read the manuscript nor would I talk about it in detail. That had to wait until publication. He didn't like that, but I did tell him my personal story, from beginning to end, including Sal and Leslie, the typewriter, my telling Sal of the Mullen cover, and the surveillance in Paris and London. I also gave him a few nuggets like the Agency's use of the American Institute for Free Labor Development and other union organizations, our subversion of the governments in Ecuador, and our intervention in Chilean and Brazilian elections.

I liked Stern—he seemed fair and open-minded. When he got on the afternoon train for London, I agreed I wouldn't talk to other reporters until his article was published in two days.

A couple of days later Stern sent me a note from London. "Philip: Saw copy of manuscript obtained through my clandestine training at the *Washington Post* . . . it's very good stuff . . . much more dynamite than Marchetti-Marks . . . needs more editing. . . ."

How had he seen it? The only copy outside Penguin is at the *Sunday Times*, with Bruce Page, where they're considering it for serialization. I wonder if that guy's letting people read it. Got to talk to Middleton. We can't let it come out piecemeal.

The day Stern came, our little red truck made four or five more trips to deliver telegrams. From then on it was a family joke—every time we saw it turning into the drive we'd yell, "Here comes the Queen's delivery service again." For a couple of weeks, it seemed, that the truck and driver were working exclusively for us. All the London papers and wire services wanted interviews, as did *The New York Times*.

I called them all, beating a well-worn path through the graveyard to the telephone booth. My only condition was I wouldn't discuss the specifics of the book. But with Sniffen and Dick Eder of the *Times*, I said I wouldn't talk until they published my denials of the first story's KGB connection.

Sniffen promised to publish my denial, and I said I'd do a telephone interview afterwards. But Eder got hysterical when I told him I'd just spent the day with Larry Stern. He drove from London that night, knocked on the door as we were having breakfast, and demanded equal treatment with the *Post*.

I repeated my position that I wouldn't see him until the *Times* published my denial. He was almost dumbstruck and walked away muttering something about troubles with his editor in New York. He spent most of the day sitting outside the red telephone booth behind the old church waiting for calls from London and New York. Pitiful sight. Next day he persuaded me to listen on the telephone as someone in New York read the denial that would appear the following morning, Thursday. I then told Eder I'd talk to him in the afternoon, knowing that he couldn't get the story out until Friday, a day after Larry Stern's. Both the *Times* and the *Post* reported that not only I, but "official sources" as well, denied the KGB connection.

In New York Melvin Wulf also helped. He told the press that the ACLU would defend my right to publish my book as they had Marchetti and Marks's. More important, he described how Greaney had interfered with my right to see my children, and how Greaney had made no denial when Wulf confronted him about it.

I spent most of the next two weeks doing one interview after another with journalists from all over Europe, even from South America and Mexico. The questions were always the same: my family background, why I entered the CIA, why I left, and why I had decided to expose its operations and personnel. The myth of reformism was a point I made constantly, along with the Agency's role in political repression and torture as the secret political police of American capitalism.

When journalists questioned the propriety of revealing secret operations and naming names, I emphasized that the American people have a right to know and judge these activities. If ours is really an "open society" then these government activities should also be part of the "public debate." And the issue was not just *what* the CIA does, but *who* does it—meaning no hiding behind, or under, the covers. In the end, the Agency should be seen as an instrument of government policy, and the real argument is with *policy*, not with the CIA.

As clippings of the interviews filtered back I found that most were fair and accurate. But there were a few others that followed the Agency's original line. One was an item on *Newsweek*'s "Periscope" page. Years before at Headquarters someone had told me that "Periscope" was a favorite Agency outlet for propaganda items, and it seemed that game had continued.

The Spy Who Came in for a Drink

That drunken CIA agent who blabbed to a Russian KGB man revealed far more than simply the use of a Washington, D.C., public relations firm as cover for some operatives. He gave his KGB friend names of a whole string of legitimate private companies in North and South America performing an identical function. The list compromised an uncounted number of agents. The man, who later tried unsuccessfully to peddle the story as a book in Europe, is still under CIA surveillance.

From the telephone booth I did radio interviews with stations from London to New York to Sidney. Television crews came too, with all their cables, trucks, cameras and cases. CBS chartered a plane to fly out Charles Collingwood and a crew of ten from London. Then came

BBC and other networks. St. Clement, that rustic little hamlet, would never be the same, although Robert and Sally and most of the neighbors were sympathetic and understanding.

Neil Middleton came out to work on a "final" edition in the midst of all the media turmoil. I told him what Marchetti had heard about Penguin possibly not publishing, but he said that would only be over his dead body. His main concern was that the book was still too long and had too much background information on Latin America and the countries where I'd worked. I fought to keep the "realities" in, insisting that for most people the true impact of the operations couldn't be seen unless set in the context of local social, economic and political conditions. If that made the book tedious or hard to read it didn't matter. I hadn't written an adventure story. Middleton gave in, but complained that we'd be criticized for the length. I didn't care a hoot about criticism.

Our summer's idyll had ended so abruptly we'd hardly had time to think about where we were going to live in the fall. And what about schools? As the interviews subsided we began discussing the pros and cons of moving back to London. The main drawback was the expense of living there—my Penguin advances were almost gone.

Maybe we could stay at Penmoor, take one of the flats in the big house, and Phil and Chris could go to school here. They loved the idea. We visited the schools each would attend, and they still wanted to stay. So we did, arranging with Robert and Sally to move in September to a two-bedroom flat they called Kingfisher.

In documents I received in my FOIA suit against the CIA, I found that the Agency about this time developed two distinct lines for confronting the problem I posed. One was a series of long memoranda stating the facts of my career in the Agency, the circumstances of my resignation, my letter to *Marcha*, and page after page, all censored, of the actions they had taken against me. These documents were clearly prepared as background briefings for the National Security Council, the White House, the State Department, and members of Congress—although probably without their schemes for a drug plant, kidnapping or assassination.

> It was inevitable that sooner or later the Central Intelligence Agency would be faced with the problem of a disaffected staff employee such as Philip Agee. He is the first one in the Agency's history and has written a book about his Agency experiences.
>
> Agee's overall performance as an operations officer was competent . . . he was regarded as bright, aggressive and well-

motivated. . . . At the time of his resignation in Mexico City, Agee gave no indication of disaffection.

In Mexico he came in contact with some people on the far-left spectrum and took some studies at the National Autonomous University of Mexico. This is where his ideological defection began at a rapid rate. . . . Only the barest outline of Agee's activities is available for the period from his resignation until he left Mexico permanently. . . . Disaffection first came to light in November 1971 with publication of Agee's letter in *Marcha*.

There is no definitive evidence that Agee's activities are sponsored by opposition intelligence services.

Another series was written as propaganda guidance for journalists and perhaps for other intelligence services. These lengthy documents were sent abroad either by cable or pouch. Although heavily censored, certain passages made their purpose clear: a classic *ad hominem* attack that would so discredit me that my book would lose credibility.

During his Agency career Agee showed himself to be an egotistical, ambitious, superficially intelligent but essentially shallow young man who was uninterested in politics and had no political convictions.

Agee was always borrowing money, his financial accountings were constantly in a poor state. . . . Agee was constantly involved in extramarital affairs . . . he had a consummate preoccupation with sex. . . . . . . in defiance of a court order Agee stole the children from their mother and flew them to Mexico where they lived with Agee and his recently acquired mistress. . . . Agee's grandiose schemes for making money in Mexico did not bear fruit . . .

Later these themes would surface in articles or commentaries which people sent me from around the world. For the moment, though, after the first torrent of media attention, Angela and I both felt we had not come out badly. The CIA had indeed gotten in the first blow with the "drunk-despondent-KGB" story, and for many that impression would be lasting. But my denials circulated even more widely, as well as my story of penury in Paris and the Agency's actions against me.

Penguin would have both hardcover and paperback printed by late November or early December, and it would be their featured New Year's publication. That was almost six months away, but there would be no resting in the meanwhile. A flood of letters from individuals and organizations had to be answered. With rare exceptions the letters were supportive, giving me a sense of relief that people were not buying the CIA line, that they believed and agreed with what I was saying. Many more press and television interviews. Visits from old and new friends. And frequent trips to London on the Penzance-to-Paddington sleeper.

In September Victor Marchetti came to London for publication of the British edition of *The CIA and the Cult of Intelligence.* It was our first meeting, and he had a strange tale to tell. On a Sunday morning some days before leaving, an old friend of his from the Agency dropped by—he "just happened to be in the neighborhood." At a moment when Marchetti and he were alone in the kitchen, the guy said the Agency had sent him. They wanted Victor to steal a copy of my manuscript.

Marchetti answered that copies of it were already circulating among publishers in New York and also in Washington. Agee had sent it to friends at the Center for National Security Studies for a conference on the CIA later that month. But Victor's friend insisted they didn't have it.

"Look, Victor, you may not agree with the Agency anymore, but you're a patriotic American. Agee's gone off the deep end. He's a radical, and he's going to jeopardize innocent people—your old buddies!"

"I'll think about it," Victor had said, but he had no intention of cooperating. I told Victor I was sure they had it, that they were probably trying to sow distrust between us. Keep us from joining forces in any way. We agreed it was a pretty dumb maneuver and we'd stay in touch.

With the many people who visited us in the aftermath of the first publicity, the question often arose: how can one defend against an organization like the CIA? Invariably I answered: exposure, both of operations and personnel, in as many countries as possible.

With several of the Americans who came I discussed how CIA people could be found, and the importance of a campaign to expose them. The easiest to identify would be the vast majority under cover as diplomats and administrative staff in U.S. Embassies. If we could somehow get the telephone directories of different Embassies, I could determine who most of the CIA people were. We could then get the names published in the local press, and they would have trouble staying in their countries of assignment. We'd give them a taste of their own medicine.

I didn't tell anybody how I could tell the CIA people from the others—obviously I didn't personally know the thousands under diplomatic cover worldwide. But I knew the State Department's *Bio-graphic Register* and *Foreign Service List* were on file in the British Museum. The first contained career histories of all the officers in the Foreign Service, including CIA officers under State Department cover. The second was a listing of assignments by foreign post. By analyzing employment histories in the *Register* I could identify the CIA people because the cover assignments were so obvious. Identification was also possible through collation of office and tele-phone extensions. Finally, the directories also had their home ad-dresses and telephone numbers. My co-conspirators came up with a whole pile of directories—all from the Department of State in Washington.

My plan was to begin the exposure campaign after publication of my book when my credibility and political motives would be fully es-tablished. But in mid-September revelations began in Washington of the CIA's subversion of the Allende government in Chile. With tor-ture and other forms of repression continuing in that country, and with the CIA's hand in Pinochet's coup now revealed, I decided not to wait.

I would start with the CIA Station in the Mexico City Embassy. The press there had carried sensational stories, based on a purloined copy of my manuscript, outlining the intimate relations between the CIA and recent Mexican presidents. The Presidential spokesman and others called for an investigation, so why not give them something to start with. But I had a problem. I did not want to reveal my method, lest the Agency convince the State Department to classify, or stop publication, of the telephone directories or my analytical tools. So I tried to cover up by attributing the list of CIA personnel to Mexicans I said I had trained. It wouldn't fool the CIA, but might prevent dis-appearance of the documentation.

With friends at the London-based *Latin America Newsletter*, which I had used extensively in my research, I organized a press conference for early October. The night before I wrote a statement in the *News-letter* office that read, in part:

> Today I announce a new campaign to fight the U.S. Central Intelli-gence Agency wherever it is operating. This campaign will have two main functions: first, to expose CIA officers and agents and to take the measures necessary to drive them out of the countries where they are operating; secondly, to seek within the United States to have the CIA abolished.
>
> Discussions are already underway for the formation of an interna-

tional committee to coordinate this campaign. There are good reasons, we believe, for waging a campaign to "destabilize" the CIA and get it abolished. CIA's promotion of fascism in Chile is no isolated case. It has intervened to "destabilize" the forces of change and to support traditional ruling elites in other countries where fascism has developed: in Brazil, Indonesia, Uruguay, Greece, South Korea, the Philippines, Iran, and Portugal.

Today we begin the campaign of exposure by announcing the names and home addresses of thirty-seven CIA operations officers and administrative employees who together constitute the bulk of the CIA Station under cover in the U.S. Embassy in Mexico City.

Next morning I made copies for distribution at the press conference, and I gave one to the Interpress wire service which put a dispatch with the names and addresses on the telex to Mexico. Then I walked through the cold and rain to the Old Bell Tavern, a pub on Fleet Street, where I'd reserved a room.

I'd never had a press conference before, and despite having done many one-on-one interviews, I was nervous. I had taken care not to reveal what I planned to do, so I was pretty sure it would be a bomb for the Agency, not just in Mexico but all over. The pub had arranged several rows of chairs and a table in front for me. As I sat down a slight, dark haired, somewhat mousy-looking man in his early thirties brought a chair to my table, sat down, and put a tape recorder in front of me. He seemed nervous and tense, and a bit out of place sitting at my table, but I didn't mind. It was all quite informal.

I read the statement and then made a few remarks. I said that anyone who opposed the CIA's operations to overthrow the Chilean government and to provoke the unspeakable repression that followed ought not to be satisfied with the recent revelations. The information was indeed positive, and it helped expose the Agency's methodology, but it wasn't enough. To really fight this kind of subversion one had to expose the CIA's personnel as well as its operations. Wherever possible their photographs as well as names and addresses should be published. People should organize demonstrations at Embassies and at their homes demanding they get out. When that happens, I said, they'd be gone pretty quick, and all their work would be disrupted.

The journalist sitting at my table asked the first question and went on to dominate the entire session. He was anything but friendly as he fired off a series of provocative questions about my personal politics, finances and visits to Cuba.

Afterwards a friend asked me, "Phil, you know who that was asking all those questions?"

"He said his name very fast and I didn't get it. Did you?"

"He's Robert Moss of *The Economist*. He was in Chile during the Allende period. Wrote articles against him. He's also an editor of *Vision*, the Latin American newsweekly with ties to Somoza in Nicaragua. Very right wing."

Robert Moss. I remembered the name. He had asked me to do an interview for *Vision*, and was quite friendly on the telephone. In recent weeks he had sent two telegrams: "Very anxious to talk with you. . . . Eager to do major interview and review of your book. . . . Interview would appear as one of a series that will include Gabriel Garcia Marquez, Galbraith and others . . . very timely to do something now in the wake of the Chile revelations . . . could offer a fee of 100 pounds plus expenses . . . grateful if you could call me collect. . . ."

My press conference was the "interview" he wouldn't have gotten. Later Moss was revealed as having been in the thick of the Agency's propaganda operations against Allende and had written a book, *Chile's Marxist Experiment*, which was financed by a CIA front in London and distributed by Chilean embassies around the world. I assumed the Agency had put him on my case, and as it turned out, he never got off it. In years ahead he wrote many scurrilous articles referring to me as "the CIA's only ideological defector."

The impact in Mexico of my press conference was immediate and everything I'd hoped for. Banner headlines, names and addresses. Associated Press, Reuters, and Agence France-Presse placed dispatches in ten Mexico City papers. The Interpress story was also widely published. Journalists were knocking on the Chief of Station's door early on October 4, and before the end of the month he and the Deputy Chief were transferred. Others would soon follow. Journalists found that at some of the CIA homes someone had hastily painted out the street number I'd given and painted in a new, false number. Not bad for a first try.

Penguin's marketing people were very unhappy about the press conference because I hadn't told them in advance. They had wanted one for early January to coincide with publication, but hadn't told me. They felt I had jumped the gun. Didn't make sense to me when I'd been doing interviews constantly for three months and had still others coming up. If Neil Middleton had been in London I would have coordinated with him, but he was in New York trying to sell U.S. publishing rights for *Inside the Company*. When he got back his news was disappointing.

Neil had talked to editors at every major publishing house in New

York and Boston, and every one of them turned my book down. Several said it was boring, but the real problem was fear of a government lawsuit to require censorship, as with Marchetti's book, and libel suits from people I wrote were CIA agents.

Knopf's legal bill in the Marchetti litigation was over $125,000, even though the ACLU had handled the defense *gratis*. British Penguin couldn't distribute in the U.S. because of trade agreements, and they wouldn't give U.S. publishers the normal indemnity guarantee for foreign rights because Penguin was already taking a huge risk.

The only company that offered to publish it was Straight Arrow, a publishing house owned by *Rolling Stone* magazine. I had already done a long interview with *Rolling Stone,* and they were also interested in buying rights to serialize excerpts.

Later we learned that the Agency, both directly and through its "old boy" network, had initiated an intensive campaign to convince publishers that my book was damaging to the national security, that publishing it would be unpatriotic, and that legal problems might indeed ensue.

Middleton made a preliminary oral agreement with Straight Arrow, but no contract was signed. Curious about their financial condition, I asked my father to get a Dun and Bradstreet report. Although *Rolling Stone* was solid, the publishing company was not. I wondered. Then I discovered that Straight Arrow's attorney had written to the CIA asking for advice on the accuracy of my book and offering to send a copy of the manuscript for review. The hell they would. I told Neil I could never agree to that and would prefer to hold a decision until after publication by Penguin. He returned the U.S. rights for me to negotiate directly.

I just couldn't imagine not having the book published in the States. Offers for publication in other languages were pouring in. Getting Americans to read it was just as important as circulation in Latin America. The whole point was to start a movement against the kind of subversion and repression that happened in Chile.

Neil said machine copies of the typescript had already made the book an "underground" classic and collectors' item in the States, and certainly copies of the Penguin edition would filter in through Canada. But that wasn't enough. I just had to get it published there. If necessary I would form my own company for U.S. publication.

Then one day at the end of November it happened. The little red truck pulled up with a "special delivery" package. Inside were six copies of *Inside the Company: CIA Diary.* Oh, Angela, just look. Doesn't Leslie's typewriter look great on the cover, with all the elec-

tronic stuff showing. Just feel it, it even smells good. And there it is:
"Dedicated to Angela Camargo Seixas and her comrades in Latin
America struggling for social justice, national dignity and peace." Oh,
god, I can't believe it. Just look at it!

Our joy was momentarily interrupted by a call from Robin
Blackburn in London. We had become friends after he put me in contact with Middleton, and I usually stayed at his apartment on visits to
London. He said Gabriel Garcia Marquez was in London and wanted
to get in touch with me. Could he be given my telephone and address? Sure, sure. You ought to see the book, Robin. It's beautiful! I
sent a copy to my father that very day.

Garcia Marquez wrote a note inviting me to testify at a hearing of
the Bertrand Russell Tribunal scheduled for January in Brussels. It
would focus on political repression in Latin America. On my next trip
to London I gave him a copy of *Inside the Company*, and we met several times afterwards to discuss specifics of the book and my long trek
to get it done. He and his wife, Mercedes, were so relaxed and
straightforward, and with such easy wit, they made me feel almost as
if I were getting to know old friends again. He didn't tell me then, but
he wrote a long and very favorable article, a combined book review
and interview, that was later published in many countries. I had participated myself in police repression. I had never spoken about the
CIA at a public meeting. Would I be jeered?

"Philip, don't worry. You're my guest."

Angela made one of her few trips away from St. Clement to have
dinner with Garcia Marquez and his wife, and she was elated with the
copy of *Cien Años de Soledad* he dedicated to her. But that was an
exception. After the first weeks of excitement at Penmoor, I was away
in London over half the time, leaving her to look after Phil and Chris,
now thirteen and ten, which she did with fully as much attention as
she would have for her own children. Both of the boys had lost a
school year because of differences between American and British cur-
riculum, and Angela tutored them with sensitivity and care. The
three got along exceptionally well, it seemed, but unknowingly I was
sowing the seeds of another personal failure.

For all my efforts to make it possible for Phil and Chris to live with
us, and to have a role in their formation, I was becoming a part-time
father, and a part-time lover as well. There had been no plan for me
to be away so much, no way to anticipate the different demands and
opportunities that would arise with all the unexpected notoriety upon
becoming a public figure.

Things just happened, and we both thought I should not shun a full activist role. If that meant traveling, Angela would look after the home front. Nobody complained, and I didn't realize then how unfair it was for her, and for my sons as well.

Christmas was approaching with two weeks' school vacation. What'll we do? What about a little trip? We can be together, see something new. Great, but where? Angela suggested Portugal, a country we'd been closely following since April when fifty years of fascism was swept away in the coup by progressive military officers.

I'd done several interviews with Portuguese newspapers, emphasizing the dangers of CIA intervention, and already my book was being translated for publication in Lisbon. We could make it a "political" vacation, try to meet people, see what's really happening. Portugal, it seemed, was becoming the first socialist country in Western Europe.

On a trip to London I reserved two cabins and a car space for the 21 December sailing of the *Panther*, picked up folders at the Spanish and Portuguese tourist bureaus, bought a two-year-old Volkswagen beetle, and headed home. We couldn't wait for our ship to sail.

V

On the Attack

The *Panther* may have been nothing but a humble, all purpose ferry-boat, but through the snow that Friday night it looked like the sleekest of ocean cruisers. On the drive from Cornwall I'd been worrying out loud about Spain, recalling all the Agency's efforts through Sal and Leslie to get me there.

"Not to worry," Angela kept saying, "you're famous now—they wouldn't dare try anything."

"Yeah, Dad, we'll take care of you."

"All right, I'm not worrying. Good thing we took the precaution to tell only a few friends about this trip, and not a word about it on the telephone. They probably don't have the slightest idea."

The line for tickets and immigration moved quickly, considering the weather, and soon I was handing our passports through the window to the control officer. But instead of just glancing at them, as he had for the cars ahead of us, the officer asked to see our return tickets, then took everything to the adjacent office. Dammit. He must have recognized the name. Can't see what he's doing in there. I'll just walk over and look through that window. Ah, he's got them on the

desk, and the other guy's making a phone call. Oh, oh. He sees me.
Here he comes.

"Please return to your vehicle, sir."

"Okay. Anything the matter?" I wasn't moving very fast.

"You are not allowed to abandon your vehicle," he said with all the
pomposity he could muster.

"It's not abandoned. See, that's my family inside."

Why make a fuss? I got back in the car and in a minute he brought
the tickets and passports over. We rolled on board, found our cabins,
and agreed this was going to be a fun trip. Chris and Phil found the
electronic games while Angela and I went up to the bar.

What was the call about? Obviously it's a lookout procedure, but
what does it mean? Who knows, probably just their watch list routine.

The ship rolled and pitched all night, but by morning as we passed
through the islands off the coast of Brittany the storm was over. Good,
I could get the article for *CounterSpy* written and mail it from Lisbon. After breakfast I sat at the little dressing table in our cabin
outlining the reasons why I thought the CIA's personnel, as well as it
operations, should be publicly exposed.

CounterSpy was the quarterly magazine of a small group in
Washington, D.C., who called themselves The Organizing
Committee for a Fifth Estate. Norman Mailer had started the magazine in 1973, at his fiftieth birthday bash, to fight what he called
techno-fascism and encroachments against civil liberties by the CIA,
FBI and other government agencies. The goal was to form citizens'
committees to monitor and expose abuses by police and security
services—hence Fifth Estate—and their apt motto was "We're
Watching Big Brother." Mailer helped finance the group which also
drew support from leaders of the anti-war movement. They were
among the first to contact me after the outbreak of publicity.

Following my October press conference, *CounterSpy* decided to
publish a list of CIA Chiefs of Station around the world. They asked
me for an article on why such exposures were justified and necessary
in defense against the Agency.

I wondered where they were getting their list, but didn't ask. Later
I learned that John Marks, Victor Marchetti's co-author and a former
State Department intelligence officer, had published an article in the
November issue of *Washington Monthly* called "How to Spot a
Spook." He described how to identify CIA personnel using the *For-
eign Service List* and the *Biographic Register:* which Foreign Service

designations to look for and how to analyze the cover histories. Using Marks's article, *CounterSpy* then compiled its list of Chiefs of Station, and Marks checked it for accuracy. Both the list and my article would be in the January issue.

I wrote of the importance of cover for CIA officers. In my own experience I had been able to handle a relatively large number of across-the-board operations because I had no opposition. My cover as a diplomat was solid, and I could go about developing all sorts of operations. These operations, in the end, helped prop up minority elitist regimes and served to promote political repression. Or, as in Chile, CIA officers under diplomatic cover undermined the elected government and provoked a fascist coup.

Exposure of CIA personnel, including publication of their photographs and home addresses, would make it difficult for them to remain overseas, and would neutralize their capability to conduct operations. I advocated a solidarity campaign by Americans to identify CIA people and to make the information available in as many countries as possible.

"This campaign," I wrote, "could remove the key to CIA effectiveness in destabilizing progressive and revolutionary forces seeking social justice in the Third World. That key is secrecy, and when it is peeled away, there standing naked and exposed for all to see, is the CIA secret policeman, who only hours before was lurking in the darkness to bribe a military officer, a student leader, a journalist, a politician, or a trade unionist. Take away secrecy and the CIA officer becomes impotent."

Early Monday morning, we sailed through the narrow entrance to San Sebastian harbor. Looked like we'd have plenty of sun on the drive west to see the pre-historic paintings in the caves at Altamira. What a change from that awful British weather. As the ship docked we went to the car below. The bows opened, the ramp came down, and off we went.

Just as we cleared the ramp, Christopher said, "Hey, look at that policeman standing there. He was just looking at our license plate and now he's making a phone call."

I looked over and there he was, standing at the ramp exit talking on the telephone. Could it be that . . . no, no, he's not looking this way. Let's see what happens at immigration control. I handed over the passports, the officer stamped them with hardly a glance, and gave them back.

"See, Chris, you and your imagination! No problem at all."

We'd be Altamira by lunchtime, see the caves, then to Burgos before dark. Good highway all the way.

We left the port and drove onto the expressway to Bilbao. It was pretty crowded, but as a precaution I took the first exit, drove a couple of blocks, stopped a few minutes, then drove on. Looking through the mirror I noticed that a couple of cars had left the expressway with us, had also stopped, and now were following. Like so many times before, I began to get that creeping feeling of fear, anger and frustration. Don't panic. Relax. Stay calm.

"Don't anybody look back," I said. "I think we're being followed."

Phil and Chris immediately turned around, all excited, asking which car, what color, where?!

"For god's sake, don't look back! Turn around! I'm not sure, but I don't want them to think I spotted them."

I drove back to the expressway and decided to continue normally while watching through the mirror. Within a few kilometers I was almost positive we were being followed by two, maybe three cars, each with two or three men. Near Bilbao we came to the first of several police check points where we had to stop, show documents, and open the storage compartment. Probably looking for members of the Basque independence movement known as ETA. I drove off as fast as the little VW would go, just to see what happened with the cars tailing us. Looked like they just flashed ID's—then were waved right through.

That call by the immigration officer in Southampton obviously started it. British told the Station in London. London fired off a cable to Madrid. Madrid put the plan in motion through liaison. These guys are from one of the Spanish security services. What are they going to do? Just follow? Or finally the drug plant, or something worse.

God, why come to Spain of all places? I knew I shouldn't have. But don't get Phil and Chris worried—just let them have their high adventure. Maybe they'll disappear when we get further into the countryside toward Santander. About two hours more to get to Altamira. Let's just see what happens.

Maybe we should get their license numbers. Angela got out a notepad and pen, and I began to slow down in the right lane. Sure enough, one of the cars kept coming in the fast lane, then another. To our surprise they passed us and disappeared over the next hill. No problem getting the numbers. But it looks like there are two more back there. They're not going to pass. Maybe we should try the next exit—no, no, that would be too obvious. Let's try to act like we haven't seen them.

I noticed a sign indicating a parking area coming up. Looked like it would be just over that rise. If we pull off there, maybe the cars behind us won't see. Without slowing I turned up the road leading to the rest area above the highway. From there we could see the other cars pass. Only two cars here. Good, we'll just park a little behind this one. Hey, what are those guys doing with their trunk up?

"Angela, will you look at that. Can you believe it?"

"What?" All three of them said it together.

"Try not to stare," I warned. "They're changing license plates. See? That man just put a new one on the back, and he snapped the holder shut. The other one must have done it in the front. The Agency makes special license plate holders with springs so you can change plates in seconds. Jesus, I never thought I'd see this."

"Look at his face," Angela said. "He knows we see him. Let's just look at the map a minute."

We spread the map over the steering wheel as two men hopped back in the car and drove back to the expressway. We followed a few minutes later. Within a minute or two, one of their cars was behind us again. We continued toward Santander as the surveillance vehicles alternated, sometimes passing us, sometimes dropping behind out of sight, but always there.

Angela and I discussed what to do. Should we try to escape? Could we? Too many of them. Maybe I should call Melvin Wulf at the ACLU in New York and tell him what's happening, see what he could do from there. Later, when he gets to his office, I could call him collect from a coin telephone. Or maybe we should change plans. Turn around and drive straight to France. It was only a couple of hours away.

By the time we got to Altamira, we'd identified four, maybe five cars following us, each with two or three men inside. Over lunch we decided to continue as planned. So far they were only following. Problem was what to do with our car at night. No matter where I parked it, they would know and could do a drug plant while we were sleeping. For that matter they could do it in whatever hotel we found. Either we had to get away from them, keep driving all night to Portugal, or head for France.

Two of the cars were already in the parking lot when we got to the caves, and several of the men were standing around up the hill toward the tourist shop and ticket office. I bought tickets and we walked across the garden to the elevator entrance. Only eight people could go down at once. A young couple, probably just married, was in front of us. Within seconds two of the surveillance agents fell in behind us. Down in the caves we stuck close to the guide, as I quietly translated her commentary. For a few minutes the marvel of these paintings, done thousands of years ago by a tribe seeking refuge from an ice age, almost made me forget our company.

Back in the elevator I stared at the two men from behind, trying to engrain their faces in my memory. As we walked through the garden toward the parking lot, I noticed a man holding a briefcase in an odd position against the front of his thigh. It was as though he were pointing the keyhole at us.

Immediately I remembered the old briefcase photography setup I'd given surveillance teams in South America. We used a "Robot" camera with a spring winding mechanism that would advance the film if you pressed a button on the handle. The camera was mounted inside the briefcase so that the lens aimed through the keyhole. I also remembered the problem with that rig was the noise made each time the film advanced. Without saying why, I steered Angela and the boys over toward the man. We passed just a few meters from him, and there it was: "zing, zing, zing," from inside the briefcase. He was so awkward turning, trying to keep the keyhole pointing at us, I nearly stopped to pose.

Very funny, those guys, but what to do now. We headed back toward the main highway from Santander running south to Burgos. We had to make a decision. Do we drive through the night toward Portugal, go backwards to France, call the ACLU in New York? By now I was getting that old feeling of being cornered, hemmed in, caught in a snare. And tired. It was after four, and we'd already had a long day. But there they were, still behind us. Bastards. What in hell did they think, that we planned to leave a message for ETA in the caves?

We drove into the last city before the main highway, a dusty place called Torrelavega. It was rush hour in the middle of town, especially at a main traffic circle where six or seven streets came together. That policeman up there, what a job with all this traffic!

Suddenly I decided to shake them. Or at least to try to. We were stopped almost at the intersection. I turned off the engine. When the policeman waved our street ahead, I didn't move. Pretended the car wouldn't start. Horns started honking. Policemen rushed over yelling for me to get moving. I gave him my best *no comprendo* shrug. People started shouting. I didn't move.

The policeman was perfect. He started waving all the cars in back of us around and into the intersection. There went our boys: one, two, three, four. And each in a different direction. But nobody down that street. Quick. Start the engine. Make a hard right down that street. That's it. Now as fast as possible for a few blocks. That dirt road over there. Let's go down there and park behind that shack. Now let's wait.

Maybe, just maybe, I thought, we'd shaken them. Our car was pretty well hidden, and we didn't see any of the surveillance cars cruising around. We checked the map. We could take a back road to Burgos, not the main highway. It looked to be paved all the way, but was very twisting where it went over the mountains. Let's hope it doesn't snow.

We waited until dark, then took the narrow, winding blacktop to Burgos, arriving about ten that night. We found a hotel with a parking garage, checked in and went to the first restaurant we saw. The day's tension had left all of wilted and weary.

After ordering, I broke the silence. "Well, folks, how do you like our vacation? Started out great, eh?"

Angela, who'd been the calmest co-pilot during the storm, just smiled and sang, "We made it! We made it! They're in trouble. They lost us."

We spent the next night, Christmas Eve, in Salamanca watching the traditional festivities in the medieval Plaza Mayor. Next day we feasted on *cabrito asado* at the *Parador* outside Ciudad Rodrigo and then headed for the border crossing less than thirty kilometers away. But then I started worrying about the Spanish immigration and customs check. The Agency may know, or assume, we're going to Portugal. Maybe they've got instructions to stop us, arrest us on some pretext, prevent us from seeing people in Lisbon.

They stopped us all right, but for other reasons. The half-dozen customs and immigration people from both sides of the border were having a Christmas blast—the kind where bottles are passed around and around and everyone either gets maudlin or superfriendly. *Ah, Ud. habla Español. Y la señora es Brasileña. Tomen, tomen!* Oh, god. This will go on forever if we start.

Angela said we couldn't refuse. Just one drink, five minutes chat, and then we could go. She was right. They were so drunk an army could have marched through that post in either direction without any questions asked. We drove on to Coimbra, spent the night, and arrived in Lisbon the next afternoon.

We found a small, cheap hotel two blocks from the Praça Rossio where most of the tumultuous political rallies of recent months took place. We'd seen them constantly on television and now we were walking around, getting the feel of the "Revolution of Carnations"— the bloodless coup that ended the longest fascist dictatorship on record. Every wall, it seemed, was papered with political posters, one on top of another as if the parties were competing for space.

Since the coup nine months earlier, Angela and I had followed events in Portugal with special fascination. The country was the poorest in Western Europe, had the lowest paid workers, the highest illiteracy, a concentration of wealth in a half-dozen private monopolies, and extreme imbalance in land ownerhsip.

The coup had released enormous pressures for change. Militant trade unions either surfaced or sprung up almost overnight to lead hundreds of strikes for higher wages. Autonomous workers' commissions took over factories. Landless peasants seized huge farms in the central and southern regions. The Communist Party of Portugal surfaced as one of the strongest political organizations and seemed to be dragging behind the general revolutionary momentum, while various parties to its left called for immediate transition to a radical socialist society.

The Armed Forces Movement (MFA), the group of junior and middle level officers who made the coup, was especially interesting to me. They had fought the colonial wars in Africa against Marxist liberation movements just as I had fought the "war against communism" in Latin America. For them the wars had been a radicalizing experience. They came to understand that the real beneficiaries of the African colonies were the monopolies at home that supported the fascist regime.

Although this group of a few hundred seized power to free the colonies, break up the monopolies, and eliminate the huge inequities between the rich and poor, they were far from united in their politics. In fact they considered themselves above the battling political parties, rather as guardians of the revolt against fascism. Already, in September, the MFA and its military units had united with hundreds of thousands of workers to frustrate an attempted right wing countercoup. Their political agenda was election of a constituent assembly in April to draft a constitution, followed by general elections and a return to civilian rule.

There was much speculation about whether Portugal was on the road to becoming a European Cuba—or a European Chile—comparisons I thought were wrong because the Portuguese situation was unique and moving in its own direction.

Talk was rife of CIA support for rightist parties, information media, and other remnants of the old regime. Much of it centered on the person of General Antonio de Spinola, the conservative, compromise president installed after the coup in the first provisional government. He had organized the September "march of the silent majority" and was forced to resign, but he was still around and clearly opposed the way the revolution was moving. Speculation also centered on intervention by European NATO governments and political parties, particularly the Social Democrats and Christian Democrats.

I couldn't imagine Ford and Kissinger, and their European allies, idly watching revolution develop in Portugal. This was a charter member of NATO, proof that even in the aftermath of World War II, Washington would embrace fascists—so long as they were anticommunist.

Western solidarity was at stake here as in other key countries. Only a few months earlier the fascist military dictatorship in Greece had fallen. Franco's health was failing, and the future in Spain was uncertain. In Italy the communists were closer than ever to participation in national government. To some the "southern tier" in Europe seemed on the verge of disintegration. And if Marxist regimes took over in Mozambique, Angola, Guinea-Bissau, and the Cape Verde Islands, they could threaten the vital African sea lanes.

Revolution in Portugal could also mean the loss of Lajes air force base in the Azores. No other NATO country, only Portugal, had permitted refueling for the American airlift to Israel during the 1973 war, and that base was vital. There were more than enough reasons, it seemed to me, for Ford and Kissinger to intervene.

Some signs were already visible. In August General Vernon Walters, the CIA Deputy Director, visited Portugal to survey the scene. A few weeks later came Spinola's "march of the silent majority" and failed counter-coup. In Brazil ten years earlier, Walters, then U.S. Embassy Military Attaché, had a key role in helping the Agency foment the military coup against the Goulart government. Some of the most effective operations in provoking that coup were huge antigovernment street marches like the one Spinola tried.

Trade unions were a key area to watch. Already the Brussels-based International Confederation of Free Trade Unions was seeking ways

to break communist and other left wing control of the labor movement. Irving Brown, the AFL-CIO European representative and CIA
bag man for labor operations since the 1940's, had also come—no
doubt looking for ways to split unions from the main federation, as he
had successfully done in France and Italy after the war.

Another postwar tactic to watch for now was CIA assistance to
right-wing Social Democrats and Christian Democrats, and support
for reactionaries within the Catholic Church hierarchy. Propaganda
and provocations designed to split the MFA would be another dish on
the menu.

The comparison with Chile, I thought, was valid in the sense that
the Portuguese economy, badly run down by the African wars, was
extremely vulnerable to any economic squeeze that Washington
might undertake, directly or through multilateral lending institutions. The difference was the Portuguese military, which so far were
under control of progressive forces within the MFA. They were dedicated to preserving and extending the revolution, not to its overthrow. No comparison here with Chile.

The April coup apparently caught the CIA by surprise, but if not,
certainly the depth of radical politics within the MFA did. Otherwise
they and the dictatorship's security services would have frustrated it.
The American Ambassador, only a year on the job, was fired, and I
guessed the same happened to the Agency's Chief of Station.

If the new Ambassador, Frank Carlucci, was any indication, the
Ford administration was determined, both alone and in concert with
European allies, to stop the revolution. Carlucci had been on the
team in Kinshasa when Patrice Lumumba was assassinated and the
Congolese revolution stopped. Then he worked four years in Brazil
following the military coup of 1964. He would be in charge of
coordinating all American efforts to "save" Portugal.

The CIA's first problem was to develop fresh sources of information. Even the outgoing Ambassador admitted the Embassy's normal
sources had disappeared with the coup. As in most NATO countries
those sources were the old regime's security services. But the services, so widely hated in Portugal, were dismantled and the leading
officers jailed. Documents made public at the time revealed that the
services, well known for torture and assassination, received training
from the CIA in interrogation and other "technical skills."

The Agency would have to bring in a new group of officers, both
under cover in the Embassy and the military assistance mission, and
outside as businessmen, students, tourists or whatever cover they

could establish. Some would be veterans from Brazilian operations. They would have the crash task of recruiting new agents and setting up new technical operations such as communications intercepts. First priority for penetration would be the MFA, where they would try to identify "moderates" who might be willing to work with them. As always, the capability for political destabilization would depend on good intelligence.

These and other ideas would be the subject of our conversations with the political contacts we hoped to make. At last Angela could speak her own language. She started calling around and soon we had a list of appointments. The group we most wanted to speak with was the Revolutionary Party of the Proletariat-Revolutionary Brigades, the PRP-BR, which had been in the vanguard of the armed struggle against the dictatorship. In two long sessions we discussed probable CIA activities with Isabel do Carmo, the party leader, and I did an interview for their newspaper. Then I did interviews with other papers, magazines and television.

The more I talked with people, the more convinced I was that an expert on the CIA was needed on the spot in Portugal. We couldn't move to Lisbon in the middle of the school year, and I had numerous other commitments in Britain. But in December I had proposed to Jacqueline Lacoste, while she was visiting us in Cornwall, that she consider moving to Lisbon for a while. She was a researcher and journalist then living in Washington, D.C., and understood the CIA's methodology quite well. I could teach her how to identify CIA personnel in the Embassy and the rest of the official mission, and also how to spot people under non-official cover. Together we could develop a model for political destabilization and apply all the elements to Portugal. And the CIA identities and indications of their operations could be published regularly in the Portuguese media, which was predominantly in revolutionary hands.

As often as necessary, Jackie could fly to London, or I could go to Lisbon, and we would work closely with the revolutionary groups there. The idea was to destabilize the CIA before it could destabilize the revolution. She wanted to do it, but the problem was money— how to finance her Lisbon living expenses and the travel costs.

We had brought with us a dozen pre-publication copies of *Inside the Company* and were giving them to people we met. One day I suggested that we take a copy to the headquarters of COPCON, the command center of the military and security forces. It was headed by Brigadier Otelo Saraiva de Carvalho, the man who organized and di-

rected the April coup. He was also one of the principal leaders of the
radicals within the MFA, and was generally perceived as the "strong
man" of the revolution.

I wrote a dedication to Carvalho, and the four of us drove over to
COPCON headquarters. I gave the book to the sentry and asked that
it be passed to the commander. He asked me to wait, made a telephone call, and came back saying Brigadier Otelo wanted to see me.
Someone from his office was coming immediately.

Our escort, a young military officer, took us to Carvalho's office.
After a short wait in an anteroom we were ushered in. I'd read some
of his press comments on the CIA, and I knew he had a keen interest
in the subject, but the meeting was a complete surprise.

Our discussion concerned how the CIA would attempt to derail the
revolution. I told him I was trying to get an associate to come and live
in Lisbon, someone with whom I would work closely in trying to
identify the Agency's personnel and operations. He liked the idea,
and by telephone he made arrangements for me to meet a subordi-
nate officer interested in the same subject. Later I had a long conversation with this officer, and it was clear they needed help. We agreed
to meet again on my return, which I hoped would be within a month.

Driving away from Lisbon, I was even more convinced that
Portugal was high on Washington's agenda. The Agency's role was to
promote the socialist Party of Mario Soares along with several small
right-wing parties. They would support General Spinola's efforts to
keep conservative media alive, to split the trade union movement or
develop alternative, social democratic unions, to support conservative leaders in the Catholic Church, and to find ways to split the
MFA. They would coordinate closely with their allies in corresponding Western European parties and institutions which were seeking
similar goals. In propaganda operations they would have to distort the
revolution, painting it as communist, Moscow-oriented, and a grave
threat to Western interests.

It was a tall agenda, maybe unrealistic given the speed with which
the revolution was moving ahead, the general effervescence of energies, and the broad hatred of the old regime. But I was certain the
Agency would be trying. Political subversion, after all, was one of the
main reasons the Agency existed. If only we could find sponsorship
for Jackie to come and live in Lisbon, totally immersed in the scene,
we might expose enough people and activity to make a difference. As
soon as we returned to Cornwall I would write her and send an
outline of what she would have to do and how much it would cost.

On the boat back to England I studied press reports of the illegal CIA domestic operations that had been revealed during our vacation. It was a scandal, so grave that Ford appointed Vice-President Rockefeller to head an investigation. What perfect timing, I thought, with my book just coming out. People will see how Watergate, and now this domestic spying, are nothing more than bringing the CIA and its methodology home.

The immigration officer at Southampton was nasty enough, asking where we'd been and what we'd done. He also asked insulting questions about the relationship between Angela and me, but then he let us pass.

We headed for London instead of Cornwall to see, finally, whether my book was actually on sale. It had to be. It was Tuesday and last Thursday, January 2nd, was the publication date. It's got to be in the stores. We'll check Collett's, the biggest bookstore on Oxford Street, where they said they'd do a window display with Leslie's typewriter. All the way I had that lingering doubt that somehow the Agency and British services could have stopped publication.

I parked the car on a back street, and we walked to Collett's. There it was. Looked like a hundred copies stacked around the typewriter, with all the electronic parts showing, and a poster-size photograph of me above. Shit, can you believe it? Just look! Let's see how many they've sold.

At the counter I said, "I want to ask a question about that CIA book."

Without looking up, the saleswoman said, "Sold out. We've placed three re-orders since last week. Maybe this afternoon we'll have more. We can't sell the display copies."

"How many have you sold?"

She looked at me, and her face lit up. "You're the author! I recognize you. Listen, you can't imagine! We've sold thousands—all the copies we could get. Can't get enough from Penguin. You should talk to them, tell them to print more."

That was all I needed. Home safe after all those years! They couldn't stop it! Sold out! Wow!

We drove back to Cornwall on a cloud, to find a huge pile of mail with the first batch of reviews from Penguin's clipping service. Hundreds more would follow. I didn't mind the criticisms of style, my political motivations, or the "realities" overkill. I knew it was hard reading. But nobody scoffed.

The London *Evening News* wrote: "A frightening picture of corruption, pressure, assassination and conspiracy." The *Economist* called it "inescapable reading." And Miles Copeland, a former CIA Station Chief in Cairo, wrote in *The Spectator*: " . . . as complete an account of spy work as is likely to be published anywhere . . . presented with deadly accuracy." Then Garcia Marquez: " . . . one reads it through without a break . . . a fascinating book."

In FOIA documents I learned that CIA Stations all over the world were asking the London Station for copies. Then Headquarters sent a secret message to all Stations warning them that my book had to be treated as classified information. That meant it had to be kept safe, that officers couldn't take it home to read, and that anyone who left it out at night would get a "security violation."

I had to prepare for the Brussels session of the Bertrand Russell Tribunal the following weekend. I was nervous about the meeting, standing up before all those Chileans and others who'd been victims of CIA operations. So I left early thinking that if I got there on Saturday I'd have that day and most of Sunday before I had to speak.

Garcia Marquez said he'd put me in contact with people so I could get a feel for what to say. But in London I got bogged down doing interviews, discovered I'd left my passport at Penmoor, then called Angela and asked her to send it via British Rail express. I got it Sunday morning at Paddington Station, took a taxi to Heathrow, and barely made the flight to Brussels. At the Palais des Congres I found Garcia Marquez finishing lunch with Regis Debray, the French writer who had been with Che Guevara in Boliva, and was captured, tried and imprisoned for several years.

I sat with Debray in the back of the darkened auditorium as the afternoon session began. It was two-thirds full with about 250–300 people, each with a headset for translations into English, Spanish and French. Speakers had thirty minutes followed by a fifteen-minute question period. I was studying my notes as two speakers came and went. Then the moderator announced that I would be the next speaker, giving a short description of my background. The hall became absolutely silent as people started looking around. Debray gave me a nod of encouragement, and I started down the aisle amidst whispers and hushed comments I couldn't understand.

At the lectern I took out my notes, took a deep breath and began. My main points revolved around the CIA's operations to train and equip police and security services, and their subversive political operations to provoke military takeovers as in Chile. I also described a program common to all Stations in Latin America—the so-called Subversive Control Watch List.

This was a requirement to maintain files on the CIA's most important political enemies, with details about their lives and movements, so that they could be found and arrested quickly. The information was kept current and ready for immediate passage to local security forces at a moment of crisis. I was certain the Agency gave this information to Chilean services at the time of the coup and was thus responsible for many of the immediate arrests, tortures and summary executions.

Stage fright made me speak too quickly. This prompted interruption from the interpreters and the Tribunal President requesting that I slow down. But then an unexpected laugh made me relax. In discussing political operations I mentioned that we had even formed our own party in Ecuador, one we wanted to appeal to a broad following, hence the name: Popular Revolutionary Liberal Party.

As people howled I realized for the first time how contradictory and ridiculous that name was. I ended with a call for an international campaign to identify CIA people and to organize demonstrations against them wherever they could be found. The loud applause made me feel that while I hadn't spoken well, and should have been better prepared, I hadn't done as badly as I feared I might.

When I finished, press and television crews crowded around with requests for interviews. I spent an hour with them. Then I met with Chileans and other Latin American exiles. It was like a side-show to the main Tribunal, with one question after another about what the Agency's doing in this or that country, why I had joined, why I left, why the Agency hadn't killed me. As I had expected some hostility, I was struck by the friendliness and the support expressed.

Too bad the CIA people on my case couldn't see this, I thought. They'd have realized that with this kind of public acceptance and approval no amount of false press plants, intimidations or threats were going to work.

I was wrong again. The Agency did know about my activities that day, as I found out from FOIA documents years later. These were lists of places and dates I spoke, with excerpts from my speeches. Starting with the Russell Tribunal, it seemed they hardly missed a press conference, a public meeting, a television or radio interview. Later, in protracted litigation, they would use these quotes to convince judges that I was a "threat to national security."

I returned to Cornwall to prepare for a promotional trip to Canada where Penguin was selling all the copies of the book they could get from London. Meanwhile television and press people were still coming to St. Clement, and every day the telephone rang with requests for more interviews.

Inside the Company quickly went on the British best-seller lists, although Penguin's marketing people went out of stock for six weeks. In Toronto they wanted 50,000 additional copies for my visit but were shipped only 30,000. Nevertheless, the book was displayed in shops and kiosks everywhere.

As I passed through passport control at Heathrow for the flight to Canada, I noticed a procedure that would be repeated every time I left Britain in the years ahead. The immigration officer recognized my name, wrote something on the departure card, and passed me through.

Looking back, I noticed he immediately put up the rope to stop the line, took my departure card over to a glassed-in office, and made a telephone call. Just like Southampton, I thought, they're getting my destination and flight number to the Agency like good "junior partners." Still, I would never understand why they had let me complete my book there.

The trip, the first of four to Canada that year, was a whirlwind of press, radio and television interviews, many with media people who came up from the United States.

Tom Snyder's *Tomorrow* program on NBC was especially pleasing. I never saw that telecast, in which I talked for an hour, mostly about the Agency's connections with political repression in Latin America. But later I learned that the Agency arranged a special showing of the program in the Headquarters auditorium. It was followed by a discussion in which, to my surprise, some younger officers stood up in my defense—or at least in partial agreement.

In the streets Canadians stopped me for autographs and congratulations. Once, in a book shop, a man came charging over. For a second I thought he was bent on violence. Then he grinned, said he'd seen me on television, and drove 150 miles from his home somewhere in New York, just to buy the book.

Then U.S. booksellers began importing shipments in the thousands both from Canada and Britain. An 1891 law made it illegal to import books in English by an American author, and the book was marked "Not For Sale In The U.S.A." Confiscation was the penalty. But when customs officials went around to bookshops in New York there were no copies left to seize. FOIA documents show that the Agency tried to keep up with U.S. sales, even quoting one press report that the book had become a collector's item.

In Toronto I had long conversations with American activists from the anti-war movement who came to visit. I was doing a *Playboy* interview and succeeded in getting several of them to write sidebars on themes like the CIA's Phoenix assassination program in Vietnam for publication with the interview. With everyone I insisted on the importance of the exposure campaign and the need to monitor the Agency's work in Portugal as closely as possible. And through members of the *CounterSpy* staff who came, I arranged for distribution of my book to every member of the Senate and House of Representatives. These contacts with American "movement" people were stimulating and full of excitement—after working in isolation and anonymity for so long I was starved to know the people who had fought the war at home.

The problem of getting a U.S. publisher came up in every conversation, especially in view of the public threats by William Colby, the CIA Director, to take legal action to prevent publication. His dubious argument was that even with tens of thousands of copies already in circulation, publication of classified information was illegal. The FOIA documents reveal that Colby tried to get the Justice Department to seek a court injunction against publication, but Justice said they couldn't get it because the book was already published in England. Exactly as I planned.

Straight Arrow still wanted to publish *Inside the Company*, and they dispatched an editor to Toronto to discuss cuts they wanted. But their proposed deletions included some of the most important political content, so I decided to put it all in the hands of an agent and insist on the original Penguin version. I chose Scott Meredith—a decision I would later lament—and told him my main concern was to get it out quickly, if possible directly into paperback with a limited hardcover edition for libraries.

Simon and Schuster, which had rejected the book with all the other "majors" six months earlier, decided to reconsider. They were distributors for Straight Arrow and already had prepublication orders for 30,000 hardcover copies. But FOIA documents showed that Simon and Schuster's lawyer, Selig Levitan, was discussing publication with the CIA and was "not enthusiastic" about it. Although he said his role was to review the book for possible libel suits, he also tried without success to persuade the editors that the book "violated national security." Later Simon and Schuster rejected it again—for fear of libel suits.

At about the same time, Warner Books, one of the country's largest mass market publishers, offered a $50,000 advance, conditioned on their ability to secure libel insurance. That seemed to be no problem

until columnist Jack Anderson published two articles sourced ultimately to CIA information, alleging that I had connections with Cuban intelligence and might even be under "Cuban discipline."

The content of the columns was not only distorted and misleading.
He wrote that people in my book were harassed with threatening
phone calls, that the daughter of one received a death threat, and that
someone emptied a pistol at the taxi of another who miraculously escaped.

Anderson called me before publishing those columns, but I only
saw them, together, several weeks afterwards. I found it difficult to
believe he could get things so wrong except by intention. If people
had been threatened or shot at, the stories would have been news
before then, and I'd have had a hundred calls about it.

I had told him about my Cuban visits. If he'd wanted to know my
purpose he could have found that in my book. But he wrote that I
"refused to go into any details." I also told him I had been to the Cuban Embassy in Paris a couple of times to ask about research pending
in Havana. But this came out as "refusal to comment on the report
that he had been seen in Paris with Cuban agents." On being "spotted in the company of Cuban intelligence agents in Paris and
London," Anderson followed immediately with: "Agee doesn't deny
this. 'I have seen them in Paris and London,' he acknowledged to us."
The *them* was totally misleading because I had not told him I saw
"Cuban intelligence agents" but Cuban Embassy officials.

In the end he did get a couple of quotes accurately: "'Whether they
were Cuban intelligence officers or not, I don't really care.' He added
meaningfully: 'I support the Cuban revolution.'"

With those two columns it seemed pretty clear that the Agency was
taking a new approach. They dropped the "drunk-despondent-KGB"
line for a "Cuban agent" version, spicing it with "mortal danger" for
the "innocent victims" I had written about. Soon they would seize on
my reference in the "Acknowledgements" to "encouragement from
representatives of the Communist Party of Cuba at a time when I
doubted that I would be able to find the additional information I
needed." I had pondered long and hard about that reference and decided to include it because I had written about my stay in Cuba and
my difficulties finding documentation. The reference would be translated in propaganda as my having written the book "under Cuban direction." Nothing could have been further from the truth, as the
Agency's FOIA documents confirmed. Yet, for years to come they
played the "Cuban agent" line to the exclusion of the simple fact that

I was just one more of thousands who had visited Cuba and seen the positive achievements of the revolution.

I wrote my denials, which the *Washington Post* published, but I obviously had no way to reach the millions who read those columns in other newspapers. Among them, I supposed, were people at Warner's insurance company because they cited the Anderson columns in their refusal to grant libel insurance. Mel Wulf at the ACLU offered to litigate any libel proceedings *pro bono,* and I suggested they keep the advance as a reserve against libel judgments, but that wasn't enough. Through Anderson, the Agency had successfully blocked U.S. publication once again.

Not for long. In April, a small, offbeat publishing house called Stonehill offered to get the book into the shops in eight to ten weeks. I accepted, and before long we had a mass market reprint contract with Bantam, the world's largest paperback publisher. They would publish their edition six months after the hardcover. Neither threats of legal action by the CIA Director nor the backdoor methods with journalists and lawyers worked this time. Finally, finally, I had an American edition coming out.

At this time, a group of former CIA officers started a retired officers association to "defend the Agency's image" and mount a campaign against its critics, notably Marchetti and me. This was the brainchild of David Phillips, who resigned as chief of Latin American operations to become the CIA's public defender. He sent a letter to a couple hundred retired officers in which he wrote:

> I have been deeply concerned about the decline of morale at Langley (headquarters) and abroad . . . . Our capabilities abroad are being damaged. More and more of our agents and friends—many of them fine people who cooperate on the basis of ideology—are saying thanks but no thanks. Friendly liaison services are beginning to back away from us. The Marchettis and the Agees have the stage, and only a few challenge them.

Phillips may not have been the best choice for image building, I thought, given his background. He had participated in the overthrow of the democratically elected Guatemalan government in 1954. He later served in Cuba during the Batista dictatorship. He worked on the Bay of Pigs task force, directed Agency operations in the Dominican Republic when the U.S. invaded that country, was Chief of Station in Brazil under the military dictatorship there, then was chief of all Latin American operations in the period leading up to the military coup in Chile. But he thought he could defend all that by getting on the lecture circuit, speaking at universities, civic clubs, veterans' organizations and other groups. He sent his résumé and proposal to 586 colleges and universities; five months later not one had invited him.

The BBC did put him on television, though, in a debate with me. Before the program I told the producer I didn't want to see him before or after the program. He happened to be Chief of Station in Rio de Janeiro when Angela was shot and tortured by services the CIA had trained and supplied. She was coming with me to the London studio, along with Dad and Nancy, who were visiting. We walked into the hospitality lounge and who should be standing there but Phillips. He got up, walked over like some hustling insurance salesman, and shook hands with my father and Nancy. Neither Angela nor I hid our contempt. We walked to a far corner of the room, without speaking to or looking at him.

On the program, the best he could do was justify the CIA because it carried out government policy. He denounced me for revealing secrets, and closed by calling me a "moral primitive." Knowing his background, it wasn't hard for me to lay the Chilean coup, torture in Brazil and other political repression at his feet. The next day a taxi driver who saw the program congratulated me and said he thought Phillips was one of the slimiest sights he'd ever seen on the tube.

Besides U.S. publication of my book, there was other good news. One of my visitors in Toronto was a documentary filmmaker from Berkeley, California, named Allan Francovich. He had made a film on the Allende government and the coup in Chile. His politics seemed good, so I agreed to help him on a documentary about the CIA that he thought he would call *On Company Business*. Already he was raising money for the project.

Another interesting film offer came from Emile de Antonio. He wanted to do a dramatic film based on *Inside the Company*.

Several Hollywood filmmakers had already approached me, and I told them I wanted to see a script before making any decisions; I was afraid they'd make an adventure movie with no political content. But De Antonio was different. I'd seen his work—loved *Milhouse*, his satire on Nixon—and didn't doubt he could do the right film politically.

He had started working on a script, and had informal commitments from Jane Fonda and Haskell Wexler to participate. Finally, Neil Middleton accepted my idea for another book for Penguin, this one a study of CIA support for political repression in ten or twelve countries around the world, including Iran, Indonesia, South Korea, Brazil and Zaire.

In contrast, my attempts to interest U.S. groups in the CIA exposure campaign and the "CIA watch" in Portugal were less than successful. I recommended both activities, offering my assistance, to progressive groups strongly committed against CIA subversion: the North American Congress on Latin America (NACLA), the Center for National Security Studies (CNSS), the Institute for Policy Studies (IPS), and its Third World subsidiary, the Transnational Institute (TNI) in Amsterdam. All declined.

Part of the problem was that these groups had to operate within "respectable" limits so as not to lose their private funding. They were a "loyal opposition." Some were even working with Congressional liberals in the House and Senate investigations of the CIA. They and others honestly believed major reforms, like prohibition of covert actions, were attainable through Congress. My guerrilla warfare approach outside reformist norms was not compatible.

The other part of the problem was that the Agency's campaign was designed to isolate me from those groups, and it was somewhat successful. About the same time the Anderson columns appeared, other articles and statements began emerging from a loose network of far-right writers and activists.

Typical of these was Larry McDonald, the Georgia Congressman and leader of the John Birch Society. While I was trying to interest groups in the two projects, he made a speech about me in the House of Representatives which began with the "Cuban agent" theme, describing me as "this defector to the Communist cause." Through the acknowledgments in my book he linked me with people in NACLA, then with CNSS, IPS and TNI in a red-baiting harangue that made us look like an international communist conspiracy, in league with terrorists and bent on destruction of the United States. For years he would play variations on this theme through speeches or insertions in the *Congressional Record*, always brokering the "red menace" conspiracy, until he finally found peace on KAL 007, the Korean airplane shot down by the Soviets.

I found the McDonald-style attack amusing. There was no more conspiracy among the groups than agreement on alternative agendas. And I certainly had nothing to do with their work at that point. But the attacks had the effect of convincing those groups to keep their distance from me, even though most of their members agreed privately with what I was trying to do. They just couldn't manage formal partic-

ipation, and rumors of a coming grand jury investigation into my activities didn't help. Jackie Lacoste thus had to search for non-
institutional support for the Portugal project, which she eventually
found, but not until months later, after the revolution had begun to
come apart.

The one group that I expected would unquestionably participate in
the exposure campaign was the Fifth Estate and *CounterSpy*, since
they had published the list of over 100 CIA Chiefs of Station in January. But they too had problems with the campaign. Financial not political. Almost overnight all of their support from liberal sponsors
dried up, largely due to attacks that they too were "Cuban agents"
and "communist conspirators."

At the same time the IRS withdrew their tax-exempt status and
slapped a $50,000 lien against Norman Mailer's property. That killed
his subsidy, but for the next issue he savaged the Agency in an article
entitled "The CIA vs. Democracy." Rumor also had it that the Fifth
Estate would be investigated by a grand jury. For the time being the
most they could do was to republish the names of CIA people that had
already come out in the foreign press, e.g., the Mexico City list.

In Europe, however, journalists had no such constraints. Among
those who visited me in early 1975 were three Americans: Mark
Hosenball, Steve Weissman and Louis Wolf, all living in London.
Hosenball, who worked at the weekly entertainment listings and pop
world magazine *Time Out*, had chanced onto a copy of John Marks's
article, "How to Spot a Spook," in the *Washington Monthly*. They
wanted to know if the "Marks method" was valid, and if so they would
write an expose of the CIA Station in London. I was appalled when I
saw the article. The CIA would now get the State Department to classify or restrict circulation of the *Biographic Register* and *Foreign Service List* which sooner or later would make identification of CIA personnel in diplomatic missions much more difficult.

But it was done. I confirmed Marks's accuracy, and before long,
two or three more journalists from other publications were
coordinating on the story with the first three. One of the most aggressive and effective was the editor of *The Workers' Press*, the newspaper of the Trotskyist Workers' Revolutionary Party in which Vanessa
Redgrave was a leading activist. I worked with them all.

We found only six or seven CIA officers on the London diplomatic
list, but then one of the journalists got a U.S. Embassy directory. It
was a jackpot, as I knew it would be. Analysis showed a CIA Station
with no fewer than sixty-two people. Then photographers got on the

job, surprising a number of them in the street outside their homes. Publication of the names, addresses, and photographs, together with organizational diagrams of the Station, caused a mild sensation.

In the British House of Commons, Stan Newens, a left-wing member of the Labour Party, raised questions about why so many CIA people were in London, considering what they had done in Chile. He made a parliamentary motion, signed by thirty-two MPs, that they be expelled. Then a group of progressive U.S. citizens, who called themselves "Concerned Americans Abroad," organized "Tours of Stately CIA Homes" with chartered buses from Sloane Square. Another American, a theater director, cast a production mocking the CIA, and his troupe accompanied the tours, performing in the streets in front of the houses. For a while, the CIA in Britain was a laughing stock.

The exposures in Britain were widely reported in the Western European press, setting off a rush by journalists throughout the region to identify and expose the CIA people in their own countries. Most of them gravitated to me and to Louis Wolf, who became an expert in analysis of career backgrounds found in the *Biographic Register*. He discovered that the British Museum had all the *Registers* and *Foreign Service Lists*, year by year, back to the 1940's. He ordered them all from a storage depot, set up shop in the State Papers Room, and spent months there hunched over a table preparing analyses of hundreds of CIA officers.

Working with the journalists and the Embassy directories provided by the State Department, I began to prepare exposés to coincide with publication of my book in other languages, among them Swedish, Danish, Dutch, French, Italian, German, Spanish and Greek. Our "guerrilla journalism," as someone called it, would soon have the CIA's stations exposed as never before—just at the time when Congressional investigations were revealing the Agency's poison dart guns, shellfish toxin, cobra venom, assassination attempts, and political subversion.

The timing couldn't have been better.

Despite the CIA's threats to block U.S. publication of my book, they never took legal action. By publication date in late July, Stonehill had orders for 70,000 copies. I went back to Canada for promotional work both prior to and after publication. More radio, press and television, and meetings with American activists. I was nearly bowled over when over the 4th of July weekend, the Pacifica radio station in Berkeley, KPFA, read all 600-plus pages of *Inside the Company* on the air.

Some journalists suggested I was putting people in danger and ruining their lives, but I had a good quote from CIA Director Colby. On my naming names he said, "I think it's terrible, frankly, because this puts people's reputations in bad shape." Does a criminal indictment hurt a mafioso's reputation? Working for the CIA was an act of choice, with risks of exposure. Colby only confirmed it was disreputable as well.

In every interview the question arose about when I would return to the U.S. I discussed this with my lawyer, Mel Wulf, told him I wanted to go back as soon as possible at least to visit, and he began negotiations with Attorney General Edward Levi. We wanted to know whether I had been indicted for revealing secrets in my book, and if not, whether if I returned I would be prosecuted.

I'd make a decision taking into account the cost of a trial and the chances for conviction. If there were no criminal prosecution, I still had to consider the effect that a civil injunction would have on my work. Such an injunction, already upheld by the courts against Victor Marchetti, would require me to submit all my future writings and speeches to the Agency for censorship before publication or delivery. I would have to weigh these considerations against my ability to continue writing and speaking from abroad, outside the jurisdiction of U.S. courts, without censorship, and immune from extradition.

Another unknown factor was whether Angela would be allowed into the U.S., given her revolutionary background in Brazil and her help on the book. The Agency certainly knew that the book was a joint project for us, and that without her I'd never have gotten it written. Surely they would oppose her entry to the States. Even if she was let in, could she be happy there? After all, for her the United States was the imperial power behind the military dictatorship in her own country. We would have to see, I told interviewers and colleagues alike.

Inside the Company was an immediate U.S. best-seller, stimulated by hundreds of reviews across the country. The *Washington Post* started them, months before U.S. publication, with a review by a journalist who had worked in the Peace Corps in Latin America. "Agee has provided the most complete description yet of what the CIA does abroad. In entry after numbing entry, U.S. foreign policy is pictured as a web of deceit, hypocrisy, and corruption . . . grist for a hundred Latin American Watergates. . . ." Countless others were just as satisfying.

One review that I especially liked was by the CIA itself, in its professional, in-house quarterly called *Studies in Intelligence*. The journal was normally classified secret, but under the FOIA John Marks got the complete review. Nothing was censored as classified, and Marks sent a copy to me, and published it in a magazine called *Bookletter*.

While the reviewer questioned my personal and political motivations, there wasn't a mention of the "drunk-despondent-KGB" or "Cuban agent" lines, and, most importantly, he confirmed the accuracy of my book. The review included the following comments:

> His most thorough revelation of sensitive information is given in his accurate descriptions of each Station's operations under identifying cryptonym.
>
> His description of the Clandestine Service's *modus operandi* is valid outside Latin America, and Agee is said to be working on a larger project describing CIA activities all over the world.
>
> The book will affect the CIA as a severe body blow does any living organism: some parts obviously will be affected more than others, but the health of the whole is bound to suffer. A considerable number of CIA personnel must be diverted from their normal duties to undertake the meticulous and time-consuming task of repairing the damage done to its Latin American program, and to see what can be done to help those injured by the author's revelations.

In my FOIA proceedings later, the CIA gave me a copy of the same *Studies in Intelligence* review. Each of the above passages relating to accuracy and damage was now censored (blacked out) as "properly classified" because, according to the Agency, they revealed "methods of analysis." But the reviewer's conclusion remained uncensored: "The book's main achievement is to provide the Communists and extreme Left with specific knowledge of CIA's Latin American operations and insight into CIA *modus operandi* in order to permit them to counter U.S. and particular CIA actions."

The Agency, if not the reviewer, would soon discover that my book would be useful to many who were neither "Communists" nor "extreme Left": social democrats, church activists, students, nationalists, trade unionists and journalists.

The Agency's internal description of my book as "accurate" contrasted vividly with their propaganda line as revealed in the FOIA documents. "Agee's book gives a distorted view of U.S. policy and CIA operations in Latin America. It contains numerous falsehoods and items of disinformation . . . it contains numerous inaccuracies designed to cause maximum damage to the CIA and U.S. Government."

Following publication of *Inside the Company*, Angela and I began to question whether we wanted to live so far from London. No question that it was beautiful out there in Penmoor, but I was away over half the time for interviews, speaking engagements, return to Portugal, or work on the exposure campaign. And when I was home, I was always at the typewriter, half hysterical, trying to write magazine articles, catch up on mail, respond to press attacks such as the Anderson columns, or read the voluminous documentation I'd ordered from research centers. These materials I needed to get started on my second book.

Angela, although she came on several trips, was still mostly stuck in domestic choies, shopping and cooking, and helping Phil and Chris with school work.

Needless to say, the stress I felt affected my relations with Angela and my sons. I hadn't yet learned to say "no" to requests for articles, interviews or speaking engagements, and the hectic pace made me tense, irritable, nervous and bad company at home. Interruptions, inevitable with four people in a three-room flat, brought on sharp words and an occasional temper tantrum.

A partial solution to these problems might be to move back to London and eliminate all the hours coming and going on the train. Angela wouldn't be so isolated when I travelled. In the spring I looked for a London flat. No success. Angela searched too. The combination of high rents and school complications seemed insurmountable.

We called Tom and Anne in Cambridge, and they encouraged us to move there—only an hour or so from London. I had already spoken at a pro-Chile rally at the university and liked the students' enthusiasm. In June, Angela found a house large enough for Phil and Chris to have separate bedrooms and for me to have an office. We moved the following month, bought bicycles, and began to settle in.

Still, there was little relief. Polarization was growing in Portugal where events were almost impossible to follow. Jackie finally got there in late July, and it seemed a civil war was looming just over the horizon. Following an abortive coup attempt by General Spinola and right-wing military officers in March, the revolution moved steadily left toward rule through institutions of "popular power," such as commissions elected by workers, tenants, neighborhood groups and peasants. Similar commissions were set up within the armed forces, breaking traditional military discipline and relations between officers and soldiers.

Controversy raged over worker takeover of the Socialist newspaper *Repubblica* and the Catholic station *Radio Renancença*. The leading political force in this movement was not the orthodox communist party but the PRP-BR, with which I had spoken in December and March.

But the center and right, led by the Socialist Party of Mario Soares, with millions of dollars from European social democrats and the CIA, were fighting back. The Soares party won a plurality in the April elections, but was denied real power and left the government. The Catholic Church, especially in the north where it was strongest, was fomenting a terrorist campaign against the communist and other left parties.

Spinola organized a paramilitary force called the Portuguese Liberation Army which staged cross-border raids from Spain and dropped incendiary bombs to start forest fires. A separatist movement in the Azores, organized from the U.S., threatened secession. Thousands of Portuguese were returning from Angola with no jobs in sight. And the economy was collapsing.

For over a year the U.S. and its allies has been calling for "pluralism" and "modernization" as conditions for economic assistance— codewords for stopping the revolution and turning power over to Soares and the right. In July the "moderates" in the Armed Forces Movement surfaced with the so-called Document of the Nine which denounced both the orthodox communist party and the more radical movement for "popular power." This document began circulating among military units and was answered by a document from COPCON under Brigadier Carvalho which reaffirmed support for "popular power." The MFA and military units then split along those lines.

In August I wrote an article, "An Open Letter to the Portuguese People," describing the different ways I believed the CIA was intervening to weaken their revolution, first and foremost by supporting Soares and the "moderates" in the MFA. I also gave the names and addresses of the CIA people in the Embassy that I could identify, together with their backgrounds.

As I had expected, the Stations was largely comprised of officers with prior experience in Latin American operations. The "open letter" was published in Lisbon and several other countries. Then the soldiers and sailors commissions in several of the radical military units invited me for lectures, but I had tours already scheduled for England, Scotland, Sweden and Canada.

In November I would go back to Lisbon. By then it was too late. A few days before my scheduled return, right-wing military units seized on the standard ruse, a supposed "communist plot," and proceeded to disarm and dissolve the radical military units.

The revolution was stalled, if not completely stopped.

Altogether in 1975 I spoke at almost forty public meetings in half a dozen countries: from factories to universities to political rallies to pro-Chile meetings, even to the staff and patients of a mental hospital. In Switzerland I found myself speaking before almost a thousand people at a rally for a cantonal candidate of the Revolutionary Marxist League. Next day the conservative Zurich press observed with alarm that it was the biggest rally of the whole election campaign.

On a speaking tour of Canada in October the possibility of my returning to the United States came up again. Jon Peters, the film producer and companion of Barbra Streisand, bought motion picture rights to an article I wrote for *Oui* magazine. It was a fictional account of the CIA's takeover of the U.S. through secretly running its own candidate in the 1976 elections. I gave it a twist at the end that I knew would please the Agency: the operation blew up after the CIA candidate was elected, when tapes of conversations in the CIA Director's office were sent to the *Toronto Star* by the KGB. Peters met me in Vancouver and asked me to go to California to work on the script at the Streisand ranch.

I couldn't. Mel Wulf had finally learned from the Attorney General that I had not been secretly indicted. But Levi would not say whether I would be indicted if I went back. After discussions with Angela and others I decided to keep working from abroad, uncensored, and avoid the risk of a long and costly trial. I wrote a statement giving all the reasons and sent it to friends in the States for publication.

The year-end school vacation was coming up, and all of us wanted to take a trip. Where to this time? Well, I said, in early January I have to be in Rome for publication of my book in Italian.

What about Italy? I have to speak at just two more meetings, one in London and one in Paris. Then I have to see people in Zurich and Geneva. We could meet in Milan, spend two weeks touring, then I'd stay in Rome for the press conference and interviews. How about it? Great! Great! Milan, Venice, Florence, Rome, Pompeii. Here we come!

My trip to Italy started with a meeting at the London School of Economics sponsored by "Concerned Americans Abroad," the same group of activists who had organized the "Tours of Stately CIA homes." The subject was the crisis in Portugal, and also in Angola where troops from South Africa and Zaire had entered the civil war to support UNITA and the FNLA, followed by Cuban troops in support of the MPLA, which controlled the capital.

Newspapers were full of reports that the Agency was backing the FNLA and UNITA, most likely from Zaire, and I didn't doubt them. Before the meeting I did an analysis of the directory of the U.S. Embassy in the Zairean capital, Kinshasa, and found eighteen I believed were CIA plus another fifteen who were possibly CIA people. I gave this list to Angolan solidarity in London for passage to the MPLA, which I announced to loud cheering at the meeting.

The Paris meeting was also on Portugal, sponsored by the Bertrand Russell Tribunal. I went on to Zurich, then to Geneva, where I accepted an invitation to stay overnight with a lawyer friend. At about seven o'clock, his roommate came home. He was surprised and enthusiastic to meet me because he was an Ecuadorean and had read my book. He was fascinated by the magnitude of the Agency's political operations in his country. But then he had a strange and bewildering tale to tell.

"You know that woman who gave you the money in Paris—and the bugged typewriter? The one called Leslie? I think I know her."

"You're kidding," I said in amazement. "She disappeared three years ago. I heard she was in Spain."

"Well, I think she's right here in Geneva. Her name is Janet Strickland and she works at the International Labor Organization of the U.N. You see, I have a friend, also Ecuadorean, whose best friend is a guy from Spain. Janet Strickland is the Spanish guy's girlfriend. A few months ago, when your book came out, my Ecuadorean friend told me that the Spanish guy had told him that Janet was the Leslie in your book. She told her boyfriend in strict confidence that the CIA had recruited her at an American university and sent her here to study French. Then they sent her to Paris to work against you, giving her a false name and identity. Then she came back here and got a job at the I.L.O."

We discussed Janet's physical appearance, and she seemed about right for Leslie. And university recruitment, Geneva studies, Spanish boyfriend—that all fit Leslie. Jorge, the Ecuadorean, worked for another U.N. agency. He got out his directory and found Janet's name and home address on Chemin du Bouchet, a luxury apartment building according to him.

Jorge and I made a plan. In the morning, early, we would drive over to her place and park across from the entrance. I could see her when she left for work.

We did just that. To keep her from recognizing me, I wrapped a scarf around my head, with just my eyes showing. We sat there for an hour in bitter cold. No Janet. No Leslie. Later Jorge telephone her office. She'd left a day early for the weekend—be back on Monday. Damn! And I had to get to Milan to meet Angela and the boys on Sunday.

"Look, Jorge, I appreciate your help. I'd really like to be sure it's the same person. I'm going to be touring Italy with my family for two weeks, but after that I'll come back here, and we'll figure out a way for me to see her. Meanwhile please don't mention this to anyone else. If Janet is Leslie, and she finds out I know, she'll disappear again. This may be a CIA spy in the U.N. that we can nail cold."

"That's okay. Just call me. You can stay with us again."

The hours on the train to Milan were seemingly endless, probably because one thought predominated: could that be Leslie? *My* Leslie?

VI

An Untimely Death

The Orient Express from London to Venice, with Angela and the boys on board, was half an hour late so I strolled around the huge Milan station, thinking of Leslie and also of Sal. With him little mystery remained. Just after his name surfaced, people in the States who'd known him in the anti-war movement got in touch with me for more details. Some said they had suspected Sal all along. Then several people contacted him by telephone at his parents' home in Chicago. Although he protested his innocence, he seemed defensive and refused to see them. Then he apparently stopped taking telephone calls.

Phil and Chris found me on the platform amidst the hordes of holiday travellers. Through the crowd they steered me to their car for the ride to Venice. Angela had arranged reserved seats—people were standing in the aisles so packed they could hardly move. I immediately told her of the possibility that I'd found Leslie, and she was elated. Well, let's see, I said. We haven't found her yet. And we've got two marvelous weeks ahead of us to see Italy.

Seeing Venice and Florence for the first time was so enchanting
that I hardly thought of "work." The day after Christmas we headed
for the Florence station and a train for Rome. At a newsstand I bought
an *International Herald Tribune*, and there on the front page was a
headline I would never forget: "CIA Man Slain in Athens." Oh, my
god, Angela, look what's happened. I could hardly speak or breathe.
My heart was racing as we read the article. Richard Welch, the Agency's Chief of Station in Athens, had been shot late on the night of December 23rd as he returned to his home from a party at the Ambassador's residence. Three masked men had driven up in a car, one got
out, shot Welch three times, then sped away. No indications of who
they were.

The article also said Welch's name and address were published a
month before in the English language *Athens News*. Goddamit! This
is going to cause an unholy uproar. Why did they do a thing like that?
Why couldn't they just demonstrate, as in London? Why'd they have
to kill him? "Thank god we're not home," I said to Angela, "that telephone must be ringing off the hook. When we get to Rome I'll call
London and see what's happened. There's going to be terrible
trouble, you can bet on that."

"Did you know this man?" Angela asked.

"No, but I know the name. Richard Welch worked in Latin
America. He was on the *CounterSpy* list as Chief of Station in Lima.
Seems odd that someone with his background would be assigned to
Athens."

All the way to Rome we talked about Welch and the CIA in
Greece. I remembered those weeks I was temporarily assigned to the
Greek desk in Headquarters, back in 1959 before I went into the
training program. I didn't understand very much, but it seemed the
Agency's hands were into everything in that country. And apparently
it hadn't changed much, because a recent mission directory showed
an enormous CIA contingent for a nation the size of Greece.

Angela thought Welch's killing had to be seen in historical context,
and she was right. The Left had been the principal resistance movement during the Nazi occupation. After the war first the British, then
the Americans, intervened to install and sustain corrupt, conservative
regimes. Through savage political repression, just as in Chile, they
tried to exterminate the Left. The CIA was the main instrument,
working through the police and security services. They set up the
Greek CIA, the KYP, trained its people and gave it money and equipment. Then in 1967, when it looked like a moderately reformist government might come to power through elections, the "colonels"

staged a coup using a sham "communist plot" as pretext. Echoes of
Latin America.

For the next seven years Greece lived under a fascist military regime, led almost to the end by the colonel who had been the KYP's
chief liaison officer with the CIA. Thousands of Greeks went through
that regime's prisons and torture chambers, and thousands were
forced to live in exile. If Turkey hadn't invaded Cyprus, the regime
would probably still be in power. But the junta collapsed, and millions of Greeks hit the streets to show their joy. Now, little more than
a year later, some group takes reprisal against the junta's main supporters, the CIA. Who should be surprised?

"You and I know that," I said to Angela, "but in Washington
they're going to blame Welch's killing on me and *CounterSpy*. They'll
use it to attack the whole exposure campaign."

"You have to put it in context," she answered. "It was a political
act. The group didn't even know Welch. They picked him as a symbol
of the CIA's role in political repression. That's different from
bombing a crowded place where innocent people get hurt. Welch was
anything but an innocent bystander."

"Yes, but what to do now? What's going to happen with the Rome,
Madrid and Paris exposures? I don't think we should try to call them
off, do you, Angela?"

"No, no. That would be a mistake. It's what the CIA wants. Besides, it's out of your hands now."

I agreed. We shouldn't be intimidated if the Agency blamed Welch
on us. In London Steve Weissman was doing the analysis of the Rome
Embassy directory for publication in a new Roman newspaper called
La Repubblica. The CIA Station there was almost as big as in
London, and the exposure would coincide with my Rome press conference and publication of the Italian edition. Another article by
Weissman, exposing the CIA Station in Madrid, was due for publication in *Cambio 16* in a couple of weeks. And at *Liberation* in Paris,
they were all set to expose the CIA Station there—timed with the
publication of the French edition and still another press conference.
Those were all big Stations, and the exposures should go ahead, no
matter how Washington reacted to the Welch killing.

In Rome we checked into the YMCA hotel, and I called Weissman.
"Steve, I just read this morning about Welch. What's happening?"

"Oh, it's you. Nice of you to call, Phil. Nothing's happening—just
an earthquake in Washington and a couple hundred people trying to
get in touch with you."

"Shit. It's bad, huh?"

"Well, yeah, I guess you could say it's bad. The CIA blames you and the Fifth Estate. They're getting all sorts of death threats. David Phillips and his old-boy network are also on the attack. They're saying your *CounterSpy* article calling for neutralizing CIA people was an invitation to murder. The whole thing is exploding."

"Steve, what about Welch's name being published in Athens? Did you know about that?"

"No, but I do now. In late November the *Athens News* published an open letter from some group calling themselves a Committee of Greeks and Greek Americans. They attacked the CIA for its work in Greece and named ten CIA people. Welch's name and address were included. A week later another group calling themselves the Committee to Keep Greece Greek—great name, eh?—wrote a letter attacking the Russians. They named ten Soviet Embassy people as KGB. Yiannis Horn at the *Athens News* wouldn't publish it, but the wire services picked it up. Did you know Welch was in the Mader book?"

"No, but that's a good thing. So *CounterSpy* wasn't the first to publish his name." Steve was referring to *Who's Who in the CIA* published in East Germany in 1968 by someone called Julius Mader. I was in it along with hundreds of other officers—and quite a few mistaken names. It was most likely a KGB publication.

"You should call the Fifth Estate. They've called here half a dozen times trying to reach you."

"Sure, I'll call right now. Say, Steve, I think the Rome, Madrid and Paris exposures should go ahead, don't you? I mean we shouldn't stop because of the Welch case, right?"

"Hell, no. They're gonna burn your ass and the Fifth Estate's over Welch, but there's no stopping that. So why should we stop?"

"Good, just wanted to be sure." I then told Weissman I was going to wait until my Rome press conference to comment on Welch. That was less than two weeks away. Meanwhile we would continue our trip, then Steve would come to Italy to review the *Repubblica* list before publication.

The mood at the Fifth Estate offices in Washington was grim. "Irresponsible Americans fingering patriotic Americans for murder" was the main theme emanating from the CIA and spread through the media. They were literally under siege—several times had to call police for protection after threatening phone calls. I gave them such encouragement as I could, and said I wasn't stopping exposures because of Welch. But I would keep quiet until the Rome press conference, when I'd answer the attacks.

Meanwhile the seven of them were working on a statement. Did I have any suggestions? Yes, I think the Welch killing should be put into context of how the CIA's operations in Greece helped the military junta take power, then supported it through seven years of terrorism against the Left. From all the revelations of recent months people the world over now know what the CIA does, and are determined to resist.

Exposing the CIA's operations and its personnel is an act of solidarity with the victims. The purpose is not to get anyone killed but to force those people back to the States. As for Welch, it's a terrible misfortune for him and his family. But why go to Greece, where anti-America feelings were so strong, after his name was published as a CIA officer?

They told me that over a year ago a Maryknoll priest who worked as a missionary in Peru had visited, and brought with him a copy of a Peruvian journal with Welch's name as the CIA Chief in Lima. So it was Mader in 1968, Peruvians in 1974, and *CounterSpy* and the *Athens News* in '75—and who knows how many other times in between. The CIA had to be blind not to realize Welch had no cover anymore. But that was not the main point. The CIA was responsible for fascist terror, torture and assassinations in country after country of the so-called Free World. Employees aren't forced to work for that Agency. If they make a conscious choice for that work, they assume certain risks of retaliation. If U.S. administrations use the CIA for political repression, and if Congress could not, or would not, stop it, then ordinary Americans have every right to work against them—including exposures of operations and personnel.

I urged the Fifth Estate members not to let themselves be intimidated by the attacks, especially those using "patriotism" and other emotive grounds. Use the press reports that Welch's house was known for years in Athens as the CIA Chief's residence. Put the blame on Presidents and Congress, and the CIA itself—first, for what the Agency does, and second, for its incompetence in protecting its people. And in the statement, tell the truth: that you only re-publish names of CIA people that have already surfaced somewhere else.

My call may have helped a little, but probably not much. They were really down, feeling the heat, and nervous about the threats.

While sightseeing in Rome we ran into the same loud American family that we'd seen in every city since Venice. Again we got the familiar greeting: "Well, halloo again," and "Ya'll-have-a-good-day-now, hear?" Same thing in Pompei. When Chris asked me if I thought they were following us for the CIA, I wondered. They seemed to go everywhere we did. No, I didn't think so. Too obvious. Still . . .

In Naples we rented a car and headed back to Milan with stops in Siena and Pisa. Welch's killing had cast a cloud of apprehension over the trip, so I was not sorry to see it end even though we'd seen new marvels everywhere we went. Through newspapers I tried to follow the continuing reactions in Washington. President Ford blamed Welch's death on "CIA defectors" who revealed agents' names—a clear reference to me that the media spread around immediately. And CIA Director Colby kept up the charge that the Fifth Estate was responsible. Even so, they stiffened and announced that the next *CounterSpy* would carry the names of seventy more CIA people.

Meanwhile in Athens a secret political group called the "Revolutionary Organization of November 17," after the date of the 1973 student revolt against the "colonels" regime, sent a statement to the press claiming responsibility. They justified the action by citing CIA intervention in Greek internal affairs and its installation and support for the junta.

The communique of the "November 17" group, which got little media coverage, revealed that they had been stalking Welch's predecessor, Stacy Hulse, until Welch replaced him, five months earlier, and moved into his house. They even wrote of where Welch ate, what cars he drove, and the hours he came and left his residence.

In a follow-up, secret Congressional investigation, the CIA revealed that its Headquarters had warned Welch not to move into the house occupied by Hulse because it was so well-known in Athens as the CIA Chief's residence and because anti-American feeling was at a fever pitch in Greece. Welch refused the advice.

The "November 17" group never needed to see Welch's name in print, and publication in the *Athens News*, much less *CounterSpy*, had nothing to do with his identification as the CIA Chief. The CIA's warning to Welch and his reaction would not surface publicly for more than a year. Meanwhile the Ford administration, the CIA and most of the U.S. media put the blame on *CounterSpy* and me.

It was a Friday when we got to Milan and found hotel rooms a short walk from the railway station. The next day Angela, Phil and Chris would take a train back to London. My press conference in Rome was not until Wednesday, so I had time to drive to Geneva and look for Leslie again. I called Steve Weissman, told him I'd be out of town for the weekend, but back on Monday night. He said he would fly to Milan on Monday, and the next day we could drive together to Rome.

I gave him the hotel address and said I'd make a reservation for him.

Saturday afternoon Angela and the boys got on the Orient Express again, and I got to bed early. I wanted to get to Geneva before dark to make plans with Jorge for Monday morning. I got up about seven, had breakfast in the room, made reservations for Monday, and carried my bag over to the parking garage. Then I headed west across the city for the A-4 *autostrada* to Torino and Geneva.

The streets of Milan were fairly deserted that Sunday morning. More from habit than expectation I started glancing through the mirror. What's that? Two or three cars a block back travelling the same speed and direction I was? Well, let's see. I turned left at an intersection, away from my original direction west, and they followed. At the next main intersection I turned right, and they followed again. Goddammit. Only way they could have found my hotel here was that call to Steve. They must be monitoring his telephone.

I started getting that feeling, like emotional choking. Fuckin' Italian services. They're even worse than the Spanish.

The Agency set them up after the war with the same officers that served Mussolini. They just got a new name. Still as fascist as ever, and up to their necks in right-wing bombings and assassinations. And I'm all alone. No witnesses. What the Christ do I do now?

I thought about Welch. Is this going to be a reprisal for his killing? Are those guys terrorists instead of an official surveillance team? Idiot! What difference does it make? They're all the same. Can't drive out of town—no deserted highways with those guys around. Besides, I can't let them know I'm heading for Geneva. That might ruin the check for Leslie. Have to do something here in Milan, and if I can't get away I'll stay here.

The combination of adrenaline and the car heater was making me sweat. I opened the window for air, hoping it would help me to think straight. I stopped to look at the map of Milan, and the three cars stopped too, about a block and a half behind. The map was too confusing—I couldn't figure out where I was. Then a voice in my head said: Look, they're only following. If they wanted to kill you they'd have done it already. They would have got you in the street outside the hotel—or just as you drove away. They're just sitting back there. Yeah, that's right. They would have done it already.

I started off again, determined to make some kind of move to shake them. Then I remembered how I got away in Spain. Something like that, maybe. I started going slowly, almost forcing them to get closer. By the time I got to the next traffic light they were only half a block

behind. Then it turned red. I stopped and they did too, right behind
me: one, two, three. Then some other cars pulled up, in the lane on
the right and on the left.

The light turned green. I let two cars on the right pull out, then I
pulled into the curb lane and stopped. They had to go ahead of me,
across the intersection, where one car stopped and the others
creeped ahead. Now! I squealed the tires as I turned right, gave it all
the power, and headed down a narrow, one-way street. Then I turned
right, went two blocks, then left, then right again. No cars behind.
Left 'em in the dust. Better keep going, though, down small streets
away from the main ones where they'd be looking for me.

After fifteen or twenty minutes I was pretty sure I was clean. No
sign of those or any other cars following. I stopped by a park to find
out where I was. I was on the east side of the city. That meant I could
drive to the south side, then westward, take a secondary highway toward Torino, then hit the *autostrada* three or four exits out of Milan.
That way, if they were watching cars entering the freeway directly
from Milan, I'd get around them.

It worked. No sign of surveillance from Milan to Torino, or from
there up the Alps. And no sign I was on a watch list at the *Mont Blanc*
passport control.

In Geneva, Jorge had bad news. He'd been calling Janet
Strickland's apartment all weekend, ready with a wrong number pretext, but no answer. She was out of town for the weekend, and we
could only hope she'd be back for work in the morning.

Next day we waited in front of her apartment, again with no luck,
then we decided to look for her at the International Labor Organization. He was going to see if she was in her office, number 159 on the
ninth floor. Ten minutes later he returned. No Janet.

We had coffee to kill twenty minutes before another try. This time
he came back with a big smile. She was there!

I didn't know why I was so nervous as I walked to the elevator, but
I was. Could I get away with this, if Janet really was Leslie, without
her recognizing me? If she did, what would she do then? Maybe she
wouldn't—my clothes were different, hair shorter now, no more
Zapata moustache, different glasses. Okay. Out the elevator, turn
right, deep breath, don't look like an outsider, just another employee. I got to Janet's corridor, watching the numbers: 151, 153,
155, 157, all with the doors closed. Ah the next one's open. As I
walked by I scratched my head with my left hand, concealing my face
a little while glancing in.

There she was! Leslie Donegan in flesh and blood! She was talking on the phone, looked up at me, then quickly back down. Shit, that was close but I don't think she recognized me. Back to the elevator and down to Jorge. "That's her, I know it is. What a miracle, Jorge."

"I thought it was her. Now what?"

"Let's not do anything yet," I said. "I have to drive back to Milan now. If we keep quiet about this, not letting anyone know I've found her, we can spring something later, some kind of surprise."

"Don't worry. I won't say a word, but I can keep track of her from a distance, you know, like if she moves to another job."

"Thanks! Thanks a lot, *compañero*. I'll be in touch real soon."

Driving back to Milan, I pondered the different assignments Leslie-Janet might get from the CIA Station in the U.S. Mission in Geneva. Obviously she could provide all sorts of internal I.L.O. documents from her position in the Central Library and Documentation Branch. But there was more. She could spot and assess potential recruits throughout the I.L.O. and in all the other international organizations in Geneva, including Third World people who would be valuable CIA assets on return to their native countries. Her cover was perfect for meeting people of interest, then introducing them to CIA officers under diplomatic cover for further development. Now what I needed was an exposure plan with maximum surprise.

Weissman flew to Milan, and we then drove to Rome without any sign of surveillance. He filled me in on latest developments in the Welch case. There were two principal features in the continuing attack. First, Welch was converted into a national hero with all the media hype imaginable, culminating with burial in Arlington National Cemetery. President Ford, CIA Director Colby and other notables were at the ceremony.

The other tactic was to use Welch's death as grounds to attack not only the Fifth Estate and me, but also the Congressional committees then investigating the CIA.

Opponents of legislation to reform and control the intelligence community found the Welch case quite useful. Colby and his allies in Congress proposed legislation making it a crime to publish information on the CIA's operations and undercover personnel. As for those of us who published names, we were providing "hit lists" for terrorists, issuing "invitations to murder," and seeking "the destruction of the United States."

By coincidence, on the very day of my Rome press conference the wire services buzzed with the latest sensational leak from

Washington: President Ford had asked Congress for $6 million in additional funds for secret payments to Italian political parties during the six months before the next elections. So I spent most of the evening discussing past Agency operations in Italy such as the splitting of the trade union movement and the socialist party after World War II.

Next afternoon I flew back to London and took a taxi from Heathrow to BBC studios for another face-to-face encounter with David Phillips. He went on at length about Welch the family man and scholar, and he accused me of inciting violence by publishing CIA names. I blamed Ford, Colby and Welch himself on the poor cover issue, adding: "The purpose of these exposures is not to get anyone killed, but to lessen as much as possible the capability of the CIA to promote the type of repression that has occurred in Chile, Brazil, Uruguay and many more countries. . . . The prudent thing for those exposed is to go back to the United States."

Back in Cambridge I found a pile of letters, articles and editorials on the Welch case, and a long list of journalists and others to call back. After four days I'd hardly dented that work, but I did manage to write responses to nasty editorials on me and Welch in the *New York Times*, *Washington Post*, and *Washington Star*. Then I headed back to London to speak at a public meeting sponsored by the Socialist Forum.

David Pallister of *The Guardian*, a journalist with whom I'd done an interview months earlier, was waiting for me at the entrance to Conway Hall. He flashed a teletype of a news article, saying it had just come in. It was pretty bad, and his editor wanted my comments before they used it. We went up to the table behind the podium, sat down, and I began to read the latest plant. It was a shocker, like the original "drunk-despondent-KGB" story in *The New York Times*.

The article was filed from Brussels by a *Los Angeles Times* correspondent named Murray Seeger whom Pallister explained was the *Times* staff correspondent resident in Bonn. Citing "qualified Western sources," Seeger wrote that I had given to the KGB, when I was in Cuba in 1971, the name of a key member of a French spy ring operating in Poland. As a result, that person and about 120 others were arrested by Polish security police beginning in June 1975. The key figure was Jerzy Pawlowski, an Army Lt. Colonel and world famous fencer, who had won the saber championship at the 1968 Olympic Games in Mexico City.

According to Seeger, Pawlowski went on to win over twenty other international fencing honors and was recognized as the greatest saber fencer of all time. He went on: "Pawlowski apparently met Agee in Mexico City where Agee was working under the cover of Special Olympic Attaché to the American Ambassador. Agee described (in his book) a contact he had in Mexico City named Besaber and said he was a local resident of Polish extraction used by the CIA to contact Polish intelligence agents."

Seeger added that Pawlowski had attempted to commit suicide, that his fencing hand was broken during interrogation, that another member of the Polish fencing team had escaped to Italy, while still another had "simply disappeared." According to Seeger, "The Polish government is expected to put the arrested group on trial early this year." To emphasize the point, Seeger wrote at the end of his 800-word article: "He (Agee) is known to have met with Cuban and Soviet espionage agents in Havana."

The Polish press agency had confirmed Pawlowski's arrest, and it was obvious the Agency was trying to pin it on me. I told Pallister that my connection with him was a fairy tale. I had never met such a person, never worked on such a case, and didn't know the names of any CIA agents working in the Socialist countries. I explained that BESABER was the internal CIA cryptonym for a man of Polish extraction, resident in Mexico, who served as an access agent to diplomats and intelligence officers in the Polish Embassy in Mexico City, adding that CIA counter-intelligence people suspected him of being a double agent. I had never met him, but had done paperwork on his security clearance. I added that I'd never learned of any French spy ring anywhere, and if indeed Pawlowski was a French agent, the French service, not the CIA, would have contacted him in Mexico City.

The Guardian printed Seeger's charge, with my denial, but I later learned the foreign editor at the *Los Angeles Times* issued a "mandatory kill" on the story because it lacked confirmation. Neither was it published by the *Washington Post* which shared the *Times* and *Guardian* wire service. Pallister sent me a copy of the original teletype which I wanted to study carefully. It seemed strange that in commenting on my exposure campaign Seeger could quote verbatim from my remarks on the BBC debate with Phillips only four days before. He also had several passages on me, unrelated to the Pawlowski case, but apparently part of the CIA's package.

In the book Agee told of his career as a CIA agent in Latin America and named many of his colleagues. He resigned from the Agency in

1969 without giving any indication of serious disaffection with his work.

Agee resigned from the CIA at a time when his marriage had failed and he was having an affair with another woman. His original intention was to remarry and live in Mexico City, but his love affair was broken off after he was divorced. Agee was reportedly desperate for money and drinking heavily when he decided to write a book about the CIA that might pay his bills.

Despite his record as a CIA agent working against communist interests in Latin America, Agee was warmly received in Havana in May 1971 when he arrived to do research.

No American publisher would accept his book, and the first draft was turned down by a European publisher also. His second attempt, a pseudo diary written with the assistance of the British Museum's newspaper files, was the version published last year.

Five years later I found in the documents obtained under FOIA that the CIA's propaganda guidance on me in the mid-1970's included such phrases as "no indication of disaffection" when he resigned; "having an affair with another woman"; and, "warmly received in Havana in 1971." Comparison of these and other phrases in the CIA documentation with the Seeger article and others suggested that the Agency had been feeding the same propaganda to various cooperating journalists who hardly changed the wording.

If the Seeger story was meant to intimidate it didn't work. In less than two weeks the CIA Stations in Paris, Madrid, Rome and The Hague were stripped of cover through the local press. Over a hundred names were published, some with home addresses and telephone numbers, along with the floors and office numbers of CIA premises within the Embassies.

The day after the Conway Hall meeting I did a filmed interview with CBS News at their London studio. In the interview I discussed the exposure campaign, my lack of involvement in publication of Welch's name, and my disapproval of violence against those exposed. A couple of weeks later I received a letter from a colleague in the States. He wrote that the CBS News program "Sixty Minutes," the most popular current affairs program in the U.S., had broadcast a report on the Welch case with the assertion that I was responsible for publication of Welch's name.

That started several years' efforts on my part to get a rectification from CBS. I never got it, and the case remains for me the best example of "media-McCarthyism" in all the years since I became a "public figure."

At first I thought there must have been a mistake. But Judy Stevenson, the "Sixty Minutes" staff person in London, sent me a transcript and arranged for me to see a video of the program.

Morley Safer, the program reporter, said in introductory comments: "The man who betrayed Welch is Philip Agee, a former CIA agent who worked with him in Latin America." Safer went on to conduct a long interview with David Phillips, the Agency's spook-turned-public-defender, in which they discussed me. They concluded together that "the possibility exists that Philip Agee could have been working for the KGB the whole time."

I protested to Stevenson that I never knew or worked with Welch, didn't give his name to *CounterSpy* or anyone else, and certainly had not worked for the KGB. CBS had my statements about Welch on film, didn't use them, and broadcast a still photograph of me as I was being discussed.

I demanded a chance to respond, both orally to Stevenson and in writing. She said she would speak to Safer. Then I waited. Months passed without a word from Safer, although from time to time I called Stevenson to enquire.

Almost a year after the broadcast Stevenson called to say that Mike Wallace of "Sixty Minutes" was in London and could see me at his hotel that night. For an hour we discussed the program and my right to reply to "personal attack." Wallace said he was certain that Safer didn't intentionally lie about me—he was "not that kind of person," and "would never do a thing like that." Wallace promised to take up the matter in New York and let me know what "Sixty Minutes" would do. I never heard from him.

Eventually Mel Wulf, as my attorney, wrote to CBS in New York, demanding time to reply under the "personal attack" regulation of the Federal Communications Commission. A CBS lawyer wrote back, enclosing a copy of a letter to me from Kay Wight, Director of Administration for CBS in New York, dated five days after the broadcast, i.e., before I even knew of the program. It was the standard letter required by FCC regulations on "personal attacks," informing me of the broadcast, enclosing a transcript, and advising "if you believe you are legally entitled under the FCC Section cited above, to respond, and wish to do so, please get in touch with me so that we may further discuss the issue." The letter was addressed in my name, with street address, "England."

Too late, the lawyer wrote. "Our letter requested that Mr. Agee contact CBS News for further discussions if he desired to respond to the broadcast and claimed a legal right to do so. No response to our

January 30, 1976, letter was ever received. We do not believe that your present letter, written nearly two and a half years after the broadcast in question, constitutes a timely request for response time on Mr. Agee's behalf."

The truth was I had been in regular contact after that—but with the London office where they must have known of the letter but played dumb. Stevenson had been in contact with New York over the video and transcripts, had spoken to Safer, and had my complaint and demand in writing. Awfully convenient, I thought, how they left Cambridge off the address. Also got the postal code wrong, just in case.

Mel wrote back, saying that I never received the letter because of the faulty address, that such notice was required by FCC regulations, and asking again for time to reply. Time passed. Next time I saw Mel I asked whether we could go to court to force CBS to give me time.

"You got a hundred thousand dollars to spend on this?" he asked.

"Oh, yeah, sure. How about just a hundred bucks?"

"Well, CBS has millions and they'll fight. That's Freedom of the Press in America, didn't you know? Why don't you just forget it. Only fifty million people saw it."

I had to drop it. Morley Safer and CBS did a job on me, just like Anderson and lots of other journalists. I'd have had to be a multimillionaire to press all the libel suits through the courts. I was determined, in any case, to continue the exposure campaign despite false blame for the Welch affair.

The "Sixty Minutes"program and other media attacks relating to Welch were effective in killing several projects I considered important. Jon Peters backed off on the film of my fiction piece on a CIA takeover of the United States. And Emile De Antonio found almost all his sources of finance unable to help on the *Inside the Company* dramatic film. We had met a number of times in the previous year to work on the script, but now it was stalled. In writing me of his problems, De Antonio said, "I have never had trouble with money, but right now I can't even get the money to get the money to get it off the ground. The conventional, liberal press is building you as a mass murderer. . . . "

George Bush replaced Colby as CIA Director in early 1976 as the·
Agency and its supporters were manipulating the Welch case to stop the ongoing Congressional investigations and meaningful reforms and controls. Eighteen months of sensational revelations and scandal, Marchetti's book and mine, and our "guerrilla journalism"—and

Welch—had indeed produced a backlash. Both the House investigation under Otis Pike, and Senate investigation under Frank Church, were wound down after year-long inquiries. In terms of reform or control of covert intervention, the most those investigations produced were establishment of intelligence oversight committees in both chambers, and recommendations for possible future legislation.

But there were a few victories still. A couple of weeks after the House of Representatives voted to allow the White House to censor the Pike committee's report, someone leaked it to the *Village Voice*. It was sensational, with details of CIA intervention in foreign elections, paramilitary operations and propaganda—along with damaging revelations of the Agency's intelligence failures. It had to come out in permanent, book form, so I wrote an introduction and published it with the Bertrand Russell Peace Foundation.

Another victory was the exposure of CIA intervention in Angola. There the Agency had spent $30 million to hire white mercenaries from Western countries and to provide military equipment and propaganda support for South Africa-backed UNITA and the corrupt, Zaire-backed FNLA. Ford and Kissinger wanted millions more, but the Congress for once said "no."

Stung by these defeats, Ford seized the initiative and promulgated a "reform" program of his own for the CIA and other intelligence agencies. By Executive Order he established new charters and duties, hyping it all as "reform," when in fact he made "legal" many activities considered to be "abuses" in the past.

The only restriction on covert intervention in other countries was a prohibition of political assassinations. For nearly every other apparent restriction, exceptions were provided. In fact the Ford "reforms" were a license for operations that must have truly pleased the Agency. The only hope for reform and controls now, such as prohibition of covert intervention, was in the Congress—and in an election year they weren't moving very fast. Ford did ask Congress for legislation, but only for laws making it a crime to reveal classified information on intelligence activities.

He certainly needed new laws to get at people like me. I learned in the FOIA documentation that Bush continued Colby's earlier efforts with the Justice Department to get a criminal indictment against me for the secrets revealed in *Inside the Company* and for the exposure of CIA officers. Bush also continued Colby's efforts to have the State Department revoke my passport for having "damaged the national security." Justice, however, told the CIA that if indicted I would get access to the Agency's documents on their crimes against me—which the Agency said could not be revealed. And Justice also told State that they could not successfully defend revocation of my passport on "national security" grounds. The Supreme Court had ruled years before that passports could not be denied because of citizen's political ideas.

Imagine, then, Bush's consternation when he discovered that the U.S. Information Agency, the official government propaganda arm, recommended *Inside the Company* as one of the "good books" in its Washington libraries. They did it in the June 1976 issue of *USIA World*. The FOIA documents showed the CIA contacting the USIA with the following argument:

> Prior to publication of his book in January 1975, Agee announced his intention of forming a campaign to fight the CIA wherever it was operating. He has used the exposure of CIA personnel stationed overseas as a means to promote and publicize the sale of his book. . . . It is therefore a surprise to find USIA advertising Agee's book as available in their libraries. We wonder if they are also distributing the book to their overseas libraries as well . . . It would be advisable to ask USIA to desist from purchases and distribution of a book which continues to cause damage to our U.S. government foreign policy.

The Agency's internal routing slip attached to the above memorandum carried a revealing question: "Have we fallen so low in esteem that USIA can recommend Agee's book to its staff as 'good reading'?"

The exposure campaign continued through the press in various West European countries and as far away as South America. For publication in Portugal I wrote an up-date on CIA Station officers and their joint intervention with European governments and parties to bring the "moderates" and "pluralists" to power. Their success in stopping the movements for workers' control and popular power, and purging radicals like Otelo Saraiva de Carvalho from the military, was fairly complete by the time an elected government led by Mario Soares took power.

About the same time the military commander who had organized the putsch against radical military units in 1975 began a long term as Portugal's president. The road was now open to begin reversing the gains made in land reform and industrial control during the first eighteen months of the revolution.

Sweden was the setting for one of the most unusual and sensational exposures. In the fall of 1975 I went to Stockholm for promotion of a

Swedish edition of *Inside the Company*. At a press conference one of the journalists asked a number of penetrating and well-thought-out questions about the Agency's operational methods. Little could I imagine that at that moment the journalist, Jan Guillou, was running a classic double agent operation against the CIA Station in Stockholm.

The agent was a journalist from Kenya whom a CIA officer under diplomatic cover had recruited—or thought he had recruited—to penetrate the African diplomatic community. In fact he discussed the "recruitment" with colleagues at Radio Sweden and then with Guillou.

For eleven months the Agency thought the journalist was a genuine recruit, even sending him twice to Angola to provide a pretext for anti-MPLA propaganda fed to him by the Station for publication in Sweden. Guillou collected every detail of the information requirements levied on the journalist. In March 1976 the whole story was published—and several CIA officers left immediately for home.

By then the number of CIA people exposed had passed five hundred, and it seemed to be having an effect. In a story titled "CIA Morale Plummets," the *Washington Post* reported: "The publication of names of CIA employees overseas has brought about a marked decline in the already low morale of personnel . . . it is affecting not only the Agency's ability to gather intelligence but also is causing severe personal strain as well . . . the year-long expose of CIA wrongdoing in Congress and the press created serious problems, not just in the office, but at home . . . the concerns were about teenage children who now questioned how their fathers made a living . . . publication of hundreds of names seems to be the final straw that is breaking the back of CIA morale. . . ." One CIA officer told the *Post*: "The Agency has really been shattered."

Steve Weissman, Louis Wolf and I began work on a book that would be a compilation of the various press exposes along with the employment histories of each CIA officer as revealed in the *Biographic Registers* and *Foreign Service Lists*. Then it occurred to me that a global *Who's Who* would be useful. After all, the East German *Who's Who* had numerous errors and was out of date.

It would take considerable financing to pay for the research and analysis required to go through thirty years of documentation. I conceived and wrote a project for a *Who's Who in the CIA* to be organized like a catalog or technical manual with snap-in pages. Once established, the *Who's Who* could be sold by subscription with supplementary pages sent out for insertion twice a year. Such a project might eventually become financially viable, but at the start it needed support. I sent the written proposal to colleagues in the U.S. for possible funding by progressive donors.

Weeks and months went by without success. Finally Angela and I decided to begin anyway, using income from *Inside the Company*. First we needed the documentation. Through the copy service at the British Museum she began accumulating *Biographic Registers* and *Foreign Service Lists*. In other libraries she copied the U.S. Embassy portions of *Diplomatic Lists* from around the world.

But how to organize the thousands of names and lengthy biographic information? A computer would be prohibitively expensive, so we settled on a manual system. Angela was a mathematician, and she thought she could organize the project using a system of large cards which would contain information on each particular officer. The cards would be in alphabetical order but with punch-out sections around the edges. Long rods would run through holes along the edges to separate cards in classes according to the punch-out system. The principal divisions would be date and place.

Angela ordered three thousand cards from a company in London that sold the manual computer system. Eventually we had several large tea chests full of documents and blank cards, but still no way to finance the project.

As the July 1976 American Bicentennial celebrations approached, I spoke at a number of "alternative" rallies sponsored by progressive groups and political parties. Following one of these, a weekend cultural fair in Copenhagen, I flew to Paris determined to do something about Leslie-Janet. My literary agent arranged for me to tell the story to Rene Backmann, an editor at *Le Nouvel Observateur*, the liberal French newsweekly. He asked me to write the story for publication in the magazine. Then he got an idea. Couldn't we get some photographs of Leslie-Janet to go with it? I said it wouldn't be difficult, and if he wanted I would take photographers right to her office for a confrontation. Perfect.

With the magazine's expense money, I flew to Geneva to make arrangements with photographers Backmann lined up. They were a team: a fairly tall, robust man and a slight, attractive woman. The Leslie-Janet story fascinated them, and we were all eager to get the pictures. The next morning we drove to the I.L.O. and went to the cafeteria. I was nervous over how she would react and unsure I would have the "cool" to carry off my plan to provoke her. But I would give it a try. I took the elevator alone to her floor, walked down the hall as nonchalantly as possible, spotted her briefly in her office, walked down several flights of stairs, then took the elevator the rest of the way down. That would be our escape route if we needed one.

Hans, Gaby and I had a final tense discussion of our operations plan, then headed for the elevator. As we turned down Leslie-Janet's corridor we smiled affirmatively at one another—but then: shit! Her door's closed. Must have gone out. Just a minute, I'll knock.

"Come in." The voice had a familiar ring.

I opened the door and walked slowly toward her desk in a far corner of the office. She was alone. As my heart pounded out of control, my prepared lines vanished from memory. Gaby followed close behind me, stationing herself in a corner next to the windows, and Hans came last, closing the door behind him. He stood with his back to the door. Leslie-Janet looked up and seemed not to recognize me.

I looked down at her with a menacing face I'd practiced in my hotel bathroom mirror. "Hello, Leslie, don't you know who I am?"

"What do you mean?" she asked with a slight quiver and still deadpan expression. She recognized me all right, but was trying not to show it. But I saw the first sign of tension: her fingers went stiff as she rubbed the cuticle of her left thumb. Hans and Gaby took their cameras out of bags and started flashing pictures.

A crooked smile appeared and she started blinking, as she often did after putting on her contact lenses. I leaned over a little closer and, faking an insidious sneer, said: "You knew I'd find you, Leslie. Now I'm here. Aren't you happy to see me?"

"What do you mean?", she repeated, this time with strained voice and a quick glance around the room. Hans and Gaby were flashing away.

In my most threatening voice I slowly said, "You could have gotten me killed Leslie. Now I'm here to get you."

The smile twisted off her face as she rose, let out a dreadful shriek, and strode toward the door. More flashing cameras. Hans, who was blocking the door, didn't move.

"Let me out of here," she yelled in near hysteria. In heels she was nearly as tall as Hans. She reached out grabbing his arm to pull him away from the door. Gaby kept shooting from her corner. Hans offered no resistance. Leslie opened the door, turned left and went bounding down the hall, screaming something unintelligible about people in her office.

"This way," I told Hans and Gaby. We turned left following Leslie-Janet, but she was far ahead. Several people were peering out of offices. A few quick steps brought us to the stairwell door. Down we went as Hans and Gaby bundled their cameras back in the bags. We ran down two, three, four flights, then emerged in another hall, hurried to the elevator and descended to the garage. Driving back to the studio we couldn't stop laughing—Leslie-Janet had put on one incredible show. Now to see the pictures.

They were terrific. I stayed in Geneva for a pro-Chile solidarity rally two days later, all the while looking in vain for Leslie-Janet's face in the crowd. Then I took prints back to Paris and gave them to an astonished Backmann. The story would just make the issue coming out on Friday. That was only three days away, so I stayed in Paris, ready for a press conference on the CIA's spy in the I.L.O. Thursday my agent called and said I should come over. She had a story I could hardly believe. Jean Daniel, the editorial director at *Le Nouvel Observateur* killed the story just as the magazine was going to press, telling Backmann that he had no interest in exposing CIA operations.

That son-of-a-bitch. I protested to Backmann, and also to Olivier Todd, one of the magazine's chief editors with whom I'd recently done another *Playboy* interview—for a Bicentennial issue of the French edition. Hadn't "*Nouvel Obs*" done a four-page article on the CIA a few months before, including a photograph of the Chief of Station? No luck. Daniel was adamant.

Later I learned that Jean Daniel was well-connected in Washington. In 1963 President Kennedy sent him as a private emissary to Cuba to explore possible ways to improve relations. Daniel was discussing this with Fidel Castro when someone walked in with the first word of Kennedy's assassination. To make matters worse, Leslie-Janet disappeared a couple of days after my visit. No surprise, no scandal. Who was this woman, anyway? I would probably never know.

I shelved the story and the photographs and went back to work in Cambridge on an article I considered much more important. Jean Paul Sartre had heard of my book. He was almost blind and couldn't read it, but someone read him parts, and he sent word to me that he wanted me to write an article for his journal, *Les Temps Modernes*. It would be a special issue on the United States to coincide with the bicentennial celebrations. He wanted me to do a critique of the various official investigations of the CIA and other security services together with all the revelations and scandals of the previous two years. What does it all mean and what does the future hold? It was a mammoth task, but I accepted, considering it a special honor to write for Sartre.

I waded through more than 2000 pages of official reports from Congressional and Executive investigations along with hundreds of newspaper and magazine clippings. In the end I had an article of nearly fifty pages, tracing the development of covert action operations from World War II, the CIA's intelligence failures, the assassination plots, the illegal domestic operations, the testing and use of drugs like LSD, and the deceitful Ford "reforms." But the worst aspect was the scant mention of the CIA's support for security services in other countries that tortured, assassinated, and imprisoned without trial the people striving for change. Nevertheless, my conclusions were upbeat.

I believe the revelations of the past few years constitute a great popular victory, even when weighed against the absence of effective reforms. In the first place, popular movements have gained a huge body of knowledge concerning the methods and specific operations of the institutions of counter-revolution. Obviously, one must know how these institutions operate in order to anticipate their moves and defeat them.

Second, the revelations served to continue the alienation process, probably in fact to hasten the legitimacy crisis that everyday is separating more and more people from the government and traditional institutions. What better subject could be found to demonstrate hypocrisy, corruption, and the ways in which the government in general tends to serve privileged, minority interests?

Third, the revelations, especially those relating to Chile, demonstrate more clearly than ever how the activities of the CIA are tailored to meet the security needs of American-based multinational companies.

Fourth, the revelations and investigations demonstrate once again what is best in the American system: separation of powers, free flow of information, checks and balances, need for protection of the individual from oppression by government bureaucracy.

Fifth, the lack of meaningful reforms demonstrates the limits of the liberal reform process. Those who may have hoped for the abolishment of the CIA or of covert action operations may well reconsider whether they have been putting the cart before the horse. Only after power has been taken away from the owners, managers, and their politicians can their instruments of repression be dismantled. After all, the law that established the CIA was based in part on recommendations made by a New York investment banker.

In June 1976 I spoke at an alternative Bicentennial celebration in Copenhagen. Also speaking was a representative of the Cherokee people of North Carolina. He described how fatuous the celebration of

200 years of conquest and exploitation was, since his people had been
in America for some 25,000 years. He also described how Native
Americans were marching across the country from the Pacific to the
Atlantic coast. When on July 4, 1976, the candles were lit on the two-
hundredth birthday cake of the United States, the Native Americans,
he said, would be there to blow them out. This attitude, the exposures
of secret intervention and repression, and the continuing growth of
popular movements in the United States are the real reasons for
celebrating the Bicentennial.

Through the spring and summer of 1976 I had far more invitations
to speak and write then I could accept—though I tried to accept them
all—and those letters I could answer were sometimes six to nine
months old.

I continued to travel, but once on return to Cambridge I had a
scare. One night I began feeling weak and short of breath, and in the
morning I had pains in my chest. Angela drove me to the hospital
where they put me in the intensive care unit for coronary victims.
After tests they said I hadn't had a heart attack, but I did have a case
of "exhaustion." I spent the week there, looking at those suffering
men who had had heart attacks, and vowed to slow down. Truth was,
the pace had been hectic during the two years since the "drunk-
despondent-KGB" article spoiled our Cornwall idyll. And I certainly
didn't want to end up an invalid.

I could slow the pace, but there were domestic problems that still
created constant stress. The owners of our house were due back in the
fall, and we had to find another place to live. Should we stay in
Cambridge?

Should we.try renting again or buy a place? Should Phil and Chris,
then fourteen and twelve, be forced to change schools yet again? And
what about returning to the States?

We decided to stay in Cambridge and look for a house we could
buy. The boys had several years' secondary school remaining, and the
best thing for them was to avoid another change of school. Angela and
I both liked Cambridge and had made friends there.

In Washington the Justice Department was still refusing to say
whether they would indict me on return, and with the change in climate following Welch's killing, going back to the States seemed more
remote than ever. But ominous signs from the British government
also gave constant cause for worry. For months immigration had de-

layed extension of my residence permit. At first they had given me yearly extensions, but now they were keeping my passport with my application "under consideration."

That meant each time I traveled I had to telephone or write, asking immigration to send the passport. Each time they gave me a couple of months, and then I would send the passport back with another application for extension. They were obviously keeping me on a leash, but I had a contract for a second book with Penguin and that seemed justification enough for continued residence.

We found a place we thought was perfect. It was a mid-19th-century end-of-terrace grey brick house on Maids' Causeway just across from Midsummer Common and Jesus Green. Only a five-minute walk across those parks was the River Cam with its cycling paths, punting and rowing clubs. The price was not too bad, we thought, but it needed a lot of work. We made a down payment and started planning how we would renovate and divide the space.

I should have known better, should have waited until the overdue payment from Stonehill in New York was in. They owed enough on royalties to cover the purchase price and renovations, but they didn't have the money to pay. Months passed with no payment, and several times I had to get extensions of the deadline for paying the balance of the house. Beginning of renovations was delayed, and it was doubtful they could be finished by the time we had to vacate our rented house. Then to our relief the family that owned our house was delayed in returning to Cambridge.

Jeff Steinberg at Stonehill finally got some money and made a payment. At least we could start the renovations: new roof, new plumbing, new wiring, new heating system, new plaster and paint. Plenty of room for all our needs plus a patio in back with covered walk to the garage with a room above—a perfect place for organizing the *Who's Who* documentation.

For me the house had a special meaning: it gave me the first real feeling of security and stability I had had since I left Mexico. For the foreseeable future we wouldn't have to move again, wouldn't have to pay rent, wouldn't be wondering where "home" was.

A couple of weeks after I left the hospital the Cuban Cultural Attaché in London called. A representative of the Cuban Book Institute was in Moscow and wanted to discuss a Cuban edition of *Inside the Company* with me. In addition, the Soviet publishing house Voenizdat wanted me to help in shortening the book for a Russian edition. For a year I had been trying to get the book published in

Cuba, the Soviet Union and other Eastern European countries. The Cuban edition was particularly important because the Spanish edition that should have been published in Mexico was suppressed. My hope was that a Cuban edition would circulate in Latin America.

Should I go to Moscow? It was obvious enough that if I did, the Agency and its friends would use the trip to link me once again with the KGB—or to Cuban intelligence and by extension to the KGB. I asked Angela what she thought. She said: Look, the CIA is going to use the "Cuban-KGB agent" line against you forever. Should that stop you from ever visiting Cuba again or from going to any socialist country? Don't you have a legitimate right to promote translations of the book?

She was saying just was I was thinking, but why give them more ammunition to use against me? Still, even if I stayed completely away from socialist countries, they were perfectly capable of creating fairy tales like the Seeger story, distortions like the Anderson columns, or slanders like the "Sixty Minutes" program.

I decided to go, and Angela went too. But we made certain to spread around word that we were going, so that no one could say it was anything secret. Both the Cubans and the Russians said the book was too long and wanted a shortened version. I had already prepared one shortened version, for Sweden, and knew abridgement was very difficult because of the diary form—so many people and operations return from time to time.

Nevertheless, I worked on it for about a week in the Intourist Hotel, taking time out for sightseeing in Moscow and a Sunday outing to the monastery fortress of Zagorsk. Not long after that trip articles began appearing that "Agee was spotted in Moscow." I remembered De Antonio saying that the American media was nothing but a ruling class sewer filled with shit and bile, and I began to think he was right.

In Cambridge I was still swamped with letters, writing projects, and trying to supervise the house renovations. One night the telephone rang, and a far-away voice said, "This is Dennis Daly in Kingston, Jamaica. I'm calling on behalf of the Jamaica Council for Human Rights. Your book has been a best-seller here, and we want to invite you for a speaking tour in September. Maybe you've read of the violence and other problems we're having. A lot of people think the CIA is involved. Could you come?"

I didn't know a thing about Jamaica and I told him. "I haven't the least idea what's happening there. I might be able to come, but first I'd have to do some reading and talk to someone who's up on things. Could you write me a letter with the details?"

"Yes, right away. And we'll arrange for someone in London to fill you in on the situation. We hope you can come."

A few days later a Jamaican called from London. He had just arrived from Kingston, and was calling on behalf of the Human Rights Council. I went to meet him and was intrigued by what he had to say. Since the beginning of the year a series of events had occurred suggesting the same pattern of economic and political destabilization as had occurred in Chile under Allende.

Many thought Kissinger and the Ford administration were responsible—and that the CIA was one of their principle tools. The suspected goal was to undermine popular support for the ruling People's National Party (PNP) and its leader, Prime Minister Michael Manley, during the months remaining before elections.

The main ingredients of the anti-government campaign were: a national and international propaganda war to discredit Manley and the PNP as "dangerous radicals" and "communists"; local and international actions to weaken the economy; attempts to form civic groups for political action; and political violence on an unprecedented scale.

The economy was in dire crisis. Local and foreign investment had all but disappeared, an estimated $200 million had left the country illegally, bauxite revenues were down 50 percent due to strikes and sabotage, sugar earnings were halved, the tourist industry had collapsed because of bad publicity in the U.S., and foreign exchange reserves were down from a surplus of $57 million to a deficit of $60 million—all since the beginning of the year. Recently the U.S. Export-Import Bank lowered Jamaica's credit rating, forcing cutbacks in essential imports. Shortages of food staples such as flour and rice were spreading. Unemployment, which the Manley government had reduced earlier through public works, was on the rise again.

Political violence, endemic in Jamaica, had surged since January with several hundred dead and many more injured—mostly supporters of the PNP. In the Trenchtown ghetto—a PNP stronghold—residents had blocked access to their own streets with old cars, trees and furniture, set up "no-go" areas, and organized nightly patrols.

Despite draconian laws against possession of unauthorized firearms, security officials estimated that more than 8000 guns had been smuggled into the country since the violence heated up. Adding to the climate of tension, a critical shipment of flour, and another of rice, were contaminated with parathion causing deaths and widespread fear.

In June Manley declared a national emergency after a defector from the opposition—and conservative—Jamaica Labor Party (JLP)

revealed that escalating political violence was part of the JLP's electoral strategy.

Security forces arrested several JLP leaders on evidence that they
were fomenting violence, and soon the number of detainees rose to
about two hundred. The violence subsided without completely disap-
pearing. Still, the U.S. press emphasized the dangers for tourists in
Jamaica, and travel bureaus advised customers to go elsewhere. The
main U.S. airline serving Jamaica stopped its daily flights from Miami
and New York.

Jamaica's principal newspaper, the conservative *Daily Gleaner*, led
the propaganda battle against the government, blaming Manley's
moderate socialist policies for the economic crisis and his friendly relations with Cuba, Jamaica's nearest neighbor, for scaring away foreign investment. Already attempts had been made to form an anti-
government "Silent Majority" and to organize a "March of Empty
Pots"—both capitalizing on middle-class discontent.

As I listened I couldn't help thinking of parallels with CIA operations in my own experience and those revealed by the Senate investigation of the Agency's work in Chile. I called Daly back, said I would
go, and got to work reading about Jamaica in London libraries.

Manley's social democratic party had been elected in 1972, ending
ten years' rule by the JLP. At that time Jamaica was a country of very
few wealthy—the "Twenty-One Families"—of mass urban and rural
poverty, of high unemployment and illiteracy, and of poor-to-
nonexistent public health care. Early on, the PNP established a literacy campaign, rural improvement programs, and a bauxite levy to increase revenues and eliminate transfer pricing by the aluminum
multi-nationals.

Manley also established full diplomatic relations with Cuba, which
then sent a technical assistance mission of engineers, construction
workers, doctors and others. They helped set up health clinics, built
an agronomy school, started new housing projects, built small dams
for irrigation, and trained hundreds of Jamaicans in technical skills.
Jamaica under Manley was also an active participant in the non-
aligned movement, and he made no friends in Washington when he
recognized the MPLA in Angola, approved Cuban military assistance
there, and called for Puerto Rican independence.

Manley's domestic and foreign policies were clearly out of line with
tradition in the English-speaking Caribbean, and he was a dangerous
example to other islands in the region. It seemed to me that Kissinger
and Ford had every reason to fear his influence might spread—and to

make sure he failed in his domestic programs. As I read I began to
agree that the signs were there, a kind of pattern of activities to stran-
gle the economy, create widespread tension and fear, blame the
government—which was really the victim—and call for "return to
reason."

The same institutional tools used to undermine the Allende government, including the CIA, now seemed to be applied against
Jamaica. The solution, though, was not to provoke a military coup,
but to defeat the PNP in the elections due in late 1976 or early 1977.
Events since January suggested they had started a year ahead—
typical of CIA election operations.

After arrival in Kingston I became even more convinced that all the
visible signs of destabilization were no mere coincidence. For a week
I spent every day discussing the patterns and giving similar examples
from my own experience: at public and private meetings, on radio
and television, and through press interviews.

The public meetings were by far the most stimulating and
challenging in two years of lectures and rallies. Jamaicans, I quickly
learned, are anything but shy. Spontaneous commentary during my
speeches was continuous. In discussion sessions afterwards there
were always applause and cheers, or boos and catcalls, depending on
what somebody said. And although the crowds were overwhelmingly
favorable to me, I never lacked for articulate and aggressive opposition.

Every public meeting had its moments of tension. At one, in a rural
school in Clarendon Parish, I was speaking to cane cutters and workers from the nearby Alcoa alumina plant. Not long after the meeting
started, a tall, silver-haired white man—probably the only white man
in the hall besides me—stood up, and with a cultivated English ac-
cent began to dispute my allegations of CIA interference. He was
about sixty, dressed in a starchy white suit, and the picture of a colonial planter.

As he rambled on, people began to stir and mumble against him.
Just as he seemed to be finishing he said, "I know my Jamaicans."
The hall exploded with outrage. People got up, stamped their feet,
shouted at him, and for a moment I feared for his safety. But he left,
and I continued—duly impressed with their strong reaction to white
arrogance and paternalism.

This was no ordinary trip in other ways. From the moment I
arrived I was under twenty-four hour protection by a police escort
and volunteers from the Human Rights Council. We travelled by

armed motorcade everywhere. On arrival at public meetings a security escort of ten to fifteen men would form a circle around me, lead me to the stage, then take seats in front of the stage facing the audience. Nobody, but nobody, was going to shoot up those meetings. Still, one meeting in Montego Bay had to be cut short because of a bomb threat.

The *Daily Gleaner* and the JLP, as expected, denounced me for interfering in Jamaican internal affairs, and the president of the Jamaica Manufacturers' Association accused me of conducting "a smear campaign against the CIA and the United States in general." But overall, people were friendly and supportive. They often stopped me in the street to say, "You got it, brother," or "Keep it hot, man."

Everywhere I went people asked who and where the CIA people were. But I saved that for last. I had brought several names of CIA officers in the Kingston Embassy that I discovered through research in London, but I knew there had to be more.

On my arrival I told the Council people the kind of information I needed to identify others. They set to work, and in the end we had nine CIA people and two more in the Embassy whose backgrounds suggested participation in CIA operations. In addition, the Council people came up with their home addresses and telephone numbers, and the make, color and tag numbers of their cars.

At the end of the week's activities the Council organized a press conference where I distributed a written statement that included the names and all the other information. Next day the Council distributed 100,000 leaflets in Kingston with the same information and a call for those people to leave: "We want good relations with America. But we don't want their spies. Let the CIA mind their own business and go back to America." It worked. Within days the CIA began withdrawing people on the list.

In the FOIA documentation I learned that the Embassy was reporting my every move to Washington. The CIA Station no doubt was doing the same, but I didn't get their documents. The voluminous State Department reports included verbatim transcripts of radio and television interviews under headings like: "Media Blitz on Agee Continues" and "Agee Visit: Media Event of the Year." One declassified Embassy cable ended with the statement: "Latest Information is that Agee is leaving on Saturday. (Thank God.)"

Back in Cambridge, Angela and I prepared things for moving to the new house. It gave me a strange feeling, especially as I watched the renovations nearing completion. It was gong to be nice, really nice, perfect for the boys and for our work, too.

VII

Yankee Go Home

Neither Angela nor I could understand how we had accumulated all the "stuff," but there it was, packed into tea chests and ready for the mid-November move to Maids' Causeway. I'd tried to write an article on Jamaica but put it aside as my papers, files and typewriter disappeared into the boxes.

Since returning from Jamaica I had spoken at several meetings about the CIA's destabilization operations in that country, and about two recent terrorist attacks by Agency allies. One was the assassination in Washington, D.C., of Orlando Letelier, the Chilean exile leader and Director of the Transnational Institute in Amsterdam. It happened while I was in Jamaica and was surely the work of the CIA's "sister service" in Chile known as the DINA. Two weeks later a Cubana airliner was bombed in flight killing seventy-three people. Few doubted it was the work of CIA-trained Cuban exiles.

One of those meetings was a rally at the London School of Economics organized by Concerned Americans Abroad. It drew a big crowd including many Jamaican residents in London. The other speakers were Richard Hart, the renowned Jamaican and Caribbean political figure, and Stuart Hall, also Jamaican and professor at Birmingham University. Elections had been announced for mid-December, and reporting on Jamaica in the London press included speculation on possible CIA intervention.

I would also be able to speak about the pattern of intervention in Jamaica on trips after we moved. First I would go to Norway for a Chilean solidarity rally, then to Algeria, and then to Iceland.

For year's end we would all go together to Greece, first to promote the Greek edition of *Inside the Company*, and then for a family vacation. None of us had ever been there, and we would see the sights as we had in Italy the year before.

Because of the Welch incident, the CIA would be especially furious, but I planned to distribute my analysis of the U.S. mission with the names of almost 250 CIA people presently and formerly assigned there. I had finished the list, and an accompanying historical article on the CIA in Greece, months before, but publication was stalled— due in part to death threats against the newspaper editor who wanted to publish it.

Although renovations on our new house were incomplete, enough had been done so that we could move in as planned. Two days before, I awoke to the sound of the doorbell. We'd been up late packing, and I was dead tired. Eight o'clock. Who could that be? Too early for the postman—probably a telegram. Why doesn't he just stick it through the slot? Guess he wants a tip. Half asleep, I put on my robe, maneuvered between tea chests, and stumbled down the stairway. I opened the door to find two men standing on the front steps.

The one closest to the door asked, "Are you Mr. Philip Agee?"

"Yes, what do you want?" If they were reporters I was going to tell them to go to hell.

"We're from the Cambridge police. I have a letter for you from the Home Office." He took an envelope out of his pocket and held it out to me. Oh, Christ, I thought. What now? I took the envelope and without speaking turned to close the door.

"One moment, Mr. Agee. The Home Office asked that you read it on delivery. Would you mind reading it before we leave?"

I sensed something, like a trap, but was too sleepy to argue. I pulled some papers out of the envelope: a two-page letter with a two-page attachment. Two passports were inside the envelope. As I began reading my breathing got short, as if the wind was knocked out of me. I tried not to show it.

Sir:

I am to inform you that the Secretary of State has decided that your departure from the United Kingdom would be conducive to the public good as being in the interests of national security. Accordingly he has decided to refuse your application for a further extension of stay, and for the same reason he has decided to make a deportation order against you . . . you are not entitled to appeal. . . .

That was enough. I glanced at the remaining pages without reading them, nodded my head to the police officers, and closed the door behind me. Goddammit, I thought, they've done it. They've finally done it. And a Labour Party government. I sat at my desk and read on:

You may, if you wish, make representations against the decision to deport you to an independent advisory panel. You will be allowed to appear before the panel if you wish to do so but you may not be represented. To such extent as the advisers may sanction you may be assisted by a friend or arrange for third parties to testify on your behalf. . . . If you decide to submit your case to the panel, a copy of the attached note will be sent to them. . . . You should inform this Department as soon as possible whether or not you wish to make representations to the panel of advisers and, in any event, not later than 14 days from the date on which this letter is handed to you. If the Secretary of State makes the deportation order you will have a right of appeal against removal to the country specified in the removal directions on the grounds that you ought to be removed to a different country specified by you. I enclose your sons' passports.

Yours faithfully,

P. L. Taylor

"Representations." What the hell does that mean? And "removal." Like a piece of furniture. I suppose they'll put me on an airplane in handcuffs. What's this attachment? The stationery had E.R. at the top—that meant *Elizabeth Regina*, I guessed—a royal proclamation from Her Majesty no less. It had my name, date of birth, nationality, immigration number, and the two decisions: to refuse renewal of residence and to deport. Then a "Home Office Statement." As I read it I thought: Those dirty bastards, here they go again.

Mr. Agee first arrived in the United Kingdom on 24 October 1972 when he was granted leave to enter as a visitor for three months. He

subsequently applied for and was granted extensions of stay as a freelance writer. . . . Mr. Agee now has submitted an application for a further 12 months' extension of stay.

The Secretary of State has considered information that Mr. Agee: (a)
has maintained regular contacts harmful to the security of the United
Kingdom with foreign intelligence officers, (b) has been and continues
to be involved in disseminating information harmful to the security of
the United Kingdom, and (c) has aided and counselled others in ob-
taining information for publication which could be harmful to the security of the United Kingdom.

In light of the foregoing, the Secretary of State decided that Mr.
Agee's departure from the United Kingdom would be conducive to the
public good as being in the interests of national security.

There it is, I thought. It's in writing, official, Queen's proclamation: He's a filthy spy. Just wait till this gets out.

I sat there with what seemed like a thousand thoughts going
through my mind: our new house, the boys' school, how soon I would
have to go, where I could go, and why this action now? Why now?

Jamaica. It has to be Jamaica. Getting rid of Manley is a joint
American-British project. It has to be. Or at least the British agreed
in principle, and are letting the Americans, mainly the Agency, carry
the ball. Now, probably under American pressure, the British are
hitting back. I must have hurt them bad, real bad. Or maybe it's the
emergency loan Britain's trying to get from the International Mone-
tary Fund. That $4 billion is crucial for the Labour government—
perfect situation for the Americans to apply pressure. James
Callaghan, the Prime Minister, must have made the decision, then
told Merlyn Rees, the Home Secretary, to get rid of me.

Angela came downstairs wondering who had rung the doorbell. I
gave her the letter and said, "Think you better read this."

"What is it?"

"Read it. It's from the Home Office. They're deporting me."

Angela's eyes opened wide as saucers. "Oh, no. Philip, they
wouldn't do that. Not now, just when we're moving to the new
house." But she read it, got angry, then wondered, "How soon? What
does this 'fourteen days' mean?"

"I don't know. I'm going to call Tony Hawley and see if he can see
me right away."

Tom Culver had put us in touch with Tony Hawley, a Cambridge
lawyer who could handle personal affairs like the house purchase.
First thing he told me when I got to his office was that his firm had

defended Rudi Dutschke, the West German student leader, in his deportation proceedings in 1970. Dutschke had come to Cambridge for medical treatment after being shot in the head by a fanatic. The government contended Rudi had violated the conditions of his coming to Britain by engaging in politics, and thus had become a "security risk." At that time a person could appeal a deportation order in the courts, but the Dutschke case was extremely embarrassing to the government because in the appeal the government had to produce evidence, and this showed they had been tapping his telephone and reading his mail.

Dutschke lost and went to Denmark, Tony explained, but the Conservative government at that time adopted a new immigration law that eliminated all appeals. It gave the Home Secretary total discretion to certify that a foreigner was a "security risk." If I wanted I could make "representations," meaning a statement of some kind, to the advisory panel, but their advice to the Home Office was only that.

The Home Secretary had absolute power. Only one "security" case had come up under the new law, that of Franco Caprino, an Italian working in Britain who the government claimed had links with revolutionaries in Italy. That was last year. But when Caprino said he would appear before the advisory panel, the government backed down and cancelled the deportation proceedings. Why? Because they knew the "no appeal" procedure went against the Treaty of Rome's provisions for treatment of Common Market nationals by each of the member countries. They were afraid Caprino would take Britain to the European Court and win.

But as an American I wouldn't have the same protection as Caprino. Tony wanted to check further. Would I mind if he talked to other lawyers? Of course not. What about costs? I told Tony I could afford some, but I had put most of my money in the house. Tony said he wanted to talk to an immigration expert, a lawyer named Larry Grant. Grant worked at Kent University, in Canterbury, as head of a law clinic that took unusual cases. If I wanted to try some kind of legal defense, perhaps Grant would take my case. That would save money and it would also mean the best possible advice.

What about the "fourteen days?" Does that mean I've just got two weeks before I have to leave? No. I had two weeks to decide and inform the Home Office whether I would appear before the advisory panel. The panel would then set a date for the hearing. They would then advise the Home Secretary who would make a final decision on whether to proceed with deportation or not.

The procedure might take a month from the time I told the Home Office that I would "make representations." Shit, two weeks from today is November 30th—they can have me out before the end of the year, maybe even before Christmas.

If I have to go, will they send me to the States? That depends, Tony said. Usually a person being deported can select the country where he wants to go, but that country has to be willing to accept him. If you fly to Paris, for example, and the French refuse entry and send you back here, then they'll send you to the States. So better start thinking about where you want to go and be certain they'll let you in.

I drove back home and told Angela what Tony said. The most important thing, it seemed, was to avoid being sent to the States. Even if I didn't go to prison, they probably wouldn't let Angela in. I had to find another country that would accept us both. But where?

Better get some advice, talk to people who can help. Bernard and Hettie Vorhaus, for sure. He's one of the leaders of the Concerned Americans group and went through this problem years ago. He was directing a movie starring John Wayne, around 1950, when his name came up in the House Un-American Activities Committee hearings on "communist influence" in Hollywood. They were shooting in Italy. At U.S. request the Italians arrested him and summarily threw him out. He and Hettie, who's British, settled in London, but he went on the Hollywood blacklist and never made another picture. Better call Mel Wulf too, but after I get back from London.

I had several appointments in London that day, beginning at Steve Weissman's flat at noon. As I drove from Cambridge I felt overwhelmed by all the complications coming up. By the time I got to Steve's I'd almost decided not to appear before the advisory panel. After all, if there was no appeal procedure, why bother making "representations." If I could find a country that would definitely let me in, and if the Home Office would let Angela and the boys stay on a little, I would leave quietly. I would try to find a new place to live, and they could join me later.

Ana, Steve's wife, let me in, and with great excitement asked, "Did you hear about Marc Hosenball?"

"No, what about him?"

"You won't believe it. He's being deported as a security risk. Got a letter from the Home Office this morning."

"No kidding," I said as I sat down, thinking I'll be goddammed, Hosenball too. Steve was on the telephone just then, talking to Hosenball at the *Evening Standard* where he'd been working since

July. When they finished he filled me in. Hosenball was at the paper this morning when two policemen delivered a letter with a statement saying he had published information that had harmed British security and endangered "servants of the Crown." Marc was stunned. He'd already spoken to his editor, who said the *Standard* would back him, and he'll be meeting with the paper's lawyers this afternoon.

"Isn't that funny," I said with a wide grin. "Take a look at this." I handed Steve my Home Office letter and statement, Ana read over his shoulder, they both whooped in astonishment, and began simultaneous questions and comments. First Hosenball, now you. That new Home Secretary, Merlyn Rees, must be crazy. Who's next? What are you going to do? Are you going to appeal? What was Angela's reaction?

"How do you like that," I asked, "especially the bit on 'regular contacts with foreign intelligence officers.' They're really trying to stick it to me this time, don't you think?"

"You have to fight it," Steve said, "can't let them get away with this. Hosenball's appealing and so should you. Phil Kelly's already getting together a defense committee for Marc—it'll be for both of you."

"There is no appeal, Steve. I already saw my lawyer in Cambridge. I can 'represent' myself in front of a three-man panel, but Rees has the last and only word. Why bother?"

Steve and Ana insisted that I talk to others, like Hosenball, Kelly (a freelance journalist who had worked on the "CIA in Britain" stories). Concerned Americans, friends in the Labour Party like Stan Newens, and other political groups I'd done meetings with: the Workers' Revolutionary Party, the International Marxist Group, and the International Socialists. Shouldn't make a quick decision. If I went without fighting it would look like I was leaving with my tail between my legs, and also confirming the bullshit reasons they gave.

By the end of the day I had talked to many interested parties, and all had encouraged me to fight the deportation, through a political campaign as well as through "representations" to the advisory panel. Sitting among the stacked tea chests with Angela and Cambridge friends, I agreed, but wondered how much we could accomplish in the few remaining weeks.

Marc Hosenball had decided not to fight the deportation, that is, not publicly. He was going to appear before the advisory panel and thought he had a good chance of convincing Rees to let him stay. By going public with me he would hurt his image and the *Evening*

Standard wouldn't pay his lawyers. Even so, he wasn't against inclusion of his name in any public defense, so Phil Kelly and the others were going to call themselves the "Agee-Hosenball Defense Committee."

Although Hosenball had been in the thick of the press exposures of CIA staff and operations in Britain, his main offense seemed to be an article he wrote for *Time Out* on Britain's secret communications intelligence center at Cheltenham. Many of us suspected that the government had no intention of throwing him out. Rather, they could have tacked him on to my case, with the idea of throwing me out, letting him stay, and making themselves look liberal.

With the defense committee I agreed to convert my defense into an attack on the CIA and U.S. for pressuring the Labour government and on Prime Minister Callaghan for bowing to the pressure. We would also attack the immigration law allowing expulsion without appeal.

The telephone never stopped ringing, neither did the stream of press, radio and television people who dropped by for interviews. With all of them I denied Rees's charges and pointed out that in the past two years the only contacts I'd had with people from socialist countries were a couple of interviews with the *Novosti* correspondent in London, three visits to the Cuban Embassy to discuss a Cuban edition of *Inside the Company*, and the 10-day visit to Moscow in August to work on the Russian edition. Besides that, I had never worked in operations involving British services, and I had no knowledge of anything that could affect the country's security.

The real reasons, I insisted, were my Jamaica trip, American pressure on the IMF loan, and the CIA's determination to stop my second book. The Home Office, meanwhile, stuck to its lie that "the action was taken neither at the behest of, nor after consultation with, foreign governments or their agencies."

Most of the avalanche of articles were fair, but there were exceptions. The right-wing *Daily Mail*, under a headline "Agee 'Visited by Soviet Spies,'" reported that meetings with "Russian and Cuban intelligence agents" was the reason for my deportation. And the Sunday scandal sheet, *News of the World*, wrote that I had said I had "frequent meetings with both the Russian and Cuban Embassies in London," that I had "spent most of July and August in Russia discussing future revelations about the CIA," and that my second book was to be published "in the New Year in Russia. . . ."

Rupert Murdoch's mass circulation tabloid, *The Sun*, which always carried a nude woman on page three, wanted something different—like maybe a sex angle. I said my deportation was a scandal, all right, but not that kind. Then I thought, why not give them the Leslie-Janet story rejected in Paris months earlier? They liked it.

What followed was a pleasing, if at first incredible, denouement to the saga of that woman. Through the American Chamber of Commerce in Caracas, the *Sun's* Washington correspondent found Leslie Donegan working as a motel clerk in Georgia. She denied everything, said she'd never worked for the CIA, never met me, never even been to Europe. As a last question the reporter asked, "And I don't suppose you have ever heard of someone called Janet Strickland?"

Astonished, Leslie answered, "Why, yes. She was my best friend when I went to school in Venezuela." After the reporter explained Janet's work against me, Leslie added, "I would have been the perfect identity for her to use as a cover. She knew all about my family history and my own personal likes and dislikes. We were such good friends."

The reporter then traced Janet to her parents' mansion in Palm Beach, Florida. Turned out that her father had been the head of the Exxon corporation's Latin American operations. She admitted she'd heard of me, but as for working for the CIA she said, "That's crazy." But she refused to discuss her Paris days, and when a photographer took her picture her father threatened to beat him up and break his camera.

The Sun ran two front-page stories on Strickland and the bugged typewriter, with huge headlines like "Blonde Who Bugged Me," "Spy Girl and CIA Rebel," and "Face to Face with a Spy." Over one of the photographs from the I.L.O. in Geneva, the story began: "This is the moment when CIA renegade Philip Agee confronted the girl he claims is at the center of a spy mystery. The picture below shows the beautiful blonde with 41-year-old Agee. . . ."

The *Sun* stories were the only laughs we had during those first hectic days after the deportation letter arrived. But dozens, if not hundreds, of people now began to join the fight. In the House of Commons, Stan Newens organized over fifty Members of Parliament to write in protest to Rees, and led a delegation to see Rees personally.

Another M. P., Judith Hart, questioned Rees in the Commons on my behalf. He hid behind the cloak of "national security and the safety of servants of the Crown," refused to say anything more than the vague charges already known, and insisted that the procedure before the advisory panel, and their recommendations, would have to be secret. But he did admit that he had been considering my case "for three or four weeks" before his formal decision—in other words just following the IMF loan application.

Winston Churchill, grandson of the wartime leader and Tory right-winger, remarked that my "contacts" were with Soviet and Cuban intelligence services. He had immunity, so I couldn't sue, but nobody took him seriously anyway.

There was an interesting political irony in the whole affair. The Labour Party had bitterly opposed Rudi Dutschke's deportation by the then-Conservative government, and the new "no-appeal" immigration law as well. None other than Merlyn Rees led the fight against the law in the House of Commons. Their position was that the new law was unfair because it would deprive the affected person from "due process of law." Now they were applying the very procedure they had opposed.

From Denmark Dutschke recalled: "There was a Conservative government in power then, but it is different now. Mr. Callaghan not only came to protest meetings about my deportation—he was actually on the platform next to me. Mr. Callaghan said on one of those occasions: 'The whole idea of deporting people after a secret tribunal, simply because of claims that they might have damaged the security of the state, is a nasty, sordid business. ' "

That hypocrisy was not lost on Labour M.P.'s who opposed the proceeding, and when some threatened to withhold their votes speculation broke out that the government might fall. Labour had only a one-seat majority, and couldn't afford a single defection.

The defense committee set up shop at the National Council for Civil Liberties (NCCL) and began organizing petitions, rallies and pickets of the Home Office. They also published a series of pamphlets on the CIA that included my *Temps Modernes* article, the U.S. Senate reports on CIA assassination plots and subversion in Chile, articles on current destabilization in Jamaica, and CIA penetration and manipulation of the Labour Party. The last was a well-researched study that included past connections of Denis Healey, the current Finance Minister, and Anthony Crosland, the current Foreign Minister, with CIA front organizations.

Both the defense committee and the National Union of Journalists (NUJ), of which later Hosenball and I were members, appealed to other unions and the Trades Union Congress (TUC) for support. Judith Hart became my leading defender in the House of Commons. Her role was critical because she was a former Minister of Overseas

Development and member of the Privy Council—and a member of the Labour Party's National Executive Committee. One of her first actions was to organize and lead a delegation from the Executive Committee to protest personally to Rees. Concerned Americans Abroad mobilized its members for action, including a protest to the American Ambassador, Anne Armstrong. And the NCCL organized its members and supporters in protest. The defense campaign was off and running.

Under a pall of gloom we moved into our new house where the various contractors still working were alarmed that I might be gone before they got their money. Because they weren't finished we couldn't really unpack, so the tea chests stacked around in the old house were now stacked all over the new one. It took heroic efforts on Angela's part to organize meals, unpack essentials, and direct the workers while I started running around seeing M.P.'s, the defense committee, journalists and lawyers.

Four days after the crisis broke I drove to Larry Grant's thatched cottage in a hamlet near Canterbury. He was a big man with a big head made still bigger by an overgrown red mane and bushy red beard. Originally from Yorkshire, he was in his mid-thirties with years of civil rights experience, much with the NCCL. That day he was miserable with asthma, not helped much by the cigarettes he constantly smoked. We spent the afternoon sipping scotch and discussing my case.

At first he thought I could sue Rees for defamation over his "contacts-with-foreign-intelligence-officers" charge, but then he decided that wouldn't work because as a Minister of the Crown Rees had immunity. When I wondered why Rees hadn't just refused to extend my residence permit, Larry explained that in that case I would have had a legal appeal, evidence would have to be presented, and witnesses cross-examined. But by designating me a "security risk" Rees put me in the no-evidence, no-appeal category. It also gave him the opportunity to make sinister allegations in the vaguest possible way to make me look bad.

He then explained that the panel members were nothing more than "poodles" of the Home Secretary. The chairman was Sir Derek Hilton, President of the Immigration Appeals Tribunal, the court that would have heard my appeal if Rees had not classified me a "national security risk."

Grant had argued numbers of cases before him in the past. During World War II Hilton had been a general in the Special Operations

Executive, the British paramilitary and intelligence agency that helped set up the CIA's predecessor organization, the Office of Strategic Services (OSS). Another member was Sir Clifford Jarrett, Chairman of the Tobacco Research Council, and former Permanent Secretary of the Admiralty, Britain's Navy Department. The third was Sir Richard Hayward, a former leader of the postal workers' union who later became a member of the National Postal Board. In 1971 the union had expelled him for siding with management during a strike. Those three establishment figures would hardly by sympathetic to the likes of me, and would surely respect Rees's "national security" argument.

One chance I might have was with the European Commission on Human Rights in Strasbourg on grounds that I was being deprived of "due process of law." Grant said he wanted to talk to several barristers about this possibility and other aspects of the case, and we would meet again the following week. Meanwhile I should prepare a draft letter to Rees for delivery on November 29, the last day of the fourteen-day period in which I could accept the panel hearing.

I would deny all his allegations, affirm that I would "make representations," and demand to have details of the allegations: who were the "contacts," what information had I "disseminated" and to whom, whom I had "aided and counselled," and how had all that harmed the "security" of the United Kingdom. I would also ask a series of questions on proceedings before the panel such as any restrictions on the number of "friends" to be present or witnesses on my behalf.

The day after I met Larry, I had an unforgettable experience, a stimulus to go all out in the defense campaign. It was a Sunday. The Trades Union Congress and the Labour Party had organized a mass demonstration in London against racism in Britain. Merlyn Rees, the Home Secretary, would be one of the speakers.

Upwards of 20,000 people assembled in Hyde Park behind their union banners and headed off in a march to Trafalgar Square. Angela and the boys and I marched with the NUJ while the defense committee handed out thousands of leaflets and petitions against the deportations. Several times during the march people watching from the sidewalks saw us and came over to express support; one was an American Catholic priest.

We stood no more than ten meters from the speakers' platform as Trafalgar Square filled to overflowing. Looking around I was almost embarrassed by the number of banners and placards condemning the deportations. Some had "Merlyn the MagiCIAn," others "CIA and Rees Out! Agee and Hosenball In!"

Several speakers came and went before the attentive crowd. But when Rees took the platform, a small group started chanting, "Merlyn Rees, CIA; Agee, Hosenball must stay." Like wildfire the chanting spread through Trafalgar Square along with a roar of heckling and jeering.

We were straight in front of Rees as he started to speak, but the roar got louder. He was looking in our direction, but I wasn't sure whether he saw us. Chills went down my back as the shouting and chanting carried on. Phil and Chris and Angela and I looked at each other in disbelief. Rees started his speech again, got flushed with anger, and after five minutes quit. Hardly a word was heard above the roaring crowd.

After the rally we were discussing with members of the defense committee whether the heckling might have hardened Rees against me when a call came from Amsterdam. Saul Landau was calling from the Transnational Institute (TNI) with an offer of a fellowship and help in getting the Dutch government to give me residence. Landau, a fellow at the Washington-based Institute for Policy Studies (IPS), had taken over as acting TNI director after Orlando Letelier was assassinated. "Yes," I told Saul, "anything you can do will help. Thank you so much."

In the days that followed Larry Grant brought in three barristers on my case: David Turner-Samuels as Leading Counsel and Lord Anthony Gifford and Cedric Thornberry as Junior Counsels. All were acknowledged as among the best legal minds in Britain of progressive political persuasion. We began a series of meetings to discuss procedures and strategy. They all helped me draft my reply to Rees, and Cedric began a petition to the European Commission on Human Rights.

When time came for the hearing, Larry Grant would be my "friend," but the barristers would also attend if I were allowed more than one. At David's suggestion I would begin drafting a detailed statement on my background: why I went into the CIA, what I did in the Agency, why I resigned, why I wrote *Inside the Company*, and what I've been doing since. I should include all my writings, speeches, interviews, and travels since first arrival in Britain, along with every contact I had had with people from socialist countries.

From the beginning of the crisis, pledges of support and protests against my deportation and the procedure employed arrived from much of Western Europe. Nobel prize winners, human rights organizations, solidarity groups, and political leaders sent messages or signed petitions. These included writers Jean Paul Sartre and Simone de Beauvoir, filmmaker Costa Gavras and Greek socialist leader Andreas Papandreou. In Amsterdam the Anne Frank Foundation offered to make me a fellow and to assist in getting a Dutch residence permit.

Americans also responded with thousands of dollars in contributions to the defense committee. In New York Emile de Antonio began gathering names of writers and filmmakers for a newspaper ad of support. Joan Baez and Jane Fonda, among others, signed a petition, and Ronald Dellums, Chair of the House of Representatives Black Caucus, sent a telegram of support. So did the New York and California ACLUs and the National Lawyers Guild.

In Britain individuals and organizations throughout the country pledged support or protested. These included local Labour Party organizations, the national students union, and the trade union movement. Eventually almost every union of importance, representing millions of British workers, joined the campaign. Even the Trades Union Congress, the national center, sent its General Secretary to see Rees.

The response to my plight from so many corners gave me the confidence and energy I needed to stand up and fight, even though my only hope was to change Rees's mind. I took the attitude that with all the support and my own efforts Callaghan and Rees could be convinced. In the press conferences and public rallies coming up I would use my defense campaign, like all my work, for political education on why the CIA exists, how it operates and how it can be weakened through exposure of its operations and personnel. And I would try always to remember to emphasize that the real issue was not the CIA but the American social and economic structure that requires such an Agency—with all the human cost, as in Chile, that its activities provoke.

On November 29, fourteen days after Rees's letter, I delivered my response in person to the Home Office. At that moment hundreds of supporters were staging a picket organized by the defense committee. At one point an official came out threatening to have the police drive them away because they couldn't get a delivery of plastic teacups through the crowd.

Along with my letter I delivered petitions signed by over 10,000 people. Then I held a press conference where I distributed copies of Rees's letter and mine demanding that I be given a chance to defend myself. It was the first of many occasions when I deliberately sought to open up my case to public scrutiny.

The next day I had another press conference with the journalists who covered the House of Commons, and afterwards I spoke with many M.P.'s who responded to an open invitation from Judith Hart to discuss my case with me. The main point I made was that Rees should bring criminal charges against me if I had committed any offense. Sources could be protected by presentation of evidence *in camera* if that were necessary. That night we had our first public rally at Central Hall, just across from Westminster Abbey. Hundreds of people crowded in to hear Judith, historian E. P. Thompson, union leader Alan Sapper, Labour's International Secretary and M. P. Ian Mikardo, and me.

While our rally was going on, Rees was on the ropes in the House of Commons. The forty Labour M.P.'s who were members of the scientific and technical workers' union, the biggest union group in the Commons, had protested the "no evidence–no appeal" procedure and forced Rees to hold an extra-parliamentary session with every Labour M.P. invited. During the, at times, angry session, Rees argued defensively that he had not made up his mind on the deportations, which was nice to hear but contrary to his letters to Hosenball and me. He said he had merely served notice of intent to deport. Then he gave the lame and false excuse that Hosenball and I were due to leave shortly anyway, since my current residence permission was to expire at month's end and Hosenball's in December. Neither of us had the slightest intention of moving from Britain and he knew it.

A couple of days later Larry Grant learned from the Home Office that my hearing would start on January 11. What a relief to know I had almost six weeks to get my statement ready, and that I wouldn't be railroaded out before the end of the year. Without any doubt Rees and Callaghan would have preferred to get it all over fast, but pressure from the M.P.s, the unions and all the others had made summary execution impossible. Thank god we'd have more than fourteen days to mobilize.

With that news Phil Kelly and the defense committee accelerated their activities. They put out a "Child's Guide" for identifying CIA officers in U.S. Embassies. Picketing of the Home Office was expanded to a march by hundreds on the U.S. Embassy and a "magical mystery tour" of the homes of CIA officers with pickets and street theater. With loud hailers and leaflets the *cherchez le spook* demonstrators advised neighbors who *their* neighbor was. *Time Out* ran an article by Weissman on the identity and background of the new CIA Chief of Station in London, and a delegation delivered a demand to the U.S. Embassy that he be withdrawn. And Claridges Hotel was picketed when Secretary of State Kissinger stayed overnight.

December 8 was a "National Day of Action" with *ad hoc* defense committees in various cities taking part. The main event was a day-long teach-in at the London School of Economics for which John Marks came from the States. Many other speakers, myself included, participated.

The Penguin Books NUJ local struck that day from noon to two p.m. in order to take part in the Home Office picket. When management said they'd have to forfeit pay the union retorted that the company had made a lot of money on my book and please forward, as a minimum, the equivalent of pay withheld to the defense committee. Other activities such as concerts, film benefits and discos were organized to raise money. All the activities were well-covered by the British press which helped keep momentum going within the Labour Party and the unions.

I participated in almost all those London events, but other speaking invitations poured in from all parts of Britain—far more than I could accept given the time needed to prepare the statement for the panel. Yet, before the end of the month I'd gone to Blackpool, Newcastle, Birmingham and Glasgow. Judith Hart spoke at the Glasgow rally as did Neil Kinnock, a Welshman with a booming voice whom many considered to be a rising star in the Labour Party, and who in fact became Party Leader in the mid-1980's.

I wrote the panel statement as if I were rebutting an imaginary dossier presented to Rees by the British security services in the hope that my information would be more convincing than anything the services, with help from the CIA, could have concocted. Rees had refused to get any more specific than the original letter on grounds that he had to protect "sources." So I was in the position of having to detail everything I had done since beginning work on *Inside the Company*, knowing that I might miss items of relevance to the panel and to Rees. At the same time I knew his allegations were false, particularly the "regular contacts" charge, but I didn't know what evidence might have been falsified. As I wrote in the statement, its preparation was like shadow boxing in the dark or firing a rifle in fog so dense the target couldn't be seen.

In the end I had an eighty-five page statement with nearly forty attachments including the fifteen volumes of the Senate intelligence investigation, the House of Representatives investigation, the Rockefeller investigation, all my writings and interviews, dates, destination and purpose of every trip I'd made since 1972, and date, place and sponsor of every public meeting where I'd spoken or lectured. The statement itself was a chronological review of my life, including an explanation of every contact I had ever had with officials of socialist countries—all of which were either press interviews or were related to research for, and publication of, *Inside the Company* and my planned second book.

The problem remained about where to go if I lost. The Justice Department had refused to say whether I would be prosecuted if I returned to the States, but they did admit prosecution was "under active consideration."

We concluded that I had better do whatever was necessary to avoid being sent to the States. But my lawyers and the defense committee recommended that I refrain from asking other countries for permission to resettle because that would look defeatist, and if a particular country did agree, that would take a little pressure off Rees and possibly deflate our campaign. Still, we didn't know how much delay there would be between the hearing and Rees's decision. He might decide very quickly, and I would have little time to make arrangements.

For insurance, in case I had to leave quickly, Tony Gifford arranged for me to meet discreetly with the Algerian Ambassador whom he knew well. The Ambassador said that I could go to Algeria if deported, but he cautioned that a West European country would be better from the point of view of image than a radical Arab state. His agreement was an enormous relief, especially since the European Commission on Human Rights rejected my preliminary petition.

More than 150 M.P.'s signed motions of protest, but Rees and Callaghan had their own way of fighting back. Early on, at a reception at the Prime Minister's residence, editors of several leading newspapers were told that the deportations were an extremely serious security matter and that journalists had nothing to fear if they stuck to traditional reporting. The editors were also asked to downplay the matter.

A directive also circulated through the BBC that any interview with me had to be cleared with senior management and that I was not to be given an easy time. On one occasion I even got an apology prior to filming. The interviewer, Ludovic Kennedy, met me on arrival at the studio with a glass of scotch and a half-eaten chicken leg. He said he had word from on high to be rough, and I shouldn't take it as anything personal.

In the face of rising protest which was inundating the Home Office,

Rees sent out a circular to union branches and local Labour Party offices. Written on the "Elizabeth Regina" stationery, the statement was extremely misleading about the causes for the deportations, the fairness of the panel proceedings and Labour's opposition to the new immigration law in 1971. The defense committee got a copy of the memo and sent a rebuttal to every local party and union branch.

Then came the rumors. Some originated in the Home Office, others with Callaghan and Rees in the corridors of the House of Commons spiced with whispers, nods, and winks. All had the purpose of making the deportations look like a grave security matter, the details of which could not be revealed. "Lives are at stake," Rees had muttered according to M.P.'s friendly to the defense. First, there was the version that Hosenball and I had developed contacts in the Irish Republican Army; then that I was going to publish a list of British undercover agents in Northern Ireland; then that Hosenball and I together were going to publish a list of British "safe houses" in Northern Ireland. Another rumor was that I was involved with the Red Army Fraction in West Germany whose activities were then at a peak.

The rumors all got into the press, including one that the CIA had asked the British to give me special police protection for fear that Cuban agents would murder me and the Agency would be blamed. We wondered if that one originated from the time Larry Grant and I were waiting to be served in a restaurant when suddenly the man eating at the table next to us began to choke, turned red, stood straight up clutching his throat, then fell over still-legged in an unconscious heap. Larry figured he got my plate by mistake.

But Rees's lowest blow was saved for David Steel, leader of the Liberal Party who was undecided on whether to line up the Liberals against the deportations. From several people I learned that Steel had asked Rees "what this Agee thing is all about." Rees apparently replied that "Agee is directly responsible for the death of two of our agents behind the Iron Curtain."

It worked. Steel did not denounce the procedure—even though defense of civil liberties was a basic party tenet—but the Young Liberals led by Peter Hain did join the defense.

At first I dismissed the story as preposterous, but I picked it up several times more. On reflection I thought: maybe they've inserted the case of the Polish fencer, Pawlowski, into the dossier.

It could be crucial to my defense, so I decided to go public on it before the panel meeting. In separate interviews with reporters from principal London papers I went into the case, explaining how the story originated a year before with the *Los Angeles Times* in Brussels. I gave all the reasons why the CIA would never have selected me for involvement in such a sensitive operation on the eve of my resignation, and I said that Rees's remark to Steel must have been based on falsified information. Besides, if it was a French intelligence operation, as Seeger reported, why would they have the CIA make the contact in Mexico City rather than one of their own officers?

The reporters contacted Steel who admitted that he discussed my case with Rees, did not deny the remark, and refused to discuss it, claiming House of Commons "privilege." The Home Office, naturally, denied.

The London papers carried long articles on the case, but five days later it cropped up in the strangest way in New York. *Newsday* came out with a front page photograph of Pawlowski and other Polish fencers positioned next to a photograph of me, with the caption: "Spies, Athletes, Treachery." The long article, by Ernest Volkman, was attributed to "U.S. intelligence sources" and told the whole story of the 120-man ring, that I was to have contacted Pawlowski during the Mexican Olympics, and that the CIA believed I betrayed the operation in Cuba in 1971. But Volkman's "intelligence sources" now described the operation as British, not French, and said my deportation was ordered after the CIA told the British that I told the Cubans or KGB about it.

Accounts of the London stories must have been picked up by the wire services, but Volkman neither contacted me for comment nor made any mention of my denials or analyses published in London. Someone was determined to keep that story alive—I had a vague suspicion who—so I included it in great detail in my statement for the panel.

By the time the hearing began, the defense campaign had widened to include repeal of the 1971 Immigration Act and passage of an American-style Freedom of Information Act as goals. On a cold Sunday two days before the hearing we had another march: from Charing Cross Embankment to the Home Office to the American Embassy to Speakers' Corner. About 1500 people turned out, and speakers included Judith Hart; Jo Richardson, another Labour M.P. who had been active in the defense from the beginning; and Ken Morgan, General Secretary of NUJ.

But the person who really moved everyone was Philip Noel-Baker, the grand old man of the British peace movement whose career went back to the Versailles conference and the League of Nations. His

Nobel Peace Prize dated from the 1950's. Now in his late eighties, he was rolled in a wheelchair up to the flatbed truck that served as our speakers' platform. Several of us had to lift him up to the truck, but once up he was able to walk over and stand behind the microphone. Pale, thin and fragile-looking, with hair as white as snow, he began with a shaky, creaky voice that seemed to come from afar. The crowd fell silent.

All the while, as he made an impassioned plea to stop the deportations, I stood on the ground below the microphone practically in awe. He was so frail I was afraid he might fall forward, off the truck, and I was wondering how I could break the fall without hurting him. But he managed, and we lowered him back in the wheelchair as the crowd cheered and applauded.

The advisory panel chose as "neutral ground" for our hearing one of those most eminent of British institutions: a men's club. The club itself was defunct, but its building was used as a government conference center. Only last year Henry Kissinger had attended a NATO conference there. It was still pure establishment: the United Services and Royal Aeronautical Club at 116 Pall Mall, just a few minutes walk from the Home Office.

Although the panel had refused our request to open the hearing to public and press, and were trying to shroud the whole farce in total secrecy, we decided to open it up as much as possible. The defense committee set up a press center at the Institute of Contemporary Arts (ICA), just around the corner from the club, and announced we would have press conferences after each session with the panel.

As P-Day ("p" for panel and "p" for piss on 'em) approached, Angela's "team" got the draft mimeographed for distribution to the press and assembled kits with the statement and attachments. Altogether we had "representations" of a half-million words, not counting attachments like *Inside the Company* and reports of the official investigations in Washington. We planned to ask at the opening session for a three-week postponement so that I could improve the statement and organize more witnesses. We would also ask that Angela and the boys be allowed to attend the hearing.

Larry Grant would be my "friend"—which in truth he had become in the weeks since we met—but we would ask that I be allowed more than one "friend" present. The second would be Tony Gifford, the barrister who was our "Junior Counsel."

I had learned in the various meetings with the legal team something of the difference between solicitors like Larry and Tony

Hawley, and barristers like David, Cedric and Tony. The barristers wear the white wigs in court and are "instructed" by solicitors on case law, the fine points of the defense, what the prosecution is likely to do and all the other particulars. So it was that Larry wrote the following "Instruction to Counsel" for Tony Gifford for the opening of the hearing. It gave the flavor of our frustration.

> Outside the Advisory Panel Hearing
> Pavement 116 Pall Mall
> January 11th, 1977
> For security reasons, Counsel will not find herewith:
> 1. (Name of document deleted)
> 2. (Ditto)
> 3. (Ditto)

Counsel is asked to attend at or in the vicinity of 116 Pall Mall, London. As Counsel will not be admitted to the hearing unless his instructing solicitor makes a successful application for a second friend, and as the weather of late has been a little inclement, Counsel is advised to wear an overcoat.

Counsel will be aware that the Panel have requested that those attending produce some simple form of identification such as a passport or a driving license. Counsel is therefore asked to ensure that he has one of these two documents in his possession and that the document is *current*.

As Counsel is a Peer of the Realm, other identification might suffice, such as a coronet, a copy of *Burke's Peerage* or a House of Lords car park permit.

Counsel should not be fearful of a number of men wearing trench coats who will be hovering around the building. I am assured that these gentlemen are all senior members of the Law Society. Similarly I am assured that the photographers are all from the journal *Country Life*.

As to Counsel's entering the hearing room, he will receive an indication by a signal: grey smoke, "no," white smoke, "yes."

In case of difficulty instructing solicitor will forward to Counsel a number of NCCL factsheets on arrest and bail.

VIII

Showdown in the Ladies Room

It was snowing as Angela, Phil and Chris and I walked up Pall Mall to the club. I had bought a dark blue pin-stripe suit and appropriately conservative tie for the occasion—first time I'd dressed like that since leaving the Agency. The hearing was to begin at ten-thirty, but we were half an hour early. Just the night before, still another motion in the House of Commons was submitted, signed by 43 M.P.'s, calling on Rees either to bring criminal charges against Hosenball and me or drop the deportations.

Reporters, television crews, and members of the defense committee were across the street behind a police picket. I didn't see the stuffed, giant kangaroo that some on the committee had vowed to bring and figured that wiser heads had prevailed. Just down the street sat a van with more police and dogs. I spoke a few minutes with the committee and press, then headed over to the club entrance.

The building was impressive: a multi-story Nash mansion with or-nate facade of fluted pillars and sculptured cornices. Several more policemen were standing by varnished double doors with polished brass fixtures. One of them led us into a cavernous vestibule where we showed identification and were given a "pass" to pin on. Then a guard escorted us up the regal stairway. Hanging on the walls were large paintings of heroic military scenes from India—British officers on the charge, horses, swords, golden epaulets, mountains, and dark-skinned natives retreating. Shining marble and glistening chandeliers were everywhere.

We were shown through a door titled "Ladies Room One" where the panel secretary, Mr. P. J. Bailey, was sitting with two assistants. Bailey, a perfect double for Casper the Friendly Ghost, escorted us down the hall to a door titled "Ladies Dining Room." It opened to a large lounge with period sofas and tables and would be our "waiting room" for the hearing.

Larry was already there and had a surprise. He had shaved off his beard, trimmed his hair, and was dressed in a dark, three-piece suit with antique watch and chain. "It's my court suit," he said defensively. "I only wear it on special occasions." Soon Tony Gifford and Tony Hawley arrived. The lawyers were tense as they discussed our first moves, but my only thought was that every word they said was being recorded.

Precisely at ten-thirty, the ghost arrived and led Larry and me to the hearing room, the door of which bore the sign: "Ladies Room Two." It was another fairly large lounge, ornate in keeping with the building, with carpet and panelled walls. The "three wise men" were sitting at a long table covered with a blue baize cloth that hung to the floor in front. They were all in their late sixties and dressed in dark, three-piece business suits. In front of each of them was an ashtray, file, legal pad and pencils, and a magnifying glass.

We took our seats facing them at a slightly shorter table with blue baize covering. To our right, against the wall, was a seedy-looking, floral-patterned sofa. To our left sat a faceless woman whose job, we soon learned, was to rise and pass papers across the three meters of space separating the two tables. A crystal chandelier was hanging over that space.

Sir Derek introduced himself and presented Sir Clifford and Sir Richard. He then gave a speech about why we were there, mentioning, among other things, that the panel had seen the evidence laid before Rees and would make their recommendations after hearing my "representations." Sir Derek's manner was starchy in the extreme, aloof and impersonal, and he hardly looked at us as he spoke.

As he talked to the wall behind us, I took out my small cassette re-corder, faced the microphone at Sir Derek, and turned it on. Eventu-ally he wound down, looked at me and said, "You may now speak if you wish."

"I would like for my friend, Mr. Grant, to comment first."

Larry began by saying that while he was there as my "friend," he intended to make a number of applications to the panel on my behalf. Our main requests were: 1) that I be informed of the particulars of the accusations; 2) that I have the opportunity to confront the people who were accusing me; 3) that I be permitted to have my family and more than one "friend" in the hearing; 4) that we be permitted to make a record of the hearing either by tape or stenographer; 5) that press and public be allowed to attend; 6) that the hearing be postponed for three weeks; and 7) that a timetable be agreed for presentation of my statement and those of my witnesses.

He went on, reading from a 25-page, 80-point memorandum justi-fying each of his applications. He emphasized that I was there be-cause I had nothing to hide, but my presence did not mean I accepted the proceedings as appropriate or fair. As we and various M.P.'s had been arguing, the Home Secretary at the time the current Immigra-tion Act was adopted promised that under this procedure the person affected would be given as many particulars as was possible without compromising sources of information. We hadn't received *one* partic-ular, not even the time frame or the continent in which my supposed actions had taken place.

An hour into the hearing, as Larry was speaking, the auto-stop on my tape recorder clicked, and I began to turn the cassette around. Sir Derek looked at me, his pop-eyes bulging in anger, and shouted: "Mr. Agee! What is *that?*"

With the most innocent air I could fake I said, "Well, as anyone can see, it's a tape recorder."

"How dare you," he sputtered, "turn that off immediately. Why didn't you ask permission?"

"Why should I? It's my hearing and I want an accurate record. You saw me put it on the table. Why didn't you say something?" A voice was telling me to stay calm but my temper was rising.

"Well. I'm not terribly mechanically minded. Turn it off. This hear-ing will not be recorded." He looked back at Larry, who was telling me in a low voice that I'd better put it away.

I put the recorder in my briefcase, thankful that Sir Derek hadn't asked for the tape. At least I had the first hour to play at the press conference. Larry went on, eventually ending with the lament that

Britain had come a long way from the time it gave residence to aliens whose political views and activities were not approved by the governments of the day: Marx, Engels, Kropotkin, Bakunin, Lenin, and Sun Yat Sen. Could I be more dangerous than the likes of those?

Sir Derek declared a recess for the panel to consider our applications. We returned to "Ladies Dining Room" where the others were waiting. When the hearing resumed a half hour later Sir Derek denied all the applications except one: my family could be present, and I could have more than one "friend." The paper-passer went for Tony Gifford, Angela and the boys. Tony took a seat at our table while Angela, Chris and Phil took the sofa to our right.

Tony and Larry then began arguing with Sir Derek over the refusal of our applications. The wrangling went on for at least a half-hour in an increasingly hostile atmosphere. Finally Sir Derek, obviously out of patience, said: "The Home Secretary has decided that this is the system. Take it or leave it."

I turned to Larry and Tony and said in a voice loud enough for Sir Derek to hear: "Let's have a recess to consider whether we should leave it."

More argument. Sir Derek wanted to proceed. We wanted to talk it over in private. Finally Sir Derek asked the other panel members, and they relented. We went back to the "Ladies Dining Room," discussed whether we should walk out, and decided to continue. On our return to "Ladies Room Two," Sir Derek announced an hour's break for lunch.

Down in the street we looked for the van from the BBC that was to do a live radio interview, but none was in sight. Later we learned that no more live interviews with me were to be permitted. All interviews had to be reviewed by the Director General or the Editor of News and Current Affairs before broadcast.

We hurried over to the press center at ICA which was packed with journalists, radio and television people and members of the defense committee. Tony, Larry and I sat at the front table, and I took out the tape recorder. I re-wound the tape as Larry began describing our visit to the "Ladies Room." When he mentioned Sir Derek's reaction to my recorder, everybody started yelling, "Let's hear it!" "Play the tape!"

I had already been playing it as Larry spoke, and I felt like a perfect fool. The tape was blank. I looked out at the excited crowd and said, "Now you'll see why I'm so dangerous. I couldn't even bug my own hearing. I forgot to press the red record button."

Howls of laughter, hoots and more shouting. When the uproar died down Larry, Tony and I went on describing the hearing, giving as much detail as possible of what had gone on.

After a quick lunch in the snack bar we returned to the hearing room. I began reading my statement, and when the session ended we returned to the press center, passed out copies of the pages I had read, and again described the hearing. The most interesting comment we could make on that session was that when I began reading about Jamaica all three panel members suddenly became alert and starting taking notes. Sir Derek even opened his 20- to 30-page folder to look for something.

The next day, Wednesday, I continued reading morning and afternoon, and we presented our first "character witnesses," Tom Culver and Christopher Roper of *Latin America Newsletter*. After each session we repeated the press conferences, passed out the pages I had read, and the witnesses outlined what they had said and gave their general impressions. Our main point was to show how farcical the whole procedure was: this bizarre spectacle of grown men sitting morning and afternoon in great solemnity in the "Ladies Room" as I read the story of my life.

Thursday morning Judith Hart and Alex Lyon, also a Labour M.P. and former Minister in the Home Office, came as witnesses. They insisted that the panel had the power to give me at least some particulars. Sir Derek got increasingly defensive. He admitted that the "evidence" file in front of him held no confidential documents and that Rees had given him no instructions on how to conduct the hearing. He didn't know who, except Rees, could give any particulars. How could telling me the time frame or the content jeopardize sources? Sir Derek didn't know. Neither did Sir Clifford or Sir Richard. Sir Derek said he was "in a straitjacket." The whole procedure was so Kafkaesque that Judith and Alex stood up and said they were going straight to the House of Commons to see Rees for an explanation, and to ask him to authorize the panel to give me at least some particulars.

We broke for lunch, and on return Sir Derek looked at me and held up his file saying: "You have told the press that I refer to this file on matters you are speaking about. It has nothing to do with anything except correspondence between your lawyers and the Home Office."

But to Alex and Judith he'd implied it was the "evidence" against me. "Oh yeah, let me see it then." I stuck my arm out his way, gave a nodding glance to the paper-passer, who started squirming, then added, "That's the evidence you're hiding. Let's see it so I can answer it. I can't defend without knowing the case against me. Why are you hiding the evidence? Because there isn't any, that's why."

Sir Derek didn't like that. With evident disgust he said, "I tried to spell out the rules on the first morning. You're wasting our time insisting on something that is already clear."

I equalled his disgust: "What do you mean wasting your time? You're getting paid for your time, not like me."

The three of them, but especially Sir Derek, exploded. "I'll have you know, Mr. Agee, that we are doing this *pro bono publico*. We are doing you a favor." A fuckin' favor, eh? I was about to say that, but Larry intervened by announcing our next witness.

For the rest of that day and the next I presented more witnesses and continued reading from my statement. Stewart Tendler of the London *Times* came, as did Ken Morgan of the NUJ, Neil Middleton, and Stan Newens. Newens told the panel that he had named CIA officers on the floor of the House of Commons and didn't think their exposure was a bad thing at all.

On Friday afternoon I reached the final paragraph of my statement. "I do not expect the panel to share my political beliefs. I do expect the panel to recognize that many millions of people in this country as well as abroad do share them. I expect the panel to respect their and my right to our beliefs. I expect the panel, however distasteful the views held by myself and other socialists may be to them, to understand that we will not be intimidated by accusations that we are traitors, that we are agents of foreign powers, that we subscribe to exotic and foreign ideologies, that we threaten the national security."

After finishing I told the panel that I was concerned about the many rumors floating around, caused in part by their, and Rees's, refusal to give any particulars. I mentioned the "death-of-our-agents" and "lives-at-stake" comments attributed to Rees. Was there anything in the evidence to this effect? Sir Derek and the others could not comment. Will you deny that there is? They would deny nothing. As for the "foreign-agents-contact," does "foreign" include or exclude citizens of the Commonwealth countries? Inappropriate to comment. That was it—my "representations" to this trio of mutes were finished.

The panel then questioned me for over an hour, at first on my trips to Cuba, then on my finances. I repeated, as I had everywhere, that I support the Cuban Revolution and have never made any secret of it. But it hardly follows that I'm some kind of spy or agent of the Cuban government. Then they started asking general questions on my opinions of intelligence work and the effects of my exposures of operations and personnel.

Finally they came to the point: wasn't there a common interest between the United States and the United Kingdom in safeguarding secrets? If my work affected the CIA's operations, might it not also have affected joint CIA-UK operations? I thought to myself: There it is, Jamaica, clear as day. I told them that if fomenting terrorism and subversion of the elected government of Jamaica was a joint operation, it deserved to be affected—exposed and neutralized. I would do it again even if I knew it meant deportation from this country.

We then asked for more time to organize witnesses who were coming from the United States. To our surprise Sir Derek agreed to adjourn the hearing for three weeks, until February 3, when I would present Melvin Wulf, former Attorney General Ramsey Clark, and Morton Halperin, a former Assistant Secretary of Defense and aide to Kissinger who was now Director of the Center for National Security Studies.

Another reprieve. It meant I had four to six weeks more. None of us were under any illusions, though, for Rees's obstinacy and the panel's attitudes gave no hope at all that he was going to change his mind.

Hosenball testified before the panel for two days the following week and made no publicity at all. Afterwards speculation was stronger than ever that I would go and Hosenball would stay.

But Judith Hart didn't give up. She co-sponsored, with Barbara Castle, another prominent Labour M.P., a new motion in the Commons. This was to establish an all-party select committee to consider the "no evidence-no appeal" procedure. By the time the panel reconvened more than 150 M.P.'s had signed it, but that wasn't enough.

Meanwhile the T.U.C. General Secretary visited Rees to protest, as did the Executive Director of the NCCL. In an uncharacteristic slip of the tongue, Rees admitted to the latter that the whole affair had been "a politically traumatic experience," and that the case had been made for changing the procedure—eventually, but not before the Agee and Hosenball cases were settled. And he was still adamant on revealing any particulars. Any details on my contacts with foreign agents, he said, would endanger peoples' lives.

The Hart-Castle motion was supported by *The Guardian* in an editorial titled: "Mr. Rees in a Trappist Trap." It summed up the government's predicament.

>   When Merlyn Rees, ten long weeks ago, decided that Philip Agee and Mark Hosenball must go, he must equally have known there would be a fuss. But did he realize the endlessly stretching, deeply embarrassing nature of that fuss—the evidence at a length to rival "War and Peace," the press conferences, the parade of fervent witnesses? Any politician in this sort of jam tends to ask himself a very

political question (a topical question, too, as Agee's three-man circus resumes business again tomorrow). Simply: what is the point of this whole painful exercise?

The editorial went on to point out that if Hosenball stays and I go, that could mean that he was just luckier at blind man's bluff than I was. Besides, if I went to another country and not to prison in the United States, what was to prevent me from continuing to harm the U.S.'s security? It ended: "The present system is a self-evident disaster and whatever happens to Agee and Hosenball, it needs rethinking from beginning to end."

Back to the "Ladies Room" with Wulf, Halperin and Clark—and still another new witness, Alvaro Bunster who was the Chilean Ambassador to Britain during the Allende period. He had remained in Britain after the coup, and he told the panel how important my work was for Chilean exiles and for hindering the CIA's subversive operations of the type that brought on the Pinochet dictatorship.

My American witnesses all lashed out at the "no appeal–no evidence" procedure and the secrecy. Mel compared it with Britain's former Star Chamber, the Spanish Inquisition, and the McCarthy hearings in the U.S., and rightly claimed it was a "free speech" not a "national security" case. Halperin concentrated on the positive results brought by my revelations and those of others, and on the traditional abuse of the "national security" cloak by security services. And Clark called the whole proceeding "utterly lawless." He recalled how Martin Luther King, Jr., had been called a "national security risk," and he condemned the fact that I couldn't confront my accusers.

As Ramsey Clark spoke, all three "wise men" looked down at their table as if in shame. Not once did they look at his face, probably because they knew that every word he spoke was the truth that they were ignoring.

The final session ended when we passed a video cassette and transcription to Sir Derek. It was a statement from Sean MacBride, former Irish Foreign Minister, former United Nations Assistant Secretary General, founder of Amnesty International—and the only person ever to be awarded both the Nobel and the Lenin Peace Prizes. We had taped the statement a few days earlier because his travel plans precluded appearing on the day of the hearing. He also condemned the procedures and, in commenting on my exposures of CIA operations, said I was not only "morally entitled" but had a "legal duty" to do it.

We had the usual press conference at ICA afterwards where

Ramsey said: "I have never before, during my forty years as a lawyer, had to appear before a tribunal and go away again without having any idea why the proceedings have transpired or what the facts alleged are." That night at Central Hall in Westminster hundreds turned out for another rally to hear my American witnesses condemn once again the Rees proceedings. At that moment, down the road at Parliament, Rees was under attack still again from Labour M.P.'s, this time led by Alex Lyon who accused Rees of reneging on his duty to give at least some particulars.

At the beginning of the crisis Rees said he would receive "representations" directly from Hosenball and me as well as through the panel. Through Judith Hart I asked Rees for a meeting to make these "representations" face to face. He refused. So I wrote him a letter noting, among other things, that both he and the Prime Minister had said that "lives are at stake" in my case.

Since that was not among the formal allegations, I challenged Rees and Callaghan to make the statement publicly and defend it in an open forum. I also pointed out how macabre the panel procedure had been, and asked again to meet him personally. At the Home Office I delivered the letter, gave copies to the press, and handed in petitions signed by some 15,000 people.

To say I was exhausted after three months of campaigning would have been an understatement. I was dead. Still, energy came from somewhere, the survival instinct probably, but it didn't prevent me from taking a Glasgow train from Cardiff when Edinburgh was my destination.

That day was a bad one all around. While waiting in the Glasgow station for a train to Edinburgh I wandered over to a newsstand, and there it was: "Americans Lose Appeals." Shit. After all this. I took an automatic deep breath, stood staring at the headlines, and thought, well, we all knew in our heart of hearts that this would happen. But at least we fought. And playing it "cool" didn't help Hosenball. I'll bet he's surprised.

I bought several papers. Rees had announced in the House of Commons that after considering the recommendations of the panel he had not changed his mind and had proceeded to issue formal deportation orders. We had until the end of the month—two weeks—to tell him where we wanted to go.

In the Commons Rees's announcement caused a storm, a furious uproar with jeers, catcalls and shouts of "shame" and "disgrace"—as one reporter put it: "a caterwaul of protest not seen in years." The ironic scene was "a deafening chorus of yells and groans" from Rees's own party while across the chamber the Tories were "loudly cheering."

When one M.P. suggested that Rees was following a demand by the CIA, Rees responded again that there had been no request from, or consultation with, any agency of the U.S. government. But he caused another howl of outrage when he said defensively that he and only he had seen the evidence. What about the panel, shouted various M.P.'s. They had seen "certain information," and he was not prepared to go beyond that. "Peoples' lives are at stake," he said once again.

On the train from Glasgow to Edinburgh I stared out the window at the snow, the farm houses, the barren trees, wondering if preparation of my "representations," the hearings, the rallies, press conferences, constant running from place to place were really worth it.

We all knew I had almost no chance from the beginning, especially if our suspicions of a Kissinger-Callaghan deal were correct. The only thing we really could do was to show up the whole procedure, and the Labour government, as squalid, hypocritical and sold out to the Americans.

Was it worth the trouble? I thought of the people who gave their time in the defense committee, the unions, the House of Commons, made huge efforts, never gave up. People like Phil Kelly, Steve and Ana, Bernard and Hettie, Larry and the rest of the legal team. And Rita Maran who worked tirelessly with contacts in the British peace movement. So many people. If it's worth the trouble to them, it's worth it to me. But where would I go?

Brian Wilson, the journalist from Skye and Labour candidate for M.P., met me at the Edinburgh station with tears in his eyes. He had organized most of the Scottish campaign and really thought I had a chance. We went over to a hotel where Tony Gifford and Larry Grant were waiting. Cedric Thornberry, they said, was writing up another petition to the European Commission on Human Rights. And next week Hosenball's lawyer would present a petition to the High Court in London.

If accepted, the decision might take a month or so, and if he lost he could go on to the Court of Appeal and finally the House of Lords. No point in my duplicating Hosenball's appeal: whatever he won would apply to me. Let the *Evening Standard* pay. But we did have to decide whether to play the "Scottish gambit." This was a possibility, first brought to our attention weeks before, that Scots law might provide a loophole to escape Rees's deportation order.

The Scots had a legal system separate from England, and a law dating from the nineteenth century might save me. A Scottish barrister, Lionel Daiches, had told me in December that the 1887 law that established the office of Secretary of State for Scotland vested all executive power in this office. According to his interpretation all decrees of the London government to be executed in Scotland required confirmation by the Scottish Secretary. The requirement had not been observed traditionally, but now, against a background of rising Scottish nationalism, we could seek to probe what some called the "Doomsday Machine" of British constitutional law.

The question was whether the Secretary of State for Scotland had to sign a Home Office deportation order against an alien who happened to be in Scotland. If a Scottish court ruled in our favor, that alone might be enough to cause Rees to back down in order to avoid the concession and precedent. If he didn't, then I could appeal in a Scottish court where evidence would be required and cross-examination possible. Rees would then have to give the particulars, and defend them, or drop the deportation. The principle of Scottish confirmation had never been established in court, but twice, in 1953 and last year (1976), when Daiches threatened to invoke it in defense of aliens resident in Scotland who were under threat of deportation, the Home Office in London had cancelled the proceedings.

Larry, Tony and I met with Daiches, who was eager to proceed. My arrival in Scotland just an hour before Rees's decision would help, and so would official service of the deportation order in Scotland. Police would bring it to my Edinburgh hotel tomorrow according to Larry.

After hearing Daiches outline our case, Larry, Tony and I looked at each other, shrugged, and agreed we should try. Why not? It'll look bizarre, as if I'm clutching at driftwood, but what do we have to lose? Daiches would draft the petition and file it early next week. He would seek to have Rees's deportation order declared null in Scotland, and he would ask that the police be enjoined from removing me from Scotland pending decision of the first issue.

If we won it would mean Scotland had been misgoverned for almost a hundred years, and hundreds of previous deportees from Scotland would be lining up to come back, but those weren't our worries. Daiches asked me for my Edinburgh address to put on the petition. I fished in my pocket and found a card from the hotel. Perfect: No. 1 Royal Circus.

As my "defection" to Scotland moved ahead, problems for Rees and Callaghan were building in the House of Commons. Paul Rose, the Labour M.P. who was Hosenball's principal Commons defender, announced that he was going to withhold his vote for an indefinite period, thus cutting Labour's majority to zero. Pressure from M.P.'s was also growing for a formal Commons debate on the deportations. All this with a critical vote only four days hence on the so-called devolution bill, a controversial Labour project to establish elected legislative assemblies in Scotland and Wales. In a move to garner support for that bill among revolting M.P.'s, Callaghan and Michael Foot, the Commons Leader, agreed to a debate on the deportations following the vote on the devolution bill.

The defense committee kept active with our supporters in the Commons. They also organized a delegation to lobby the T.U.C. for strike action against the deportations. Regina Fischer, 63-year-old mother of Bobby Fischer, the former world chess champion, started a hunger strike at the entrance to the Home Office. She set up camp in snow and rain, with sleeping bag and folding cot, protesting that Hosenball and I should not be used as "pawns" by the British and American governments. After two days the police arrested her for "obstruction," carted her away on her cot, kept her in jail overnight, and released her on twenty pounds bond the following morning. She went straight back to the Home Office, cot and all, and continued painting posters for the defense committee, playing tapes of Gilbert and Sullivan, and sipping tea and water. Overnight she became a tourist attraction and focus of worldwide press attention.

But then a dramatic event no one expected. In London, the night Regina started her fast, three supporters of the defense committee were arrested under the Official Secrets Act—the British law against espionage. For almost three days the young men were held incommunicado, then formally charged for passage and receipt of classified information. They were Duncan Campbell, Crispin Aubrey and John Berry.

Campbell, a graduate of Oxford, was Britain's original "phone freak," had become an expert in communications technology, and had been responsible for almost all of the *Time Out* article which everyone thought was the reason for Hosenball's deportation. Aubrey, also a graduate of Oxford, was a journalist at *Time Out* and one of the most active volunteers on the defense committee. And Berry was a former corporal in the Signals Corps. Police had captured a tape recording in which Berry was describing to Campbell and Aubrey certain British intelligence communications monitoring activities. Predictably the right-wing press played up the case as "Three Agee Men on Secrets Charge" and "Agee Defenders in Espionage Arrest."

So began the infamous "ABC" case. For twenty-one months the

government sought to put Aubrey, Berry and Campbell in prison through two trials that brought monumental embarrassment and discredit to the British legal system and security services. In the end all three were convicted but remained free, Berry with a six months' suspended sentence and Aubrey and Campbell with conditional discharges. The real losers were the proponents of "state secrecy" and the use of "national security" to justify and cover up political crimes.

Angela drove with the boys to Edinburgh to join me for my speaking tour in Scotland. First event was the election for Rector at Dundee University. It was an ancient tradition in Scotland that the students elected their spokesperson, the Rector, to the university governing council, and I had been asked to stand as candidate of the Socialist Society. Faced with deportation I questioned the propriety of accepting, but did so at the insistence of the student group and the defense committee. Clement Freud, an overweight Liberal M.P. and grandson of Sigmund, was the incumbent standing for re-election. Three years earlier he had taken over the job from Peter Ustinov, and his face was equally recognizable: he made TV commercials for a leading brand of dog food and looked every bit the morose basset hound.

The other principal contender was Fiona Richmond, one of Britain's most famous women. She was the beautiful and voluptuous vicar's daughter who had become the country's sex queen. Readers of British "tits and ass" magazines knew her body as well as she did, and she wrote a regular column for *Men Only* on her on-going sexual adventures. She also starred in London revues with upbeat names like "Let's Get Laid" and "Come into my Bed." Her current show was "Erotica." Although she quickly became known as candidate for "Erector," she promised not to campaign with her car—which bore plate number FU-2—nor would she take her clothes off at the "hecklings," the election rally where all of us would speak.

Tradition held that candidates arrived a day or so before the "hecklings" to campaign at the student union and other places on the campus. So we did, Angela and the boys included, and in several impromptu meetings I talked about my experience in student government, my CIA career and the other usual questions, and the deportation.

Clement Freud and Fiona Richmond were doing the same, and our paths crossed several times. To my surprise Fiona was far different from her sex queen image. She was a beauty all right, but also spoke with wit, intelligence and real concern for students' welfare. In contrast with Freud, who came across as a sour-puss, she was open and friendly with everyone.

The night of the "hecklings" several thousand students jammed the auditorium, even broke the fire doors in the rear, to get a glimpse of Fiona. They took "heckling" literally and energetically as each of us gave our fifteen-minute speech and answered questions amidst constant cheers and jeers.

Fiona was a natural for focusing on one of the main problems at Dundee: student housing. Said she would fight for more beds. But the shouting unsettled her. At the microphone her hands started shaking with her written speech—which prompted Freud to needle her mercilessly from our table just behind. Stage fright could get anybody, I guessed, even a women who'd ridden naked through Piccadilly Circus. In the end Freud won the vote, but Fiona won the fantasies.

The day after the "hecklings," I spoke at a meeting with Dundee shipyard workers and rushed to catch a plane for London and the House of Commons deportation debate. As it happened, that day Lionel Daiches submitted my petition to the Scottish court. In the Commons that night, after the government lost the crucial vote on devolution, the Speaker of the House announced that my case was in the Scottish court and therefore *sub judice*. That meant it could not be subject to public debate, as in parliament or the media, until after the court's decision. When he added that the deportation debate was cancelled, another tumult broke out. Finally Michael Foot, Labour's Leader of the House, promised that the House would have a debate at some later date, presumably when Hosenball's and my legal appeals were over—if we lost.

Another reprieve. Hosenball's petition to the High Court in London was going in the next day. Rees, meanwhile, promised our Commons supporters that we would not have to leave before the debate.

I was flying back to Edinburgh just as Daiches's petition was under argument in court. He hadn't objected to my trip back to London for the Commons debate, but when the Solicitor General for Scotland, representing Rees, asked if I was still in Scotland, Daiches couldn't say "yes." So the judge refused our request for injunction against my removal and went on to reject the position that the deportation order was invalid in Scotland. His reasoning was too obscure for my understanding, but the point was we lost the "Scottish gambit" in a walkover.

Word reached us in Scotland that the High Court accepted Hosenball's petition. Thank God. I'm safe as long as his appeals are in, and then the Commons debate. Hope that court takes its own good time. One day between meetings we drove the entire length of Loch Ness, slowly, cameras at the ready, thinking that to be the first to get a good photo of the monster might somehow change my destiny. It didn't show.

Following my speaking tour in Scotland my defense campaign continued in England, only now the rallies were organized jointly with the "ABC" defense committee. But I was fast running out of steam. I had spent over half of the last four months on the road, fighting a losing battle, uncertain from month to month when I would have to leave. It was still a matter of how long Hosenball could keep his appeals going.

In mid-March, while in Cambridge between rallies, I had a call from Mel Wulf in New York. He had sensational news. After weeks of insisting, he and Ramsey Clark had finally gotten the new Carter team at the Justice Department to state what the consequences would be if I returned to the States on deportation from Britain. It was "no prosecution."

Benjamin Civiletti, the new Assistant Attorney General, Criminal Division, announced that the investigation had come to its logical end and that there were no grounds for prosecution. However, he did not rule out the possibility of prosecution if new information came to light. Reaction from the CIA was totally negative with complaints that new laws were needed to protect their secrets.

The announcement was both surprising and perplexing. Should I go back to the States? Hosenball had already lost in the High Court and would go to the Court of Appeal in a few days, then to the House of Lords. It was just a matter of weeks before he would lose. Anticipating that, I had made a formal request to the Dutch government to go there.

Louis Vellemans, a Dutch television journalist resident in London with whom I had done several interviews, had begun lobbying on my behalf with his high-level friends in the governing Dutch Labour Party (P.v.d.A). And Ian Mikardo, International Secretary of the British Labour Party, had asked his counterpart in the P.v.d.A., Harry van den Bergh, to help. I was to meet van den Bergh in London in a week. Cedric Thornberry was also contacting his friends in the Swedish Social Democratic Party for permission for me to go there.

Ramsey and Mel suggested that I not make a quick decision because there were potential dangers other than criminal prosecution. First there could be no doubt that the Agency would seek and get a civil injunction against me, forcing me to submit all my writings to

The author's family home in Tampa, Florida.

The author, then 23, after entry in the CIA and assignment to U.S. Air Force Officer Candidate School, 1958.

Paris café, Le Yam's, where author, who lived at Minerve Hotel, right, was befriended by journalist Sal Ferrera. (Photo: Colm Foy)

Passage des Eaux, Paris, where author lived "underground" in 1972 (building far left) and was found by CIA through "bugged" type-writer. (Photo: Colm Foy)

The author in confrontation with Janet Strickland, who used the name "Leslie Donegan" when she met the author in 1972. Strickland gave the author the "bugged" typewriter that led to discovery of his "secret" residence. Confrontation was at the International Labor Organization, Geneva, 1976.

Janet Strickland, who used alias Leslie Donegan, struggling with photographer during confrontation with author at International Labor Organization, Geneva, 1976.

Author addressing the International Tribunal of the 11th World Festival of Youth and Students, Havana, 1978.

The author showing his passport from Grenada at Managua press conference, 1981. At left is Freddy Balzán, editor of the magazine *Soberanía*.

The author with Maurice
Bishop, Prime Minister
of Grenada, August 1981.

The author addressing Nicaraguan troops in southern battle zone, 1983.

Author and family on fishing expedition at Varadero, Cuba. From left to right: Burnett Agee (author's father), Therese Roberge (author's mother-in-law), Philip Agee, Jr. (son), author, Giselle Roberge-Agee (author's wife), and Christopher Agee (son).

them for censorship. If I published without submitting, or refused to delete objectionable material, I would go to jail for contempt of court. That would certainly affect my second book with Penguin, and it would make the *Who's Who in the CIA* impossible. Another threat was grand jury proceedings in which I could be subpoenaed to testify. If I refused to answer questions on principle I could be jailed for contempt of the grand jury. And, as always, the question remained whether Angela could, or wanted, to go to the States. Mel would be in Europe in the summer, so I decided to wait until we could discuss the whole matter face to face.

Civiletti gave the wrong reasons for the no-prosecution decision, I learned much later from FOIA documents. The same day in December that the Chief of the Criminal Division wrote to Mel Wulf that prosecution was "under active consideration," he forwarded a 26-page analysis of my case to Attorney General Levi recommending that the case be dropped. Not for lack of grounds, as Civiletti said, but because the CIA continued to insist that their "illegal acts" against me had to remain secret.

Levi ordered my case closed on the final day of the Ford administration, and he sent the file to the Civil Rights Division for possible prosecution of the CIA officers who had committed the crimes against me. Civiletti then came under fierce attack from right-wing organizations for a decision he hadn't made and couldn't fully explain.

Hosenball lost in the Court of Appeal, Britain's highest court. The opinion, announced by Lord Denning, Master of the Rolls, was pure "national security" doctrine. "This is no ordinary case," he said, "it is a case in which national security is involved. Our history shows that when the State itself is in danger our cherished freedoms may have to take second place. Even natural justice itself may suffer a setback." He followed with a justification so sinister I burst out laughing when I read it: "Spies, subversives and saboteurs may be mingling among us, putting on a most innocent exterior. If they are British spies we will deal with them hard. If foreigners, they can be deported."

The next day Michael Foot announced in the Commons that the debate would be April 5th, five days later, during the closing session before the Easter vacation. But the day of the debate Hosenball appealed to the House of Lords. The case was again *sub judice*, and the debate again postponed. Another reprieve. We packed our sailing gear and drove that very night to Cornwall.

One day a telegram arrived. Larry Grant wanted me to call him. Did I want to go to Sweden or to Holland? Both countries would take me. I selected Holland because it was closer. Later I would go to Sweden to see the situation there. It was a relief to know where I was going, although by now a little anticlimactic.

The sailing was a nice escape, but not really relaxing. There were too many things to think about. Would Rees allow Angela and the boys to stay until the school term ended in July? Would he let me stay until then? What to do with the house? What would resettlement in Holland be like? What about schools for Chris and Phil? How much would all this cost?

The day after we returned to Cambridge I left again, this time for Yorkshire to address the annual conference of the National Union of Journalists. More than four hundred delegates representing 28,000 members would be there. My union had fought the deportations every inch of the way, mainly inspired by Ron Knowles, editor of the union newspaper.

By now my speeches had changed from fighting the deportation to campaigning for change in the immigration law, repeal of the Official Secrets Act, and defense of Aubrey, Berry and Campbell. In thanking the union for their support, I nearly choked with emotion, but went on and pledged to keep my membership current no matter where I went. The standing ovation was still ringing in my ears as I drove away.

A week later the Law Lords rejected Hosenball's appeal, and the Commons debate was set for the evening of May 3rd.

Angela, the boys and I arrived early and got our tickets to the visitors' gallery from Stan Newens who was to be one of our principal defenders. Just after ten, Merlyn Rees opened the debate, which was limited to two hours, with a review of the immigration act and his decisions. Various M.P.'s rose either to criticize or support him, citing the "no evidence–no appeal" procedure or the needs of "national security." Stan Newens raised the strange anomaly that the U.S. Justice Department had decided not to prosecute me and questioned the validity of the evidence Rees had seen. And Alex Lyon denounced the panel hearing as "the most farcical procedure I have ever heard in all my life."

With a half-hour remaining, Stephen Hastings, a far-right Tory, stood up to play a new variation on the KGB smear. He read from the latest *Foreign Report* of the *Economist* magazine, a weekly "confidential" newsletter circulated through restricted subscriptions and edited by Robert Moss. The article said that former CIA officials believed my first "significant contact" with Soviet intelligence was back in 1964 in Montevideo where I met a "senior KGB officer" named Semenov. Later Semenov was in Cuba when I was there in 1971, and still later in Moscow when I went there. The clear implication was that I'd been working for the KGB all that time.

As I listened, I could feel nothing but anger and frustration. The article read like a "scoop," with no mention of the fact that I had told the story of Semenov and other KGB officers I knew in *Inside the Company*, including CIA Headquarters' encouragement and close supervision of those contacts.

Hastings went on to say I had admitted frequent meetings at the Soviet and Cuban Embassies, parroting the false press reports that came out when the deportation crisis started.

Rees ended the debate. His only remark of interest was that my writings on the CIA had nothing to do with his decision. And as before, he insisted: "The decision to deport has been mine and mine alone. . . . It was taken neither at the behest of, nor after consultation with, the government of the United States or its agencies, including the CIA."

Rees was lying through his teeth, I thought as I watched him from the crowded gallery, but I would never be able to prove it. I was wrong. Strong evidence of American pressure came five years later at the end of my FOIA case. The State Department refused to give me a number of documents relating to my Jamaica trip, but under the law they had to index them and justify their refusal.

The index showed that on Thursday, 30 September 1976, the week I returned from Jamaica, the Department cabled a seven-page classified memorandum on me and Jamaica "to the Secretary of State in London." On Saturday, 9 October, the Department sent a six-page cable "to Embassy London for the Secretary of State." This cable, classified secret, had originated in the U.S. Embassy in Kingston on 25 September, and it too discussed me and Jamaica.

I didn't remember Kissinger making trips to London after my return from Jamaica, so I checked *The New York Times* for the dates when the cables were sent. There was not a word of Kissinger travelling to London on either weekend. On 30 September he was at the United Nations in New York, but he dropped completely out of the news for the next five days. Similarly, he met with the Chinese Foreign Minister in New York on 8 October, but then he dropped out of the news for five days again. The *Times* of London index showed no Kissinger trip to London on either of those dates.

Why weren't the two trips announced? In all probability because

Kissinger took up my case with the British Prime Minister, James Callaghan, and wanted to hide his intervention. He needed to avoid any appearance of "cause-effect" when the deportation proceedings began a few weeks later. Also, he had to avoid making the British government look like it was doing his dirty work for him. Callaghan surely knew my deportation would bring an uproar of disapproval, but all Kissinger had to do was to threaten to block the IMF loan.

Other entries in the State Department index showed coordination between the two governments that they both denied at the time. On 6 November, just over a week before delivery of the deportation notice, the U.S. Embassy in London sent a cable about me, classified secret, to Washington. It reported "information given in confidence to an official of the U.S. Embassy in London by a British government official."

Enough was said in the index to conclude that the British had informed the CIA of the action they were about to take against me. Another secret document mentioned in the index is one called "Contingency Press Guidance concerning Mr. Agee." That document was dated 11 November, five days before delivery of the deportation notice.

If I had known of Kissinger's personal intervention I would also have better understood the Home Office's statement on "regular contact with foreign intelligence officers." That was written to substantiate the "KGB-Cuban agent" line of long standing. The agreement was not just to deport me, disrupting my work and family situation, but to tarnish me worse than ever with the "communist agent" lie.

Under FOIA I also got a heavily censored, five-page CIA memorandum about my trip to Jamaica. The main section included word-for-word transcripts of comments I made about British intelligence during interviews on Jamaican radio and television. It looked as though it was prepared for use with the British to show I pinned the "destabilization" label on them too. Reading the transcripts I realized I was a lot less discreet about possible British involvement than I thought I'd been.

The vote at the end of the Commons debate went against us, as everyone knew it would. Afterwards, I wrote to Rees asking permission to stay until late July when Phil and Chris would finish school, but he would only agree to one month for settling "personal affairs." His removal directions to the Netherlands arrived, and I made reservations to take the ferry from Harwich to Hook of Holland on June 3rd. The intervening days were as hectic as ever, with defense expenses to review and pay, powers of attorney to arrange, more press interviews, and selection of files and papers I would need in Amsterdam.

Nevertheless, I continued the exposure campaign even as I was packing. A national scandal broke out in Australia over CIA interference in trade unions and political parties, with evidence that the Agency had been involved in the 1975 "coup" against the Labour government of Gough Whitlam.

The London bureau of the Australian Broadcasting Commission (ABC) wanted me to comment on the scandal in a television interview. I agreed, studied the press reports, and analyzed the U.S. mission in Australia for CIA officers. I found seven whom I named in the interview as people who could clarify the facts of the scandal.

The interview was broadcast live on morning news in Australia, and journalists immediately descended on the homes of the CIA men. Later that day at a news conference the Foreign Minister, Andrew Peacock, unthinkingly confirmed the identifications, causing still more storm in the press.

In Greece, my publisher put me in contact with Christos Papoutsakis, editor of *Anti*, the leading left-wing political journal. He wanted to publish my year-old analysis of the CIA Station in Athens that had more than two hundred names. The conservative government tried unsuccessfully to block publication, then tried to buy up all the copies from the newsstands. Papoutsakis printed another edition, while opposition members of the Greek Parliament called for expulsion of all on the list who were still in Greece.

With two weeks remaining, Angela and I gave a combination house warming and deportation party in Cambridge for the defense committee and other friends. To identify the house Chris and Phil painted a superb coat-of-arms like those that hang outside British pubs. Replete with lions and crown, they named it "Merlyn's Head." To prove I was a Cuban agent, Angela prepared a huge pot of *garbanzo* beans, I wore my white *guayabera*, and we played *mambo* records and sang *La Guantanamera*.

But the bitter day got closer and closer, and my spirits lower and lower. Less than a week before I left, Hettie Vorhaus had a heart attack. She had worked in the defense campaign practically full time since day one, and more than anyone else was responsible for the tremendous backing from trade unions which she tirelessly wrote and telephoned. Many times I'd had meals or stayed overnight with her and Bernard at their Primrose Hill house. She was hospitalized and expected to recover, but it would be slow and painful.

The night before I had to go, the defense committee organized a farewell party at Conway Hall in London with music by a rock group called "High Speed Grass." About four hundred people turned out to say goodbye, and with each embrace, each handshake, I felt more and more forlorn.

I hated to leave. I couldn't stand the thought of leaving behind all those friends I'd come to know so well since my first desperate arrival more than four years before, all the people who had given so much time and energy in the defense campaign.

Among them was Heinz Norden, one of the leaders of Concerned Americans. He was my father's age, a long-time resident of London, and an antique dealer by trade. Like Bernard and Hettie, he and his wife Clair had entertained us at their beautiful home in Hampstead. With his flowing white mane and deep booming voice he would usually start the collection at rallies by putting in a ten pound note. His partner in conspiracy, Bernard Vorhaus, would do the same. Heinz handed me a well-worn miniature chess set as a parting gift. I pulled myself together for a last short speech in which I called for a John Berry in every government department.

The next morning we drove to the ferry terminal at Harwich. I was wearing the same defense committee lapel button I'd had on from the beginning: in yellow and black it read "I am a Security Risk." Some reporters and more friends, including Larry Grant, were waiting to say goodbye. Richard Fletcher, a university professor and defense committee activist, was going with me to Amsterdam and would bring the car back to Angela. More sad farewells and embraces.

As the ferry pulled away I raised a defiant clenched fist from the railing, but inside I felt defeated and hopelessly cut off. About halfway across to the Hook I went up on deck alone to look at the sea. Sitting there I felt Heinz's chess set in my jacket pocket where I'd put it the night before. I took it out, opened it, and noticed for the first time a dedication that Heinz had attached to the inside of the lid.

Dear Phil,

   This pocket chess set was given to me thirty-five years ago as a going-away present, when I went off to war, having fought my way into uniform because of my heinous record as an organizer of slum tenants in New York City. It went with me from Greenland to the Philippines, and many points between. I now pass it on to you with the hope that it will give you as much pleasure as it has me, and that it may serve as a life-long reminder of your friends and admirers in Britain. We expect great things of you, Phil, and we know that you will never disappoint the people of the world, the people that really count. I am proud to call myself your friend. Heinz Norden.

Oh, Heinz, Heinz. I closed the lid with shaking hands as suddenly all the pent up emotion of the last six-months surged to my chest, throat, nose and eyes. I held my head in my hands and wept until I had no more tears, no more.

IX

Retracing a Refugee: Eight Generations On

As the Netherlands coastline appeared I thought of my ancestor, Mathieu Agé, the first of the family to emigrate to America. He was from a noble Huguenot family, one of thousands forced to flee religious persecution in France after Louis XIV's revocation of the Edict of Nantes in 1685. He found refuge in the Netherlands, joined the forces of William of Orange, and probably fought in the Battle of the Boyne.

William and Mary then granted 10,000 acres on the banks of the James River in Virginia for "French refugees," Mathieu among them. He emigrated to America in the 1690's, had four children and twenty-four grandchildren, and eventually Anglicized the family name. From Mathieu's sons to my father all the men in our line were born in Virginia. I wasn't exactly reversing Mathieu's odyssey, but in a certain way I felt I was. I wondered if I would find the same tolerance in Holland that he found.

The immigration officer was expecting me, stamped my passport with a three-month residence permit and said I should register my address with local police within a week.

As I drove out the customs control exit, reporters and camera crews waved and yelled for me to stop. I found a place to park not far from the gate, got out of the car, and was immediately surrounded.

How did it feel leaving England? How does it feel coming to the Netherlands? How long will you stay? What will you do here? Where will you live?

"Look, I don't really have anything to say except that I'm happy to be here, and I appreciate the government's decision to let me come. For the moment I'll be staying at the Transnational Institute in Amsterdam, looking for a place to live, and waiting for my family to come over after school is out."

It was almost dark when we arrived at the TNI building, a five-story red brick turn-of-the-century house facing the Vincent Van Gogh Museum. Basker Vashee, TNI's local director, welcomed us and showed us to the fourth-floor dormitory. I called my Ministry of Justice contact to tell him where I was, then started unpacking the car, which was crammed with clothing, papers, typewriter, and boxes of writing materials. I found an empty desk at the rear of the dormitory, which had seven or eight steel beds scattered around, and proceeded to set up my little corner. At the moment there was nobody visiting but me, and Richard soon went to see some friends with whom he planned to stay the weekend.

Basker showed me around. We had a drink, and I knew immediately that he would make a good companion in Amsterdam. He was soft spoken, quick to laugh, and, like me, a current affairs junkie. Through London papers he had followed the deportation saga, and he too was convinced an American hand was behind it.

Basker had been at TNI a couple of years. He was from Zimbabwe, of Indian parentage, thin and strikingly handsome with dark skin and eyes, flowing black hair and clipped beard. Now in his early thirties, he had joined the independence struggle at fourteen, later left university to fight with the ZAPU liberation movement, but was captured by the security forces of the Ian Smith regime. For three years they kept him in solitary confinement, allowing him only one thirty-minute visit per month by his mother. Thanks to a campaign by Amnesty International he was released to exile in Britain where he worked in a TNI-sponsored research project before coming to Amsterdam.

I told Basker of my plans: my second book, the global index on CIA personnel and fronts, and the *Who's Who*. To avoid making any problems for TNI, I assured him I wouldn't work on either project while living there, and in any case I needed books and files that wouldn't arrive until I found a place to live.

Was there any group or institute in Holland that might be interested in the index project? I couldn't, or shouldn't, try to organize the project as if it were mine, because the Americans might bring pressure against the government as in Britain. I had to find an established organization to sponsor this work, and then Angela and I could help as informal advisers.

Basker didn't know—maybe Chilean solidarity. But he recalled they received Dutch government money and probably wouldn't want to risk that subsidy. Besides, they were already overextended.

I wondered. Could be that Holland wasn't the best place to resettle. I told Basker I was going to take a look in Sweden, France, Switzerland and Algeria before making a final decision. Maybe one of those countries would have advantages over the Netherlands. My top priority was to find some established group that could do the index project.

One of Amsterdam's most attractive features, which I noticed the first day, was its "outdoor" nature. Lots of people in the parks and streets, sidewalk cafes everywhere, constant bicycle traffic, music from organ grinders and buskers, and more noise from conversation than from cars. Everyone, it seemed, spoke English, and several people that weekend came up to me on the street and said, "Welcome to the Netherlands," and "Keep up the good work." So many people speaking English made communication easy but wouldn't help a foreigner learn Dutch. Later, if I stayed here, I would take classes. For the moment I enjoyed the relaxed atmosphere and thought Amsterdam was a nice place in which to resettle.

On Sunday, Richard and I had a late breakfast with Basker and his friend Gretta Bedier at the Keyzer Bodega, a popular traditional restaurant next to the Concertgebouw.

She would help us settle in in every possible way, but she warned me to prepare for problems if we wanted to live in Amsterdam. People waited years for rent-controlled apartments, and the free market was limited and extremely expensive. And forget the inner canals— what's available is tiny and overpriced. Schools? There's an International School with English instruction on the south side of town. It is said to be quite good.

Richard headed back to England with the car. At TNI I started making notes of things to do and people to see. First on my list was an appointment with Willem van Bennekom, a lawyer who specialized in immigration matters and who could help me get my residence permit extended from three months to one year.

Van Bennekom's office was in an old canal house on Prinsengracht. He was wearing a sport shirt and round steel-rimmed glasses, and had his long blond hair cut in classical "dutch boy" style. Actually he looked more like a laid-back professor than a lawyer. He spoke perfect English in a direct, crisp, authoritative but friendly manner.

Van Bennekom knew the broad outlines of my deportation from press accounts and was quick to assure me that immigration laws in the Netherlands differed greatly from Britain's. Extension of my permit was simply a matter of filling out a form at the Aliens Police office. Shouldn't be any problem since the principle that I could live in Holland was already settled.

Just to be sure, I told Willem of the two projects I wanted to get going. He responded that Holland was a liberal country with freedom of press and speech. No problem with the book. Better to be discreet about the index though, until I get the residence extension and permits for Angela and my sons. I asked how internal politics might affect my status, since the Labour Party was having difficulty getting together a new coalition following elections two months before. That shouldn't affect me, he said, because Labour had increased its Parliamentary seats and the coalition would eventually work out.

The senior government official in charge of alien affairs was Henk Zeevalking, the Secretary of State for Justice, who belonged to a party called Democrats-66. At the request of Labour, the senior coalition partner, he had given approval that I go to Holland on deportation from Britain, so extension of my permit should be automatic. In the worst of cases, if for some reason extension were refused, I would be able to appeal the decision, see and dispute evidence, and eventually go to the Raad van State, the Council of State, which was the highest court in Holland. The appeal process itself would take a couple of years.

The next day at the Aliens Police I was received by an officer named van den Brink. To my surprise he already had a folder with my name on it and what looked like 15 to 20 pages inside. I wondered what those documents were. He was friendly enough and I filled out the request for extension.

During the next two weeks I visited the International School, checked in with a real estate agent, and started planning my travel itinerary. I also made a substantial dent in the pile of unanswered letters.

At Phil Kelly's request, I wrote an article, titled "A Letter from Exile," for *The Leveller*, the radical London magazine run by Kelly and other journalists who had worked in the defense committee. It was an account of first impressions in Amsterdam and a pledge to continue working with the ABC defense and others who had opposed my deportation.

In mid-June I flew to Stockholm where I contacted people I knew in the Chilean solidarity movement. They filled me in on such things as housing problems and the political climate. I wouldn't have any problem writing another book on the CIA, but the index on CIA personnel might be interpreted as violating Swedish neutrality. Either I should do it quietly or get good political advice before talking about it.

They recommended a lawyer who represented Chilean refugees. He told me I shouldn't have any problem getting a residence permit as a journalist—no need to apply for refugee status. Foreign writers, he said, were paid by the government to study Swedish in the belief that they would eventually write in the language. I also looked up my editor at Prisma, the publishing house of the Social Democratic Party that put out the Swedish edition of *Inside the Company*.

Stockholm's "old city" was a fascinating place to walk. I was strolling along one of the canals and stopped in a cafe for a beer. I'd been sitting at a table no more than five minutes when a police patrol car parked alongside. The three officers got out, took a table, and ordered orange soda pop.

Before they were even served, one of the officers walked over to my table and asked in English to see my passport. He opened it, nodded, and told me to wait. For god's sake, I thought, what now? He went to the car, made a radio call, and waited. After about ten minutes he came back, handed me my passport, and said he'd recognized me and just wanted to make sure I was permitted to be in Sweden. I was nervous, and didn't want to show it, so I didn't speak. I just put the passport in my pocket, looked the other way, and wondered which of the CIA's media plants that officer had been reading.

Eventually I saw various journalists I'd met previously. Everyone was encouraging about my resettling there, but they also pointed out some disadvantages. The main drawbacks to Sweden were the remote location, the long, depressing winters and the cost of living. Compared to Britain, prices were sky high. Nevertheless, there was an English language school for Phil and Chris, and I carefully studied the U.S. Embassy's briefing memorandum for new arrivals. After a week I decided to reserve judgment until I'd visited the other countries.

From Stockholm I went to Paris. As usual, I stayed with my friend Karl van Meter, an American journalist and mathematician. He lived in the Latin Quarter, just in front of the Jussieu metro station. Across from his apartment were the university science buildings where I had escaped from the surveillance teams before going to Britain. Just around the corner from Karl lived Therese Roberge, the Canadian friend who typed my first manuscript and was in the thick of the Sal-Leslie episode. It was kind of like coming home, and often Karl, Therese and I had dinner together at neighborhood restaurants like Lulu's bistro or the Saigon.

I talked with Karl, Regis Debray, Claude Bordet and others about my plans. As in Amsterdam and Stockholm, people in Paris encouraged me to resettle there. What about the global CIA index? Was there any established organization in Paris that might take on this project, organizing volunteers or semi-volunteers for the first step of cutting and pasting?

Maybe Action Tricontinental, the solidarity center sponsored by progressive Protestant church groups. They supported all sorts of activities with political refugees from Third World countries, particularly Latin America.

Karl and I went around to see François Charbonnier, a bearded former missionary who ran the center. I outlined the index project, pointing out that it should be under the auspices of a legitimate local organization without the appearances of being mine.

I had my second book to write and could only serve as an adviser. I could make the materials available and train people to analyze biographies in order to separate CIA people from State Department officers. And Angela could help with the manual computer cards. To make it work, the project needed sponsorship. Otherwise pressure from the U.S. government, and the CIA in particular, might be able to stop it.

Charbonnier liked the idea. He could see right away the value of the project in the international solidarity movement. We talked about Chile and how things might have been different if the names, addresses and photographs of CIA officers had been published during the Allende period. Demonstrations could have been organized to force them out and the whole process repeated as new people came in.

At his request I wrote a ten-page outline of the project, dividing it into several phases: analysis of the documentation, cutting and pasting for the initial index, transfer if possible to a computer, publishing the *Who's Who*, and permanent updating. I calculated preparation of the index and detailed biographies on six to seven thousand people would take two years, forty thousand hours of work, and would cost about $250,000.

A few days later Charbonnier told me he would take the project under Action Tricontinental, but all costs would have to be paid from new funds. He had nothing in his budget for the project. What he could do was provide space and recruit people, such as Latin American exiles resident in Paris, to work on the index. Oh my god, I thought, this is too good to be true. A perfect arrangement. I hadn't felt such an uplift since Neil Middleton gave me the contract for *Inside the Company*. Now the task was to publicize the project and circulate the written outline to possible donors in the United States and Western Europe. Getting the money to start would not be easy, but now we could try.

Regis Debray thought substantial funds could be raised in France. He wrote a two-page description of the project and an appeal for the equivalent of $150,000. He would send it to people he knew, asking for donations during the coming two months.

With Charbonnier's decision it seemed that Paris would definitely be the best place to resettle. I called Angela, as I did every few days, to give her the news. She wasn't too pleased about returning to Paris. She hadn't liked it when she lived there earlier, and was hoping Algeria would work out better. We would see.

I continued on to Zurich, which I ruled out as much too expensive. Then I flew to Algiers. During two weeks I roamed the city, visited beaches and spoke with various people who worked in Algerian solidarity organizations. There were problems of all kinds. There was no school with instruction in English. They taught only in Arabic and French. Housing was scarce. The index project *could* be done there, but finding people to work on it would be difficult. Finally, there was the political factor, negative in a certain sense, of doing the index in a radical Arab country. Inevitably the project would be attacked as having been done under government auspices.

I returned to Karl's flat in Paris at the end of July and enrolled in

the *Alliance Française* to study French. Phil and Chris had gone to
the States to spend the rest of the summer with Janet. In Cambridge,
Angela was making final arrangements for rental of the house to a visiting professor from Canada. She had also arranged to sell it, the sale
to be effective the following summer. With all that she still had to
pack our household effects again and buy new furnishings for the Canadian family. She would drive over around the middle of August,
and we would decide whether to stay in Paris or not. As for me I was
strongly inclined to stay.

I plunged into the intensive, four-hour-per-day French course, determined to master the language in the shortest possible time.

Outside of class I relaxed with friends. It was the first time in years
that I felt no tension. Paris was so different from before, when I lived
in secret and fled the surveillance teams. Now I had friends, felt secure, and had no one to fear. Almost overnight, it seemed, the emotional strain and depression of the British deportation had disappeared. Paris was warm, sunny and wonderful—and I felt the same.

Angela finished packing and turned the house over to the Canadians. She would drive from Cambridge to Dover for the evening ferry
to Boulogne-sur-Mer and then on to Paris. I guessed she would be
pretty tired, so I said I would take the train up to Boulogne and meet
her just outside the customs gate for the drive back to Paris.

I arrived early and sat in a cafe reading *L'Etranger*, an assignment
from my French class. As it started getting dark I strolled over to the
ferry dock. The customs and immigration control where Angela
would drive out was an old multi-story brick building with lanes from
the ground level and a ramp from above leading to inspection stalls. I
stood just inside the building about twenty meters from the control
points as cars from the ferry began passing through. The yellow
Volkswagen eventually appeared. Angela showed her passport and
drove over to the side where I was waiting. The car was packed to the
roof in back with boxes and clothing. She got out and we started to
embrace.

Suddenly a car stopped next to us, two men jumped out, grabbed
my arms, and started frisking me for a weapon. In broken English one
of them said they were police and wanted to see my passport. They
held my arms as I got it from my carrying bag on the pavement. The
senior officer who did the talking was so nervous and excited his arms
and hands shook as he held me. He looked at the passport and said I
had to come with him. I was completely bewildered as well as surprised, as he led me up a couple of flights of steps to his office. What

the Christ is this all about, I wondered. He sat me on a bench and told me not to get up.

A few minutes later the other officer brought Angela in and sat her on the same bench. She had moved the car to a parking area. But the minute we started talking the officer in charge told us to be silent or he would separate us. He took Angela's passport and left the room.

For thirty minutes we sat, watched continuously by a couple of plainclothed police. We asked if we were under arrest and, if so, for what offense. We also asked to speak to a lawyer. No response. I began to wonder if they were planting drugs in the car for "discovery" later.

They took me to another room, out of earshot of the first room where Angela stayed, and I waited another half-hour or so. Several times the bearded arresting officer looked in, and each time I insisted on being told if I was under arrest, for what offense, and that I be permitted to speak with a lawyer. At one point he responded that I was in France and would follow French procedure whether I liked it or not. I asked several of the police to identify themselves by name or service number. They got nasty and told me to shut up, but from conversation among them I caught the bearded pig's name as "Vassilin" or something close to that.

About an hour after our arrest, "Vassilin" told me to follow him and another policeman. Thank god, finally getting out of this hole and back to Paris. I looked for Angela, but didn't see her. Then a surprise. Instead of leading me down to the ground floor, they took me out to an upper level ramp where they handcuffed me. This made me a little panicky, and my panic was mixed with gloom. Before I could discern what was happening, they walked me to an unmarked car with driver inside and engine running. Oh, oh. They're not driving me away in that fuckin' car.

"Hey wait," I said to "Vassilin." "I've got my own car. It's right downstairs."

"You're under arrest," he said.

"For what offense?" My temper was flaring up, and I was about to call him "Vasoline jerk-off" or something like that, but before I could he said,

"You will know later. Get in the car."

He held the back door open, but I hesitated. "Where are you taking me?"

"You will see soon enough. Get in the car."

"Where is Angela? What's happening to her?"

"You do not have to know. Get in the car or we will put you in."

"Look, I want to talk to a lawyer." He called over two other police-men, and I knew they were going to use force if I didn't move pretty quickly. I got in the car, the two other policemen got in on either side, and the driver headed down the ramp. We drove from the port into the city, eventually stopping at the main Boulogne police station. After a brief wait they took the handcuffs off and led me to the cell area, took away my carrying bag and watch, made me empty my pockets and take off my belt and shoe laces. Then they put me in a small room and locked the door.

I looked around, thinking about the women's drunk tank in Rye, New York, twenty years before. It was the only other time I'd been in jail. One night a policemen caught me speeding, and I didn't have enough money to pay the fine. Since I had Florida plates he took me to the Station where they let me call a friend in New York City to bring money the next morning. I hadn't had anything to drink, but their men's dry-out tank was full, so they put me in the empty wom-en's cell.

Boulogne was not Rye. There was no cot to sleep on, just a low narrow bench a little less than two meters long. The room was nar-row, only about a meter and a half wide, about three meters from end to end, with a ceiling some four meters high.

The cell was lit by a single bright bulb in the ceiling, but there was no switch inside the room. The thick wooden door went almost wall-to-wall and had a window-like opening covered with steel mesh and screening that obstructed vision to the sides. At the other end, begin-ning some two meters up, was a frosted glass window the width of the room. The window couldn't be opened, and lights from the street showed bars on the outside.

The white washed walls were grey with age and covered with graffiti from the floor to a height of two meters. It read like a hotel register with names, dates and number of hours' occupancy. Some wrote slogans: *"Vive la Liberte!" "J'ai souffert beaucoup ici." "John F. Kennedy was here: June 1975."*

I sat on the bench next to two foul-smelling blankets that I tossed in a corner and began to think. What the hell am I doing in here? There's no charge against me. I haven't done a thing against the law in France. What can that fucking CIA and their French cronies be up to now? And Angela? What are they doing with her? Would these bas-tards send her back to Brazil? Back to prison and the torture cham-bers of the Agency's "sister" services? The thought was terrifying. A feeling of claustrophobia came over me as the room seemed to get smaller and smaller.

At intervals of fifteen or twenty minutes the guard would look at me through the window. I asked him several times for my Camus book, but each time he said he wasn't authorized to let me read. So I just sat there as the night wore slowly on. I thought of Karl. Today is Wednesday. He expected us back this evening. If we don't show he'll probably think we spent the night along the way. Maybe by tomorrow afternoon he'll realize something's happened and start checking. By Friday maybe he'll have a lawyer on the case who can get us out. Shit. August. *Vacances.* Claude, Regis, Frederic—everybody who could help politically is away for the month.

The bench was too narrow to be a bed, and the cement floor was filthy. I tried to lie on the bench, balancing in the middle, but each time I dozed off I woke up falling. I'd only worn a polo shirt that day, and the cell was frigid. The blankets stank, but I had to wrap up in them to stop shivering. I thought day would never come, but through the frosted glass I eventually saw dawn.

When the guard peeped through the window I asked to use the toilet and for some coffee and bread. I also asked if Angela had been brought there for the night. He hadn't seen her but had heard she would be there about eight-thirty. He managed the coffee and a *croissant.*

Eight-thirty came and went, and no sign of Angela. More sitting and waiting. After several long hours, the door opened. It was one of "Vassilin's" assistants. He took me to the desk, had me sign for my possessions, handcuffed me, and took me to a car. We drove back over to the border police offices at the port.

Back in "Vassilin's" office I noticed a changed atmosphere. The hostility and threats of the night before had changed, if not to friendliness, at least to straight-forward attitudes and tones. Someone brought me coffee, and when I asked about Angela "Vassilin" said she had been released about nine o'clock the night before. Shitheads, I thought. They could have told me that last night, but no, they just let me worry. In any case she must have gone on to Paris and raised the alarm.

"Vassilin" told me the government had decided I was not to be allowed in France. He acknowledged that the stamp in my passport showed I had entered legally, but that was a mistake by the airport control officer. Prior to my entry at the end of July, an exclusion order has been issued, and I should have been stopped.

What was the reason for the decision? He didn't know. Again I said I wanted to see a lawyer and to know the charges against me. "Vassilin" said I wouldn't have time to see a lawyer, that I was to be expelled that very day at the border crossing of my choice. Where did I want to go?

Look, I said, I entered France legally. I'm sure I'm entitled to some kind of appeal against arbitrary arrest and expulsion. It's not my fault the control officer didn't stop me. Besides, I've entered France five times this year. When did this so-called exclusion order go up?

"Vassilin" didn't know. His orders were to take me to the border of my choice. I insisted on seeing a lawyer. Otherwise their action was nothing less than kidnapping. Could I make a telephone call? No. And there would be no lawyer. Did I want to go to Belgium? That was the closest border, and the government there had told the French that I could enter the country in transit back to Holland.

"Vassilin's" telephone rang, as it would again and again for the next four hours. Most of the calls, it seemed, were from reporters asking about me. I couldn't understand very well what he was saying, but I thought he was refusing to let them speak to me and to say anything about where I was going. Between calls he told me that if I didn't choose my border, the Ministry of the Interior would, and that could be a flight to the United States. Did I want to go there? No, I admitted to myself, I didn't want that right now. Okay, Belgium.

"Vassilin" disappeared, but returned later with a statement and an official interpreter. The interpreter translated the statement. By my signature I acknowledged that I was not allowed to be in France, that I was therefore being expelled, and that I had chosen Belgium as the country to which I wished to proceed. When I told "Vassilin" that I wanted my lawyer to see it before I signed, he nearly blew up. Either I signed it or I went back to the Boulogne jail where I would stay until the Ministry decided where to send me. Fuck it, I thought as I signed, I don't want to go back to that cell. The sooner I get away from these creeps the better. But then I said, almost as an after-thought, that I wanted a copy of the document I signed. "Vassilin" said it was *his* document and I wouldn't get a copy.

One of "Vassilin's" assistants took me for lunch at the police mess down the hall, then to an upper parking lot for "a breath of air." I was walking around for no more than a few seconds when another officer appeared with a camera and started taking pictures of me. Then back to "Vassilin's" office where he and others were checking on trains from Lille to Belgium, and on roads from Boulogne to Lille. Their

major concern, it seemed, was to avoid any contact with the press before they put me on the train.

At two-thirty a call came from the Ministry of the Interior in Paris
authorizing "Vassilin" to take me to the border. He handcuffed me
again, put me in the back of an unmarked car, got in on the other
side, and an assistant drove. The route they had chosen—secondary
roads serving farms and small villages—required constant checking of
the map, but we got to Lille in two hours.

The driver stopped in front of a modern seven-story apartment
building, but as we walked in the entrance I noticed there was no sign
that these were police offices. We took the elevator to the top floor
and entered an office with no sign on the door. Two or three
plainclothed officers were waiting. After a half-hour or so, two of
these went with us to the train station, but they wouldn't let me approach the ticket counter for fear someone might recognize me. I
would have to buy my ticket from the conductor. We waited in the
station police office until the train was about to leave, they took the
handcuffs off, and two of the local officers got on the train with me. At
the Belgian border they got off, and I was alone and free.

For the first thirty minutes, as the train rolled on to the first stop
inside Belgium, I sat there thinking about what had just happened. In
less than twenty-four hours my hopes and plans for resettling in Paris
were destroyed. They had grabbed me in the customs station, put me
in jail overnight, refused me a lawyer, even a telephone call.

Why were they so afraid of me? What kind of intervention did the
CIA make this time? Is the Agency so powerful in France that it just
snaps its fingers and the French government complies? Nothing I
planned affected the French, not the index or my second book. Neither project was illegal, not in France and not even in the United
States. But the Agency has its ways. In 1975 they threatened to cut off
intelligence sharing with the Whitlam government in Australia, and
the next day, boom, the Governor General dismissed the government. I guess if they can do it there, they can do it in France.

Dammit. They've cut me off from all my friends in Britain, but that
wasn't enough. Now France. What exactly are they trying to do? For
one thing they want to stop the index and my second book. If they can
keep me moving, on the run from country to country, I'll never have
a home base from which to get going. My files, papers, books will
always be a couple of steps behind me, and without them I couldn't
work.

They were also trying to isolate me: physically by limiting the countries I can visit or live in; and politically by building a public image as "communist agent" and "subversive." Why now and not before? If they had taken these actions five years ago they could have stopped *Inside the Company* and everything I've done since. Maybe they underestimated. Jamaica, that was the turning point. First Britain, now France.

This isn't going to help in Holland either. Strange thing. That ancestor of mine. First I felt I was following his steps backwards, from America to Britain to Holland, now I'm going in his original direction, from France to Holland. What next? From Holland to America with love?

I thought about Jon Steinberg and my plan for a speaking tour of the United States in coming months. In Paris I had agreed to a four-to-six-week tour to raise funds for *Seven Days* magazine, of which Steinberg was foreign editor, and for the index project. I'd even talked it over with Mel Wulf and decided to take the censorship injunction just so that I could visit the States, maybe even to return permanently at a later date. Now I'd better rethink the whole idea of going back.

At six-thirty the train stopped, and I got off to call Karl in Paris. "*Salut, mon ami.* Guess who."

"Don't tell me. Let me guess. We thought you got lost. Where did you wander to this time?"

"I was tired of Paris, Karl. Thought I'd spend a night in the Boulogne jail for a change of scene. Great graffiti, good food, nice company. You ought to try it sometime. Some friends gave me a lift to Lille where they even helped me get on a train to Belgium. I'm in a town called Tornai. Where's Angela?"

"She's on her way to Brussels with Steve Weissman. Should be there about nine. The Interior Ministry announced this morning that you were questioned last night and taken immediately to the Belgian border. Everybody knew they were lying. Angela and I and lawyers and press people were calling Boulogne all day but your friends there refused to say anything."

"They were just protecting me, Karl. Do you know whether Angela called my father to tell him I'm all right?"

"She called him, but I don't know whether she said you were all right. Nobody knew. I got you a lawyer recommended by a friend. He's Jean-Michel Braunschweig. He's going to file a court appeal but says it's a slow process. The whole procedure was illegal. If a foreigner is in France legally, they can't just throw you out like that."

"Yeah, well they did it. Those police are criminals, Karl, they kidnapped me."

"Sure, but don't expect them to go to jail for it. That's the way it is in France. The police and security services don't give a shit for legalities. Everybody here thinks Giscard or the Interior Minister decided to do it that way to keep you from a legal appeal. They saw what happened in Britain."

"Well, so much for Paris. I'm getting the next train for Brussels, should be there about eight."

Karl went on to explain how he had arranged with friends in Brussels to get support from a group called *Service Social des Etrangeres*. It was run by Marco Sbolgi, a Protestant Minister, to help foreigners. Someone from the group would meet me on arrival in Brussels and arrange for Angela and Steve to find me. I took the Brussels number, and Karl said:

"Wait till you hear what happened here last night."

"What do you mean, what happened?"

"Telephones all over the fifth arrondissement went out just when you were arrested. Angela couldn't call me when they let her go, so we didn't know anything until she got here after midnight. By then it was too late to alert people in the press and National Assembly who could have done something, even though nobody's in Paris in August anyway. And an unmarked police car with four plainclothed officers was prowling back and forth in front of the apartment all that time. Guess they thought if you escaped you'd come back here."

At the Brussels station two people were waiting, one from the foreigner's support group and another from *Hebdo 77*, the main Belgian left-wing political magazine. The reporter said there was a lot of media interest. Would I like to have a press conference tomorrow at the *Hebdo* offices? Maybe, but first let me talk it over with Angela and Steve. They left me at a hotel where the first thing I did was call my father to tell him not to worry. Then I took a long hot shower.

Angela and Steve got to the hotel about nine-thirty with a copy of the Interior Ministry statement put out just before noon.

Philip Agee, alias Anderson, American citizen, who served in the secret services of the United States, was questioned during the evening of August 17 by the border police at the maritime terminal at Boulogne-sur-Mer, and was informed of an order against his entry to and residence in France. He was conducted immediately to the Belgian border. His presence on French soil is judged undesirable by reason of his past activities and the effects that certain of his present activities might have on the relations that France maintains with certain friendly nations. He has already, in November 1976, been made the subject of an expulsion order from the United Kingdom.

Steve asked about the "alias Anderson" reference. I hadn't the slightest idea. Could be I used that name once to buy an airline ticket. I used funny names sometimes because the computer reservations system was monitored by the goons. They had a watch list, and names on the list popped out on terminals in police offices the minute they went into the reservations system. That was the only explanation for surveillance teams waiting for me in different countries on arrival at the airport. But I didn't remember "Anderson." Maybe they invented that one to make me look more like a subversive.

Angela and Steve both thought I should do the press conference: partly to show how the Interior Ministry lied about my expulsion, but mostly to explain what I was doing in France and how the French were pressured by the Americans. I agreed.

The following afternoon some fifty journalists, including radio and television people, crowded the *Hebdo 77* offices. I used that morning's editorial from the *Guardian*, entitled "Agee Goes Bouncing Along," to begin. I said there was nothing "enigmatic, baffling or puzzling" about me—as the editorial had suggested—nor about what I was doing or what the French had done. My expulsion from France could only have happened because of American pressure. There was absolutely nothing illegal about my second book or the index.

I discussed in great detail how I hoped the data bank on all the people and organizations revealed as having connections with the CIA during the past thirty years would serve researchers, journalists and others to help prevent repetitions of the Chilean experience, the Brazilian, Uruguayan and Argentine coups, and U.S. supported repression elsewhere. The new Carter administration, if it was really concerned with human rights, would stop the CIA's support for security services of fascist dictatorships the world over that torture and murder their opponents.

As for France, I said, the people there ought to keep in mind that the CIA has sixty-odd people under cover in the Paris Embassy. That's far more than they need for the simple exchange of information and normal liaison. The conservatives now in power are facing elections in just seven months. If President Ford could approve $6 million for secret intervention by the CIA in Italy's election last year, those sixty people are perfectly capable of doing the same in France to defeat the socialists next March.

"They know I have a nose for spotting those operations, as I showed last year in Jamaica, so maybe that's one more reason they wanted me out of France. But we're going to appeal against the illegal kidnapping procedure and against the grounds stated by the Ministry of the Interior."

A few weeks later Braunschweig filed an appeal against the Ministry of the Interior before the Administrative Court of Paris asking for annulment of the order against my entry and a declaration of the illegality of my expulsion. He argued that my "activities" were nothing more than dissemination of information and expression of opinion, both of which were protected by the European Convention on Human Rights and the laws of France itself. We waited. Months passed and I practically forgot the matter.

In 1979, two and a half years after my appeal, the Interior Ministry responded. In a seven-page statement they listed eight articles published by *Liberation* in 1976 in which members of the U.S. Embassy in Paris were named as CIA employees, adding that although my name did not appear in the articles, I was the source. They also quoted from my Brussels press conference my statement about setting up the index project in Paris. Citing the Welch case, they said that the "fatal consequences" of such activities were "dangerous for public order" and that the Minister's exclusion order was issued to avoid "violence, deaths or assassinations."

For further justification they cited publication of a list of CIA officers by the Popular Front for the Liberation of Palestine in 1978, adding that my name and activities were mentioned in the same article—as if I had been the source of the CIA names, which I wasn't. Not satisfied, the Ministry went on to allege that I had "close ties" with the lawyers of "the Baader-Meinhof gang" and that at a press conference following my rejection as a defense witness I had made "remarks favorable to their action." Nothing could have been further from the truth.

To further justify their action, the statement noted that prior to my expulsion from France I had been expelled from Great Britain for having "disseminated information prejudicial to the security of the United Kingdom," and that I was considered "an undesirable" in Belgium—where I'd never had a problem. As I read that document I couldn't understand why they hadn't dredged up the "Soviet-Cuban agent" bugaboo as well.

But the surprising revelation in the reply was that the Interior Minister's decision to bar my entry to France was taken back in January when I was making my "representations" to Rees's advisory panel.

While admitting that I had entered France five times after that, the Ministry said it didn't matter. I was "discovered" at the Boulogne entry point, and the exclusion order was then put into effect. The truth, of course, was that they knew I was in Paris and, by monitoring my telephone conversations with Angela, they were able to set the trap in Boulogne.

We answered with an affidavit from the publisher of *Liberation* that I had nothing to do with the articles listing CIA people. On the contrary, we said, the lists were based on analysis following the method described by John Marks in his 1974 article "How to Spot a Spook."

We also submitted the statement of the November 17 Revolutionary Organization showing they were following Welch for months before his name was published in the *Athens News*, along with Morton Halperin's article in the *Washington Post* showing that the CIA had warned Welch not to live in the notorious "CIA house" occupied by his predecessor.

Finally, we pointed out that no violence of any kind had befallen CIA people as a result of publication of their names, no "fatal consequences, violence, deaths or assassinations." Therefore I in no way threatened "the public order."

Sounded good, but no chance. Eventually the court ruled that the Minister of the Interior had the power to exclude any foreigner whom he designated "dangerous for the public order." He didn't have to justify such designation, and it didn't matter that the expulsion procedure was illegal. When Jean-Michel Braunschweig told me we could appeal to the Council of State, France's highest court, but that it would cost several thousand dollars, I told him to forget it. I'd seen enough of French justice. Mine was a political, not a legal case, and they'd made a deal with the Americans.

A day or so after the Brussels press conference, as Angela and I were driving to Amsterdam, we discussed the index and *Who's Who* project. Francois Charbonnier at Action Tricontinental had told Karl that despite my expulsion he was still enthusiastic about it, if we could get enough money to start.

I suggested to Angela that she could be in Paris as often and as long as necessary to organize and train the people. And I could help resolve any doubts about analytical methods and specific cases.

One thing was certain: we would do nothing in Amsterdam that could jeopardize my residence status. This project, far more than my second book, was surely the reason for U.S. pressure on the French. Whatever participation I had, such as reviewing the computer cards, would have to be outside Holland.

This solution, mainly Angela's participation in Paris, was the first time I had brought up, even indirectly, the possibility that we might live apart, or somewhat apart. It was cowardly on my part, but at that time it was the only way I could address the looming crisis between us.

I couldn't explain to her, or to myself, why I couldn't continue as before. We had been together for nearly five years. She had done everything imaginable to help me get the book written and then to manage things at home while I travelled from country to country. But something happened with the deportation crisis in Britain. I was trying so hard to win, and she was doing the same. Somehow during that long campaign I began seeing Angela as one more source of pressure, as if she had blurred into the whole array of people and situations that were squeezing me and pinning me down.

I thought maybe we had worked too closely and too intensely for too long. Every minute we were together was like being "at the office." Even when we travelled or took vacations it was the same. Often I had felt I needed to catch my breath, turn outward to something other than this monstrous CIA question, but I couldn't with Angela.

We'd tried sailing, walking in the countryside, motoring in Switzerland and Germany, but with Angela I just couldn't relax. From the moment the publicity started that summer in Cornwall, I had the feeling of becoming an instant one-man institution struggling vainly to defend myself from all the accusations and at the same time to fulfill all the requests for articles, interviews and speaking engagements.

Angela never badgered or pushed me to accept this or that. But she was so supportive that the effect was the same: like a huge conscience casting a long and constant shadow.

If Angela spent most of her time in Paris, I thought, maybe that distance would be healthy. But I couldn't articulate the reasons. I dreaded hurting her and didn't realize how patronizing that was. How could I tell her, after all she had done, that I wanted to separate, at least as man and wife?

I wondered what was wrong with me. One thing, certainly, was a bad conscience that she did all the domestic work—shopping, cooking, washing and cleaning—besides the office work with me. She tutored Phil and Chris in their schoolwork and was more sensitive to their needs than I was. I hated to think what a separation would mean to them. Still, I felt pressured, threatened and unsure, and I somehow saw Angela as one of the sources of my anxieties.

The sudden shock of arrest and expulsion from France only aggravated the tension I felt with Angela. Those two or three weeks studying French and relaxing with friends in Paris were so marvelous, such a relief from the physical and emotional demands of the British defense campaign and all that went before. From one day to the next that short interlude became a memory, and I was back in a crisis. But rather than finding support and comfort in Angela, she seemed to be one more element of pressure.

The meaning of my suggestion that Angela work in Paris was not lost on her. She was not enthusiastic. She said: what about us? What about our getting a place in Amsterdam? Setting up a new home? I couldn't answer her honestly. I couldn't even discuss my feelings with her. I was evasive, and said let's see what happens. Maybe we won't get the money to start the thing in Paris. Failure to be honest with her made me feel more anguish and guilt because I knew she was suffering from the fears and doubts I had raised.

In the weeks ahead, my refusal to bring things into the open only made matters worse. I went into a whirlpool of depression that almost paralyzed me, making a nightmare out of administrative chores like opening a bank account, registry and insurance for the car, medical examinations and enrollment for health insurance, and, worst of all, searching for a flat.

With such pervasive gloom I began to imagine all sorts of disastrous problems if I went ahead with the U.S. fund-raising trip. Jon Steinberg came up to Amsterdam before returning to New York, and I told him I had to postpone going back until next spring. After the no-prosecution commitment from the Justice Department, and even with deportation from Britain, I thought I could do it. But now with this expulsion from France, I just didn't know.

I'll do it, but later, after I get a little organized in Amsterdam. Truth was, my expulsion from France brought back all the psychological paralysis and paranoid fears I'd first experienced trying to get *Inside the Company* done. Angela had saved the day before, but this time my ability to accept her support was limited.

In early September Angela went back to Cambridge to separate the seven or eight tea chests with the index documentation from the rest of our things that were awaiting shipment to Amsterdam. She had the chests delivered to a friend in London who had agreed to store them in his basement until they were needed. Under no circumstances, we decided, should that material come to Amsterdam and be used as evidence that we planned to do the index project there. Then she picked up Phil and Chris at Heathrow.

In Amsterdam they enrolled in the International School, as we more or less took over the fourth-floor dormitory at TNI. By now there were several others besides us and Basker living there, and although everyone got along well, I found the communal living just one more irritation.

I wasn't the only person with problems. I had kept up fairly close relations with the *CounterSpy* staff in Washington through correspondence and their occasional visits to Europe. During the past year personal and political differences within the group had paralyzed the magazine. Ellen Ray, a member of the staff, her husband Bill Schaap, and Louis Wolf, who had moved to Washington, D.C., from London, were thinking of starting a new magazine.

Schaap was a lawyer and editor of *The Military Law Reporter*, a Washington-based journal on developments within the military justice system. He and Ellen had worked for several years during the Vietnam war, in Okinawa, Japan and West Germany, helping dissident G.I.'s in a project sponsored by the National Lawyers Guild.

Bill was looking for an American publisher for the book on the CIA in Western Europe that Steve Weissman, Louis Wolf and I had started putting together in London before my deportation crisis. It was an anthology of articles on Agency operations that had mostly appeared in European publications, and it also had an annex prepared by Wolf giving the career biographies of hundreds of CIA people.

Ellen wrote that she wanted to come to Amsterdam to discuss the magazine problem, the book publication, and other projects. I was so worried about my situation in Holland, which was distorted out of all proportion by my emotional state, that I refused to meet in Amsterdam. How about Brussels? Fine.

Ellen and I met at the end of September. The good news was that Bill had arranged with Lyle Stuart to publish the CIA-in-Europe book. The advance would be enough to finish the editing and buy reprint permissions for certain articles. Already Bill had formed a company to receive the advance and any future income from the book which would be used to finance *CounterSpy* or, if internal problems persisted, a new magazine.

Ellen and I agreed that we should all meet together to resolve the magazine question and other matters. Canada was obviously the best place if I wasn't going to the States, but I was even afraid to go there—afraid they might dump me across the border. We settled on Jamaica where we knew people and wouldn't have to worry about government harassment. Perhaps November, I said, but not until I found a flat and got unpacked.

While I was in Brussels, Angela found a flat, big enough and in a good location for the boys' school, but extremely expensive. The TNI annual fellows conference was coming up in four weeks, and they needed the dormitory space—one more source of pressure—so we took the three-storey, five-room apartment on Olympiaplein knowing that money from the sale of the Cambridge house would go straight down the drain for rent in Amsterdam. We would move in the beginning of November even if the shipment from Cambridge hadn't arrived.

I was back from Brussels only a couple of days when Angela raised a question that went to the core of the problems between us. She said she wanted to participate more in the various projects I was involved in. The Brussels trip for discussions with Ellen was only the latest example of her staying behind while I ran off working. She was tired of being on the margin, looking after domestic affairs.

I said she was right, the situation in the past three years had gotten progressively unfair. But what to do about it? Neither of us wanted to continue like that, but I didn't see any easy solution: maybe her direction of the index project in Paris if that could ever get going, but not together.

Two of the most agonizing days I can remember followed that discussion. Not that I remember them exactly, because memory's protective mechanism has long since blurred the details. I only know that all of us, Chris and Phil included, went through a wrenching weekend of exposed resentments, sorrow and despair, and emotional disintegration. I can't remember how I said it, but I told Angela I wanted to separate, at least for awhile, or until I could sort out in my mind the reasons why I couldn't go on.

I called Steve and Ana Weissman in London, and they flew over the next day. They and friends at TNI did help calm the situation, but wounds were already too deep. In anguish and pain, Angela decided to return to London.

Sunday night Steve and Ana, and Angela and I, walked almost in silence to the KLM airport bus terminal across Museumplein from TNI. The three of them got on, and as the bus pulled away I felt no relief, only guilt and failure.

X

"We Hoped He Would Improve His Life"

The day after Angela left, Gretta suggested I see her former husband for a medical examination. It must have been pretty obvious I was having a bad time. And my smoking again, after a five-year break, didn't help either. He prescribed Valium and said I had to get as much rest as possible.

With Angela gone I would have to take care of shopping, cooking and other domestic chores. That didn't seem like a bad thing. For too long my energies had been focused almost entirely on "work." I wanted, and needed, some kind of distraction—something that each day would take me away from the piles of letters and papers that all related, in one way or another, to that three-lettered obsession.

Not that I lost interest in the index and *Who's Who* project or more writing about the Agency. I just felt I could no longer allow the anti-CIA struggle to be my whole world. From now on, I decided, I would work a reasonable day, then shut the door of my office and live my life. I would also get a telephone I could turn off, or better yet, an answering machine, so I wouldn't have to take calls in the evenings.

Keeping the household running would also help me develop a deeper relationship with my sons. We could do some domestic things together. I also wanted to take a much broader interest in their lives. For three years they had lived through the media attacks, attended three different schools, and endured the long British deportation campaign. Now it was time to stabilize, to try to take up the slack resulting from Angela's departure, to be a real father rather than a distant figure always away or under pressure when at home. Within a month we would be in our new flat. We would have our bicycles and could begin exploring the countryside around Amsterdam, and with the car we could see other parts of Holland.

October 12 would be Phil's sixteenth birthday. The day before, I took him to the guitar shop where he'd been eyeing equipment. Both he and Chris had studied acoustical guitar with teachers in Cornwall and Cambridge, but now his heart was set on an electric bass with amplifier and speaker console. It seemed extravagant, what with all the moving expenses, but that wasn't his fault, so I bought him what he wanted. Then I went to Olympiaplein to sign the contract for the apartment and pay three months' rent. Gretta and the rest of us at TNI planned a little party with birthday cake and candles.

On the morning of Phil's birthday, Mr. van den Brink at the Amsterdam aliens police called. He said he had some papers for me and asked if I could stop over after lunch with our passports. Sure, I said, thinking that at last we'll have the one-year extension in writing. I had checked with him in early September when the original three months was ending, and he had said the decision was delayed but not to worry. Now, finally, I would get one more administrative nuisance out of the way.

Van den Brink kept me waiting only a couple of minutes. As I sat in the chair by his desk, he told me he had the decision of the Ministry of Justice on my June request for extension. He knew I couldn't read Dutch, so he offered to translate the key paragraphs, adding that it seemed a strange decision to him. With that word "strange" my heart started pounding, and as he read it my breath got short, as in every shock before.

The Secretary of State for Justice,
    Considering that the petitioner was given permission in June of this year to reside in the Netherlands for the duration of three months, whereby he was notified to refrain from activities which could endanger "public order" or national security, including the good relations between the Netherlands and other countries;

Considering that, during his stay in the Netherlands since June 1977, the petitioner has shown a disinclination to heed this notification and has undertaken activities which are detrimental to Dutch foreign affairs, while said activities have resulted, among other things, in his removal from France;

Considering that consequently there are grounds for refusing petitioner the requested permission to reside in the Netherlands;

Considering on the other hand, with regard to all relevant circumstances of the case under consideration, that there are grounds for allowing him an opportunity to remain in the country, though for a shorter time than requested;

Has decided:

1. To grant a permit of residence to Philip Burnett Agee, which shall be valid from September 1, 1977 until November 30, 1977;

2. To affix to said permit the precept that the petitioner shall refrain from activities which could endanger "public order" or national security, including the good relations between the Kingdom and other powers.

I sat there unable to believe what I was hearing. I asked van den Brink what activities against Dutch foreign affairs they were talking about. He said he had no idea, and he then translated a paragraph on the back of the page that said I could petition for revision of the decision within one month of notification.

He handed me that written decision, and I noticed it was dated September 7, over a month before. Why so long to let me know, I asked. He had no idea about that either. He asked for the passports, stamped them with permits through November 30, and gave them back. Completely bewildered, I told him I would see my lawyer and attempt to get an explanation.

During the taxi ride back to TNI I looked out the window thinking it wasn't possible. What in Christ did they mean by "disinclination." I hadn't done a thing. So the French threw me out. What did that have to do with Holland? Not a damned thing. What activities are they talking about? Shit. I can't go through another appeal and campaign like in Britain. I just can't do that again. I haven't the energy, and I don't have the will. Christ almighty, what have I got myself into this time?

At TNI I showed the document to Basker. We asked a Dutch member of the staff to translate it just to be sure I hadn't misunderstood van den Brink. No, he had translated it accurately, and I had understood. I had "undertaken activities detrimental to Dutch foreign affairs." Instead of simply refusing the extension they gave me an additional three months.

I recalled that Willem said I could appeal an adverse decision, and would be entitled to see evidence against me, but I couldn't bring myself to call him that afternoon, couldn't even think of starting another legal appeal. I decided to think it over for a few days. That evening we had the birthday party for Phil, but acting festive was impossible for me.

The next day I began a week's trip to Zurich, Geneva and Barcelona—the first violation of my new resolutions to stay at home and spend time with Chris and Phil. But the meetings were too important to cancel.

Before leaving I prepared an itinerary for Basker with the dates and times I would call him after each arrival. If I hadn't called by a certain time, he would get word to my lawyer in the city in question that I had probably been arrested at the airport. And each time I waited in line for passport control I got those knots in my stomach, expecting to be called aside and told I could not enter. But each time they waved me through, and as I left the booth I heaved a silent sigh of relief.

While away I kept thinking about the November 30 deadline. Just a month and a half. And where to go then? Should we move into the Olympiaplein apartment, or should we forget it and try to get the money back? I wondered if someone at the Ministry of Justice had deliberately held back the decision until they knew I had made the payment on the apartment and arranged for shipment of furniture and other household effects from Cambridge.

We couldn't stay at TNI with their conference coming up. We'll have to move in, unpack a few essentials, and see what happens. Maybe I should go to Havana to see about moving there. It had been more than three years since I was in Cuba, but I thought I remembered someone at one point saying that if things ever got too difficult, I could live there.

Then I realized: shit, that's just what they want. If I go to live in Cuba they'll have every newspaper in the world saying, "We told you so. Agee's defected to the Cubans." Better wait and talk with Willem van Bennekom and Harry van den Bergh before making any decision.

The day after I got back to Amsterdam I took the decision to Willem. He said he'd never seen such weird reasoning in an immigration case. If I had damaged Dutch foreign relations, how could they justify renewing my residence for ninety days? And they couldn't get away with that vague allegation. They had to state exactly what I had done and how it had damaged foreign relations. I told Willem I hadn't done a thing except write letters and try to get settled. I'd even decided not to ship the index and Who's Who materials over from England. And my intention to write another book here was perfectly well known to the Justice Ministry when I asked to come to Holland.

Willem said the document was utterly ridiculous, and not just for the faulty reasoning and lack of specifics. Henk Zeevalking, the Secretary of State for Justice, made a political commitment that I could resettle for a reasonable time in Holland, not for six months. He had signed the September decision just two days before he left the Ministry for appointment as mayor in a provincial city.

With the continuing government crisis, no new Secretary of State had been appointed, and matters were largely in the hands of senior civil servants. That long delay in getting the decision to me smelled to Willem like a maneuver by the Secretary General of the Justice Ministry, a man named Albert Mulder, who was well known for his right-wing views and his imperious conduct of Ministry affairs.

Of course we'll appeal this, Willem said. We'll get their "evidence" file and then prove to the Advisory Committee for Alien Affairs that you didn't do anything to justify this refusal. The chances are the decision will be reversed within the Ministry when Zeevalking's successor is appointed, and Harry van den Bergh can help on this. But even if the Ministry refuses to change the decision, assuming Mulder gets his way, the decision would never hold up before the Council of State. Meanwhile you'll have a year or two before the final decision.

As he talked I thought: get the time, get some time to settle in, to get at least a little stability again. Can't start looking for still another country right now. Can't force the boys to change schools again now that they've started in Amsterdam. Willem is right. We have to appeal.

In late October I again decided to leave Amsterdam, but this time it had nothing to do with "work." Therese Roberge's daughter, Giselle, invited me over to Hamburg for a party she and others were giving on the weekend of Halloween. It was to be a costume affair, not exactly my cup of tea, but the weekend would surely be an escape, I thought, from the worries of residence permits, hostile propaganda and a new apartment.

Giselle had left the New York City Ballet a couple of years earlier and had come to Europe to continue her dancing career, first with the Stuttgart company and then with the Hamburg Staatsoper. On one of

my trips to Paris, she was visiting her mother when I called to invite
Therese to lunch. Giselle came along, and our paths crossed from
time to time afterwards. I always found her interesting. Not that she
knew much about my main concerns. Her whole life was bound up in
the ballet world. But she had read some of my articles and interviews,
so she knew the broad outlines of what I'd been trying to do.

I enjoyed seeing Giselle for many reasons. She was bright, witty,
curious and glamorous—so much so that when she walked down the
street people stared as if they were seeing a fashion model. Because
of my friendship with her mother and the adventures we'd gone
through in Paris, together with Therese's frequent talk about her children, I felt I'd known Giselle for years. Maybe she felt the same, I
didn't know, but I found it refreshing and relaxing, when we were
together, that we didn't talk so much about my work and problems as
about the books she was reading, the ballets she was dancing, the
movies we'd seen or just plain trivia.

True, I didn't know the difference between a *tendu* and a *plié*, but
just watching her walk, with quick-step swagger, turned out legs, and
perfect posture, I was certain she would be spectacular to watch on
stage. Once when she was performing in Paris she tried to get me a
ticket, but the performances were sold out. So she smuggled me
through the stage entrance of the Theater de la Ville claiming to the
doorman that I was another dancer's husband.

I stood in the wings watching with open mouth as she jumped and
turned and did a hundred steps too fast for me to follow. From her
dark red hair and big wide eyes to her muscular calves and thin an-
kles, she was probably the most beautiful woman I'd ever met. But
we had our different lives and no pretensions about intruding the one
on the other.

Before leaving that Friday I wrote a note for Basker giving him the
time I would call from Hamburg and the names and numbers to call if
I didn't call: lawyers in Hamburg and Amsterdam, and Giselle and
her flatmate, Michael, another dancer from the States. As usual I approached passport control with trepidation, but once again they
waved me through.

The party was packed with members of the ballet company and
their friends, most in more or less outlandish costumes including a
leather queen or two. Several people put on skits, and the dancing
was wild enough at times, as these slightly crazy people really let go,
but eventually the rock music blasting from the stereo was too much

for the neighbors. When police arrived about three A.M. I hid in a
back room, sufficiently paranoid to think they might check identities.
As it happened, they just wanted a little quiet.

From Friday afternoon to Monday morning something changed between Giselle and me. Nothing dramatic but nonetheless real. She
was free the whole weekend, and we spent every minute together
walking along the Alster, the lake in the center of Hamburg, or sitting
in cafes. We talked about how we could spend more time together, a
lot more time, and determined to find the way to do so.

I knew she was an "escape" for me, but that didn't matter. I
needed it. I loved her raucous, irreverant laugh, her free-spirited
way, and her unusual physical beauty.

Back in Amsterdam we were almost a community moving into the
spacious Olympianplein flat. Besides Chris and Phil and me, there
was Rodney Larson, a California researcher and writer on trade unions who was visiting; Karl van Meter who came from Paris for the
TNI fellows meeting; and Louis Wolf who arrived from the States to
work on our book. It would be titled *Dirty Work: The CIA in Western
Europe*.

Angela also came to help unpack and see friends, and a few days
later Larry Grant came over from London for a weekend. Despite the
chaos of moving in and the memory of our last weeks at TNI, Angela
and I spoke not a word of recrimination or resentment. On the contrary we continued a working partnership that now, at least, was bal-
anced and relaxed. Our friends Ken and Margo also helped unpack so
that in just a few days we had enough in place for meals and basic
necessities.

Lou Wolf had brought stacks of biographic sheets on CIA people
assigned at one time or another in Western Europe. These were the
result of several years' research in the British Museum and the National Archives in Washington and would constitute the personnel index of the Europe book. Using *Biographic Registers* and other
sources, he had zeroed in on about a thousand people. Trouble was
there were a lot of doubtful cases, and only those we were certain
were CIA employees could go in the book. So Lou and I worked day
and night for a week reviewing one career biography after another,
eliminating every doubtful case.

Rodney Larson's interest was both similar and different. For several years he and others in the California union movement had been
following leads of CIA penetrations of U.S. unions for access to foreign national and international unions.

Inside the Company had been useful to them for the Latin American scene, but in fact they were far ahead of me in their knowledge of CIA labor operations generally. Still, Rodney had an unending string of questions and our discussions broadened my knowledge considerably during his six-week visit. Eventually he and a British writer published a book on CIA trade union operations, *Where Were You Brother?*, which at the time was the best on the subject.

In mid-November Willem van Bennekom filed for an extension of my residence permit from 30 November 1977 (the strange September decision) to 30 November 1978. This request was separate from our appeal of the September decision and refusal would give us grounds for a separate appeal. Willem's purpose was to gain additional time and build our case for eventual appeal, if necessary, to the Council of State. A week later I had a most unusual visit.

A little before noon the doorbell rang. I was alone and went to the top of the long entrance stairway to pull the cord that unlatched the door below. Without a greeting or identifying statement a stranger began walking slowly up the steps. He had a briefcase and was wearing an overcoat and a hat that obscured his face as he looked down at the steps. I never had unarranged visits from strangers, and I got a little nervous. When he was halfway up I called down asking what he wanted, but he kept coming without answering. As he reached the top I saw a middle-aged man with grey face and hair. The stairway was fairly narrow, and I was blocking most of it, but he slipped by into the foyer as he asked my name in English and handed me a calling card.

Perplexed, I glanced at the card. It read "R. Scherer" and below there were three lines, unintelligible to me, beginning with "Inspecteur der Rijksrecherche." Before I even looked up he asked:

"You are Mr. Agee, aren't you?" He extended his hand which I accepted.

"Yes. Who are you?"

"I am Inspector Scherer of the Royal Investigations Police. I've come to ask you a few questions." With that he began walking slowly into the living room almost as if he were at home.

"What do you mean questions?" I followed him into the living room as he strolled to the back and looked out the window. Then he came back my way saying,

"You are appealing a decision by the Ministry of Justice on your permission to reside in the Netherlands. I have been asked to prepare some questions for you and to provide your answers to the Ministry.

May I sit down?" Without waiting for an answer he sat down slowly
into the chair next to him and placed the briefcase on his lap.

Everything about him was methodical, as if he had planned his
moves carefully and had done the same many times before. I had the
feeling I was with a pushy but cool salesman, and I didn't like it.
There was another chair there, but I decided not to sit down.

"Inspector, I believe I should have my lawyer, Mr. van Bennekom,
present if you want to ask questions. If you like I can telephone him
to see if he is free."

In a relaxed, almost intimate tone he said the questions were routine and nothing to worry about. We could just proceed and get it
over with quickly, Oh, oh, this guy's trying to con me, I thought, he's
too slippery.

"Inspector, I want to call my lawyer first. If you don't mind waiting
a moment, I'll be right back."

As he nodded, I went upstairs to my office, called Willem, but he
wasn't in. Then I went back down, determined not to talk, only to
find him poking around among the ten or fifteen unpacked tea chests
standing against a wall. I told him van Bennekom was not in and that I
preferred to wait until I could speak with him. Scherer was obviously
disappointed, tried not to show it, but agreed reluctantly.

Then he asked: "Do you mind if I look around the rest of the apartment?"

I said, "I certainly do," thinking that he'd come not just to ask questions but also to case the apartment. "I suppose in the Netherlands
the police need some kind of warrant to carry out a search, and if
that's the case I want to see one and call van Bennekom's office
again." He quickly backed off the idea, said it didn't matter, and
agreed that we could make an appointment through my lawyer to
meet later. As he walked down the steps, I was pleased: the snake had
tried to ambush me in my own house.

When I told Willem about the visit he was puzzled but agreed that
Scherer had purposely come without an appointment in the hope that
I would answer the questions without checking with him. The real
question, Willem wondered, was why a senior police inspector from
the elite *Rijksrecherche* came when normally any questioning before
an appeal hearing was done by "contacts officers" of the Aliens Police.

Three days later when we met Scherer in his office, Willem's first
question was why an officer of his rank was involved in my case.
Scherer's answer was revealing. Mr. Mulder, Secretary General of
the Justice Ministry, was personally handling my case, had composed

the questions with Scherer, and had asked Scherer to conduct the interview.

Scherer was different now. No games with van Bennekom, whose firm manner put conduct of the meeting in his, rather than Scherer's, hands. According to plan, Willem let Scherer take out his papers. As we had anticipated, Scherer had about five pages of questions prepared with spaces between each, presumably where he would write the answers. An official interpreter was present to provide translations. Also according to our plan, Willem told Scherer we wanted to hear all the questions first, before any answers, so that we could decide whether I should give the answers orally or send them back in written form.

Scherer didn't like that, but yielded before Willem's insistence.

After confirming my name, citizenship, and date of arrival in the Netherlands, he asked: "Will you tell me the names of your friends and contacts in the Netherlands?"

I looked at Willem, whose eyebrows were rising, and he asked Scherer if that meant *everybody* I knew or had met here. Scherer answered affirmatively and asked if I would like to answer, naming at least some of the people if I couldn't remember everyone on the spot. Willem said we wanted to hear all the questions and asked him to go on.

"Who is paying rent for your flat?" We kept silent. "Do you still receive royalties from Penguin? How do you maintain yourself financially? Are you now writing Part II of *Inside the Company?* What is the writing about? Do you consider your activities political?"

Then he got to one of two main themes. "Did you write in Holland an article for the *Leveller* magazine that was published in the United Kingdom? Did you expose in this article two officials of a foreign security service? Did you understand that the *Leveller* article was a political activity? Did you realize that the *Leveller* article might damage the good relations between the Netherlands and a foreign country? Do you realize that aliens are not permitted to engage in political activities in the Netherlands?"

Willem was listening intently, and his expression suggested something strange was going on.

Scherer went on to his second main theme. "Are you now engaged in establishing a computerized data bank on all the people and organizations known to have, or have had, connections with the CIA? Please explain this project in detail. Mr. Agee, you continue to travel widely in Western Europe. Are these travels connected with your work on this computerized data bank? Does your work on this computerized data bank require you to maintain contacts with foreign intelligence officials, and do you maintain such contacts? Was your expulsion from France caused by your work on this project?"

He finished with three more questions. "Do you think that your activities since your arrival in Holland violate your promise of loyalty to the State of the Netherlands? Were you deported from the United Kingdom because you . . . [Rees's three allegations]? And finally, Mr. Agee, you are well known as a man who wants to open doors and to lay things out in public. In this same spirit of openness would you kindly tell me whether your activities are really political?"

As Scherer went through the last question I started to smile, was about to laugh, but turned to Willem who was intent and serious. He said he wanted to consult with me in private. We went out into the hallway where Willem told me he'd never heard such an outrageous questionnaire. I had better answer in writing and show him the answers first.

We returned to Scherer. Willem said he had a pressing appointment in court and had to leave. We would take the questionnaire, I would have it translated into English, I would write the answers and have them translated into Dutch, and we would have it all back within a week. Scherer agreed that we could take the questionnaire but was concerned that I had not answered a single question. Mr. Mulder, he said, was waiting for a telephone report that very moment. Couldn't I stay with him and the interpreter to answer some of the questions, anything at all that I could recall? I insisted on written answers, Willem took the questionnaire, and we proceeded to the door.

Like an afterthought, Scherer told Willem that the questions and my answers were to be treated as confidential and were not for publication. Willem flipped through the questionnaire and told Scherer he could find no "confidential" markings. For us to consider it secret was most unusual.

Back in the hallway Willem and I agreed we would not get sucked in like that. We would not take the questionnaire with us. Willem gave it back to Scherer saying that he and I had to discuss it further, and he would call Scherer in a couple of days.

When they spoke again, Scherer said he had only meant that the questions and answers should not be made public before he had received them. Willem said we would accept no "confidentiality" arrangement, and Scherer said he would check with Mulder.

We never heard from Scherer again.

The next day Willem and I discussed the whole matter with Harry van den Bergh. I asked if they wanted the honor of being at the top of my "friends and contacts" list. Outrageous. How dare they even ask. It was obvious from Scherer's questionnaire that the *Leveller* article and the index project were the pretexts. I showed them the article, the "Letter from Exile" I'd written in June, and they both looked blank.

"Well, so you like it here," Harry said. "What's wrong with that?"

Then I explained the idea of the index project emphasizing that it would be a compilation of information from already published sources, mostly U.S. government publications like the *Biographic Register* and Congressional investigations. It was still just an idea, not even mine in origin, and no financing had been found. Harry said Zeevalking's commitment to him was not for three or six months, but for resettlement, for a couple of years to begin. Zeevalking also knew perfectly well I intended to continue writing and speaking about the CIA. Harry said he would talk to the Foreign Minister, Max van der Stoel, a Labour party member, to get his opinion, and also with Zeevalking.

Two days later Harry had good news: the Foreign Minister said he did not know of any foreign complaints about my activities and had nothing to do with the September decision. Zeevalking said his original intention was to grant me a year's residence permit, and even after his September decision he intended to grant an extension beyond November 30. He added that refusal of extension now, on grounds that I hadn't observed the conditions, was absolutely ridiculous.

Even with the *Leveller* article, according to Zeevalking, there were no grounds for refusal of extension. Harry had written a letter to Mulder at the Justice Ministry citing Van der Stoel's and Zeevalking's remarks and protesting the Ministry's conduct of the case. If the Foreign Minister himself had no complaint, and if Zeevalking's intention was to extend, how could the Justice Ministry now refuse?

My sense of relief, however, lasted only a couple of days. At the beginning of December Willem called and asked me to come over for some bad news. The Justice Ministry had refused to reconsider the September decision, and the Advisory Committee for Alien Affairs had set December 19 as the date for our hearing. Willem had never heard of such speed, and he was certain they were trying to prevent me from appealing to the Council of State.

What? I thought I had the right to appeal to the Council of State. Willem explained: Every foreigner who has lived in Holland for one year has an automatic right to appeal beyond the Justice Ministry to the Council of State and to remain here until their decision. If you've been here less than a year, you only have the same right if no final decision is made by the Ministry within ninety days of our appeal. Our appeal went in October 27 which makes January 25 the ninetieth day. By setting the hearing so quickly they want to get the Committee's advice so they can beat the January 25 deadline.

I felt like a punctured balloon. Mulder was going to override the political decision that I could resettle here using the flimsy pretexts of the *Leveller* article and the index project. Willem said Mulder had another man on the case, according to a contact in the Ministry, a senior civil servant in the Aliens Affairs Department named Max Wendt. Ah, yes, he was the person I had to call on arrival to report my address. Not very friendly. Maybe that's where the American hand comes in, with these little Napoleons in the civil service, because it's certainly not on the political level.

What to do now? We could appeal to the Advisory Committee, but they'll be just like "Rees's poodles."

Willem took a positive line. He said he would ask for postponement of the hearing to late January, citing my travel plans and our other request for a one-year extension from November 30. Postponement would be logical, so that both cases could be heard at the same time.

As Willem went on, a feeling of fatigue crept into my brain, all the more so when he started talking about how we could develop a support campaign.

Somewhat in a daze and thinking of all the losing effort in Britain, I nevertheless agreed to everything he said. Willem would arrange the press conference for early next week, and I would start getting the documentation together.

Back in the flat I discussed the situation with Rodney and Angela who had returned a second time to get the car and take some of her things back to Britain.

The phone had been ringing constantly with calls from journalists who wanted comments on the decision. While I was with Willem, the Justice Ministry had announced that I must leave the Netherlands because I was "a danger to public order and national security." I had been allowed to come here, they said, on condition that I refrain from political activities. By publishing articles and giving interviews of a political nature, I had violated that condition, and my residence permit, therefore, would not be renewed.

The U.S. Embassy in The Hague said they had nothing to do with it. Sure. I asked Angela and Rodney to continue taking the calls and saying I wasn't there. Better to save comments for the press conference with Willem.

You know, I said to Angela and Rodney, I haven't given a single interview in this country other than the comments for television, when I arrived in June, that I was glad to be here. The only interviews were in Paris with Karl in July and *Newsweek* in August. Then the press conference in Brussels. They're using the *Leveller* article and the index project, neither of which relates to Holland, as pretexts to railroad me out of here.

We discussed a defense campaign. I said I just couldn't go through that whole thing again. Angela and Rodney said they would help, so would others, and I could do it differently: a slower pace without the travel and speeches.

Willem's request for postponement of the hearing was rejected immediately. We had the press conference at which I distributed a four-page statement giving all the background, from the decision I could come to Holland to the unseemly haste to get me out. I also distributed copies of the *Leveller* article, Willem's appeal against the September decision, and Scherer's questions—as nearly as Willem and I could remember—with my answers. Willem spoke on the legal and political aspects, particularly the Zeevalking commitment and the importance of protection by the Council of State.

I ended by comparing the action of Britain, France and now Holland with the South African practice of "banning," and I asked for help from journalists and others to uphold my right, supposedly protected by the Universal Declaration of Human Rights and the Helsinki Accords, to collect and disseminate information without hindrance.

During that same week following the Justice Ministry's decision some unexpected visitors popped up. Mel Wulf was in town for a day, and we again discussed my returning to the States. Maybe, but it seemed to me from this Dutch decision that the Agency was going all out to stop the index and my next book—not the "Europe" book with Lyle Stuart, but the historical survey with Penguin.

If I went back they might even impound my passport to keep me there and make sure I complied with the censorship injunction. Worse was the humiliation of having to ask permission from that band of thugs for what I could or couldn't write. Where to go if not the States?

I didn't know. But in talking with Mel I remembered that Judith

Hart had spoken to Dom Mintoff, the Prime Minister of Malta, about me during the British deportation crisis. As I recalled he said I could go there. I decided to see if Malta was still possible.

The day after Mel left, a woman called from Paris and identified herself as Mary Pickens. Who? Mary Pickens. Weren't you expecting my call? It's for an interview. I thought: Mary Pickens, Mary Pickens, who could that be? Ah! It's the Abbie Hoffman contact. What a bad time for him to show up. He had gone underground several years before to escape a mandatory life sentence for a New York drug bust, a police set-up, had plastic surgery on his face, and successfully eluded the FBI dragnet. Through intermediaries he'd sent me a couple of "Dear James" letters praising *Inside the Company* which he read in hospital after falling off a Mayan pyramid in Guatemala. He fell, he wrote, from joy on hearing of Nixon's resignation. He also urged me to go back to the States to fight the fight from there.

After my deportation from Britain, Abbie sent word that he wanted to do an interview. I said yes, but no date was set, and my only condition was that I didn't want to see his face. If he ever got caught I didn't want to be suspected by all those clever people who thought that because the Agency hadn't killed me I must still be with them in some sophisticated deception operation. But now he was here, and my instincts were telling me I should do the interview another time. I told "Mary" I was swamped with preparations for a press conference and my Advisory Committee hearing and didn't have the time. She said she and her friend had come all the way from the States and asked me to reconsider. We left it that she would call again the next day.

Next morning around eleven the doorbell rang. After Scherer's visit I no longer pulled the cord from above but walked down for the option of letting people in or not. I opened the door and there standing in front of me was a beautiful woman. My first thought was to ask the old question whether she'd walked off the cover of *Vogue* or *Harper's Bazaar*. She said she was "Mary" and asked if we could speak. I hesitated, then led her up the stairs to the living room, but she was seated less than a minute when she took out paper and pencil and wrote me a note. "Could we go somewhere outside to talk?" I nodded, got my coat, and walked with her to a corner cafe.

Look, she said, we're here, not in Paris. *Penthouse* has given an advance and expense money for the interview. It'll be called something like "The Hunted Meets the Watched" or "The Wandering Jew Meets the Jumping Jesuit." We've taken all sorts of precautions, and you can be sure there's no problem. He's waiting not far from here to talk to you. will you come and discuss it with him?

I told "Mary" I couldn't. If I got caught meeting with Abbie, technically a fugitive from U.S. justice, my case in Holland would be even worse. Yes, they had read about the problem, but arrangements were all set up and quite secure. I said I didn't want to go through a clandestine routine. I was overwhelmed with problems and didn't want to ask for more.

I also didn't want to take any risk that Abbie might get caught because of me. I repeated the fear that if he did get caught, even later, people might believe I was responsible. I'd do an interview some other time but not now. Tell Abbie I respect his work, think he's got an unbeatable sense of humor and theater, but the timing's bad. "Mary" countered that Abbie had written articles on tours of the FBI building and nuclear facilities and did radio and video interviews. He wasn't afraid. I still refused.

"Mary" called the next day, Abbie took the phone, said he had to fulfill the commitment to *Penthouse*. He'd brought books and articles for me and had many things to discuss. I still refused.

He hung up, wrote me an indignant letter signed "Your KGB Contact," and later published the non-interview with typical Abbie humor as "Philip Agee Won't You Please Go Home." The place he had intended to do the interview was the Anne Frank house, now a museum.

Perhaps he was right. Perhaps I was getting paralyzed with paranoia and guilt-tripping. Whatever the problem, it didn't get any better after Abbie's call.

As in Britain we formed a defense committee to circulate petitions; to stimulate political, media and union support; and to mail out press and information kits. And a steady stream of journalists came through the flat for interviews.

I waited impatiently for Willem to get the "evidence" file which we would use to prepare for the Advisory Committee hearing. According to law the file had to contain all the evidence against me that pertained to the September decision and that the Committee would see.

Willem called at last, and I rushed over to his office. He handed me a thin tan folder. I opened it to find some ten documents. We went through it. The first was a four-page Ministry of Justice fact sheet on me: when I came to Holland, when I registered with the police and applied for one year's residence, Willem's name, the September decision and date of our appeal. The last page was a seven-paragraph re-

sume of my work going back to my resignation from the Agency in
1968.

Facts on my deportation from Britain were there along with Rees's
phony allegations. So were the "conditions" about not endangering
Holland's relations with other countries. Then it mentioned my letter
to the *Leveller*, my expulsion from France and my Brussels press conference.

Underneath were copies of my correspondence with the Dutch
Embassy in London and a telex from the Embassy with the text of my
Leveller article. The next was a telex from the Dutch Embassy in
Paris about my arrest and expulsion in August, followed by a Reuters
dispatch from my Brussels press conference with a description of the
index project. Then the shocker: a collection of clippings on me from
right-wing London newspapers forwarded by the Dutch Embassy
there. Among these were scurrilous articles by Robert Moss from the
Daily Telegraph and *Foreign Report*.

Willem had seen plenty of files from the Aliens Affairs Department
but never one with press reports as evidence for decisions on residence permits. Much of the London press material was from before I
came to Holland and should have had no bearing on the September
decision. The file was obviously cooked to put me in the worst possible light, but Willem saw a positive side. If this was all they had, cen-
tering on the *Leveller* article and the data bank, and if there had been
no foreign complaints, our job would be easy.

This time I would not have to present the story of my life. We knew
the allegations and had the evidence. But three days before the hearing the favorable political atmosphere became a disaster. Instead of a
new coalition led by Joop den Uyl and the Labour Party, the Christian Democrats formed an alliance with the Liberals and set up a new
government with a slim majority. The new Prime Minister, Dries van
Agt, was Minister of Justice when the September decision was made.
And the new Secretary of State for Justice was Mrs. Elberta Haars, a
lawyer and conservative Christian Democrat. Neither Van Agt nor
Haars would have any sympathy for me. How, I asked myself, could
my luck be so bad?

The day the new coalition assumed power, Chris and Phil left for
Virginia to spend the year-end holidays with Janet. Because we didn't
know how long I could remain in Holland, I told them they might
have to stay with their mother for the spring school term while I
looked for another place to live. But we would see. If I was lucky and

could go to the Council of State, they could come back and continue school in Amsterdam.

Prior to the hearing, several journalists came out with articles on a behind-the-scenes struggle over my presence in the Netherlands. Senior civil servants in both the Ministries of Justice and Foreign Affairs had opposed my acceptance on deportation from Britain. But Max van der Stoel, the Foreign Minister, and Henk Zeevalking had overruled them.

During the summer after my arrival the civil servants seized on the *Levelier* article and my comments on the data bank to create a case against me. Max Wendt, Albert Mulder's executioner, told a reporter that I should have avoided "politically sticky issues" and refrained from activities "directed against a particular country."

For Wendt the index project was not just a CIA affair but was also "directed against the British, Germans, Dutch and French." Other Justice officials suggested intervention by the CIA when they admitted that while there were no government-to-government complaints about me, there had been "service-to-service" complaints.

Harry van den Bergh agreed to be a witness at the hearing, as did Hendrick van Niftrik, the General Secretary of the journalists' union. But the person who could have helped the most, Zeevalking, refused. His testimony was extremely important because the Justice Ministry had meanwhile refused our second case, the request for extension beyond November 30. He would have been able to argue that the reasons for his September decision were insufficient to refuse renewal and that his intention was to extend. None of us could understand why he refused, but he seemed to be under extraordinary pressure not to appear before the Advisory Committee.

The hearing was set for ten A.M. at a Justice Ministry building in The Hague. During the drive from Amsterdam, Willem filled me in on the "independent" committee members. The chairman would be a Mr. Rosen Jacobson, Vice-President of the Court of Appeal in The Hague and a leading figure on aliens law. He normally heard politically sensitive cases and we could expect a certain arrogance and condescension from him. The same from Mrs. Barendsen-Cleveringa, a lawyer and judge. The third panel member would be F.J. Willems, a conservative former trade union official.

Not much different from Britain, I told Willem. All establishment figures to make it look "serious and fair."

This time there was no "neutral" club, no trappings of empire, no

"Ladies Room." Just an ugly modern office building. A professional interpreter was waiting for us outside the hearing room. Less than five minutes after the hour we were shown into a fairly spacious, sterile-looking room where grey tables were arranged to form a square.

Committee members were seated on one side, backs to the windows, and we were placed opposite them with our backs to the door. The committee secretary, a man, was on the left, along with the transcriber, a woman. On the right sat a representative of the Foreign Ministry, a man named Simons, and to his side sat two representatives of the Ministry of Justice: a woman named Pos and the famous Mr. Wendt.

After introductions Jacobson began a little speech which he directed at me with intentionally aggressive tones. As he spoke, the interpreter sitting next to me translated in a low voice. "Mr. Agee, there is something I believe I should clarify for you at the beginning of this hearing. You may not know it, but here in the Netherlands we have a history, more than eight hundred years, of fighting against the sea. Even now you probably will find yourself below the level of the sea. Our experience has made us a free and independent land. . . ."

As I listened I couldn't repress a slight grin. Shit, I thought, this guy should be a tourist guide on an Amsterdam canal boat. But he quickly came to the point: "I have read various statements by you that the CIA is behind certain measures taken against you. I would like to know whether you now think that the CIA is present in this room or will have any influence on the findings of this committee."

I looked at Willem, and he too had a slight, quizzical smile on his face. For a second I thought I should offer to check the room for bugs, but I decided to play the game. "Well, no, I suppose not, I certainly hope not. But I did read just recently that during those eight hundred years you've been just able to hold even with the sea. Nothing lost, nothing gained. Hope it doesn't get any worse than that."

From Jacobson's introductory remarks on, everything he and the other committee members said showed hostility and disapproval of me and my work. Far from being "neutral" advisers, the three committee members took positions as accusatory as the Foreign and Justice Ministries' representatives. I didn't have the slightest doubt that they too wanted me out of the country.

Jacobson told me why I was there, reviewed the facts of the case, and started asking questions about why I wanted to live in Holland and for how long. He returned to my allegations of CIA influence, citing a statement I made on VPRO radio a few days before. Luckily I had brought along a copy of the statement, and I gave it to the interpreter who read it in Dutch.

I had indeed said I thought the CIA had convinced the security services in Britain, France, and now Holland that I was a threat to their security. Jacobson also asked if since coming to Holland I had declared that Merlyn Rees had it all wrong if he thought he could stop my work. That was obviously from the *Leveller* article. I answered that I hadn't said it precisely that way, but one could give my words that interpretation.

Jacobson then asked about the data bank, and I told them what it was all about: an idea in which people in many countries, above all the United States, were interested. It would *not* be done in Holland, and if it ever got going I would probably be an adviser.

Jacobson turned the discussion to the "conditions" contained in the letter from the Embassy in London acknowledging that I could go to Holland, i.e., that I was not allowed to engage in any activity which would endanger the public order or the national security, including the good relations of the Netherlands with other countries.

I said I saw no way the *Leveller* article or the data bank could violate those conditions. Jacobson admitted that certain activities, taken separately, were not actual dangers, but then he took off on a fantasy flight about "potential danger," "actual danger," and my "intentions."

Willems, the former trade union man, said that he could imagine my activities were highly irritating to American authorities. Wasn't that enough reason, he asked, that I shouldn't be allowed to continue in Holland? I said a statement like that goes against all the human rights conventions. and so it went, with occasional interjections against me by Wendt and Simons.

Van Bennekom eventually turned the subject to our witnesses and asked that the committee hear van den Bergh and van Niftrik, adding that we had asked Zeevalking to appear but he had refused.

Harry came in first. He related the history of his intervention on my behalf, but his most important remarks were on conversations he had with Zeevalking and Max van der Stoel, the former Foreign Minister. Zeevalking, Harry emphasized, intended from the beginning to give me a year's residence. But because of opposition within the Ministry of Justice he compromised on three months with possibility for extensions. He would have extended my residence permit beyond November 30 even after he knew about the *Leveller* article.

As for the Foreign Minister, after he had initially told Harry that he

knew of no damage to Holland's foreign affairs, he later said that the
Leveller article had caused problems. When Harry asked how, van
der Stoel would only say that a member of the British Parliament had
commented on it, but he would not say more. Still, van der Stoel
confirmed to Harry that no government had complained about my activities, that the article was the only problem, and that since September nothing new had arisen.

At one point the Foreign Ministry representative, Simons, interrupted to dispute Harry's interpretation of van der Stoel's remarks.
Simons went on to say that the then Prime Minister, Joop den Uyl,
had intervened early on with Zeevalking to get permission for me to
go to Holland and asked if any other Labour Party people had done
the same. The mention of the former Prime Minister's intervention
clearly irritated Jacobson, but before he could change the subject
Harry named two other Labour members of Parliament who also intervened.

I sat there listening as my interpreter struggled with all the who-
said-what-to-whom, and wondering if it all mattered. Harry certainly
was trying to show that someone had changed the intention behind
the September decision. And even the Foreign Minister was vague
about damage by the *Leveller* article. But the attitudes of Jacobson
and the others, everybody in the room except my team, were so hostile that I felt we were arguing with people whose minds were already
made up. As in Britain I was sitting through another farce, giving it
respectability, and giving myself false hopes.

When Harry left, Hendrik van Niftrik came in. He said the Dutch
journalists' union took a serious view of my case because the *Leveller*
article seemed to be the cause of the trouble. The question of principle involved was whether freedom of the press applied to everyone in
Holland, foreigners included, and refusal to renew my residence permit for something I wrote violated this principle. If I were forced to
leave Holland all other foreign journalists would have to work under
the constant fear that the same could happen to them for writing
something displeasing to the government. Other countries might begin treating Dutch journalists the same way, and even Dutch journalists working in Holland would be threatened. He closed by saying the
union strongly urged that the importance of the case required consideration by the Council of State.

After van Niftrik left, Willem said we wanted answers to some
specific questions. According to the press, a Ministry of Justice
spokesman said that friendly countries had complained about me.

Which ones? Simons, on behalf of the Foreign Ministry, said none as far as he knew. Wendt didn't know of any either—or the grounds for the spokesman's statement. So there we had it: no complaints.

Willem went on to attack the vagueness of both the original conditions and the September decision. But Wendt came back to the two reasons: first, I had written an article insulting to England, and second, I had given a press conference in Brussels. For him those were activities that could not be tolerated of any foreigner. Willem asked if the committee had been asked to handle my case quickly, to which Jacobson, after first evading the question, replied that indeed they were giving priority to my case to keep within the three-month deadline.

Willem asked the committee to advise the State Secretary that the issues in my case were too important to be decided by decree and that she should delay her decision until after the deadline so that we could go to the Council of State. He proceeded with a long defense statement.

The only concrete fact stated in the September decision was that I was expelled from France, hardly a disruption in Dutch foreign relations. No concrete allegation that I had violated the conditions had been made. Nothing to that effect was in the evidence file. Exactly when, he asked, did my offense occur? Even van der Stoel, who said the *Leveller* article disrupted foreign relations, did not say how or when.

Simons interrupted to compare my activities with the drug problem in Holland. Just as the country had become known for a "permissive" attitude toward drugs, and therefore had to impose restraints, so also van der Stoel must have concluded that the country could not be "permissive" with respect to Agee and the country's foreign relations. If Agee had kept quiet there would have been no problem. Then he added: "We had hoped that Mr. Agee would improve his life when he came here."

As the interpreter finished with Simons's remarks I was caught between shouting an insult or laughing. This clown is nuts, I thought, comparing me to the drug problem. Improve my life? Like I was some reprobate? A sinner in need of reform? A juvenile delinquent? Like Holland was a halfway house for a criminal released on probation? Before I could react Willem went on, and I thought, hell, the guy's out of his mind. Willem discussed the Scherer questionnaire, pointed out that no intelligence agents were named in the *Leveller* article, and repeated that the data bank does not exist and would not be established in Holland. He passed a copy of my December 6 press statement with Scherer's questions and my answers.

At that point we had been going for well over two hours, and Jacobson said he wanted to consider an adjournment. He asked all but the committee to leave the room. Ten minutes later he called us back and announced that we would reconvene at two P.M. on Thursday, December 22.

That afternoon Willem and I had a press conference at which we described what had happened in the hearing, the vagueness of the charges against me, and our continuing inability to discover exactly what in the *Leveller* article had disrupted Holland's foreign relations. We were still in the dark, but I said I thought we were in a good position because the case against me, as it came out in the hearing, was so weak. Afterwards Willem said he would try to get Max van der Stoel to appear as a witness on Thursday. As Foreign Minister at the time of the *Leveller* article and my Brussels press conference, he was the one person who could clarify the damage-to-foreign-relations charge.

The Amsterdam apartment was empty now except for me. Angela had gone to Cambridge to spend the holidays, and Rodney went to London. I called friends in London who told me of their protest picket of the Dutch Embassy that day. Then I called Giselle to tell her of the hearing and my delay in going to Hamburg to spend Christmas with her and Therese. Thinking the hearing would be over in one day, I had made reservations for Tuesday. Now I would change them for Thursday night after the second session.

How do I feel? "I can't wait to get to Hamburg and forget about this mess. Improve my life—that's what I have to do."

Van der Stoel refused Willem's request to testify, pleading lamely that he no longer had access to the files and that he could say no more than the representative of the Foreign Ministry. No more than Simons, the reformer? Of course he could. Like Zeevalking's refusal, we were mystified: did they want to avoid testifying for me? Or against me? At Willem's suggestion I prepared copies of the statements Sean MacBride and Ramsey Clark made at the British appeal hearings, together with Cedric Thornberry's petition to the European Human Rights Commission, for submission to the committee.

The theater and cast were the same as we started the second performance. At Jacobson's request Willem told the story of what had happened with Scherer. Wendt confirmed the facts, adding that Mulder had simply wanted "a little more information" before the hearing. Jacobson pointed out that the law required me to answer questions, and Willem responded that the secrecy procedure was irregular. I had made my answers public and would answer any other questions the committee wanted to ask.

Willem then went point by point through our arguments. Refusal by Zeevalking and van der Stoel to testify handicapped our appeal, and evidence by Harry van den Burgh was in conflict with the Justice and Foreign Ministries. Moreover, my second case—the request for extension from November 30—merited a separate committee hearing after we appealed. All of this meant the committee should delay its advice, and my case should go to the Council of State.

Willem passed to Jacobson our additional documentation and went on, arguing that my writing was protected by the European Convention on Human Rights. He also cited legal experts on "public order" and said publication of an article and a press conference, both outside Holland, could hardly disturb tranquillity inside the country. As for my having violated "conditions," the onus was on the government to make them specific, and in any case the *Leveller* article was no grounds for refusing extension of residence.

Jacobson interrupted with the opinion that the article was a sharp personal attack against a decision-maker in England. I thought: Rees, that's it, my reference to Rees. Jacobson mentioned him during the first session. I found the article in my papers and there it was: "Who said deportation was a punishment? Must have been Merlyn Rees quoting from a security services manual. Who said deportation would stop anything? Rees again, but only in his dreams." That's the offending phrase? That's sarcasm. How ridiculous, I thought.

I was about to comment on that passage when Jacobson looked my way and said he understood that after Watergate and Chile much criticism of government had occurred in the United States, especially against the CIA. Why didn't I want to get on the bandwagon there? I outlined the injunction problem and said I wanted to continue writing a while longer without censorship. Then I criticized the clippings in the evidence file from the British press and said I had plenty of approving press comment.

As an example I passed Jacobson a copy of Gabriel Garcia Marquez's review of *Inside the Company* from the *New York Review of Books*. Jacobson said I was putting too much value on the clippings. Did I have any concrete evidence to add? Concrete evidence? That's what we expected from Wendt and Simons. Nothing concrete on my breaking "conditions" had come up, only ideas and possibilities.

After more discussion, Willem told Jacobson that we wanted to be present when Simons and Wendt made their formal presentations on behalf of their Ministries. He refused, thanked us all for our help, and asked us to leave. As we walked away I told Willem I had the same feeling after the hearings in London. Vague, unsubstantiated allegations, flimsy pretexts, a charade for appeal hearings, and no evidence against me.

We talked again to reporters and headed back to Amsterdam. Jacobson and the others went out of my mind like a light turned off. I had only one thought and that was to get on that plane for Hamburg.

XI

Codeword "Brown as a Berry"

I was laying my passport on the shelf in front of the immigration officer at Schiphol when he said, "Hello, Mr. Agee. Been reading about your case. May I see your ticket?"

"Sure." I gave him the ticket, wondering if he had orders to see if I was using my own name or an alias for travel. He kept them both for a while, looking down at his desk which I couldn't see. I supposed he was putting them on some kind of video system for copy or computer input.

He returned the passport and ticket saying, "Thank you. Have a nice trip."

As the plane rose in the black sky I gave a sigh of relief. New Year's Eve and my flight to Jamaica were a whole week away. I could spend at least five days in Hamburg with Giselle, Therese and their friends, forgetting at least for now my struggle to stay in Holland. Giselle would still be at the theater when we landed, but after tomorrow's performance she would have four or five days free. Her flatmate, Mi-

247

chael, had already gotten a Christmas tree, and tonight a group of friends were coming over to decorate it. I couldn't wait to get off the plane and into a taxi.

As I rode on the bus to the terminal I had second thoughts about passport control. Expulsion from France had made me wonder, every time I travelled, when the "invisible hand" would strike again. My heart was racing as I handed over my passport, and when the officer looked at it and picked up the telephone, it sunk like a stone in water. Oh no, it can't be, it just can't be. Routine, just routine, it has to be. But it wasn't.

He put down the phone, came out of the booth, and led me to a chair on the side. He said I had to wait there. I asked what the trouble was. He said someone was coming to see me. What about? You're not allowed to enter the country. Oh my god, no, no, it can't be. God-damned bastards, they've done it again.

I looked at my watch. It was just seven P.M. Giselle wouldn't be home for a couple of hours, but Therese would probably be there. Wonder if they'll let me make a telephone call. I sat in gloom for fifteen or twenty minutes until a Lufthansa supervisor arrived and told me I had to stay in Border Police custody. There was nothing Lufthansa could do, and they didn't know the reason.

I gave him Giselle's telephone number and asked him to call, tell anyone who answered what was happening, and say I would call as soon as they would let me. A while later a policeman took me to offices somewhere up in the terminal, made me take off my clothes, including my shoes, gave them all back to me, and told me to wait. Could I call a lawyer? No. My friends in Hamburg? No. Just wait.

I sat thinking about these West German Border Police. Some-where, probably not in the CIA, I had read that the Agency set them up in the early 1950's as the first quasi-military unit in postwar West Germany. They were supposed to be the first line of defense against "communism, terrorism and subversion." And it was one of their elite units that stormed the hijacked airliner in Somalia last fall. The Agen-cy's liaison with this service must still be pretty good—all they had to do was ask.

About a quarter to nine a policeman told me I would be sent out of the country the next morning.

"Why? What's the problem?"

"You're not allowed in the Federal Republic."

"But what's the reason?"

"We don't know, your name is on the list. Where do you want to go?"

"Amsterdam, I guess."

"Next flight is at seven tomorrow morning. You will spend the night in the Hamburg central prison."

"Can I call a lawyer?"

"No, but if you wish we will advise the U.S. Consulate here that you are in custody."

"No, I don't want anything to do with them."

He turned me over to three others who put me in the back of a VW minibus. Policemen got in on either side of me, and we started off toward the city. About fifteen minutes later, as I looked out the window, I noticed something familiar. Shit, this is Hallerplatz—there's Giselle's apartment. Are these bastards just trying to make me feel worse? We kept on going, eventually turned into a drive, and stopped before a steel door in a red brick wall that must have been two stories high.

The door opened, we drove to a building entrance, got out and went to "reception." It was like Boulogne: they took everything including belt and shoe laces, let me try some cold leftover soup, and then an attendant marched me down a corridor. Along the way I looked up through the round, five-story light well with its railings and barred doors all around the circle. Down some steps to get a sheet and blanket, through another hallway, and into a small cell with thick wooden door and small peep window. First thing I noticed was the barred window at the rear. The bottom of the window was level with the ground outside, revealing that I was in a kind of semi-basement.

I sat on the bed as the door closed, looked around at the walls, the toilet, the old radiator, and concluded the prison was probably built in the thirties by the Nazis.

It was not quite nine-thirty. Giselle would have just come home, and if the Lufthansa man had called she would know what happened. Maybe she and Therese would call a lawyer, maybe get me out of here. I began to worry about her and Michael and whether, since I was coming to visit them, this would cause them any problems. Goddamned CIA pigs. Why now? I've been in this country half a dozen times without a problem. Why now, just when I come to spend Christmas with friends?

Eventually I turned out the light, lay down on the sheet and covered up with the blanket. I must have just dozed off when the light went on and a key went in the door. It was after eleven. Maybe Giselle had come to get me out, I thought excitedly.

The attendant said something I couldn't understand, but it was obvious he wanted me to follow him. Saved! I'm getting out of this hole!

I put on my shoes in a flash and fell in behind the jailer. I was smiling all the way as I imagined Giselle and Therese waiting for me in the "reception room." We got to the area with the cold soup, and there sitting at a table nearby were a grey-haired man and a woman about my age.

As he stood and introduced himself my spirits sank. "I'm John Peters of the American Consulate, and this is Miss Hurley. We were informed by the German authorities that you were here, and we've come to see if you have any problems. We understand you are flying back to Amsterdam in the morning."

"Any problems? Sure I've got problems. I want to get out of here, and I want to know why I was stopped. I also . . ."

The woman interrupted: "Phil, don't you remember me? I'm Sharon Hurley. We were in the Embassy in Quito at the same time."

I'd hardly noticed her, but sure enough, there in front of me was the Deputy Chief of Mission's secretary whose desk had been a minute's walk down the hall from mine. "Well, what a surprise. How are you? Didn't think I'd run into you again in a place like this. What can you do to get me out?"

"I'm fine," she said. "I've been all over since Quito. Buenos Aires, Moscow, lots of different posts."

Peters broke in: "There's nothing we can do to get you out tonight. It's a German matter. We understand it was a decision in Bonn, but that's all we know. We're just here to see that you have humane treatment."

"Look," I said, "I came here to see friends, to spend Christmas with them. Humane treatment would allow that. Which reminds me: I want you to know that the people I came to visit don't have the slightest participation in anything I do with respect to writing or other work. They're just friends and ought not to have any problems with the Germans because of me."

"I'm sure they won't. Do you have any complaints about the way you are being treated.?"

"Goddamned right I do, starting with being in this place. I didn't ask them to notify you. I wanted to call a lawyer, but they wouldn't let me. Don't I have that right?"

"We have a treaty under which the authorities have to notify the Consulate when an American is arrested. That's why we came."

By now my frustration was turning to anger. "Mr. Peters, the Germans don't have to notify the Americans that I was arrested. Maybe you didn't know it, but the CIA office in your Consulate did. The whole thing was planned. They knew of my plan to come here from my telephone in Amsterdam and the airlines reservations computer. The Dutch confirmed my departure. The passport control people here were waiting for me. Don't give me this stuff about 'being notified.' "

He didn't respond. I talked to Sharon a little more, and twenty minutes after it started the conversation ended. The jailer took me back to my cell where I lay back down on the cot.

Sharon Hurley. Ecuador. How I loved that country. Snow-capped volcanoes and eternal Andean springtime. The bullfight the day Janet and I arrived. The party afterwards with the President's nephew. Dancing at every party: the *pasa a calle, San Juanito, cumbia, mambo.* Our house with walled garden up on the hill. The panoramic view of Quito and Mount Pichincha beyond. Whole thunderstorms passing down the valley in front of us.

And the arrogance! God how we manipulated that country. Out with Velasco. Out with the Cubans. Out with Arosemena. In with the junta. Hundreds of arrests based on our lists. Drunk with secret power, that's what I was. Thank god, thank god I quit!

At about five-thirty the next morning, the jailer took me to "reception," made me sign a receipt for my money and other things, and put me in a room where another man was waiting. He was Yugoslav, spoke a little English, said he was being deported too. A half-hour later three border policemen arrived for me. The leader had grey hair, cut quite short, and barked German like he was Adolf Hitler himself. I calculated he was mid-fifties, which would mean twenties during the war. Probably a former Gestapo or S.S. man "rehabilitated" for the Border Police.

When he gave the word to leave I grabbed the handles of my bag, which was on top of a table. But as I pulled it away, turning, it knocked over a chair. Without stopping I walked in the direction of "Gestapo Gus" who suddenly burst with rage over the chair. I couldn't understand a word, but I knew it had to do with the chair. I kept on walking, acting like I didn't understand.

He grabbed me by the shoulders, turned me around, and marched me back to the chair. I stood there asking him a series of questions in English, as fast as I could make them up, while he ranted and blew saliva and sour breath in my face.

Then I decided I'd better placate this caricature of a World War II movie prison guard. I didn't want to miss that flight. I picked up the chair, pushed it with some force against the table, enough to aggravate him some more, and turned toward the exit. He went on shouting, now to the two junior officers, as we walked to the olive drab minibus. Back to the airport by a different route, not by Giselle's flat. One of the junior officers waited with me, then accompanied me on the bus to watch me get on board.

As I sat on the flight sipping coffee, I could imagine the glee among the CIA people who were in charge of closing all the doors in Europe to me. Britain, France, now West Germany, and probably Holland. They've got a system going, just as I suspected, where they alert the Station where I plan to travel, and that Station convinces its local security cronies not to let me in. They're doing all they can to make it impossible for me to continue living in Western Europe.

At Schiphol airport I hurried to the telephone in the transit lounge without going through passport control. It was only eight-thirty, and Giselle should still be at home. She was. Lufthansa had called, her friend Trixie called a lawyer, but there was nothing he could do.

If I wanted, she and Therese could come to Amsterdam for Christmas.

"Wonderful! Come as quick as you can!"

"Tomorrow morning," Giselle said, "because tonight there's a performance and the Christmas party at the director's flat. But we'll be on the early flight, the same one you took this morning."

"Terrific. Can't wait to see you."

I spent the rest of the day answering calls from reporters and phoning family and friends to tell them I was all right. The West German action was in all the newspapers because the government in Bonn had announced my arrest and intended expulsion as *persona non grata.*

No charge was made against me, and no reason given for my arrest.

I waited until it would be morning in Tampa before calling Dad and Nancy. They had already read the news.

"Yeah, I'm fine," I told them. "Why don't you meet me in Jamaica? I'll be there the first of January and finished with work in two weeks. Come on down. I'll tell you all about the inside of a Nazi prison. Great! See you next month."

Amsterdam was cold, damp and foggy during all five days that Giselle and Therese were there. On Christmas we visited with Gretta and Basker, and in the evening I forgot about the chicken in the oven. Looked like the coop burned down, but we ate it anyway.

The next day Giselle came up with a surprise. Therese had stayed in the flat reading, and we were having lunch at Leidseplein after walking around the Dam area. I was speculating that the Agency and the Germans had stopped me because they were listening to our telephone conversations and feared I might move to Hamburg if I lost the case here.

"The solution," she said, "is simple. We need the document."

"Document? What document?"

Giselle answered: "I think we should get married. The lawyer I talked to while you were in jail said that foreign workers in Germany have a right to have their families with them. If we were married I would have the right to have you with me in Hamburg."

I was so startled by her suggestion I couldn't respond. Marriage? Again?

"You're joking," I said.

She wasn't.

I began cataloging in my mind a list of reasons against the idea as Giselle went on.

"I don't want the document just for Germany. I want to live with you, forever, and that's the way it's going to be. I want to be legally married, and I won't let you go. I won't divorce you, and I won't let you divorce me. I want to make it as hard as possible for you to quit. You'll come to Hamburg and be dependent on my residence permit for yours. And I already checked: in Hamburg there's an International School with English instruction for your sons." She paused. "Don't you see how right I am?"

Eventually I responded. "You know I've told you all about the past, all the failures, so you know what a bad risk I am. You're still in your twenties with a career ahead of you, and I'm forty-three and being hounded off the planet. Being married to me would bring all these problems into your life and wouldn't help your career.

"You would never have a minute of privacy again. Every telephone call would be monitored, and apartments probably bugged—and these days they have video. I love you immensely, in so many ways, but you don't know how rough things can be. And Germany. I can't even say my name in German. That country gives me the creeps, especially after the other night."

"It doesn't have to be Germany," Giselle said. "I'm a good dancer. I know that. I've never had trouble getting a job, and I've been on stage since I was fourteen. But I put family first. You know that from how I missed the '72 Russia tour with Balanchine.

"Pat Neary, my old friend from City Ballet, is now director in Zurich, and she said I could go there anytime. They dance the

Balanchine ballets that I grew up on. If you have troubles, I'll take care of you. You know how strong I am. The question is, do you want me to be your wife? If you do, then we have to have the document."

On we went, discussing the pros and cons. By the time the tram brought us back to Olympiaplein we had decided. I would look into the requirements for marriage of foreigners in Amsterdam, and Giselle would contact Kurt Groenewold, a Hamburg lawyer and friend of Bill Schaap's, about my eventually going there. If I couldn't, then Giselle would talk to Pat Neary about joining the Zurich company. At least in Switzerland I'd never had any problems and didn't anticipate any. Therese's reaction was to wonder if either of us knew what we were getting into. Truth was, we didn't, but to us it really didn't matter.

Our decision brought an upswing in spirits that changed my whole outlook. For over a year, I'd taken one blow after another, seen one disillusion follow another. But this was different. We would find a place, somewhere, to start a life together. Even if I lost in Holland, as seemed likely, and even if I couldn't go to Germany, there had to be a country where Giselle could dance and I could do my work.

The prospect of that life brought me new confidence, new hope, and new determination. It was like spring had suddenly burst into my psyche after a hard winter.

As for Holland, Harry van den Bergh had not given up. In early January, after the year-end recess, he would take my case to the Parliament. He would submit a number of written questions to Mrs. Haars, the State Secretary for Justice, in order to show how lame the Ministry's pretexts were, i.e., the data bank idea and the *Leveller* article, to get confirmation that there had been no foreign complaints, and to get the reasons why the Ministry wanted to prevent me from going to the Council of State. Willem van Bennekom, for his part, was appealing the negative decision on my request for extension beyond 30 November which could mean another hearing before Rosen Jacobson and Co.

For my Jamaican trip, Larry Grant had asked the British Home Office for permission for me to change planes at Heathrow so that I could fly direct to Kingston. Joan Lestor, now Chair of the Labour Party, had made the same request of Merlyn Rees. But the Home Office answered that they understood there were other ways I could get to Jamaica and that an exclusion order against me was still in effect. So on New Year's Eve I got on a KLM flight to Curacao and the next day made a connection to Kingston.

Bill Schaap and Ellen Ray were already there. Within a couple of days Lou Wolf arrived with Elsie and Jim Wilcott and several other friends from the States. Elsie and Jim had both worked in the Agency, in the fifties and sixties, he as a finance officer and she as a secretary. Besides Washington, they had served in Tokyo and in the huge anti-Cuban Miami Station. After quitting the Agency in disgust, they settled in California and became active in progressive political movements. They wrote me of their Agency experience after *Inside the Company* was published, but this was our first meeting. Not surprisingly we spent long hours discussing the Agency and how to fight back.

As a group we decided to launch a new magazine which we would call the *Covert Action Information Bulletin*. Bill, Ellen and Lou would put it together in Washington, and Jim, Elsie and I would help with articles and advice. The most important financial supporters of the old *CounterSpy* had already pledged support for the new magazine, so the financing was nearly assured. The main focus would be on the Agency's covert action operations wherever we could find them, and whenever they surfaced in the "straight" press. We would also publish the names of CIA employees around the world in a "Naming Names" column which Lou would research in Washington.

We also worked on *Dirty Work: The CIA in Western Europe*. It so happened that Lyle Stuart, his friend (and later wife) Carole, and several of their friends were at that time vacationing at his estate on the north coast.

They invited us up for a day, and I had my first conversation with this man of most unusual background. He had started as a reporter in New York, knew Che Guevara in the fifties, turned *Mad* from a comic book into a magazine, helped to found the "Fair Play for Cuba Committee," and eventually became a millionaire publisher with books ranging from *The Anarchist Cookbook* to *The Sensuous Woman*.

During the fifties he had been called before the witch-hunting Senate Internal Security Committee. When they started the questioning by asking him why he had no lawyer with him, he replied that he wouldn't waste his lawyer's time. When one of the Senators raised his voice, Stuart told him, "Don't shout at me, Senator. You don't frighten me. I eat Senators for breakfast."

Stuart wanted *Dirty Work* as soon as we could get it ready, and he said he would publish as many books as I could write.

The new magazine and *Dirty Work* naturally brought up the possi-

bility that I could return to the States to help promote them. Everyone thought I should go, and again I decided I could live with the
censorship injunction. But it would mean I could not have a major
role in the index and *Who's Who* project if I wanted to avoid contempt proceedings. Before I went back, though, I would have several
questions to resolve: the deportation proceedings in Holland, Giselle
and marriage, and my residence with her in Hamburg. Maybe I could
do a speaking tour in April or May, but it would depend on how these
other matters developed.

About ten days after arriving in Jamaica I called Willem for the latest news on my appeal. It was bad. The Advisory Committee had
ruled unanimously against me, and Mrs. Haars's final decision would
be announced any day. Our other appeal would be rejected summarily with reference to the first one. At Schiphol on return they might
give me a notice allowing just two weeks to pack and leave, and I'd
better start arranging where I wanted to go.

While in Kingston I saw many of the people who were involved in
my earlier fateful trip to Jamaica. They had all seen the junk published by Moss and others whose "great conspiracy" looked more ridiculous than ever.

After the others left, I stayed on. Dad and Nancy, whom I hadn't
seen for nearly three years, flew to Montego Bay, and we spent several days catching up on news and exploring the north coast from our
cottage at Runaway Bay. They thought it odd that I should have a
24-hour security escort from the police Special Branch, but I explained it wasn't my decision. Violence was continuing, and the government wasn't taking any chances.

One day we were eating lunch at the Casa Maria Hotel, not far
from Lyle's place, when a bus with a British government delegation
and their Jamaican hosts arrived. Suddenly I spotted Judith Hart in
the crowd. She was again England's Minister of Overseas Development and on an official tour of Caribbean countries.

We chatted about my problems in Holland, and I told her I might
need to find a country that would take me in less than a month. I had
already written to friends in Malta, and they replied that I should go
and discuss the matter there. Judith said she would telephone Dom
Mintoff on return to London, and she didn't think I would have a
problem.

From Montego Bay we started our separate journeys home. With
flight changes in Curacao and Caracas it took me thirty hours to get
back to Amsterdam. It was my birthday, and I fully expected greet-

ings at passport control: a notice to leave within fifteen days. But no, they let me pass unmolested. I called Willem and Harry. Their news was encouraging. Harry had succeeded in getting the Parliamentary Commission on Justice to schedule a discussion of my case. It was set for January 24, just five days away and one day before the ninety-day limit for automatic access to the Council of State. Mrs. Haars had postponed her decision until after this meeting.

Willem, for his part, had discovered a Treaty of Friendship, Commerce and Navigation between the U.S. and Holland signed in 1956. The treaty provided among other things that nationals of each country resident in the other had to receive equal protection and could not be treated any less favorably than nationals of a third country. Since Dutch citizens resident in the U.S. had access to the courts in immigration as in other matters, I should have access to the Dutch equivalent, the Council of State.

On the morning of the Justice Commission meeting, which was to begin at three P.M., I met with Harry in the Parliament building to give him my memorandum on the data bank which I emphasized was still only in the idea stage. He had one particularly good piece of news. Joop den Uyl, the Labour Party leader and former Prime Minister, was a member of the three-man Commission for Intelligence and Security Services. He had asked the BVD, Holland's principal security service, if they had information that I was a threat to Dutch security. They answered that in my case there was "no security risk."

"Wonderful," I said to Harry. "That puts to rest Rees's slanders because the British, Dutch and American services work so closely. It's proof that the 'Soviet-Cuban agent' charge is a lie because if any evidence existed the BVD would have it."

Harry said he would mention this in the Justice Commission hearing.

Harry also had Haars's answers to his Parliamentary questions, and it was clear that she still intended to prevent me from going to the Council of State. Athough she confirmed that no foreign complaints had occurred, she insisted that my "intended activities" would cause damage to Dutch foreign relations. But she didn't say how.

According to Harry, the Ministry's position was still as vague as it was at the appeal hearing, and he thought we had a good chance of prevailing during the Commission meeting. He said there was no point in my attending, since I wouldn't understand anything. He would call me afterwards.

When Harry called that evening he was pleased. The discussion had gone on for nearly three hours. Haars had argued that my work was a threat to Dutch foreign relations, but she couldn't say how, much less how I had already damaged relations. Of the twenty-one Justice Commission members, not one had spoken out in support of her position. Everyone, Harry said, even members of Haars's CDA, had said my case should go to the Council of State because the details were unclear and it was full of confusion and contradiction. Haars surely would not go against the opinion of the Parliamentary Commission that oversees her own Ministry.

I went to bed that night believing I had at least won time enough for Giselle and me to be married and for us to resolve the question of where to live: maybe Germany, maybe even the States.

The first telephone call in the morning was from a reporter who wanted my comments on Haars's decision. Well, what did she decide? She upheld the earlier decision. No extension. A Justice Ministry spokesman said I would have to leave by the end of March.

I said I was disappointed and couldn't understand how she would ignore the opinion of the Parliamentary Commission, but I wanted to read the decision and would comment afterwards.

That problem was solved just after noon when a policeman brought me a copy for which I had to sign a receipt. The decision was five, single-spaced pages dated yesterday, the 24th. I couldn't read it, but I knew one thing. The Commission discussion had lasted until six P.M., and I could hardly imagine Wendt, Mulder and Haars laboring over the written decision until midnight. It meant the decision was already drawn up before the Commission discussion, and Haars hadn't the slightest intention of taking others' opinions into account.

Another charade.

I called Willem who said he would arrange a press conference for later, made a copy of the decision which I took to a translator, then went to Willem's office to hear what it said.

The main part of Haars's decision was the unanimous advice of the Advisory Committee, sixteen numbered paragraphs beginning with "Considering" and ending with thumbs down. Willem found the reasoning tortuous and bizarre. They said the original conditions were that I refrain from activities that "could" endanger the public order, whereas in fact the word "would" was used. For Willem "could" had a different and much wider meaning than "would." The *Leveller* article, they wrote, "could" damage Dutch foreign relations—nothing said that it did cause damage. Then an outright fabrication: "the organization of an institute for information on Dutch and/or foreign security services, with or without the use of a so-called data bank, endangers national security . . . this leads to the conclusion that the alien is a danger to public order and national security."

Willem commented that the reference to *Dutch* services was concocted to make the index project look dangerous to Holland. He went on: they wrote that Holland is densely populated and immigration is restricted to people doing things to benefit the country or with urgent humanitarian reasons.

"You're neither of these," he said. "In the end Haars accepts all the points made by the Advisory Committee and concludes that the data bank 'could' be detrimental to Dutch foreign relations. It's all semantic juggling."

"It's like Britain," I said. "Rees said I hurt their national security, but expelling me would not stop what I was doing. Here the same. The data bank wouldn't even be done in Holland, and expelling me wouldn't stop it, if it ever gets started. They state false grounds and then a solution, my expulsion, that in no way solves the problem they construct. Descartes had it all wrong. 'I *might* think, therefore I am.' "

At the press conference Willem did most of the talking.

I sat listening, then answered questions about how I felt about the situation, mostly disappointment. My thoughts were on Giselle. In two days she would be back in Amsterdam for a long weekend.

Like Willem, Harry van den Bergh didn't give up. With the backing of the Labour Party and some Liberals from the government coalition he tabled a motion for full parliamentary debate. It called on Haars to reconsider her decision and allow me access to the Council of State. The debate would be on the afternoon of February 2, just one week away. Before that Harry wanted me to speak with a number of Liberal and Christian Democratic M.P.'s to clarify the *Leveller* article and the index project.

With Willem's discovery of the U.S.-Netherlands Friendship Treaty, I wondered about other countries. At the U.S. Consulate in Amsterdam I found that the United States had similar treaties with West Germany and France. They provided explicitly that in both Boulogne and Hamburg I should have been informed of the reasons for my arrest and the charges against me, and I should have had access to a lawyer. When I wrote to Peters at the Hamburg Consulate about this, he responded that it was not a matter for them. I should contact the West German Consulate in Amsterdam. So much for treaties and the governments that ignore them.

Giselle brought news of the legal situation in Germany. Kurt Groenewold was not able to handle my case because he was about to go on trial for his work in defending members of the Red Army Fraction. His partner, Petra Rogge, was expecting to be indicted any time for similar offenses. In fact some thirty lawyers involved in the various RAF trials were facing charges for, in effect, having conducted effective defenses.

Kurt in particular was charged with having helped his clients maintain their "identity." But Kurt and Petra recommended other lawyers, friends who specialized in immigration matters, and they were on the case trying to find out why I was arrested in Hamburg.

The German question was going to take time, and I didn't want to wait until the end of March to decide where to go, assuming our last moves in Holland failed. So I arranged with friends in Malta to go there following the debate in Parliament to check the possibility for temporary residence after Holland.

Harry expected the vote on his motion to be close. Although Labour was the largest single party in the 150-seat Parliament, the Christian Democrats and Liberals together held 77 seats. Four smaller parties allied with Labour brought our "safe" total to 67, while four smaller right-wing parties accounted for the remaining six seats.

The key person was Annelien Kappeyne van de Coppello, Deputy Leader of the Liberals, who had argued against Haars at the Justice Commission meeting. If she could swing a few of the 28 Liberals our way we could win. Another possibility was Hans van den Broek, a Christian Democrat and also member of the Justice Commission. I spoke with both of them and with others M.P.'s the day before the debate, trying to convince them that the index project was only an idea and that the "would" to "could" to "is" reasoning was voodoo logic. I could hardly hurt the Netherlands if I stayed while the Council of State considered my case.

Ken and Margo came with me to The Hague to translate the debate. As we walked across the Binnenhof, the inner courtyard of the Parliament, with its stately 17th- and 18th-century buildings, I told them about my ancestor who had come to Holland as a refugee.

"Do you suppose he walked through here to offer his horse and sword to William of Orange?"

"No," Ken said, "he came through here to get his residence permit, but they found out he wanted to do a data bank on Louis IV's secret service. William said that endangered public order so he made your great-great join the army to keep him out of trouble. Now they punish by banishment."

An attendant showed us into the Public Gallery of the Second Chamber's main hall where a couple dozen M.P.'s were listening to a speaker going on about some economic issue. The rectangular hall seemed smaller than the House of Commons in London and in some ways more elegant. The walls and ceiling were white. Golden draperies hung in upper boxes, like in an opera house, and on the floor level in arches and doorways. Red carpeting covered the floor, but overall the dominant color was green. Chairs and benches were upholstered in green, and the writing tops of members' benches had green leather surfaces.

About half the thirty-odd gallery seats were occupied. Down to our right was the speaker's platform and chair and a rostrum just beyond. In the middle was a wooden enclosure with tables for stenographers. Labour and other opposition members had their benches below us, while the government parties were on the far side of the enclosure.

As two P.M. approached the benches began to fill. Harry came in with other Labour members, and Margo pointed out Haars, whom I had never seen. I had read her official biography, knew that she was about sixty-five, and had wondered what she had done during the Nazi occupation. Her biography jumped from 1937, when she became a lawyer at twenty-four, to 1950 when she became a member of the Utrecht provincial government. Holland had its share of collaborators during the war, but nobody seemed to know about Haars. After the war the Dutch swept the whole question under the rug in the interest of "national unity."

Harry was the first to speak. He began with the background of my case and how I had been permitted to come to Holland from Britain, the Zeevalking decision, the Advisory Committee hearings and the Justice Commission meeting. His principal point throughout was that my research and writing on the CIA was well known before I came, as was my intention to continue, and that these activities were protected, for me as for any Dutch national, by the constitutional right to freedom of expression.

He brought up the Friendship Treaty, pointing out that all EEC citizens have access to the Council of State, and that denying me access was discriminatory and in violation of the treaty.

After speaking for perhaps a half-hour Harry yielded the floor. The speaker who arose to defend Haars was Hans van den Broek. During our conversation the day before he had not been especially sympathetic, but I had no idea he was to lead the debate against me. He set out the familiar Haars position, but then he went into a discussion of the data bank and the dangers this would bring to CIA people, alleging that exposure had already caused one death and could cause more. Then he asserted that any former Dutch intelligence officer attempting to do in the U.S. what I was doing in Holland would have the same problems, but he wondered if it would cause such a storm of protest over there.

Eventually Harry brought up the question of damage to foreign relations, no complaints, and the difference between possible and actual damage. For thirty or forty minutes he and Ven den Broek argued various points back and forth. Other speakers joined in on our side. Then Annelien Kappeyne van de Coppello made a speech on the Liberals' position. Her main point was that my legal position was unclear and that the Council of State should consider the possible conflicts between Dutch aliens law and the Friendship Treaty.

Mrs. Haars finally stood up and tried to strengthen her arguments by mentioning Rees's charges against me in the British deportation. Harry and other Labour M.P.'s rebutted that trick which led Haars into Rees's old game. Ominously, she said state security prevented her from laying on the table the proof against me. She then went into the dangers represented by a public computerized data bank, which brought shouting about computers in general and the Justice Ministry's computer in particular. She said she was basically against computers, especially computers that give personal information about CIA people and endanger their lives.

As the various arguments went on, I sat listening as Margo and Ken alternated with the interpreting. Why, I wondered, didn't Haars or Van den Broek simply say the truth: the Netherlands is dependent on the CIA for foreign intelligence. They can be cut off if they don't take action against Agee. That's why he doesn't have the same rights as others in this country. But no, she went on as if the index project were already set up and about to open its doors to assassins and terrorists.

After several hours, with interjections from ten or fifteen M.P.'s, the Speaker called for summing up statements on Harry's motion. Harry, Van den Broek, Kappeyne van de Copello and others repeated their arguments. Haars hid behind the "public order" clause in the Friendship Treaty and insisted that an exception in my case would open the door for others, thus throwing an unacceptable case load on the Council of State.

But then the climax. Hein Roethof, a Labour M.P. who had spoken often, compared my case with safety on the highways. If for unclear reasons, he asked Haars, a particular car is a risk to traffic safety, would you not then find that all cars are a risk? She said no, and statements followed about getting rid of dangerous cars.

It had to end pretty quickly, but I hadn't expected more suspense. Instead of voting on the motion, the Speaker proposed that the vote be taken when Parliament convened the following week. Agreed.

"I'll be damned," I said to Ken and Margo. "Don't you find this Dutch way of doing things a little strange? In the appeal hearing they compared me with drug trafficking and now with highway safety. And no vote for five days."

"Yes," Margo said, "we have a national gift for rumination."

The day after the debate I flew to Malta and while there read of the vote. Several Christian Democrats and Liberals voted for me, but they weren't enough. We lost by eight votes, just about the difference between the government coalition and the Labour-dominated opposition. I was disappointed, but I certainly felt no shame.

The whole Labour Party had backed my right to go to the Council of State, and as a by-product it came out that Dutch security services admitted I was no danger to "national security." The CIA surely was active behind the scenes, perhaps with contacts in the Justice Ministry, but no government had formally protested my work. My last hope now was Willem's direct appeal to the Council of State under the Friendship Treaty.

The welcome I received in Malta helped cushion the loss in the Hague. Besides Judith Hart's intervention, I had help in Valetta from my friend Derek who had a business there. He was a former British intelligence officer and champion squash player who was married to a Greek. He despised the CIA because of its role in the 1967 coup in Greece and the seven-year fascist "Colonel's Regime" that followed. In fact he had worked in the underground resistance. Following publication of *Inside the Company* he contacted me to exchange experiences, and we met from time to time afterwards.

Derek opened all the necessary doors. Yes, I could come to live in Malta for as long or short a period as needed. Derek showed me all over the island, a simply fascinating place with palaces and castles and ruins dating back to the Crusades and even before. It would be a beautiful place to live, and I liked the people immediately. And no problem with schools for Chris and Phil. Only trouble was, no ballet company for Giselle. We would see what happened, but at least I had another country that would take me.

On my return I planned to stop in Rome for discussions with the producers of a film about the CIA. They had called me in Amsterdam about technical advice and promotional assistance. On the way to Malta I had changed planes in Rome but didn't have to show my passport because I remained in the transit lounge. I assumed the Agency was well aware of my travel plans from the telephone and reservations computers.

Now I was back at Fiumicino standing in line at passport control wondering if they were going to close out Italy too. As usual the knot formed in my stomach even though I could see that the officer wasn't checking the passports of people ahead of me against any list. I laid it on the counter, he looked at the name, and then he looked in his book. The counter was fairly low and narrow, and I could see my name in the book. Oh my God, not again. The officer looked up and said I had to sit in a chair over on the side.

I went over and sat down. Shit. Just like Hamburg. I wondered how much the Agency was paying its liaison contacts for this service. Well, too bad. I might have made a little money on that film. At least it's not yet noon, and I won't have to stay in a Rome jail overnight. Lots of flights out of here today. After all the passengers were gone, the officer called me over to his booth. He filled out a form, gave me my passport, and motioned me through.

This is crazy, I thought, as I hurried for my bag before he called me back. They're reporting my arrival but not stopping me. I took a deep breath of relief, got out of the airport terminal as fast as I could, and took a taxi into Rome.

The film was called *Covert Action*. Seemed odd, my giving technical assistance, because shooting was almost over. But then they told me the story. David Janssen was playing a former CIA officer who had written a sensational expose of the Agency. He was on the run in Athens and Rhodes, trying to write a second book, and Arthur Kennedy played the CIA Station Chief trying to catch him. Corinne Clery was the lady in the middle.

An American publicist had prepared promotional materials comparing the film to my life. Well, yeah, I told him, sounds a little familiar. Think I'd better get a lawyer. Through friends I met Giovanni Arnone, a specialist in film and performing arts contracts, and he began negotiations with the *Covert Action* producers. I would return in a few weeks if a contract went ahead. At Fiumicino passport control the officer stopped me, filled out another form, and passed me through.

Giselle's performance schedule was tight, but she managed a few days in Amsterdam in late February. We filled out forms and turned in documents at the Civil Registry, where the friendly, grandfatherly man with bright red face set nine A.M. on March 13 as our appointment at the Old Town Hall marriage bureau. He would perform the ceremony in English, and Gretta and Basker would be our witnesses. Later in the day Giselle would fly to Stuttgart for a performance, and I would fly to Rome to start work on *Covert Action*.

In early March the Council of State accepted my appeal under the Friendship Treaty but refused to order that I could stay until their decision. That was it. I had to go.

Eventually, I won my appeal to the Council of State. The decision was that under the Friendship Treaty I should have been allowed to stay until their decision. At the same time they ruled that the government indeed had the power to refuse extension of my residence permit.

The decision was a valuable precedent for me and every other American resident in countries having such treaties with the U.S. It recognized our right to a court appeal. No longer would we be at the mercy of administrative decrees. Moreover, every foreigner in Holland whose country of citizenship had similar treaties with the Netherlands would also have the right to remain while appealing to the Council of State. At last I won something, although the decision didn't help when I needed it most.

Three days before Giselle and I were to be married I was called to the Aliens Police. The officer showed me an official notification that I was to leave the Netherlands no later than March 31. He had similar notifications for Angela, Phil and Chris since our residence requests had all gone in together the previous summer. Angela at that moment was in Amsterdam to arrange a shipment of household effects back to Britain where, through Larry Grant, she was going to ask for political asylum. The officer said he wanted all the passports and our point and date of exit. We would get the passports back on departure.

I explained that the boys were already in the States while my mind raced ahead. What if they don't let Angela back into Britain? The political asylum plan is supposed to be secret, but if the British find out about it, they may stop her entering. I lied to the officer that Angela was in Britain and not coming back, even though I knew that from the telephone it was no secret she was in Amsterdam. God hope they don't coordinate so well, I thought. Then I told him I had to work in Rome for a week starting Monday and asked if I could bring the passport when I returned. He resisted but finally agreed.

Back in the flat Angela and I decided we should avoid the departure ceremony. If either of us were refused entry by another country and returned to Holland, the Dutch would then send her to Brazil and me to the U.S. I would not return from Rome, and she would leave as quickly as possible for London. In a whirlwind, and with help from Ken and Margo, we packed everything into tea chests in one day.

Angela got on the boat train for England. She called from Harwich. They'd let her in again. She was safe for a couple of years at least.

Monday morning at Old Town Hall we were in line behind a young "punk" couple and their friends, but soon enough Giselle and I, Basker and Gretta, Ken and Margo, and Therese and Karl took our places in the chapel-like wedding salon. The little red-faced man read to us our duties, I said "no" when I should have said "yes," and he corrected me. I said "yes," and we collected the Family Book and the seven copies of the marriage certificate that I'd ordered. If Giselle wanted "the document," she would have plenty for herself, the lawyers in Hamburg, the West German government and some to spare.

Our afternoon flights left Schiphol about the same time. Giselle would transfer in Frankfurt for Stuttgart, and my flight was direct to Rome. During the flight I had plenty to think about. If the Italians didn't let me in this time, I could either continue on to Malta, try Switzerland where I never had trouble, or return to Amsterdam where I had two weeks remaining.

If only Giselle could have come with me. She gave me a special feeling of stability and strength. But increasingly in recent months, as I faced the ups and downs of another resettlement without her presence, I was nervous and afraid of what would happen next. Our legal measures in Hamburg were moving at a snail's pace with no sign of when I'd get permission to go there. With the Netherlands episode now closed, I looked to the immediate future with no confidence or self-assurance. It was going to be a lonely, anguished and angry time.

At Fiumicino the passport control officer seemed to have been expecting me. As before, he made me wait, filled out the form, and let me through. Around midnight I called Giselle's hotel in Stuttgart knowing she would be back from her performance. She told a tale that nearly made me apoplectic.

At the Frankfurt airport she was walking toward passport control when a man tapped her on the shoulder, showed a badge, and asked for her passport. Obviously he was waiting for her and had a sufficient description to pick her out from the other passengers. He took her to an interrogation room where a woman police officer was waiting, and he asked to see her ticket.

"What were you doing in Amsterdam?" he asked, as he started searching her purse.

"I went to see friends."

But he found the Family Book and said accusingly: "You didn't tell me you went to Amsterdam to be married." He began a series of departures from the room, only to return with other questions. Obviously he was in conversation by telephone with some central office. "Your husband is not allowed to enter the Federal Republic. Tell me why, because the reason is blurred in the computer."

"We don't know the reason," Giselle answered.

"When is your husband coming to Germany?"

"When the decision is reversed."

He insisted, asking a number of times when I was coming, while at the same time saying I was not allowed to enter West Germany. Each time she answered that we were working with lawyers on the problem, and she didn't know. He went through everything in her purse, sticking his fingers in the stage makeup she was carrying.

He made her write my name as if she might not know whom she married, then asked her where was Takoma Park, my birthplace from the Family Book. She said somewhere in Florida, knowing I grew up there, but not knowing it was a suburb of Washington, D.C. He insisted still more that she say when I was coming, then left her with the policewoman who ordered her to remove all her clothes. As she stood there naked the woman went through everything, especially the lining of my old leather coat that Giselle was wearing. Eventually she dressed and they released her.

That was bad enough but not the end. While waiting for her onward flight Giselle ran into two American friends from the Stuttgart ballet who had been on tour in Israel. Eileen had had a nervous breakdown, and Billy was bringing her back to a hospital. When they got to Stuttgart they all stayed together, intending to share a taxi. Bad luck for Eileen. The customs police, who were waiting for Giselle, grabbed both her and Eileen—who was already frightened and disoriented—and took them to an inspection area. The police went carefully through their bags, purses and pockets. They stuck their fingers in makeup containers and wanted to know all about the jars of vitamins, the pain killers and the liniments.

Billy protested that Eileen was sick, but that didn't bother the police. The whole scene made Eileen all the more freaky, and when

Giselle asked what it was all about the police simply said, "We don't know. It's in the computer."

Guess what they missed, Giselle asked me. All that and they missed the little cellophane envelope with the white powder. It was in the pocket of your coat. Remember? The "food" for the roses Gretta gave me. If they had found that I'd still be in Frankfurt waiting for the analysis.

Small consolation. By the time Giselle finished the story I was livid, so angry I could sputter nothing more than "Nazis, fucking Nazi pigs." She had never had the slightest problem in West Germany, was not a political activist, and didn't use drugs other than what doctors prescribed for injuries. But now, because she had married me, they were giving her the treatment—probably in the hope she would get the message and leave.

As I ranted on about World War II having changed nothing, Giselle kept saying: don't worry, it was nothing. I couldn't understand it: she wasn't the least upset. After all, she said, didn't we expect this? Besides, you ought to hear the stories about people flying into New York—much worse than here.

That Frankfurt-Stuttgart episode set the stage for the weeks ahead. When I was alone, which was most of the time, I had the constant feeling that something unexpected and drastic was about to happen, some new blow that would make a bad situation worse.

There were signs that the Agency and its friends were still on my case. The gossip columnists, for example, ran stories that "Philip Agee has secretly married Giselle Roberge, an American ballet dancer," adding falsely that Amsterdam officials said I had asked that our wedding be kept confidential. When Giselle went to Luxembourg on tour a week after we were married, I called friends and asked them to see if the Belgians would let me in. They would, but fearing that somehow the Luxembourg authorities would stop me, I flew to Brussels and rented a car. Instead of using the super-highway I drove by secondary roads, eventually finding a farm road with no controls to make the border crossing.

Every week or two Giselle could get two or three days off. We had a "honeymoon" in Rome over Easter, and some weekends if she sprinted she could catch the Hamburg-Zurich sleeper train after a performance. I'd found a relatively cheap hotel in Zurich's "old town" with two topless go-go bars and wall-to-wall carpeting on the walls as well as the floors. They seemed to rent rooms by the hour at that hotel, but for us it got to be "home." We used lots of room service, visited with her friends in the Zurich Opera Ballet, saw movies, and fed the ducks along the lake.

Every time Giselle left I got instant palsy of the brain and fear of my own shadow. I was afraid to contact political friends in Zurich and Rome for fear that would be used as a pretext for action against me. It became like those months in Paris and London all over again. Giselle tried to help by bringing me a tape recorder and a pile of classical and rock cassettes, along with books by Dashiell Hammett, Lillian Hellman and Henry Miller. I played the music in the hotel but was too distraught to read.

Once she told me by phone not to worry if I felt paranoid. Some people, she said, are paranoid for no good reason—they're the sick ones. You've got plenty of reason, so don't worry. I certainly did have reason. One day I walked into my sleazy hotel in Rome, and the manager took me aside to tell me in a quiet, confidential tone that the secret police had come to check on me and had mentioned the kidnapping of Aldo Moro, the former Prime Minister and leader of the Christian Democrats. Oh, no, I thought, not *that* pretext. In gloom I assumed my arrest and expulsion were imminent, just a matter of time.

A few days later I saw an excited crowd around a news kiosk. I walked over and discovered that the Red Brigades had that morning delivered Moro's body in a car trunk. The news caused a national outcry approaching hysteria. I was due to meet Giselle two days later in Zurich, but almost in panic I decided to leave immediately. I rushed back to the hotel, packed as fast as I could, and caught a taxi for the airport. Halfway there we were stopped at a roadblock, but they let us through. There was another roadblock at the airport entrance but we got through that one too. The test would come at passport control when they checked my name against their book. With trembling hands I put my passport on the shelf. The officer looked at it, but for the first time didn't check the list. My god, with Moro, the roadblocks, and heightened security everywhere, he didn't check. Out of here, quick, get on the plane.

Those days I could be with Giselle were practically all I lived for. I had spent several days with David Janssen posing for promotional photographs, and with the *Covert Action* producers discussing a statement by me to open the film. But when I eventually saw an edited first version, I realized it was a terrible picture, with all sorts of gory special effects to salvage credibility. So it wasn't disappointing when my participation dwindled and eventually disappeared.

Most days I spent alone in my hotel trying with little success to write articles or the story for another CIA film. This was Ellen Ray's project. She had convinced Santiago Alvarez at the Cuban Film Institute to do a joint U.S.-Cuban production about a CIA attempt to destabilize a Caribbean government as they had in Jamaica. She wanted me to write the story, but in my state of mind I made scant progress.

After the Moro scare I stayed in Zurich. My Hamburg lawyers were being stonewalled by the border police and the Interior Ministry. A Bundestag Deputy, Klaus Thusing, asked formally why I was not allowed into the Federal Republic, but the State Secretary for the Interior Ministry would only say "state security," refused to give reasons, and referred to my expulsions from Britain and France. We could try legal steps "A, B and C," leading to a court appeal, but the whole matter would take a year or two before a decision. On a trip to Zurich Giselle told me our lawyers said the simplest and fastest way was for me to somehow get safely across the border and go to Hamburg. If I could stay there for two weeks without getting caught, the jurisdiction for my case would pass automatically from the authorities in Bonn to the Hamburg state government. The system, wherein each state government had its own aliens department, was part of the "decentralization" of Germany after the war.

I thought about that long and hard. If I did it that way, I would find myself again in a whirl of controversy, a legal battle, and a defense campaign. The very thought of going through that again made me go limp with despair. And my chances of winning? Article VI of the West German constitution gave explicit protection for families, and it had always been interpreted as giving foreign workers the right to have their families with them in West Germany. As a soloist at the Hamburg Staatsoper, Giselle was an employee of the state. Hamburg authorities would be ruling on the right of one of their own employees to have her husband with her. And that government was a Social Democratic-Liberal coalition. I might just have a chance.

In solitude I fantasized about how to get across the border. The Chilean solidarity people I knew in Denmark might be able to smuggle me on a fishing boat or yacht. And Margo had mentioned once in Amsterdam that she used to ride in a forest on the border between Holland and Germany. Maybe she could lead me over on horseback.

I asked my Zurich lawyer, Gian Andrea Danuser, to check on the "green border" between Switzerland and Germany, but anti-terrorist operations on both sides made that route too dangerous. In early May he went to Hamburg to discuss the matter with our lawyers there, and he came back convinced I should try to get across. I agreed. By now I was so desperate to be with Giselle I was ready to try anything.

I needed a residence permit somewhere, so that if I were caught I would not be sent to the U.S. Rather than return to Malta to solve this problem, I talked with Giovanni Arnone in Rome. He got me a contract with a Florence publisher for participation in a book on political repression in Argentina. With this he got a work permit and then a six-months residence permit.

How he got it I never knew, but at least I could now start planning. Lou Wolf was due in Zurich about May 20 for our final editing of *Dirty Work*. After that I would make my move, which at the time seemed like a real matter of life or death.

Giselle was in Zurich the weekend before Lou arrived. A few days earlier I had noticed what I was almost sure was a surveillance team following me. It so unnerved me I didn't leave the hotel room until Giselle arrived. To avoid any bugs in the room we walked along the lake discussing every possible way I might get by the German Border Police. She thought maybe I should just get on the train and hope. But nothing seemed hopeful. With no solution we headed back to the hotel. As I got the key I noticed for the first time a poster behind the reception desk. It looked old, and I must have passed it everyday for a month, but it flashed to the core of my brain. I put the key back and pulled Giselle back to the street.

"Did you see that tour poster behind the desk?"

"No," she answered, "what poster?"

"It's there! Six daily bus tours, one of them to Germany—an all-day tour through the Black Forest that ends back in Zurich. I'm going to ask Lou to take that tour. If they stay on the bus at the border, with no passport check, I'm taking the tour as soon as Lou and I are finished working."

I was almost breathless as I went on. "Look, we have to cover my disappearance from Zurich if I get across the border. They're watching me here and listening to us every day on your telephone. They know how desperate I am. If I disappear for two weeks they may start looking for me in Hamburg. We have to throw them off.

"I'll tell you what. If I decide to try it, I'll call you that morning early because the tour leaves about eight. I'll tell you I'm starting a trip without saying where to, like we're being discreet, and I'll say I'll miss you but I hope I'll be back in Zurich within two weeks, three at the most. And I'll say, 'but I'll come back looking brown as a berry.'

"This will mean Lou's passport wasn't checked, and I'm heading for Hamburg. That night you have to call Therese, lament that I've gone away a couple of weeks, and tell her I've gone to Cuba to help with preparations for the World Youth Festival coming up this summer. Since we didn't mention that I went to Cuba, maybe they'll think you're indiscreet by telling your mother, and they'll believe it."

Another idea came to mind. If Lou has time, I told Giselle, we'll rent a car in Zurich, in his name, and before the tour I'll find out where in the goddamned Black Forest we're having lunch. I'll tell Lou and he'll drive the car there. Then he and I will head straight for Hamburg. But in Hamburg I shouldn't go to your flat. Too dangerous if they start looking.

Giselle got out a pencil and wrote an address. "That's Vickie's and Richard's apartment. Remember them from the company? You met them in Luxembourg."

"Sure, I remember. The two Americans. Do you trust them to keep quiet? Our future is riding on this."

"Totally," Giselle said, "they're my best friends."

"All right, if I get there it'll be pretty late, but I'll ask Vickie to call you about anything innocuous and you'll know I'm there."

Lou arrived on a Saturday evening, but before I could think about *Dirty Work* I had to convince him to take the Black Forest tour. True friend that he was, he got on the bus Sunday morning at the Zurich opera house. It rained and rained as I sat in the hotel watching the hours go by. But Lou didn't get back when he should have. Another hour went by, and I couldn't imagine what had happened to him.

At last a knock at the door, and there stood Lou soaked from head to foot. I led him down the hallway to get away from my room and any possible bugs. The long ride had so numbed him that he forgot to get off the bus back at the opera and had ridden to a maintenance garage outside Zurich. For more than an hour he stood in the rain waiting for a bus back into town.

I couldn't stand it another minute. "Lou, Lou, what happened at the border?"

"Oh, nothing."

"What do you mean 'nothing'? Did they check the passports or didn't they?"

"No. The bus driver told us to get our passports ready, but instead of collecting them he got out, saying that if we're lucky the Germans won't check. He came back in a couple of minutes and drove on."

I couldn't suppress my excitement as we worked on the book that night and the next day. We rented a car, and Tuesday morning I called Giselle.

"I'll miss you, but I'll be brown as a berry when I get back." I put on my checkered "American tourist hat" and mirrored sun glasses, both bought just for this occasion, and drove with Lou to the opera house.

I asked the tour guide where we would be having lunch, found the tiny town on the map, and wrote out the bus's license number for Lou. He would follow the bus to the border crossing and bring me back if the Germans took me off. If I continued with the bus we would meet at lunchtime.

I slouched against a window as the door slammed and the bus pulled away. It was only thirty or forty minutes to the border crossing, a bridge over the Rhein, but that was enough to imagine a thousand times how shattering it would be when they caught me.

We got to the river, crossed the bridge, and stopped at a German customs post. The driver said he hoped we'd be lucky and not have to show passports, but he had to check with the border police. He got off, and for what was without doubt the eternity of my life, I waited, almost unable to breathe. The driver came back, said nonchalantly "Well, they let us go this time," and started the engine. I could have wept with joy right then and there, but I simply closed my eyes and thought: It's not true, it's not true, I didn't make it, did I? But off we went, and within a minute or two I was hiding a smile with my hand.

After finding Lou at the lunch stop I told the tour guide I felt ill and was driving back to Zurich with a friend. We drove to the nearest *autobahn* and headed north. Soon it was raining. Spring floods were all over the place, and we had to take one detour after another. Darkness came and the rain continued. Lou and I switched driving every hour or so because both of us were exhausted from the tension.

Lou suggested we spend the night somewhere along the way, but I couldn't think of stopping short of Hamburg. It was midnight when we crossed the Elbe and arrived at the main Hamburg railway station. I got out and hugged Lou. As he headed for a motel back down towards Hannover, I got into a taxi and gave the driver Vickie's and Richard's address.

They were still awake. Vickie telephoned Giselle and asked about a step in one of their ballets, and within fifteen minutes she was there. We celebrated with several rounds of vodka while I, in a hyper, nonstop speech, told the story of the trip. Vickie made us a bed on the floor, and Giselle covered me up.

I was an emotional basket case, still trembling when I went to sleep.

XII

Bieber Haus Blues

I spent my first morning in Hamburg peering around curtains for a glimpse of the street below, certain for all the world that a police car would soon arrive. Helicopters flying overhead only added to the tense and eerie atmosphere as I paced alone from window to window.

Giselle had gone to the theater with Vickie and Richard about nine with a note I had written to our lawyers, Hartmut Jacobi and Winfried Gunnemann. I asked to see either of them as soon as possible outside their offices. She would take the note when her rehearsal ended at one-thirty, then come to the apartment with food, and return to the theater about five for the evening rehearsal.

She had good news. Gunnemann would meet me at eight that night at a restaurant about twenty minutes' walk from the apartment. I started early but wished I had taken a taxi. It wasn't even close to getting dark, and my catastrophe complex was in full swing.

Twice I saw green-and-white police cars in the distance, and both times I turned around looking for doorways, hedges or trees where I could hide. But I made it to the restaurant. Gunnemann spotted me immediately, and I sat down to tell him how I got to Hamburg and to begin a list of questions. First, though, he said he had been wrong before. I had only to stay here secretly for one week, not two, in order for jurisdiction to pass from the Interior Ministry in Bonn to the Hamburg authorities. That means only six more days.

What if police arrive at the apartment looking for me? What should Giselle or our friends say? What if I get caught? What if police go to the theater or Giselle's flat to question her—what should she say? If I make it through the week, how soon can we relax after I make my application for a residence permit? Could police arrest me after the week is up? Would it make any difference if I stayed at Giselle's flat this week?

Gunnemann's answers to all my questions pointed to the same conclusion: I had to conceal my presence in Hamburg through May 30. If police approached Giselle, she should refer them to Gunnemann. But if they came to Vickie's and Richard's apartment there was no way anyone could prevent a search. If they found me, they would probably take me back to the Hamburg prison where I spent the night before, then give me the choice of where I wanted to be sent.

In this instance I would be allowed to call him and he would come to see me. Gunnemann gave me an application form for residence permit and asked me to deliver it to his office on May 31. After that the Border Police couldn't touch me. And in the event I were denied the residence permit, we could probably win on appeal, a process that could last a year or two. I wrote down his home address and telephone number, hoping I wouldn't need them.

I passed each day with curtains drawn and that old feeling of imminent disaster. Giselle brought me books and the *Herald Tribune* each day, but I could hardly concentrate. It was like Catherine's room in Paris: my only escape was crossword puzzles.

Giselle promised she was being careful to see whether anyone was following her from the theater, but how could she be sure. And the closer we got to May 30, the worse it would be if I were discovered. But apparently our "Cuba trip" ruse worked because nobody seemed to be looking for me in Hamburg.

The seventh day passed without incident. That night, May 30th, we celebrated in a restaurant with some of Giselle's dancer friends, and the next day I delivered the application form to Gunnemann and Hartmut Jacobi. They were as happy as I was, and they said the application would be filed right away.

Giselle's four-and-a-half-room flat was already pretty full when I moved there, with three other ballet dancers besides Giselle along with three cats. But Michael and his friend, Thomas, were leaving in a week for New York, and after the summer vacation Maderique would find another place to live. I began to call around to let people in Washington, Amsterdam, London, Paris, Zurich and other places know that I was safe in Hamburg. Then I sent Chris and Phil pre-paid tickets to fly over when school ended two weeks hence.

After they arrived we went regularly to see Giselle's performances, and the company voted her Mother of the Year for having produced an "instant family." As I had expected, she and the boys got along just fine—as if they'd known each other for a long time. It was not surprising, since Giselle was as close in age to them as she was to me, and she had no pretense to being anything more than a friend to them.

I had a long conversation with Kurt Groenewold and his law partner, Petra Rogge. They agreed with Gunnemann and Jacobi that I shouldn't attract publicity about being in Hamburg. No interviews about the legal situation and how I got here. Better simply to keep my head down and wait for the decision on my application.

After the flimsy arguments against me in Holland, I had no trouble accepting their advice. This time I wouldn't give anybody the slightest pretext for saying I was damaging diplomatic relations or threatening "public order."

It should have been a relaxing time, a relief from such a long period of tension and uncertainty, but it wasn't. The feeling persisted that something drastic had to happen, and I spent many hours reading with the door closed, unconsciously trying to isolate myself from the next calamity. My constant thought was a knock on the door and police taking me.

When I had to go to the Aliens Affairs Office at Bieber Haus for a stamp in my passport that would indicate I had applied for residence, I insisted that Giselle come with me just in case.

Even when Therese arrived, or when Larry Grant and Tony Gifford visited, I wouldn't go to the airport to meet them for fear of being arrested again. Not that I was totally paralyzed, but it took a huge effort to arrange such things as physical examinations for health insurance and a visit to the International School where Phil and Chris would study.

Toward the end of June I answered the telephone, and on the other end was a man speaking Spanish. He identified himself as Jose Martinez, the Press and Cultural Attaché of the Cuban Embassy in

Bonn. He had an invitation for me to the 11th World Festival of Youth and Students to be held in Havana in mid-summer. Could he come to see me tomorrow? Of course, I said, any time.

I put the telephone down thinking, oh shit, they're going to put a story out that I'm starting a revolutionary conspiracy with Cuba again. But the invitation was interesting. Six months earlier I had started correspondence with the National Union of Students in London on the possibility that I might go to the Festival as a member of the British delegation. Surely, I had thought, the Festival organizers would be interested in seminars or lectures on how the CIA works.

Martinez brought a letter of invitation for me and my family as "Guests of Honor" of the Festival with the instruction that we should contact the Cuban Embassy in Madrid for visas and tickets. He said that although the Festival was still a month away, the organizing committee wanted me to go as soon as possible to help with preparations for the central political activity, an International Tribunal against imperialism.

I told Martinez I considered the invitation a special honor, not only because it came from one of the countries most victimized by CIA-sponsored terrorism, but also because I myself had worked many years in operations against Cuba. I wanted very much to go, I told him, but I wanted to check first with my lawyers since my application for residence was pending. When I saw Winfried he said I would be taking a huge risk if I left the Federal Republic before I had a decision on my application. If the decision were negative and I was out of the country, I wouldn't have the right to re-enter and remain here while my appeal went forward. And that might take a couple of years.

Once again I faced a dilemma. Twenty thousand young people from all over the world were coming to Havana. I would have the chance to speak about the CIA with many of those delegations and also give testimony at the Tribunal. Should I pass up this opportunity and avoid the risk that Gunnemann mentioned? Days went by as I pondered what to do.

I hadn't been to Cuba for four years, and the friendly environment there would be a welcome relief. The Festival would coincide with Carnival in Havana, probably the most colorful and lively street parades in the Caribbean, and with the 25th anniversary of the assault on the Moncada barracks. It would also be the first possibility for Giselle and the boys to see Cuba. I talked to Bill, Ellen and Lou. They were all going, and so were Jim and Elsie Wilcott. The first is-

sue of the *Covert Action Information Bulletin* was almost ready, and
they hoped to make publicity for it at the Festival.

Phil and Chris were anxious to go, but Giselle worried, as I did,
that the Hamburg authorities would rule against us while we were
there. But this was the biggest event Cuba had ever put on. If they
wanted my help to make it a success, especially from the political
viewpoint, I was not going to refuse. Gunnemann agreed to write a
letter notifying the Border Police that I was travelling and asking that
they provide confirmation that I would not be harassed on my return.
Giselle's season would end a few days before the Festival began, so I
would go a week ahead of the opening and she and the boys would
follow.

On arrival in Havana the first thing I noticed was the way buildings
had been painted and the city cleaned up and decorated for the Festival. The Organizing Committee had a full schedule for me in the
week prior to the Festival: television, radio and press interviews,
and, most interesting, planning sessions for the Anti-Imperialist Tribunal.

This event would be in the former legislative palace which now
housed the National Academy of Sciences. From the street on the
fringes of "Old Havana" it looked like a scaled-down copy of the Capi-
tol in Washington. I remembered visiting this impressive building on
my first trip to Havana twenty-odd years before, but I didn't remember the formal debating chamber where the Tribunal would take
place. It was a semi-circle of benches and railings carved from mahog-
any and other fine woods with a raised speaker's platform in front.
Members of the Tribunal who would conduct the hearings would sit
on the Speaker platform while a rostrum for witnesses was set up on
the main floor of the chamber. Overhead and facing the speaker's dais
was a gallery where Festival delegations would be seated. All in all a
serious and dignified setting.

During the days before the Festival opening I sat with the Tribunal
organizers listening to some of the Cuban witnesses go through their
testimony to help the sound, film, video and other technical people
prepare, along with technicians for the simultaneous translation system for six or seven languages. It was immediately apparent that the
Cubans were putting together an impressive array of witnesses, some
of whom had worked many years as double agents against the CIA.
Listening and talking to them about their "CIA years" was simply
fascinating.

One was Manuel Hevia whom the CIA thought they had recruited in the early 1960's through a member of the Uruguayan diplomatic mission in Havana. But he reported the approach, and for the next eight years he "worked for the CIA" under direction of Cuban counter-intelligence. Early on he obtained asylum in the Uruguayan Embassy, got a safe conduct pass to the U.S., and went to Uruguay. In Montevideo he was hired by the USAID police training mission which I had helped set up in the mid-sixties, and he worked closely with the man who replaced me and others I knew. Hevia passed the Agency's lie detector test at one point, and later returned secretly to Cuba. His testimony would describe how Daniel Mitrione, the chief of the police training mission who was kidnapped and executed by Tupamaro revolutionaries, established a center in Montevideo for torture of political detainees.

Another witness was Nicolas Sirgado who "worked" ten years for the Agency but was also under Cuban control from the beginning. He was an official of the Cuban Ministry of Construction whose work required him to travel with some frequency to western countries. The Agency trained him in sophisticated communications systems and photography, and he passed the lie detector test three times. At one point the Agency used him to place a "state-of-the-art" bugging system, complete with micro-scrambler, in the office of the Executive Committee of the Cuban Council of Ministers.

The disinformation the Cubans sent to the CIA through Sirgado was considered so important that an officer I had known brought him a letter of thanks from Henry Kissinger, then Secretary of State, and a gold Rolex watch as a gift of appreciation. The operation ended just after the October 1976 sabotage of the Cuban airliner off Barbados. At the memorial ceremony in Havana's *Plaza de la Revolucion,* with nearly a million people present, Castro read the CIA's latest secret radio message to Sirgado. It asked for details on Castro's movements during an expected trip to Angola, details obviously needed for another assassination attempt. There were others: one had infiltrated the counter-revolutionary organizations in Miami for seven years, another had become a top leader of the Agency's "Rat Line" of logistics support to anti-government guerrillas in the early sixties. Another, who was not Cuban-controlled but was discovered and served a long prison term, was to have poisoned Castro at the Hotel Havana Libre, formerly the Hilton. And still another witness would be the Cuban Consul in Mexico City at the time of the Kennedy assassination. He would show how the CIA tried to pin the blame on Cuba through stories that Lee Harvey Oswald had received money from Cuba. Finally there was Rolando Cubelas, code-named AMLASH in the U.S. Senate Assassinations Report. His connection with the Agency had been discovered by Cuban security forces, and he was still serving a long prison term. He would testify by video recording on his role in assassination plots against Castro.

These were the main Cuban witnesses. Many others from around the world would testify during the morning and afternoon sessions of the week-long Festival. I gave my recommendations on Tribunal procedures and on improving the general topics for each session, and began preparing my own remarks. The point of the Tribunal was to show the effect on young people everywhere of the industrial world's efforts, led by the United States, to maintain control over the resources and people of the developing countries.

There was much more to the Festival. After Giselle and the boys arrived we went through the official program, and it was staggering. Day and night there were scores of activities: from solidarity meetings of all types, to folk dancing and art exhibits, sports events, bus tours to visit schools, factories, housing projects and other achievements of the Cuban revolution, to organized political discussions on every imaginable topic. Take your pick, I suggested, and take advantage of the organizing committee escorts—they'll get us wherever we want to go.

There were two other "Guests of Honor" from the U.S.: Saul Landau of the Institute for Policy Studies, and Michael Tigar, a Washington attorney. Both had worked relentlessly to bring out the truth behind the assassination of Orlando Letelier, including sponsorship by the Chilean secret police and the fact that the CIA and FBI probably knew of the plan and could have prevented it.

We were all on the same floor of the Havana Riviera Hotel, overlooking the sea and the Malecon, but each of us had so many separate activities we hardly had time to chat. On the night of the Carnival parade we watched from the hotel as one colorful float after another passed, music blasting and dancers shaking in phrenetic Afro-Caribbean rhythms. As far as one could see the Malecon was one gigantic *fiesta*, alive with movement against a background of bongo drums, *comparsas*, and eye-popping costumes.

The six of us involved in the *Covert Action Bulletin* organized a press conference at the Hotel Havana Libre the day before the Festival officially opened. Over a hundred journalists attended. We distributed copies of the first *Bulletin* and discussed what we hoped to achieve with the publication: a worldwide campaign to destabilize the CIA through exposure of its operations and personnel, thereby making it as difficult as possible for the Agency to carry out subversive operations against governments and political movements as they had in Chile.

At the press conference Bill Schaap described how we hoped to organize a worldwide group of researchers, tentatively to be called "CIA Watch," through which CIA officers and employees under diplomatic cover could be identified and exposed in the local press. Such exposures, Schaap said, would make it impossible for them to remain in the country of assignment, and constant rotations of personnel would disrupt their operations. Lou Wolf then went through the method of separating CIA people from "legitimate diplomats" and said he would be preparing a "Naming Names" column for each edition of the Bulletin.

We also had advance copies of *Dirty Work: The CIA in Western Europe* which would go on sale in September. Our final version was an anthology of some thirty-five articles on the Agency's European operations and an index giving biographic information and career histories of over 700 CIA employees who had served or were serving in Western Europe.

Lyle Stuart's hardcover edition was over 700 pages long and had a $25 price tag, but I didn't doubt that it would circulate widely and cause a sharp reaction from the CIA. In fact the Agency had written to Lyle two months before saying they had "learned that you may be prepared to publish a book entitled *Dirty Work*. It is our understanding that this book contains the names of many CIA employees, and we have some reason to believe that the author may himself be a former employee of CIA."

Without mentioning me by name, the letter went on to cite the court ruling in the Marchetti case upholding the Agency's right to censor the writings of former employees. Publication of the book, the Agency's General Counsel wrote, would be "a violation of our contractual rights," and he asked Lyle to meet with John Greaney, the same Agency lawyer who had been on my case from the beginning.

Lyle responded that as a matter of policy he did not submit his books for censorship, and if the Agency wanted to stop it they were welcome to go to court.

With questioning, the press conference went on for a couple of hours and brought a flood of requests from journalists for personal interviews. By previous plan I told everyone I was living in Rome, in order to avoid complications for my residence permit in Hamburg. Press reaction was not disappointing. In the next few days we learned by telephone from friends in the States and elsewhere that most of the major publications carried stories about the *Bulletin* and *Dirty Work*. Perfect. Now to build up subscriptions and use the proceeds from *Dirty Work* to publish the magazine.

I attended most of the Tribunal sessions to hear the Cubans and other Latin Americans, Africans, Palestinians, Vietnamese and many more. All had horror stories of political repression of one kind or another. My first testimony was on day three. I concentrated on the CIA's liaison and support operations for other intelligence services, especially those in countries ruled by military dictatorships. These operations, in which the Agency gave information, training, equipment and guidance, made the CIA an active partner in the torture, assassination and disappearance of progressive political figures from Chile to South Africa to Iran, South Korea and the Philippines.

As long as these operations continued, I emphasized, the Carter Administration's concern for "human rights" should be taken more as an exercise in public relations than as serious policy. The following day I spoke about the CIA's operational programs to penetrate and manipulate the supposedly "free" institutions of "democratic" countries: their elections, political parties, trade unions, youth and student organizations, and information media.

With the *Bulletin* staff we scheduled evening visits to as many national delegations as possible for conferences and discussions about the CIA. These took us to the outskirts of Havana where the delegations were staying, usually in modern new boarding schools.

For me one of the most interesting visits was with the large U.S. delegation, which was immersed in a political battle over priorities: feminism, Native Americans' rights, Third World matters, arms control, and environmental protection. I had a number of visits from members of political parties and revolutionary movements who sought advice on identification of agents and technical penetrations of their organizations and on how to prevent such operations.

Before we knew it the Festival was over. Giselle had seen a couple of performances of the Cuban National Ballet and had accompanied me to Tribunal sessions and on visits to delegations. Phil and Chris had done the same and had also visited the José Martí Pioneer Camp outside Havana and made several other excursions. We stayed on a few days to relax at the beach, and before leaving I agreed to return in September to help plan a book based on the Tribunal testimonies. It would depend, however, on the situation with my residence application in Germany.

With all the Festival activities I had hardly thought about that problem. On arrival in Madrid I called Winfried Gunnemann. So far there had been no decision on my application, but the Border Police hadn't answered his letter asking confirmation of my right to re-enter the country.

The next day he had bad news. The Border Police said my name was still on the list of persons excluded from the Federal Republic. The Interior Ministry in Bonn refused to take it off the list even though I had applied for residence in Hamburg. We could go to court to establish my right to live with Giselle in Hamburg, as before, but again there could be long delays before a decision. However, if I could get across the border without getting caught. . . .

Oh, no. Not that again. I can't get away with that Black Forest bus tour a second time. Have to think of something new. But what? The Agency and its friends are going to watch my every move. This time they'll do everything they can to prevent me from slipping across the border again. Dammit, dammit. How am I going to get back to Hamburg? The very thought of going through the fear and tension of another entry put me in a blue funk of constant anxiety.

Giselle had two weeks before she had to be back at work, and she wanted to take classes in Paris for at least one week before starting the new season. For my part I needed a few days in Amsterdam at the warehouse where everything from the Olympiaplein flat was stored in order to arrange a shipment to Angela.

We flew to Amsterdam, and after a couple of days Giselle went on to Paris. Phil and I then started separating the household effects as I constantly pondered how to get across the border again. And Chris. He had said he wanted to stay in Virginia with his mother and attend school there. So he flew from Havana back to the States.

Why, I wondered, didn't he want to live in Hamburg? He'd seemed to like it before going to the Festival, but the man at the Hamburg school seemed to scare him. Then he said he preferred the school in Virginia. Maybe he was just tired of the uncertainty and other problems I brought to all our lives. Well, I wouldn't try to force him to live with me, but I knew that the suburban Washington environment, with almost no supervision from Janet, was not a healthy one. There was not much I could do about it at this point, but my worry and disappointment were always just below the surface.

A week went by. Giselle was due back in Amsterdam Friday evening to spend the weekend before beginning work Monday morning, and I still had no idea how to get back into Germany.

At lunch on Friday Margo mentioned that she wanted to spend the weekend with her parents in the south of Holland, but had decided not to get mixed up in the crush of travellers that weekend. I asked what she meant. It's the last holiday weekend of the summer, she said. The trains and highways are going to be choked with people. I asked how long it would take to drive from Schiphol airport to the nearest border crossing into Germany. A couple of hours with the traffic, Ken said.

That was it. With so much traffic maybe they wouldn't check passports at the border. But we needed a car. I couldn't rent one in my name because the rental companies might have to report customers' names to police under the anti-terrorism controls.

Ken agreed to rent a car in his name, but not at the airport. Phil and I would leave our bags at TNI, just in case the building was being watched, and take a taxi to the airport to meet Giselle. Then with her we would take another taxi, as if going back to TNI. If we weren't being followed, we would have the taxi take us to a pre-arranged meeting point with Ken and Margo. Then we would head for the border.

Giselle's flight from Paris was only a few minutes late. As we hurried out of the terminal I told her we were driving with Ken and Margo straight to the border. It looked like nobody was following our taxi, so we met Ken and Margo and piled into the rented car.

On the way to the border I thought of a precaution. Phil's name in his passport is the same as mine except for the "Junior" after it. I would get out of the car at the last service stop on the Holland side. If the German Border Police check the passports, they'll probably register a hit with his name that will require a clarification that he's my son and not me. That would tell us it's no use to try. But they would also see how close the passports are being checked. Then Ken could drive back across into Holland by a different route and pick me up.

I got out at the last restaurant before the control point and they drove on. I ordered a cup of coffee, sat waiting, looking repeatedly at my watch, as the minutes passed like years. I had to make it across, I just had to. But that Black Forest tour was pure luck. And so was the week I stayed in Hamburg in secret. I wondered if I would have to stay another week in secret if I got across the border this time. Just get across, that's all.

And if I don't? Back to TNI. On Sunday Giselle and Phil would go on to Hamburg, and I'd be sitting in Amsterdam alone trying to figure out another route. Where are they? What's taking so long? After nearly an hour, when I thought I couldn't stand the suspense another minute, they returned with mixed news.

The line of cars crossing the border was continuous, and the Border Police were checking some passports but not others. They had waved Ken on through, so there was no check of Phil's passport. What to do now? Hell, let's try it, I said, as my heart started sinking with expectations of failure. I got in the back of the car, on the side away from Ken's window where the Border Police would take the passports. It was only ten minutes' drive to the long line of cars that was moving at barely a crawl. As we approached the West German control booth Giselle put her hand on my knee for reassurance, but by then I was so certain of disaster that I began wondering what the Dutch immigration people would do when the Germans sent me back.

But then we stopped. Three cars were ahead of us, then a hippie-looking couple on a motorcycle. The Border Police had stopped them, made them get off, and put their bedrolls on the road. They were examining everything. I looked behind. For as far as I could see cars were waiting. And only one lane for passage through the control booth.

Finally the couple put their bedrolls back together and were allowed to pass. Then the car behind them was waved on through, then the second one, then the one ahead of us. As Ken slowed momentarily, they waved us on through. I was half-covering my face with my hand, rubbing my left eye, as we drove by the control officers. Then off we went into the dark, as everybody gave a sigh of relief in perfect harmony. We'd made it. Again I couldn't believe it.

Ken and Margo left us at the Osnabruck railway station and headed back to Holland. We took a midnight train for Hamburg and in a couple of hours were back in the flat. Next morning I checked with Gunnemann. No, I didn't have to stay for a week in secret again. I had the application stamp in my passport and that was sufficient protection from arrest by the Border Police. This time, I decided, I'm not going anywhere until we have the decision. No more risks, no more tense border crossings.

In the weeks that followed I put in a residence application for Phil, and he began classes at the International School. I called Martinez at the Cuban Embassy in Bonn and asked him to inform the Festival organizers that I wouldn't be able to return for work on the book until after the decision on my residence permit.

In Amsterdam, Ken rented a van and drove over with all the household effects, except for my voluminous files and papers which I

had stored in the attic at TNI. We started painting and other renovations in the flat. I also enrolled in a language school to study German.
For the first time in recent memory I was beginning to relax, even
laugh again, but still the pending decision on my application was
hanging overhead like a dark cloud.

From Washington and New York I began to get clippings on the
press reaction to *Dirty Work*, the *Bulletin* and our activities at the
Youth Festival. They couldn't have been more encouraging. One
Washington Post story, entitled "Worldwide Effort Being Launched
to 'Destabilize' the CIA," described the entire background on the
Bulletin and "CIA Watch," with ample quotes from the first issue.

> The new publication, which is expected to appear roughly six times
> a year, is called the Covert Action Information Bulletin, and its tone is
> uncompromising. Urging a worldwide effort to print the name of any-
> one who works abroad for the CIA, Agee advises readers of the pre-
> mier issue not to stop there. Once the names have been made public,
> he recommends:
> "Then organize public demonstrations against those named—both
> at the American Embassy and at their homes—and, where possible,
> bring pressure on the government to throw them out. Peaceful protest
> will do the job. And when it doesn't, those whom the CIA has most
> oppressed will find other ways of fighting back."

The article went on to quote reactions from the CIA press spokesman: "This thing is incredible . . . unbelievable. . . . These people
are operating under the overall pretext that everything we do is
wrong." Exactly.

William F. Buckley, Jr., also plugged the *Bulletin* and "CIA
Watch" in his syndicated column of reaction, lamenting that I'd probably get a Pulitzer Prize for exposing CIA people. And Jack
Anderson, whose column appeared in hundreds of newspapers,
wrote:

> CIA defector Philip Agee, working with known communist agents,
> has appealed to disgruntled CIA employees to send him "leads, tips,
> suggestions." He wrote in a widely circulated bulletin: "We are partic-
> ularly anxious to receive, anonymously if you desire, copies of U.S.
> diplomatic lists and U.S. Embassy staff and/or telephone directories
> from any countries." Agee has already laid out the biographies of 700
> U.S. undercover agents in a book published by Lyle Stuart, Inc.
> CIA Chief Stansfield Turner told us that Agee's publications have
> been "very damaging." Turner said that a CIA agent who has served

his country anonymously, "suddenly is made public by somebody like Agee and his usefulness, his career, his prospects, are greatly reduced from then on through no fault of his after he has spent years of deprivation and sacrifice."

Eat your heart out Stan, I thought as I read that column, but what's this he said about "deprivation and sacrifice." When I was in the CIA, the Station paid my rent, the salaries of three servants, my gasoline, and booze and catering expenses for every party I ever threw—all on top of a salary that was not bad by the standards of the day. Anderson didn't bother identifying the "known communist agents" I was supposedly working with, but the reference was colorful.

UPI also circulated a widely published article on the *Bulletin* and *Dirty Work*, describing them as "do-it-yourself guides on how to find and unmask CIA agents abroad." Exactly. And the *Village Voice* had a full-page review of *Dirty Work* with references to the *Bulletin* and the conclusion that our aim was "to defang and lobotomize" the CIA. Exactly.

The fringe right was even better. In remarks entitled "Agee's Covert Action," Larry McDonald inserted a seven-column statement in the *Congressional Record* that included a long article by John Rees from *Information Digest*. Lamenting the lack of legal protection for the intelligence agencies, McDonald denounced my "newest sabotage tactics":

> Our Federal intelligence agencies lack legislative mandates to take action, while our enemies are redoubling their efforts to demoralize and destroy the remaining U.S. intelligence operations. CIA defector Philip Agee, who could have taught the notorious Kim Philby lessons in treachery, joined by a handful of U.S. radicals, has launched a new attack on the CIA's covert capabilities.

McDonald went on to call for support for a proposed law already introduced in the House of Representatives that would make it a crime to reveal the identities of undercover intelligence officers. The Rees article was "the whole file." He was especially helpful because he detailed Bill Schaap's 17-year background in political activism, Ellen Ray's work with *CounterSpy*, Jim and Elsie Wilcott's political work after leaving the Agency, and Lou Wolf's research talents.

The "Agee apparat," as he saw us, intended to "develop a worldwide network of agents that will expose CIA personnel and methods of operation." Exactly. Then he gave a plug for *Dirty Work*,

quoted verbatim from my remarks on Cuban television during the
Festival, dredged up the Welch and Pawlowski cases, quoted from
David Phillips of the Association of Former Intelligence Officers and
old Jack Anderson columns, referred to Angela's background as a revolutionary, and ended with a well-selected quote from my introduction to *Dirty Work*:

> Together, people of many nationalities and varying political beliefs
> can cooperate to weaken the CIA and its surrogate intelligence ser-
> vices, striking a blow at political repression and economic injustice.
> The CIA can be defeated. The proof can be seen from Vietnam to An-
> gola, and in the other countries where liberation movements are rap-
> idly gaining strength.

Then there was *Human Events: The National Conservative
Weekly*. "Lives of CIA Agents Deliberately Imperiled" ran the headline of an article occupying the entire front page and continuing inside. The article began: "Remember Richard Welch?" and went on to
describe our Havana press conference, the first issue of the *Bulletin*,
Dirty Work, our backgrounds from the Rees article, and ended with
an alarm: "A concerted effort has been launched from Havana to sabotage U.S. intelligence around the globe, to make U.S. officials vulnerable to terrorist attacks."

Poor things, I thought, as if Agency officers hadn't tried time and
again with impunity to assassinate Fidel Castro and various other political leaders over the Agency's thirty years of existence. So they'll
feel vulnerable. So fine. In reality, though, violence against CIA people was the last thing we sought. It would only bring them sympathy
they didn't deserve.

Our Havana press conference, the first *Bulletin*, and *Dirty Work*
provoked further reactions in Congress. Senator Barry Goldwater
said he was asking the Carter Administration to take away my U.S.
citizenship. When I read that I smiled: a native-born American's citizenship can't be taken away, but Goldwater is no better informed
now than he was in 1964 when Lyndon Johnson wiped the sewers
with him in the presidential election.

Joseph Biden, like Goldwater a member of the Senate Intelligence
Committee, called for a new law to stop my revelations by
criminalizing the exposure of undercover intelligence officers. And
Lloyd Bentsen of Texas stood up on the Senate floor saying I "should
go to jail" and calling for passage of a so-called "Intelligence Identities
Protection Act" that he had introduced two years earlier:

I ask my colleagues to . . . join me in sponsoring S. 1578, a bill that
will state our clear condemnation of Mr. Agee's activities, our support
for the protection of our agents, and our desire to punish those who so
gravely jeopardize our intelligence service, its agents, and our country.

Our country? *Our* country? Once again that rhetorical unity, like
the flag, that pretends Americans are "one" when all the historical
facts show Humpty Dumpty fragmentation from the start. *Your* country, Senator, is corporate America. *Our* country, the rest of us, is
something quite different.

There were many more hysterical reactions, all confirming that our
aim was well taken. But as satisfying as they were, they only increased my worry over the residence permit. Although all the articles
had me living in Rome, the Agency certainly knew I was in Hamburg,
and I couldn't understand why they hadn't gotten a journalist on my
case in Hamburg in order to bring pressure on the government to
make a decision against me.

By the end of September, despite regular inquiries by Jacobi and
Gunnemann, the Hamburg aliens police at Bieber Haus were still
saying they needed the file on me from Bonn before they could make
a decision. We threatened to go to court to force the decision, but by
early October they got the file and promised a decision before the end
of the month.

About this time Giselle went on tour to Helsinki. The Hamburg
ballet was the main cultural presentation in a week-long trade fair to
promote commerce between the two cities. A couple of nights after
performances, Giselle sat in the hotel bar having a snack with the
Mayor of Hamburg, Hans Ulrich Klose, and his wife Elke. Back in
Hamburg I suggested to Giselle that she write to Frau Klose about
our problem and ask for advice and help.

The letter was hardly in the mail when I was contacted by two
members of the Young Socialists (JUSOS), the youth organization of
the Social Democratic Party (SPD) which was the senior governing
party in both the Bonn and the Hamburg coalitions. They were also
active in Latin America solidarity work. The Hamburg JUSOS had
heard I was there and wanted to know if I needed any help.

Well, yes, I'm going slightly nuts waiting for a decision on my application. I outlined the history of my troubles with the British,
French, Dutch and West German governments. Anything they could
do to help get a positive decision from the Hamburg government
would be wonderful. We had several meetings with a young lawyer,

Harold Muras, who was one of the JUSOS leaders in Hamburg, and
he intervened on my behalf with the member of the Senate in charge
of aliens matters but got no clear commitment.

Lyle Stuart invited me to visit him at the Frankfurt Book Fair so we
could discuss my participation in promotion of *Dirty Work*. As I was
still afraid of the Hamburg airport I sat ten hours on the train that
day, down and back, but it was worth it. Lyle had a substantial budget
set aside for the book, and he wanted to know if there was any way I
could come back to the States to help spend it.

God, how I would love to, I told Lyle, but I don't see how I could.
First, I can't leave this country again until I get a decision on my residence permit. Second, the Federal District Court in Virginia ruled
against Frank Snepp, the former CIA officer who wrote the book
about the fall of Saigon and the Agency's leaving behind its records on
the Vietnamese who were working for them. Nobody even claimed
he revealed classified information, just that he violated the "secrecy
agreement," i.e., the obligation to submit the book for censorship
prior to publication. The Court ruled he has to pay the government
all the income from the book: that's $140,000 which he, like a fool,
put in a trust fund with the ACLU. He's appealing the decision, but
who knows if he'll win. If I go back now they could try the same
against me despite the earlier decision not to prosecute. This would
be a civil rather than a criminal prosecution. And I need the income
from *Inside the Company* and other things I haven't submitted in order to keep working.

Lyle understood. I recommended that he get Marc Stone to organize a promotional campaign like he did so effectively for *Inside the
Company*. I would do as many interviews as he could line up, but
they would have to be in Hamburg or by telephone. And isn't it
great, all the free publicity we're getting in news reporting, in Congress, and from the Agency itself. We probably couldn't have bought
what we've got so far for a million dollars. Two million, Lyle said,
with no apparent sorrow.

At the Book Fair I also saw editors from Editorial Laia, the
Barcelona publishing house that was about to bring out a Spanish edition of *Inside the Company*. At long last. The original Spanish contract was with Editorial Grijalbo, another Barcelona house with major
operations in Mexico. But they delayed, giving no credible reasons,
and the contract lapsed. Later I learned that Mexican government
pressure was the reason Grijalbo didn't publish. With the Laia editors

I agreed to go to Spain to promote their edition as soon as I could get a decision on my residence permit.

At the end of October my lawyers got the bad news. By telephone the chief of the Western Hemisphere section of the Hamburg Aliens Affairs Office, a man named Hunderlage, said their decision was negative due to immense pressure from the Interior Ministry in Bonn. He said we would have the decision in writing within a week, but he acknowledged that I could stay in the country if we appealed to the courts.

I told Winfried that of course we would appeal, but I was pretty sour on the idea. He said we had a good chance to win, but I kept thinking the opposite. There seemed to be nothing I could win against concentrated U.S. pressure. Well, at least I could stay until Giselle's season ended in July. And in the meantime she could talk to Pat Neary in Zurich about a contract for the following season.

I got in touch with my contacts in the JUSOS and asked if they could try again with their party people in the Hamburg government. They were more than glad to, and were disturbed by the news from Hunderlage. I asked them to pass the word from me that I was quite willing to meet with anyone, in Hamburg or in Bonn, to discuss my activities and to refrain from anything that might cause embarrassment or problems. They would get back to me when they had any news.

Just then I got a jolt that I knew would do me no good. *The New York Times* ran an article from Moscow, reprinted around the world by the *International Herald Tribune*, about an interview published in the Soviet magazine *Zhurnalist*. In the "interview" I described methods used by the CIA against Soviet missions in Latin America with various examples from my own experience.

The interview highlighted my work in provoking expulsions of Soviet diplomats based on documents we had falsified to show Soviet interference in certain countries' internal affairs. It couldn't be. I hadn't done any interviews in Hamburg and none with a Soviet journalist since I was in Britain.

As I read the article a second time I realized that all the information was taken from *Inside the Company* and rearranged as an interview. What could I do? Anybody who read that story would think I was trying to make the CIA look bad by doing interviews with the Soviets in Hamburg.

Ten days after Hunderlage told Gunnemann of the decision, he said by telephone that he had been trying to write the decision but couldn't justify it. He had passed the file to Gunter Empen, the Chief of Aliens Affairs, who then told Gunnemann that he himself would write the decision. We would have it within two weeks.

Less than a week later Empen said he couldn't write the justification either. The next day, he said, I should go to Bieber Haus for the permit. I don't understand, I said to Winfried, does that mean I got it? The huge smiles on his and Jacobi's faces were the answer. I told Giselle, and said I couldn't believe it. But the next morning I went to Bieber Haus and twenty minutes later I had the stamp in my passport: a permit linked to Giselle's, good until next summer, valid anywhere in the Federal Republic of Germany.

I went home and wrote the event in my diary, and suddenly I noticed: It was November 16, two years to the day after delivery of Rees's deportation notice in Cambridge.

We celebrated quietly that night as I pondered what I had to do now to avoid cancellation of the permit. I would make no comments to the press, just keep on with a low profile and continue with the renovations in the flat.

Were the JUSOS the key? I called to thank them, and they didn't say exactly what they'd done. And Giselle's letter to Elke Klose? We didn't know about that either. But a few weeks later she answered, saying she was happy to see in the press that our problem was solved.

Despite my keeping quiet about the matter, the West German newspapers ran stories with headings like "Super-Spy Allowed to Remain in Hamburg." And *Der Spiegel*, the mass circulation newsweekly, had a long article with reference to my expulsions from Britain, France and Holland, the Pawlowski case, and Bonn's pressure on Hamburg to deny the permit. An unnamed senior Border Police official had told the magazine in disgust: "He simply slipped through our fingers'

That wasn't so bad, but over in London my old friend Robert Moss was at work. In *Foreign Report*, the "confidential" newsletter of the *Economist*, the lead article was entitled "Agee's New Base." This was the "surfacing" of my arrival in Hamburg that I'd anticipated, but never understood why they'd waited so long to publish.

As evidence that I had "already joined forces with the Radical Left in Germany," Moss wrote that I lived in a house owned by the convicted RAF lawyer, Kurt Groenewold. Two elderly sisters, who had probably never heard of Groenewold, were the owners of the house. And in the same passage he said our flat "was formerly occupied by

Giselle and another American, Robert Michael Steele, who has disappeared from the scene since Agee arrived in town." Giselle whooped with laughter when she read that passage, poor Michael, at the bottom of the Alster in a concrete-filled oil drum.

That was the beginning. A couple of weeks later Moss published a long article in the *Daily Telegraph* under the title "Agee and the Ballerina." It was another "full file" piece with so many embellishments and misstatements of fact that Giselle and I howled with laughter. His thoughtful conclusion: "All in all, Agee's surprise wedding in Amsterdam last spring has proved to be a convenient marriage, if not a marriage of convenience."

Moss also wrote that I was working with groups in other Western European countries, including West Germany, which were using "the same techniques that were employed to disarm the CIA and FBI in the United States." The purpose: "to duplicate the successful anti-CIA campaign by disrupting other Western services." And he concluded: "Agee's activities in Hamburg present the intriguing spectacle of the intermeshing of the anti-intelligence lobby, the terrorist support network, and Soviet and Cuban intelligence services."

Whew! I'd done nothing in Hamburg except sand floors, scrape off wallpaper, paint ceilings and varnish shelves—in fact a much-needed and long-overdue therapy that was making life exciting again. In one fell swoop these "activities" were about to demolish NATO, motherhood and Robert Moss's dream of "Western strength."

The day after that marvel of reporting appeared, as if by magic the main Hamburg newspaper, *Hamburger Abendblatt*, carried a front-page commentary based on the Moss article. With a photograph of me on one side of the page, and Giselle in ballet costume on the other, "Agee und die Ballerina" raised the alarm. "The man who emasculated the CIA" had already established contacts with the West German radical left, just as they were pushing an "Agee-style" campaign to discredit the West German secret services. In condensed fashion the article repeated Moss's fable that Kurt Groenewold owned the house where we lived, and it highlighted my various expulsions from NATO countries as a "security risk."

I thought that would be the end of it, but a week later the national daily *Die Welt* carried a long, slightly altered version of Moss's *Daily Telegraph* article. In this article I was not only living in a house owned by the lawyer and conspirator of the Red Army Fraction, but the house itself was red (in fact it was yellow).

Friends told me not to worry about *Hamburger Abendblatt* and

Die Welt. That reporting was entirely predictable because they were publications of Axel Springer, the right-wing West German press baron who had the biggest media empire in Europe.

(My friends' suspicions that Springer had ties with the CIA were later confirmed in the U.S. press. *The Nation* ran an article sourced to former CIA officers who revealed that the Agency had given Springer millions of dollars to get him going after World War II and that they had no reason to believe the relationship had ever ended.)

As I went back to building kitchen shelves, I kept wondering how a man like Moss could have the slightest self-respect as a journalist. In his articles about me he not only invented and twisted facts without shame, he also made no effort at all to cover up the fact that his information was coming spoon-fed from the CIA or its "sister" intelligence services.

But then I considered why those attacks were necessary. In the space of a few months, and against all odds, I had finally found stability with Giselle and a place to live. Not just any place. With my lawyers Harmut and Winfried, with Kurt Groenewold and his friends, with the JUSOS who helped me, and with Giselle's friends in the company, I was beginning to know Germany and like it—so different from my earlier, unpleasant impressions.

Then too, my second book, really a collective effort with Lou, Bill, Ellen and others, was out and causing wide controversy. Our *Covert Action Bulletin* had also started and was getting plenty of publicity. And reactions from the CIA, Congress and elsewhere confirmed that our work was taking a toll on the U.S. government's ability to subvert and destroy progressive political movements. Far from being intimidated or smashed, we were as much on the offensive as ever before.

But there was one thing I didn't know then, and would only learn later in my FOIA suit. At the time *Dirty Work* was published, President Carter's Justice Department began another criminal investigation to see if they could put me in prison once and for all.

XIII

A Fateful Telephone Call

My editors in Spain had a full week of activities planned, first in Barcelona and then in Madrid. These were the usual media interviews and press conferences, and as happened everywhere the journalists wanted comments on what the CIA was doing in their country. Only a few days before I arrived a military coup against Spain's "transition to democracy" was averted, and many believed the Agency might have had a hand in it, even in the terrorist operations of ETA and GRAPO that would have justified it.

I didn't think so. First, the Carter administration wanted to see Spain integrated with the rest of Western Europe, both in the European Economic Community and in NATO. And the only way Spain would be acceptable to other members was as a parliamentary democracy, not as a continuation of the Franco regime. Second, unless the Communist Party was a threat to taking power through elections, which it wasn't, terrorism would not serve U.S. goals.

I did not believe the CIA could infiltrate a revolutionary organization like ETA or GRAPO to the point where they could influence pol-

icy and operations. If in fact they were successful in penetrating these
groups at all, they would give their information to government security services to help in operations against them.

Then where were the CIA offices and what were they doing? I
guessed the Station in the Madrid Embassy was still about thirty-five
strong, as it was when exposed in the press a couple of years before,
and there were probably small offices of three or four in the U.S.
Consulates in Bilbao and Barcelona.

Again speculating, I suggested the information media and trade unions as prime targets for operations: in the first instance to promote
themes favorable to the EEC and NATO, and in the second to
weaken the communist-dominated unions, the *Comisiones Obreras*,
in favor of others such as those affiliated with the Socialist Party
(PSOE). And, of course, operations against Soviet Bloc missions, the
Cuban mission, radical Arab missions, and any liberation movements
operating in Spain like the PLO. All were obvious targets that conformed with overall American policy in Spain. Finally, I said, the
Agency no doubt had liaison connections with the various Spanish security services for exchange of information and joint operations—and
for recruiting the officers of those services as penetration agents.

Most of the editors at Laia had worked in the underground against
the Franco dictatorship. Because of this background and tension over
the failed coup, they felt I should not stay in a hotel. So I stayed with
one of Laia's marketing managers and his family in a village outside
Barcelona.

One night late, after I finished a radio program, Frederic Pajes was
taking me in his little Renault back to the village. As we drove along
the narrow winding road through the hills, he was telling me of the
continuing dangers from the security forces, which hadn't changed
much despite the end of Franco's regime.

Through the darkness ahead I noticed a faint light, like a flashlight,
some ten meters back from the road. Frederic, who was talking,
didn't notice it until we were abreast of the light. He suddenly
slammed the brake to the floor and the car skidded to a halt.

"Guardia Civil," Frederic said. "Put your hands behind your head
and don't move."

I'd hardly got my hands back when out of the dark stepped four
uniformed police with automatic weapons pointing at our heads. One
of them pointed the flashlight at Frederic and asked to see our documents.

"Get your passport out, slowly," he told me. I did just that without saying a word. They looked over his carnet and my passport, returned them and waved us on.

As we continued I told Frederic I thought the light was from somebody wanting a lift. I never would have stopped if I'd been driving. You'd probably be dead, he said, and he went on to describe recent cases of innocent people shot by security forces in anti-terrorist operations.

In Madrid I stayed at the apartment of Frederic's friend, Chini, and each night two men sat in a car watching the apartment until well past midnight. Frederic was the first to notice them, which prompted me to tell him the story of the trip several years before from San Sebastian to Altamira to Torre la Vega.

I told him not to worry, if they were just observing it was all right with me. But it seemed so stupid and wasteful, since my trip was totally public, and whatever service it was must have known that nobody was going to be intimidated.

The trip ended with a meeting at the International Press Club which the U.S. Embassy Press Attaché later complained about in a letter to the Spanish Information Secretariat. Mine was one of a series of meetings and press conferences at the Club, he wrote, "whose purpose—manifestly political—has been to spread minority and anti-democratic ideas that in every case constituted a constant criticism against the policies of both the Spanish and the United States governments." In fact I hadn't criticized the Spanish government in the least, and the letter showed pretty clearly who was "anti-democratic."

Frederic and the others at Laia were pleased with the broad media coverage we stimulated, particularly with my appearance on a Sunday afternoon television program called "Fantástico." This was a variety program, not very serious. Half the population of Spain were said to watch it. The moderator's questions were typical of those I'd had constantly from journalists of scant political depth. How could the CIA tolerate my disclosures? Why hadn't they killed me? The fact that they hadn't suggested I wasn't a genuine political dissident—rather, some kind of sophisticated deception operation. Nothing *fantástico*, I said, and then went through the usual background.

Between interviews, Frederic took me around to meet friends and comrades. They revealed a world I hadn't known. Most of them had risked their lives in the anti-Franco underground, some had been imprisoned and tortured, others hounded from place to place and job to job. All were certain that the recently aborted coup was not the end of such attempts to restore fascism.

To a person they were determined to stop it, no matter what the cost. I had the feeling that in just one week I'd learned more about the long struggle against Franco than I could have from a shelf of books.

At the Madrid airport I was surprised by the friendliness of the immigration officials. They had seen me on television and joked that I'd better be careful or the CIA would "get me." No, no, I said, the CIA was incompetent, couldn't shoot straight, nothing to be afraid of. Then I got on my morning flight to Rome.

I had a noon appointment with Giovanni Arnone, my lawyer, about a lawsuit he had started against the producer of *Covert Action*, the CIA movie starring David Janssen, for payment of my fees and expenses. We also needed to discuss the problems he was having with my Italian residence permit.

Arnone had applied for extension when the permit expired in September, but strange things began to happen. Police had called him at least twenty times to ask questions about me, twice questioned him in his office, and once took him to a police station for questioning—Italian-style intimidation even though Giovanni was well-known and prominent in the field of writers' and artists' contracts. The police approach was suggestive: Why do you represent a man like Agee? You might get in trouble. Agee makes problems. Don't you think you would be better off with other clients? Why make problems for yourself?

As I stood in the passport line at Fiumicino I knew the officer would find my name on the list, tell me to sit down, and then after everyone was gone he would fill out the form. It was as anticipated. He directed me to a bench. But after the last person passed he walked over and told me to come with him.

I asked where we were going, but he just said to come along. We went up steps to the main terminal level for outgoing flights and then to the main immigration police office. He took me to an inner office, told me to sit down, refused to say why I was there, and left, closing the door behind him. I could hear lively chatter in the front office but couldn't understand anything.

After ten minutes or so the door opened and in walked another officer. He asked to see my ticket which showed me booked on a flight late that afternoon for Hamburg. Then he said what I already knew: I would not be allowed to enter Italy.

I asked why not and got the expected answer: an order from the Interior Ministry.

"On what grounds?"

"We don't know, it's just an order."

"Can I call my lawyer to cancel our meeting?"

"No," he said. He told me I would have to wait in custody until my flight to Hamburg. Shit, I thought, six hours to wait. The officer took me out to the main waiting area and put me under watch by two uniformed *carabinieri* with automatic weapons.

They allowed me to change some money, buy magazines, have a drink at the bar, and later some lunch. I sat there thinking, wondering, "Why now?" I'd been to Italy any number of times without a problem except for the police visit to my hotel during the Moro affair. *Why now?*

All I could surmise was that the "invisible hand" had finally found a cooperative partner, maybe a new Interior Minister. After a seemingly endless afternoon and as darkness approached, the immigration police put me on the crowded flight to Hamburg.

We had a stop in Milan. As the DC-9 taxied to the terminal the flight attendant asked that all Hamburg passengers remain on board. I was sitting alone in the last row in the back as about half the passengers filed past me and down the exit. After thirty minutes or so, people began to look around and murmur about the delay. Eventually I heard people coming up the steps, but instead of passengers they were two burly *carabinieri* in black leather boots and jackets. With their helmets and machine pistols, they looked every bit like anti-terrorist commandos out of central casting. As they marched up to the cockpit, the chatter and glances increased. Then the flight attendant announced in English: "Would Mr. Philip Agee please identify himself?"

Oh, no, I thought. What's going to happen with those bullies? It seemed that every passenger on the plane was looking around at me, mostly in fear, as I rose without enthusiasm and weakly held up my hand.

The policemen walked back to me, and one of them, with gruff voice and arrogant manner, asked for my passport. I handed it over. He took out a notebook, filled out a form, gave the passport back, and together they disappeared down the exit. People were still peeping around at me, probably wondering if I was a criminal or a terrorist, when other passengers boarded and we took off for Hamburg.

Without any difficulty I settled into my new life as a ballet groupie, washing Giselle's tights and leotards, shopping, cooking and continuing renovations on the flat. Giselle had arranged for Phil, who was in his last year of secondary school, to audition for the Staatsoper ballet school. He was accepted, and three or four afternoons a week he went to ballet class. Through him, and through Giselle, I was beginning to learn how appealing ballet was, in particular the combination of music, movement and concentration.

I also discovered that self-concern was not lacking in the ballet world. There were endless conversations among Giselle and dancers who came over after rehearsals or performances. They would sit at the kitchen table for hours talking nothing but ballet: the "true" *tendu*, the proper *port de bras*, the perfect "fifth position," the ideal *sissonnes*. And incidents, hundreds of incidents, it seemed, every day, from class, rehearsals and performances. Did you see how Gabrielle did her *pirouettes* tonight? Was she ever spas. And Richard. He never got on his legs. But wasn't Annette just dreamy, especially in the second act *pas de deux*. And on, and on. Not even in the CIA was attention so exclusively focused on work and colleagues. In ballet, it seemed, there was little else the dancers could think about when they were together.

Giselle had warned me that ballet companies were one constant intrigue, and I soon understood. A never-ending soap opera, "Peyton Place" with daily renewal. Gossip and speculation: who's sleeping with whom, or not talking to whom, or depressed, or injured.

Everybody had injuries. A hip, a back, a neck, an ankle or knee—with some people you could always count on a long answer to the question "How are you?" And the choreography. They could go on for hours about steps and combinations, always certain there was a better way to do it.

From the beginning I saw that Giselle was different. She was a good listener, better than most, which was partly why the other dancers liked her. But she didn't complain much, only when she was in great pain. Mostly she found humor in the each day's high drama at the theater, and she stuck to the highlights when I asked her, "What happened today?" In fact I didn't mind hearing about the latest blow-up between the director and one of the dancers, or somebody's crisis over casting.

Her world was a welcome distraction after years of research, writing and talking about American foreign policy and the CIA. I went to most of her performances and was always just as thrilled to see her dance as I had been the first time in Paris.

Our flat was ideally located, one subway stop from the theater and only a block from the university, which meant we had all necessary shops and services within a few minutes' walk. No need for a car or even bicycles.

I often had to write out my shopping list using a dictionary. One morning I decided to buy a fresh ham, and I wanted it with the skin for crackling. I looked the words up in the dictionary and at my corner butcher's, after waiting my turn in line, asked for *schweinebraten mit pelz*. All six women behind me broke out in laughter as the butcher gave me a look of incomprehension.

I knew I'd said something wrong but didn't know what. As my face grew redder, a woman asked in English if she could help. I explained what I wanted, and she told the butcher I wanted *schweinebraten mit haut*.

"What did I say," I asked her.

"Pork roast with fur," she said, and they all started laughing again.

For the next year I bought only pre-packaged meats at the super-market.

In early 1979 Ellen, Bill, Lou and I thought we could repeat the success of *Dirty Work*, which was selling very well, by putting together a similar book on the CIA's operations and personnel in Africa. Lyle Stuart agreed, and we brought Karl van Meter into the project in Paris as well as others in London and the United States.

At several meetings in Amsterdam we planned the book, began looking for recent materials, and commissioned new articles. We would concentrate on sub-Saharan regions with emphasis on southern Africa, including clandestine activities of former colonial powers such as Britain and France, and others such as Israel and South Africa.

Sean MacBride, the Irish barrister and former United Nations Commissioner for Namibia, agreed to write a preface. I wrote a couple of articles for the book, and Lou got busy in the National Archives in Washington digging up names and career histories of CIA officers in Africa. Bill and Ellen coordinated the project and together we set mid-summer as a target for having it ready.

A month or so after we began, Kurt Groenewold called to tell me he was going to San Francisco for the National Lawyers Guild convention. He would meet Bill and Ellen there and could take anything I wanted to send. Sure, I said, I've just written a long letter on progress with *Dirty Work II* and things relating to the *Bulletin*. He took the letter with him, and on arrival in Seattle immigration officials took

him aside and looked through the hundred or so pages in his
briefcase. They found my letter and copied it. Not the slightest attempt to conceal that their "tip" came from telephone monitoring.

At about that time Lyle Stuart came through Hamburg on his way
to Sweden. It was the depth of winter, and snow was piled all over,
but he wore no overcoat, just a light sport jacket. I supposed his considerable girth gave some protection, but god, that was taking fresh
air therapy a little far. He told me he hadn't owned a topcoat in thirty
years.

We sat in the flat and talked about his publishing career and his
struggle against the old obscenity laws and establishment mores of all
kinds. Somehow we got on the subject of my problems: the bugged
typewriter, Sal and Leslie/Janet, surveillance in different places, the
expulsions from country to country, and how I managed to get residence in Hamburg. Lyle interrupted, saying I had to write those stories as a book. He would call it *On the Run,* and he was certain it
would be successful.

I told him I didn't much like to write or to talk about myself.
Everywhere I go, I said, people seem more interested in me as a person than in what I can tell them about what the CIA does and why.
They always want to know why I went into the Agency and stayed in
so long, why I quit, why I took a stand, why the Agency hasn't killed
me—all those personal things. I want to write more books and do
more lecturing, more political education of all kinds, but I hate the
fascination with personality.

"Phil," Lyle said, "you don't understand. Your life is unique. People are naturally fascinated by the unusual. You should tell your life
story to put across your political message. That would be a much
more effective method than dry exposition."

I told Lyle I would have to think about it. In any case I couldn't
write such a book from memory, and all my personal papers were in
Amsterdam in utter chaos. Two weeks later an Italian film producer
came to Hamburg to discuss the same subject. He wanted to do a film
on my life since leaving the Agency. Maybe. But first I had *Dirty
Work II* to think about. Maybe afterwards.

In the spring I rented a van and drove over to Amsterdam for my
files. I hadn't realized how many clippings, magazines, papers, books
and reports of all kinds I had accumulated since beginning *Inside the
Company.* I spent half a day at TNI loading filing cabinets and boxes
before starting off for the German border. For months I had worried
about this day, dreading that the Border Police would want to review

every last paper. When I handed over my passport the officer recognized my name, then told me to park. He walked over to the van, asked me to open it, and stuck his head inside. All he could see were drawers and boxes of papers stacked to the roof.

"What is all this documentation?"

"Ah," I said, "just personal papers and research materials I use for writing books and articles. Nothing too important."

He shook his head in dismay, pulled the door shut, and passed me through.

Several publications requested articles, and I decided I would do them all through the *Bulletin* in Washington rather than directly from Hamburg. It was a transparent fiction, of course, but I thought that if my writing was attributable to a U.S. publication, even though it carried my signature, a case against me for "damaging foreign relations" might be a little harder to make.

One such article concerned revelations of U.S. espionage against Italian security services. Anonymously from Washington, the Rome daily *La Repubblica* received a copy of a secret intelligence report from the U.S. Embassy in Rome about the inner workings, effectiveness and leadership of the Italian anti-terrorist campaign. A reporter from the paper called me and asked if I would look it over for authenticity.

It was a gem, and authentic without the slightest doubt. Not only was the report classified "Secret," it was also marked "Noforn," which meant the information was considered too sensitive for passage to any non-U.S. services. The 4000-word document, written by Dominic Perrone, an official of the Embassy's Military Liaison Office, was documentary proof that the Defense Intelligence Agency was using its official connections with Italian services to recruit agent penetrations of the same "sister" services.

In keeping with standard intelligence reporting practice, Perrone gave only general descriptions of his six sources. They ranged from junior grade to General rank in the Italian military and *carabinieri* intelligence services, and he gave them a "B" rating which meant "usually reliable." The report itself was a scathing criticism of anti-terrorist operations, described variously by Perrone's sources as "totally ineffective," "in violation of the law," "in chaos," and "led by unqualified persons."

I told the reporter the document was authentic and sent him an article giving the reasons why. *La Repubblica* published the report and my article, and the same day the Italian government declared

Perrone *persona non grata*, the first such expulsion of an American since World War II.

Neither Perrone nor the State Department denied the report's authenticity. The case made headlines throughout Italy and all the wire services carried it. Most intriguing for me was the speed with which Perrone's report leaked: only two weeks to get from his desk in the Rome Embassy, to Washington for distribution, and then back to Rome for the newspapers.

I wrote a long article based on the Perrone report, sent it to a dozen publications in Europe, and in the *Bulletin* we published the entire document and my commentary.

Another leaked "Secret-Noforn" document, this one a CIA study, was equally damaging. Phil Kelly called me from the *Leveller* to say they had received through the mail a copy of an 18-page analysis entitled "Director of Central Intelligence: Perspectives for Intelligence, 1976-1981." He sent me a copy, and this too was doubtlessly authentic. With no date but clearly from the first six months of 1975, it was a projection by the CIA Director (then William Colby) of the problems and requirements that the entire U.S. intelligence community would likely face during the coming five-year period.

In the study Colby presented a broad analysis of world problems and the corresponding intelligence priorities (U.S.S.R., China, Western Europe, and continuing regional crises—in that order), and he lamented that recent revelations of intelligence operations had caused some of his most pressing problems. We also published the full text of this document in the *Bulletin* with my commentary.

La Repubblica and other European publications also asked me to write articles on the current state of the U.S. intelligence services. I framed them in the perspective of the five years that had passed since initial revelations of the Agency's subversion in Chile, followed by exposure of illegal domestic operations, the Rockefeller, Church and Pike investigations, and the movement to "reform" the CIA, FBI, military intelligence and other agencies.

Several bills had been introduced in Congress including one in the House of Representatives that would have barred all covert action operations abroad during peacetime. The Senate also began consideration of "charter legislation" that would establish responsibilities within the intelligence community and outlaw U.S. participation in assassinations, terrorism, torture and the overthrow of governments. But the "national security establishment" won the battle with "civil libertarians" in the first two years of Carter's administration with the result that no "charter legislation" reached the floor of either house.

"Reform" was effectively dead by the spring of 1979. With revolution in Afghanistan and the fall of the Shah of Iran the political climate changed. Carter had already issued an Executive Order that appeared to restrict the CIA's use of U.S. media, clergy and academics, but through exceptions it provided options for every conceivable covert intervention save assassination. Carter also introduced the most comprehensive bureaucratic transformation within the intelligence community since the CIA was established in 1947, and he gave his CIA Director, Admiral Turner, the power needed to control the budget and tasking of all the agencies. These were the real "reforms," and they were all designed to improve the CIA and other services. As for covert interventions abroad, Turner began restoring the Agency's capabilities that had declined with the scandals under Nixon and Ford.

Rebuilding, though, would take some time. Two years into the Carter administration, Henry Kissinger could still lament with alarm: "We have practically deprived ourselves of our covert capability. This is especially dangerous in areas where there is a huge grey area between military intervention and normal diplomatic processes."

Reports from Washington continually cited low CIA morale and many security problems. Admiral Turner's style of running the Agency had provoked hundreds of officers to resign or retire early. His emphasis on technical collection as opposed to "human sources" reduced the quality of intelligence reporting and analysis. And even President Carter complained about the CIA's poor coverage of events leading to the overthrow of the Shah.

For his part Turner publicly complained that his biggest problem as leader of the intelligence community was plugging the continual leaks of secrets.

The CIA was incapable of keeping its documents, like Colby's five-year plan, under wraps. A series of Soviet penetrations had compromised some of the most important secrets. Christopher Boyce had passed the product of satellite electronic intercepts, and William Kampiles had sold the "Top Secret" technical manual for the most important photographic satellite.

John Paisley, one of the Agency's senior analysts of Soviet weapons and military strategy, disappeared. A body found in the Chesapeake Bay near Washington was said to be Paisley, but identification was cursory and so doubtful that insurance companies refused to pay policies to his wife. Some believed he escaped to Moscow. So rampant were the theories of a KGB "mole" at the highest level in the CIA that even James Angleton, the Agency's former counter-intelligence chief, and Colby himself were suspect.

At the end of May I returned to Bieber Haus to sit and sweat after applying for extension of my residence permit. I got it, but instead of a year they gave me only until mid-September. The woman in charge told me that was because Giselle's permit was valid only until then, and she refused to extend Giselle's permit on the basis of her contract for the coming season. We would have to go back in September for extensions for both of us.

Again I began to imagine catastrophe lurking just ahead. We had almost finished *Dirty Work II*, and Lou Wolf's appendix would include the names and career backgrounds of more than 700 CIA officers who were now on post, or had recently served, in Africa. So, too, the *Bulletin* continued under fierce attack in Washington for Lou's regular "Naming Names" column.

I became so worried about the residence situation that I called Bill Schaap in Washington and asked him to take my name off *Dirty Work II* as editor. That left me only as author of the two articles I had written. I also removed my name as editor of the *Bulletin* but left it as editorial advisor. How that would save my residence in Germany was a little obscure, as Bill and others pointed out, but such was my fear that I was hardly rational—at least on this point. Lyle Stuart had already announced the book with all five of our names as editors, but he agreed to take mine off.

Publication of *Inside the Company* in German presented the same problem. West German and Austrian publications called for interviews, and I was determined to avoid any journalists who might intentionally distort what I said or put words in my mouth. I checked with Kurt Groenewold, who was part-owner of the publishing house, on every request before accepting.

It was an opportune time for interviews. In Nicaragua the final insurrection against the Somoza regime was underway. News media were carrying daily stories of atrocities by the U.S.-trained National Guard. Somoza's air force was bombing Nicaraguan cities.

In the interviews I was able to cite CIA support for that fascist dynasty over many years. Meanwhile I turned on the radio at least six times a day for news of gains by the Sandinista Front (FSLN) against the Guard and of the Carter administration's efforts to mount a joint U.S.-Latin American military intervention.

Any intervention to prevent the FSLN taking power would, of course, be 95 percent U.S. But times had changed since Lyndon Johnson's invasion of the Dominican Republic in 1965. Costa Rica, Panama, Venezuela and others, as well as Cuba, had supported the FSLN, and for once the Latin Americans stood firm against intervention. On July 19, as Nicaraguans poured into the streets to celebrate the Sandinista triumph, I was packing my suitcase for a trip to Cuba.

I had to fly to Madrid for a visa and the Cubana flight to Havana, and I decided to try a little experiment. I wanted to see how the CIA and other security services used the airlines computer reservations system for control of travellers. Surveillance teams had followed me on other trips to Spain, and this time I wanted to see what the reservations system might produce. I said nothing by telephone about flying to Madrid, and neither Giselle nor I spoke about it in the flat. I made no prior reservation, but on the day of the flight I wanted, I went to the airport and bought the ticket. About five hours would elapse between the moment my name went into the computer on buying the ticket and my arrival in Madrid.

As I stood in line at the Madrid airport passport control I noticed two men in civilian clothes behind the control booth. I passed on through, and they seemed to disappear. I got my bag and told the taxi driver the name of a hotel on the Gran Via in central Madrid. There was so much traffic on the expressway into the city that I couldn't be sure if we were being followed. But once we turned into the narrow winding streets leading to the rear entrance of the hotel, the car was obvious: a white sedan with three men inside. As I paid the taxi driver the surveillance car parked half a block away.

Well, I thought, my clever little scheme worked. It meant my name was on some kind of computer control within the reservations system, and it probably rang buzzers or printed out automatically at security service terminals. Maybe directly in Madrid, maybe at a CIA terminal, maybe in West Germany—and maybe all three.

I immediately began to worry about staying in the hotel, where I was subject to any provocation, so I called my friends Alberto and Milagros for advice. They invited me to stay at their house. For two days the surveillance agents followed me around, without the slightest discretion, from their base in a school parking lot across from the house.

Imagine my disappointment when they failed to show up for my flight to Havana. I'd planned to congratulate them on a job well done, but as luck would have it, the computers had probably spewed out another name.

Only a week after the Sandinista triumph, the Cubans held their annual 26th of July celebration. In my Havana hotel room I turned on television to watch Fidel's speech in Camaguey, the provincial city awarded the main ceremony this year. Just before he was to start, an amazing scene took place on the platform. A ten- or twelve-member delegation of Sandinistas appeared, almost all with beards, guerrilla uniforms and rifles. From one side of the TV screen to the other, all I could see were *abrazos*, euphoria and sheer joy. No wonder such emotion, I thought to myself. It wasn't just that the Sandinistas had defeated one of the longest and cruelest "Made in USA" dictatorships in Latin American history. For twenty years the Cubans had struggled against CIA subversion and U.S.-imposed isolation. Now, at last, they were joined by the Nicaraguans in another giant step in the centuries-old Latin American revolutionary process.

I sat, my attention riveted to the TV. I was positive that the "U.S. Interests Section," Carter's diplomatic mission in Havana, was recording the history-making scene in Camaguey for viewing in Washington. They'll never stand for this in the States, I said to myself, never, no matter which administration or party is in power. The Sandinistas, like the Cubans, had fought for generations to eliminate U.S. dominance and exploitation of their countries. Now they've shown that armed struggle can still be successful, even against Latin America's most servile and favored U.S. client. Carter couldn't intervene militarily, but neither could he rescind the Monroe Doctrine. It didn't matter that no Soviet hand was involved. The Sandinistas had broken free. And the revolution was not just to overthrow Somoza. It had been fought in the name of the poor, it stood for land reform and social justice, for redistribution of wealth and income, and for nonalignment in foreign policy. The Nicaraguan example, like the Cuban example, was too dangerous for U.S. interests in the rest of Latin America.

I remembered my memorandum for the Allende government in Chile eight years before. I got out paper and pencil and began making notes on all the ways I could imagine that the CIA would be called on to subvert the Sandinista revolution. First the structure and cover of the Station in the Managua Embassy. Then the likely covers of

officers in Nicaragua posing as "private citizens." I made lists of the
Agency's probable information needs and the ways they might proceed to get it, how they would target for agent recruitment and what
technical operations they might try. Then I described the likely covert action methods and the institutions through which they would
work: political parties, trade unions, media, the anti-Somoza middle
class, perhaps the Catholic Church. And their goals: split the revolutionary leadership; build up Agency-controlled and supported institutions; organize a political opposition; begin a propaganda campaign.

For several days I worked on the analysis with the intention of
getting it to the Sandinista security service, although I had no idea
what sort of service they had. But I knew they must have had some
intelligence organization in the struggle against Somoza and assumed
that this would develop into a formal, established counter-
intelligence structure. And hopefully soon, because the Agency was
surely already at work reorganizing its Nicaraguan operations. In the
end I had a long memorandum with as many details as possible, and I
hoped it would help the Nicaraguans anticipate and thwart the Agency's certain task to derail and destroy the revolution. I got the document to a member of the Sandinista Front and offered to go to
Managua anytime to discuss it and related matters. They would let
me know.

While in Havana I met with a member of the Grenadian mission
and offered to help them in any possible way. Only five months
earlier in Grenada the New Jewel Movement (NJM) had overthrown
another tyrannical regime supported by the U.S., that of Eric Gairy,
in a lightning, nearly bloodless coup. The NJM's revolutionary plans
were similar in principle to Nicaragua's, although application would
obviously be different in an Eastern Caribbean island nation of only
100,000.

Already Maurice Bishop, the Grenadian leader, had denounced
several cases of arson as suspiciously similar to the CIA's operations
against Michael Manley's government in Jamaica in 1975-76. Bill
Schaap knew Bishop and other Grenadian leaders through solidarity
work with the NJM in the States, and had told me they all knew my
work in Jamaica and from *Inside the Company*. I sent word to Bishop
through Bill that I would go to Grenada anytime they wanted.

Giselle, Therese, my sons, and my mother and father all flew to
Havana for a kind of family reunion. I hadn't seen Dad and Nancy for
a year and a half, and they had never met Giselle and Therese. We

rented a house in beautiful Varadero, the world-famous beach resort east of Havana, and spent a week there swimming, fishing and just relaxing.

As soon as I was back in Hamburg I wrote an article outlining probable CIA operations against the Sandinista revolution which I called "The CIA's Blueprint for Nicaragua." Recalling elements of Agency operations in Chile, Angola, Portugal and Jamaica earlier in the decade, I suggested "pluralism" and "moderates" as two catchwords likely to be used to create an international "cause" as revolutionary programs moved ahead. Alleged Nicaraguan support for liberation movements in El Salvador, Guatemala, and Honduras would be another propaganda issue, as would "free elections," "betrayal of the revolution," and "substitution of one dictatorship by another." It was published in Managua, in the *Bulletin* in Washington, and in several other countries.

My older son Philip was now enrolled in New York University, and Christopher, now fifteen, was at the International School in Hamburg. After one year in Virginia, he had decided Hamburg would be better.

Chris's first friend was a classmate named Joe Stebbins, son of an officer at the U.S. Consulate General. The Stebbins family were very friendly to him and apparently didn't know who his father was. Shortly after school started in September, Chris took a fall in a basketball game and needed to see a neurologist. I called the Consulate for a recommendation and was referred to a man who answered "Stebbins." He gave me the name of a doctor from the Consulate list, and in closing I gave my name and thanked him for the attention he and his wife had shown to Chris. Stebbins, who seemed not to have caught my name, replied that he was happy Joe and Chris were friends.

Within a week we learned from Joe that all officers in the Consulate had been instructed that their children were not to visit the notorious Agee home. The result, of course, was that Joe and other children of the Consulate staff came over "secretly" several afternoons each week and on most weekends.

In mid-September my fears of continuing residence problems were finally put to rest. Both Giselle and I received one-year extensions, and it now looked as though I was safe. Much later, in my Freedom of Information Act documentation, I discovered that a few weeks earlier the Justice Department had decided not to prosecute me for revelations in the first *Dirty Work*. It was the sixth such decision since publication of *Inside the Company*, and all were based on the Agency's continuing insistence that their crimes against me could not be subject to revelation through discovery procedures in a criminal trial. Whatever those crimes were, they were in effect the CIA's own guarantee against prosecution.

Giovanni Arnone received a court order that I appear in Rome for a hearing in our lawsuit against the producer of the film *Covert Action*. He sent it to me by mail, and the day before the hearing I again flew to Rome. His partner, Marina, was at the airport to meet me. At passport control four officers were waiting to take me into custody. Back up to the same police office as before. I showed the court order, duly signed by the judge, but they wouldn't let me in. Marina argued, but to no avail. After a few hours' wait, they put me on a flight to Geneva.

The Italian newsweekly *Panorama*, in a story on the refusal to let me appear in court, revealed that for at least three years U.S. missions had been circulating requests to various governments, including the Italians, that I be denied entry.

Meanwhile in Washington our "guerrilla campaign" of exposures continued. With each new edition of the *Covert Action Bulletin* and the wide press coverage of Lou Wolf's "Naming Names" column, the CIA and its supporters in Congress and the media reacted with continual references to the Welch case and accusations that we were publishing "assassination lists."

Two new "pro-intelligence" foundations popped up in Washington, one headed by former CIA counter-intelligence chief James Angelton, and the other headed by former CIA Deputy Director Ray Cline. Both pledged support for "restoration" of the CIA's effectiveness while lamenting the damage done by revelations and criticism.

In the months that followed, Admiral Turner and the CIA Deputy Director, Frank Carlucci, made speeches and testified before Congressional committees urging passage of the proposed Intelligence Identities Protection law, now known as the "Anti-Agee Bill." They also campaigned for exemption of the Agency from provisions of the Freedom of Information Act.

Turner compared exposure of his young officers to "cutting off the hands" of a young surgeon. By his count we had exposed some 1,200 CIA employees, not bad considering that *Dirty Work II* would bring the total to about 2,000, and that Turner's own personnel cutbacks had reduced the number of people in the Directorate of Operations to around 4,000. Elsewhere he said, "The professional effectiveness of officers so compromised is substantially and sometimes irreparably damaged. They must reduce or break contact with sensitive covert sources . . . some CIA officers must be removed from their assignments. . . . Replacement of officers thus compromised is difficult and, in some cases, impossible."

Turner and Carlucci both lamented that our revelations were making it harder to recruit foreigners to work for the Agency. They also blamed the Freedom of Information Act, even though this law had specific provisions for protecting secret information. The problem was, according to Carlucci, that potential foreign agents didn't know that, and therefore they were afraid any collaborations with the CIA would become public knowledge.

The "pro-intelligence" campaign was gaining strength by summertime when Carlucci announced that the Agency was to seek legislation that not only carried the "anti-Agee" provision. It would also criminalize exposure of Agency personnel by people who had never served in the government, never had access to classified information, and worked only through analysis of public documents. This was an "anti-Wolf" provision, destined to stop his "Naming Names" column. Most lawyers and even some members of Congress saw it as clearly unconstitutional. For his part President Carter said, in a speech about the famous Soviet Brigade in Cuba, "We will increase our efforts to guard against damage to our crucial intelligence sources and methods of collection."

In mid-October, all thirteen members of the Intelligence Committee of the House of Representatives sponsored a new bill, written by the CIA itself. It contained both the "anti-Agee" and the "anti-Wolf" provisions. As for constitutionality, Representative Boland said, on introducing the bill, "I fully realize that this ["anti-Wolf"] provision will be controversial. It could subject a private citizen to criminal prosecution for disclosing unclassified information obtained from unclassified sources."

Another sponsor added, "We must provide all appropriate protection for the brave men and women who serve our vital national interests by working for our country undercover in foreign lands—often at their own peril." Sure, like those brave CIA men working with the Somoza regime, with the Argentine, Chilean, Uruguayan and Brazilian generals, with the Shah before he collapsed, and with torturers in many other countries.

Typical of the false emotional arguments was the following, from Rep. Wyche Fowler, another sponsor: "About two years ago the Agee crowd named almost everyone under cover in Western Europe, almost everyone in the NATO countries. Families were harassed . . . and bombs discovered." As the *The Real Paper* in Boston put it: the proposed bill was "Save-a-Spook" legislation.

In Hamburg I finally found time to read the books written by other former CIA officers after *Inside the Company.* I was both fascinated and astounded by the amount of historical information contained in those books, most of which were exercises in self-justification. Those officers told of their experiences and of operations from Europe of the late 1940's to Vietnam of the 1970's, from recruitment of Nazis for anti-Soviet operations to abandonment of thousands of Vietnamese agents when Saigon collapsed. Taken together one got a pretty good history of the Agency's work all around the world, and from a personal viewpoint they gave me added incentive.

The best of those books by far, as an exposure of a single large political, paramilitary and propaganda operation, was John Stockwell's *In Search of Enemies.* He wrote it in secret and published without submission to the Agency for censorship. It told the story of the blundering, lying and corruption in the CIA's 1975–76 intervention in the Angolan civil war of which he was Task Force Chief in Washington. After that operation ended he resigned in protest.

I met Stockwell for the first time the year after his book was published. We met in Cuba of all places, where he had gone with a friend for spearfishing. We spent several days together, and found ourselves in general agreement on the destructive role the CIA plays in Third World countries.

Although Stockwell had come under fierce attack from the Agency · and its supporters for publishing the book without submission, he was determined to keep on writing and lecturing in the States. It was a strange experience, speaking for the first time with a former Agency operations officer whose experience was rather like mine, and whose reaction was not so different either. He too had served about twelve years, from the mid-sixties to mid-seventies, in various African posts and in Vietnam where he met his wife. And he too had gradually turned against the work. We exchanged many tales, and stayed in touch afterwards for mutual support and encouragement.

When the hostage crisis in Iran broke out in early November, I was not surprised. During the preceding months of mass demonstrations and agitation the U.S. Embassy had been occupied rather easily by young revolutionary militants. No one should be shocked at anything against the U.S., I thought, after all the years of American support for

the Shah and his SAVAK secret police. The surprise came when the
militants started almost immediately to distribute copies of secret
documents they had captured. Journalists started calling me and
sending copies for verification and interpretation.

The first batch showed the militants had gotten into the CIA Station's vault area—offices usually protected with massive steel doors
and combination safe locks. These documents were copies of false
identity papers issued to CIA officers: one a set of Belgian documents
including passport, and another of West German papers also including passport. Instructions for use of the documents were also there as
well as Agency correspondence showing they came from the regional
support base in Frankfurt. Other documents revealed the identities
of four or five Station officers, all but one of whom were among the
hostages.

If these were a sampling of what had fallen into the hands of the
militants, the whole affair was probably going to be the worst disaster
in the Agency's history.

As the hostage crisis continued to be front page news, I wondered
how the documentation could be used most effectively. At the same
time I was appalled at the emotional "let-our-people-go" reaction in
the States. Not just from government leaders but overwhelmingly
among ordinary people. No question it was a tragedy for every one of
the hostages, but nobody carrying out U.S. policy in Iran was an innocent bystander.

For god's sake, I wondered, doesn't anybody realize how dreadfully Iranians suffered under the Shah? And how important U.S. government support, especially the CIA's, was for him to stay in power
all those years? I thought of the scene on television some months before when people discovered a secret torture center in Tehran. It was
a basement with steel beds that had horizontal wire mesh at different
levels. An Iranian was explaining that coal fires were started under
the beds, and prisoners were strapped to the mesh, then gradually
lowered until they were barbecued. At the end he held up two se-
vered, charred human hands that torturers left behind. But that film
segment was from Dutch television and probably never seen in the
States.

Praise the power of the flag. All those ordinary people in the States
thinking that Americans working in that Embassy were representing
them, doing jobs that were in their interest. They seemed not to have
a clue that American foreign policy, and those who execute it, serve

first and foremost the interests of the small minority of people who run the country for corporate America. Such delusion! But then, wasn't that my belief when I went into the CIA? But after the Vietnam War, Watergate, and all the other scandals one would think the country would be a little more aware.

As the crisis continued and efforts to secure release of the hostages failed, I kept thinking: the Iranians want the Shah in exchange for the hostages. Carter can't send him from a New York hospital back for trial and execution. He just can't. What other solution would the Iranians accept? Copies of Embassy documents kept arriving, and one morning I thought: what about the CIA's files on its operations in Iran? The whole warehouse back to the 1940's: cables, dispatches, memoranda, agent files, descriptions of operations, financial statements, everything! Those files, tens of thousands of pages, probably hundreds of thousands, would make a whole research institute. Journalists, historians, scholars of all sorts could get out to the world for years to come the details on how the CIA helped create a real Frankenstein monster. And as they did, maybe more Americans would understand the hatred and outrage they were watching on television.

Would the Iranians accept a "files-for-hostages" deal instead of "Shah-for-hostages"? Who knows? Those files are their history, all the details on how the Agency set up the SAVAK, trained its officers, supported that murderous institution in every way possible. They would learn the name of every Iranian who ever worked with the Agency, how much they were paid, what their jobs were.

And Carter. What would he do if confronted with the choice of "files-for-hostages"? Protect the CIA? Or make a deal? The files, after all, were nothing but paper in one sense, and truth in another. Would U.S. public opinion, so distorted over the capture of these "innocent" Americans, favor prolonged captivity over humiliation of the discredited Agency?

If the Iranians made a "files-for-hostages" proposal, the pressure on Carter might be strong and would grow. And if he did give up the files, that would be the end for the CIA. Any successor organization would be years in developing new covert capabilities.

Reports coming from Tehran suggested the possibility that the hostages might be put on trial before some kind of tribunal, something the Carter administration quite obviously feared.

If the "files-for-hostages" idea was accepted, then the CIA rather than the hostages would be put on trial. But how could the Iranians be confident that they would get *all* the documentation? That they wouldn't be cheated? I knew the Agency's filing systems and could tell if they got everything, and other former officers would probably help too, if that were the solution.

If a "files-for-hostages" deal were made, the *Bulletin* could ask for the files under the Freedom of Information Act, and the Carter administration would have to declassify them. Later, after the exchange, the documents could be used at a tribunal organized by the Bertrand Russell Peace Foundation, the Iranian Students Association or some other group.

Crazy as this idea may have seemed, I discussed it with several people who were involved in the crisis, or were close to people involved. One was Sean MacBride who had made a couple of trips to Tehran to mediate. He thought the idea had possibilities and would pass it along. My lawyers knew the Iranian Consul General in Hamburg, and we discussed the idea with him. He said he would discuss it with the Foreign Ministry in Tehran.

Most of my conversations about the idea were over my home telephone, which I knew was no more private than a Washington, D.C., radio station, but I didn't care if people from the Agency on up to Carter knew. It was just an idea, and I had nothing to hide. But nothing happened. No response anywhere. Except in the United States.

On December 17th, a Monday, Mel Wulf called from New York. He said I was in the news again. The *New York Post* that morning had headlines covering most of the front page reading: "CIA Traitor May Judge Hostages." Mel read the text.

> Iran wants Philip Agee—the CIA defector believed to have sent at least one agent to his death—to help judge the U.S. hostages. A leading Iranian diplomat in the U.S. told the Post: "There will be an anti-imperialist, anti-Zionist American on the tribunal and Philip Agee is at the top of our list of candidates. He is a true enemy of American imperialism and we respect him greatly."

The article went on to quote David Phillips, former chief of the Agency's Latin American Division, the officer who had retired in 1975 to organize a defense of the Agency and a campaign against me, *CounterSpy* and later the *Bulletin*. Of Iran's interest in me, Phillips said,

> I suspected that would be the case. Agee has a talent for creating mischief. He has been active like this. He's an articulate guy. He can

do a great deal of damage. He certainly would work hard to spread the propaganda. If I were a hostage, he'd be the last guy I'd want to see.

Then the article repeated the Agency's accusation that I was responsible for Welch's death and alleged that attempts to reach me for comment were unsuccessful. It was unsigned, but Mel had found out that it was written by a *Post* writer named Gregory Rose. As if to drive home the danger factor, a front-page box opposite my photograph read: "Exclusive: Iran hit team is on the loose in U.S.—See Page 3."

"That's wild Mel," I said. "Absolutely crazy. I haven't been invited to serve on any tribunal, and I wouldn't go to Iran as long as the hostages are held. The *Post* didn't try to contact me for comment—I was home all day yesterday and this morning. That story's a plant because I did propose an idea: The Agency's files on all its operations in Iran since the forties in exchange for the hostages. But there's been no response. Things are just too confusing out there."

"Well," Mel replied, "I already contacted the Iranian mission at the U.N., and they said none of them gave the story. That's what I'll tell reporters along with your denial."

Not long after Mel's call, the telephone started ringing, and I told all the journalists that the story was a plant, totally without substance. As the week went by, I wondered again and again what the point of that story was. It didn't make sense to me.

On Saturday I was filing some papers when I came across a little booklet published by the State Department for Americans travelling abroad. It listed the addresses, telephone numbers and principal officers of every American diplomatic mission in the world. I thumbed through it and found the section on Iran. There were four different telephone numbers for the Embassy in Tehran. Then I checked my telephone book and saw that I could dial direct to Tehran. Should I or shouldn't I?

Why not? I dialed the international code for Iran, then the Tehran code, then the Embassy number. To my surprise it started ringing, and to my greater surprise someone answered.

"Hello," I said in English. "I'm calling from Hamburg in West Germany. Is that the American Embassy in Tehran?"

A man responded in English but with obvious irritation. "No, this is the nest of spies. What do you want?"

Not a good start, I thought, but I went on. "My name is Philip Agee and I. . ."

He interrupted. "Ah, I know you. I read your book—we all have—
it's been very helpful to us. Why are you calling?"

"Look, I have an idea I want to pass on, an idea that might be a
solution to the crisis there."

"Okay, wait just a minute. I'm going to transfer the call to the recording room."

He came back on, and I went through the whole "files-for-
hostages" idea. Afterwards the Iranian responded that he thought it
might be a possibility and that he and the others would discuss it at
the next meeting of their "Revolutionary Council." He asked for my
number, which I gave him, and said he would call me back in a few
days. I asked him his name and got the answer, "Mehdi." When it
was over I thought, Well, that's done. The right people have the idea.
Now just wait and see.

The next morning I started cooking early. Therese had arrived from
Paris for Christmas, Phil had flown over from New York, and Lou
Wolf was visiting. For the following afternoon, Christmas Eve, we
had invited about forty people over, including members of the ballet
company, friends I had met in the solidarity movement, and school
friends of Chris and Phil.

I was preparing a big pot of black beans with knuckle of pork and a
variety of sausages that had to be diced. About two in the afternoon
Therese and I were chopping onions in the kitchen, and Giselle and
the boys were decorating the Christmas tree, when the buzzer from
the street entrance sounded. Giselle went to the inter-com phone,
then came into the kitchen. "Joe Stebbins's father, from the Consulate, is downstairs. I just rang him in."

Wonder what he wants. Could he be bringing a present for
Christopher? I walked to the door and looked down the staircase as
Stebbins walked up. I didn't see any package.

"Bob Stebbins," he said as he reached our landing. He was about
my age, a little younger maybe, with a somewhat meek but perfectly
friendly appearance. For an instant I wondered why he was dressed
in a suit and tie on Sunday. He held out his hand. I took it and invited
him in.

"Uh, Mr. Agee, I've just come for a minute. I was asked to bring a
letter over to you." He reached into his coat, pulled out a sealed envelope from Consulate stationery, and handed it to me.

I could feel my breath getting short. I saw my name on the envelope but didn't open it. "Is this all?"

"Yes," he replied, and then as if forcing the words out, he added, "but I think you ought to read it."

"What's it about?"

Looking everywhere but at my face, he said in a barely audible, halting voice: "The Consulate has been instructed by the Department of State in Washington to inform you that the Secretary of State has revoked your passport. Sorry to bring bad news at Christmas."

XIV

Man Without a Country?

My reaction to Stebbins's surprise was automatic and by now familiar. Taking short, shallow breaths, I felt that involuntary protective mechanism, something like a tent sliding up the back of my brain, along the top and sides, and coming to a stop around my eyes. Like a lens, it focused my attention with such intensity that my face felt like stone.

I glanced at the letter and back at Stebbins saying: "I'll read it later." Then I turned to the door.

"Mr. Agee," Stebbins protested mildly, "I'm supposed to bring your passport back to the Consulate. For your trip back to the States the Consulate is authorized to issue you an identity card which you will have to surrender on arrival."

Almost straining to speak, I answered: "I'll call you after I've spoken with my lawyer." Stebbins acknowledged and turned toward the steps while I entered the flat and closed the door. In the hallway, I opened the letter.

The Department of State has requested the Consulate to inform you that the Department has revoked passport number Z3007741 issued to you on March 30, 1978. . .

The Department's action is predicated upon a determination made by the Secretary . . . that your activities abroad are causing or are likely to cause serious damage to the national security or foreign policy of the United States. The reasons for the Secretary's determination are, in summary, as follows:

Since the early 1970's it has been your stated intention to conduct a continuous campaign to disrupt the intelligence operations of the United States. In carrying out that campaign you have travelled in various countries (including, among others, Mexico, the United Kingdom, Denmark, Jamaica, Cuba, and Germany), and your activities in those countries have caused serious damage to the national security and foreign policy of the United States. Your stated intention to continue such activities threatens additional damage of the same kind.

You are advised of your right to a hearing. . . You are requested to surrender the passport to the Consulate forthwith. . . . Any future use of the passport could constitute a violation of Section 1544 of Title 18, United States Code. . .

As I read the letter one thought dominated all others: what happens now? Will this action really force me back to the States? Will I have to leave Giselle and Chris? Will the Germans start a deportation proceeding? Will I be imprisoned and put on trial when I get back?

The shock was such that I had hardly noticed everybody looking at me, waiting for an explanation. "They revoked my passport," I said, trying to be calm and to conceal my fright. I handed Giselle the letter which she began to read without speaking. But Therese and the boys shouted: "Out loud, out loud!" I stood there as Giselle started again, reading to the others, and thought, I'd better call Mel Wulf right away.

I went to the office, dialed his home number in New York, but no one answered. Must be at his country place for the weekend, I thought, and I didn't have that number. Then I called Ramsey Clark, also in New York, and read him the letter. He said the revocation was illegal. The Secretary of State couldn't revoke a passport if I hadn't been indicted for a crime. He didn't have Mel's country number either, but he would find him and ask him to call me.

I walked into the kitchen to find Giselle wiping her eyes as the others watched. As I put my arm around her she said, "They're going to send you to the States. I know it, I know it."

"Don't worry. Ramsey just told me it's illegal. They can only revoke a passport if you've been indicted. And that hasn't happened."

"And the German government? If you don't have a passport they'll probably send you to the States. You shouldn't have made that call to Tehran yesterday. That's the reason."

"Maybe. But now I understand *The New York Post* article on Monday. They planted that story about the 'tribunal' to justify revoking my passport. They knew about the 'files-for-hostages' idea and were afraid it might work. My call yesterday gave them the final jolt. Let's not worry, not yet. Ramsey's going to get Mel to call. Let's see what he says."

I called Harmut Jacobi, but he was away for the weekend. Then I called Kurt Groenewold, and he said he did not think the German government would act quickly. He would speak to several people about both the political and the legal situation. At his suggestion I started writing a statement for use when the inevitable calls from reporters would start. That reminded me to call Dad and Nancy to give them the news before they heard it from others.

Lou Wolf was out Christmas shopping when Stebbins came, and when he got back and read the letter he seemed more shocked and outraged than anyone. He helped me write the press statement, in which I ascribed my passport revocation to the "files-for-hostages" idea. Since the false "tribunal" invitation from the *Post* story was sure to come up, I decided to mention that the militants at the Embassy had asked if I could go there but not to serve on any "tribunal." Lou suggested that I include a strong statement that I would not go to Iran for any reason until after the hostages were released. "You just can't imagine," he said, "how chauvinistic the country is over the hostages. People really mean that 'Nuke Khomeini' nonsense."

Then the calls from reporters started, hardly an hour after Stebbin's visit. A State Department spokesman had announced in Washington that my passport had been revoked, giving the reasons contained in the letter. He also said efforts to revoke my passport had been going on for several years, but only recently had Cyrus Vance, the Secretary of State, concluded that the case was strong enough to hold up in court. He also said I had been ordered to return to the States, which I declined, that I had refused to turn over my passport, and that West German authorities had been advised.

The press agencies had checked on my status with Bonn and Hamburg officials who said foreigners in West Germany need valid passports to remain here. But apparently no decision had been made on deportation proceedings. One reporter read a quote from a Bonn Interior Ministry official who said, "We would be hardhearted to do this

at Christmas, but afterwards it is another matter." I refused to specu-
late or to be drawn into discussion, limiting my comments to a reading of the prepared statement. But I confided to Lou, beyond earshot
of Giselle, Chris, Phil or Therese, that things looked awfully bad.
I just couldn't imagine being separated from them by force, for
months, maybe years, maybe the rest of my life.

In the midst of constant calls from the press, Mel Wulf finally got
through. I read him the letter and his response was positive, almost
brash. "No, no. They can't do that. The Supreme Court settled passport matters years ago. Without an indictment they can't revoke a
passport. This isn't England, or France, or Holland. Here you've got
rights, protections. This is a constitutional question. You've got a constitutional right to travel. I'll talk to the State Department tomorrow,
and if they refuse to cancel the revocation we'll go straight to court.
You're gonna win this one."

Mel's remarks were encouraging. But the more immediate cause
for anxiety was wondering what the Germans would do. We continued preparing the meal for Christmas Eve and decorating the tree,
but our earlier festive mood had turned to eerie silence. I put the
"Hallelujah Chorus" on the stereo but it didn't help much. When we
went to bed that night Giselle was still in a state of gloom, and I didn't
feel much better.

Next day friends began arriving in early afternoon. My *bohnen
eintopf* was a hit, but our sudden crisis was the main topic of conversation. About three o'clock Kurt, Petra and Hartmut arrived, the latter with a couple of thick lawbooks. The apartment was crowded, so
we went back to my office to talk in quiet.

Hartmut showed me something he had found in the West German
laws on foreign residents. The law required foreigners to have valid
passports, but there was an exception. One section, dating from the
early post-World War II period, allowed U.S. citizens to reside in the
country if they had a "Card of Identity and Registration" issued by
the Foreign Service of the United States. In a footnote Hartmut
found that this document was simply an identity card confirming U.S.
citizenship and issued by any Embassy or Consulate.

"You mean," I asked Hartmut, "that if I get one of these I can stay
here without a passport?"

"That's what the law says."

"Well I'll be goddamned," I said. "They'll have to give me one of
those. The passport is just a travel document. Revocation doesn't affect citizenship." I went running to the kitchen to tell Giselle. She

was relieved but wondered if the Consulate might simply refuse to give me the card. "I'll ask Mel to check with the State Department," I said. "I don't think they can refuse."

Hartmut said he would immediately write a letter to the Hamburg authorities advising of the passport revocation and of the legal recourse that I was taking in the U.S. He would also insist that they take no step against me pending the outcome of those proceedings. If I could get the "Card of Identity and Registration" it would be better, but he was almost certain I'd be safe in the meantime.

We opened presents late into the night, now with a little more hope and cheer. Next morning I was still asleep when the telephone started ringing. I reached under the bed for the phone. "Hello."

"Mr. Agee, this is Mehdi in the nest of spies."

"Ah! Yes, good morning." I sat straight up on the edge of the bed.

"I'm calling to tell you that we considered your idea. We have decided that we only want the Shah. People in Iran know what the CIA did. The farmers know from their lives of poverty, the intellectuals and students know from repression they suffered, and the clergy know from years of prison."

"All right, well. . ." I started to comment, but he went on.

"We think the CIA's files would be useful, but we already have a collection of the CIA's documents. We don't need any more to learn what the CIA was doing here. If you want to come and see all these documents, we're very glad to show them to you and. . ."

I interrupted. "You know what? The day after I called you the Secretary of State revoked my passport. I can't travel anywhere, and I may be sent to the States."

"Yes," he replied, "we read about your passport. Don't worry. Most of us spent years without passports of our country. If you want to come here we will get you an Iranian passport. We also have some CIA spies in the group who are telling us things."

"I don't think I will go anywhere right now. My lawyer is going to try to get my passport back. I'll think about going later. I've also been getting copies of CIA documents that you've been distributing there."

"You can come when you want. Goodbye." Well, I thought as I hung up, that was that. An idea, a telephone call, and now no passport.

I wasn't the only one with travel problems. Lou Wolf flew to London and called me a day later with a new "Believe-It-Or-Not" tale. At Heathrow the immigration officer stamped his passport, passed him through, then came running after him in the baggage claim area. They searched his luggage, found a copy of *Dirty Work*, saw my name with his as co-editor, and took him into custody. Later the immigration officer cancelled his entry permit with the statement: "I understand you are an active associate of Mr. Philip Agee who is persona non grata in this country and in view of your character, conduct and associations in this connection it seems right that your exclusion is conducive to the public good. . ." They kept Lou locked up overnight and planned to send him on a flight back to Hamburg, but he was able to call Larry Grant who successfully intervened. They cancelled their cancellation of his "leave to enter" and gave him a four-day entry permit.

Mel Wulf had no luck insisting with the State Department that the regulation under which they had revoked my passport was illegal. We decided to skip the appeal hearing provided in the regulation and go to court. On New Year's Eve the Federal District Court in Washington heard our request for a temporary restraining order directing State to restore the passport. In the hearing David Newsom, the Under Secretary of State for Political Affairs, filed an affidavit attempting to justify the revocation.

> In recent months and particularly in recent weeks the citizens of various foreign countries, particularly the Islamic countries, have demonstrated an increasing sensitivity to allegations that the government of the United States has conducted and is conducting intelligence operations within their borders. Allegations and suspicions of such United States intelligence activities have contributed in some areas to an intensification of anti-American feelings which have the potential to cause serious damage to the national security and foreign policy of the United States. Examples of actual damage may be found in the recent attacks on the United States Embassies in Iran, Libya and Pakistan.

Newsom went on to describe my travels and exposures of CIA operations and personnel, said that these exposures "have endangerd the lives and well-being of many United States employees," and cited the bogus *Post* article about my possible participation in the Tehran "tribunal." He added that my ability to travel would likely cause serious additional damage to the national security. He concluded:

> Among the adverse consequences which could result from such activities would be that United States diplomatic facilities, including Embassies and Consulates, would be taken over by force and that

United States diplomats and other nationals would be physically harmed.

Mel testified that the *Post* article was false and that I would not go to Iran while the hostages were being held, but Judge Barrington Parker wasn't about to allow such a dangerous man as me to travel. We would have to file suit.

In the days after Christmas I began to get copies of U.S. press comment on my case. The earliest highlighted the false claim that West Germany was proceeding to deport me to the U.S., while others depicted me as a "man without a country." Many were laced with invective. A UPI dispatch, based on interviews with former CIA officers, quoted one as saying: "If I can get him with my bare hands . . . I'll kill him, I'll kill him." Others called me an anti-American, a Soviet or Cuban agent, a vile human being, and a Judas who "devastated the Agency's operations in Latin America," and who "may have single-handedly done more to wreck the operations of the CIA than any other single person."

Time, in a nearly full-page article, quoted CIA officials as saying I was a "traitor" with "close ties to the other side." And *The New York Times*, in an editorial containing such words as "hatred," "suspicion," and "offensive," accused me of bringing discredit on those who wanted to reform the Agency—presumably those "respectable" critics like the *Times* itself.

In early January my case was taken by Judge Gerhard Gesell, known in legal circles as a leading "liberal" in the District Court. By now three lawyers from the American Civil Liberties Union had joined the case on my side. Counting quickly, I calculated that over twenty lawyers in ten countries had helped me in the previous five years. And the ACLU had agreed to pay most of the costs. That was a relief because there were lots of potential expenses down the road.

Our argument in the District Court was based on the First Amendment to the Constitution (Freedom of Speech) and the Fifth Amendment (Due Process of Law) as well as previous Supreme Court decisions in passport cases, principally: *Kent v. Dulles* (1958), *Aptheker v. Secretary of State* (1964), and *Zemel v. Rusk* (1965). In these three cases the Supreme Court held that Congress had not authorized the Executive to restrict an individual's freedom to travel, a right protected by the Fifth Amendment, on grounds of political beliefs and associations, or for vague "national security" considerations, or in limitations of a person's exercise of First Amendment rights, i.e., speech. On the contrary the Court held that passports could be denied or revoked for only three reasons: when a person's citizenship was in doubt, when a person was engaged in criminal activity, or when a person was seeking to escape prosecution.

In order to go straight to the constitutional questions we avoided contesting whether my activities had in fact damaged the U.S. national security. We conceded that I had. That converted our argument into a "pure question of law": whether the Secretary of State had the authority to revoke my passport because of words I had spoken or written under protection of the First Amendment.

Our written arguments were submitted in early January, as were those of the Justice Department arguing on behalf of Secretary Vance, and arguments were heard the middle of the month. Meanwhile the Department of State agreed to issue me the Card of Identity and Registration whenever I wanted it, but I decided to keep the passport and await the judgment. From German authorities we didn't hear a peep. On January 28 we had the decision. Mel was right. We won without a problem. Judge Gesell ruled that Congress had not authorized the "national security" regulation under which Vance revoked my passport and that the document should be restored.

Wonderful! Only trouble was, Gesell suspended for a week his order to revalidate the passport so that the Justice Department could appeal to the Circuit Court of Appeals. More arguments followed with the Justice Department pleading not only that the Court of Appeals review the case, but also that the Court extend Gesell's stay against restoration of my passport.

At this point the CIA entered the case with two affidavits from John McMahon, the Deputy Director for Operations, designed to support the pleading of the Justice Department. His admissions of the damage I had done were surprising, without precedent, and truly satisfying. He acknowledged that I worked for the Agency from 1957 to 1968 in Washington and Latin America where I learned "the secret methodology used by the Agency to provide cover for its employees and cooperating sources." He went on to quote from my London press conference in 1974 announcing the exposure campaign, and he listed over a dozen countries where the exposures were carried in local media. He continued:

> Mr. Agee has engaged in a program designed to expose CIA activities and personnel, through publications, personal appearances and press conferences throughout the world. [He has] stated his intention

to destroy the clandestine capabilities of the CIA through exposure of
the identities of undercover employees and agents on many occasions. . . . Although there have been numerous instances in which
American officials have been subject to deliberate public exposure as
alleged CIA officers, these exposures generally have been identified as
propaganda originating with opposition intelligence services or political groups hostile to the United States. While such exposures may, in
fact, have caused some measure of damage . . . there is, in my judgment, an enormous difference between an allegation . . . by hostile
foreign governments and foreign publications, and a similar allegation
by a former CIA employee such as Mr. Agee.

Mr. Agee . . . is perceived abroad as a highly credible source. His
efforts . . . to expose undercover CIA employees and provoke action
against them has [sic] disrupted the activities of the CIA. Given the
current dangerous situation in which official American personnel find
themselves in Iran and elsewhere, if he continues these efforts it will
certainly place the lives and safety of American officials in jeopardy. . .

It is clear that Agee cannot personally conduct all the investigative
efforts which are an essential element of his program to expose undercover CIA people. As Agee himself has acknowledged, he employs
agents and collaborators to assist him in his efforts. To assure the effectiveness of his collaborators he must train them in the clandestine techniques needed to expose . . . CIA employees abroad. Agee's ability to
travel thus enables him to find, recruit and train his collaborators. . . .
Without the ability to travel Agee will be severely handicapped in
locating, recruiting, training and receiving reports from foreign nationals who, for whatever reason, may be willing to support him and his
program.

The ultimate effectiveness of Agee's program, to destroy the CIA's
operations abroad, is dependent on the activities of hostile foreign
groups. Such groups, depending on the degree of their political ex-
tremism, will engage in actions designed to harm the CIA: such as
physically surveilling U.S. officials abroad; harassing them by other
means, such as demonstrating and picketing their homes and offices
and, in extreme cases, committing murder.

(I do not intend here to claim that Agee has specifically incited anyone to commit murder . . . [but] Agee's actions could, in today's circumstances, result in someone's death. . .) In order to incite hostile
groups to action, Agee has during the past several years made personal
appearances before hostile groups in his travel abroad. Similarly, press
conferences, press releases, and appearances on radio and TV have
significant impact only when they take place within the country in
which Agee seeks to incite anti-CIA action.

Recent events, particularly the hostage situation in Tehran as well as the attacks on our Embassies in Islamabad and Tripoli, demonstrate clearly that the political instability and anti-American feelings in certain countries have increased to the point of making open violence probable with little provocation. Agee's program of exposing Americans abroad by accusations of their involvement with CIA has markedly increased the likelihood of individuals so identified being the victims of violence. Agee's lists of people alleged to be CIA officers now constitute convenient "hit lists" for terrorist groups and radical political organizations anxious to find a means of gaining instant notoriety and national politicial prominence.

For the reasons stated herein, Agee's continued ability to travel will clearly increase the likelihood and probable extent of serious damage to our Nation's foreign affairs and greatly increase the threat to the safety and lives of American officials abroad.

As I read McMahon's statements I kept thinking how cleverly the Agency had colored the exposures with references to the hostage crisis, the burning of Embassies, and physical danger. It was as if the CIA people among these "patriotic Americans" had every right to go about their dirty work unopposed. Was McMahon exaggerating the damage in order to impress the Court? I couldn't tell. But taken at face value the admission was clear: they had been hurt.

The Court of Appeals agreed to review the District Court's decision, and they extended Gesell's stay of his order to restore the passport. Their decision would take four to five months, and if my case went to the Supreme Court, as seemed increasingly likely, another year would pass without restoration of the passport. In order to preclude any surprise action by the West German authorities, I turned the passport in at the U.S. Consulate and got the Card of Identity and Registration. Then I took it to Bieber Haus where they gave me a new residence permit on a piece of paper that tied the permit to the Identity Card. I was now about as safe from deportation as I could be, but I couldn't leave Germany.

About this time, early February 1980, Bill Schaap telephoned from Grenada. He was an old friend of Maurice Bishop, the Grenadian revolutionary leader, and he said Bishop wanted to invite me to the first anniversary of the overthrow of the Gairy dictatorship. The celebrations were being organized for mid-March, and many people from progressive political movements in the Caribbean would be there.

One of the main activities, Bill said, would be an international seminar on the CIA. My role would be to lecture on my experiences and on probable current CIA operations in the region: in particular their operations against the Grenadian revolution.

I said I would like to go, but obviously couldn't without a passport. Bill checked with Bishop and called back to say that Bishop was going to send me a passport with the invitation. Then I began to worry about possible complications with the West German authorities or getting stranded in one of the Caribbean countries where I would have to change planes.

Still, I was excited and grateful. International solidarity, I thought, really is a two-way street. I would receive a travel document from a revolutionary government while both the District Court and Court of Appeals were conniving to prevent me travelling even though I had won. If those judges in the "great democracy" cared the slightest for a U.S. citizen's right to travel, a fundamental constitutional right going as far back as the Magna Carta, they would have restored the passport while appeals went ahead. But no, they treated me as an accused criminal too dangerous to allow free on bail.

The Grenadian High Commission in London sent me the invitation and passport. At Mel Wulf's suggestion, to protect my U.S. citizenship, I had them write on the "Comments" page that I was a U.S. citizen with Card of Identity and Registration issued by the Consulate in Hamburg. But the West Germans, probably under American pressure, refused to cooperate. I took the passport to Bieber Haus and asked them to stamp the residence permit in the passport so that I wouldn't have trouble with the Border Police when I returned.

They refused, saying that the permit was attached to the Identity Card which reflected my true nationality. Since I wasn't a Grenadian citizen they had no obligation to recognize the passport. This meant I would have to get a visa at a West German Embassy, perhaps Trinidad, for re-entry. If they refused or delayed I might be stranded with no way to return. For days I tried to figure out a way to get to Grenada and back, but in the end I had to pass it up. I returned the passport to London and wrote Bishop a letter of congratulations on the anniversary. He answered that the invitation was open for whenever I could go.

Early February was full of surprises that required constant transatlantic telephone calls costing a small fortune. On the very day that the Court of Appeals agreed to take my passport case, the Justice Department brought another suit against me in the District Court seeking a court order, or injunction, requiring me to submit all my writings to the CIA for censorship prior to publication.

For years I had avoided this kind of injunction, first brought against Victor Marchetti and approved by the Supreme Court, by staying out of the States and away from any U.S. legal jurisdiction. But a couple of months before the passport revocation, Mel Wulf and Bill Schaap had filed suit under the Freedom of Information Act (FOIA) against the CIA and other agencies for documents they had about me. Now Justice, in the name of the United States, was filing a "counterclaim" based on my submission to the Court in my FOIA suit.

The FOIA suit by itself was unique. The State Department had hundreds of documents about me, as did the FBI. The Justice Department also had a large number. But the CIA was my main target, and they refused to respond according to the requirements of the law. Nevertheless, we had learned a little. In late 1978, a year after Mel Wulf filed the FOIA administrative request, which should have been answered within thirty days, Stansfield Turner, Carter's CIA Director, commented on my case to the National Press Club. He said the Agency had already spent nine "man-years" reviewing their documents on me.

A year after that, when we filed suit, we drew Judge Gesell. At the first hearing the Agency admitted to having some 45,000 pages on me, about 90 percent from the period after my resignation. That would cover about six years, from the time in 1971 that they learned I was writing a book to the date of my FOIA request in late 1977. During that period the CIA produced an average of 18 pages per day on me, weekends and holidays included. Those tens of thousands of pages comprised 8,699 separate documents, 7,771 of which originated during their six-year "counter-intelligence" program (three to four documents per day on average).

I knew a volume like that had to be transcripts of telephone calls and audio penetrations of places I lived, along with copies of my mail and reports based on sources like Sal, Leslie/Janet and other spies sent to contact me. Details of their work against me through other security services, such as the French, British and Spanish, would also be there. And I was just as certain that somewhere among those documents I could find proof that on many occasions the Agency had acted illegally against me, not excluding assassination plots. Gesell gave the CIA and other agencies a practically indefinite period to process their documents, while advising Mel that he should get a younger lawyer on the case—one who would still be alive at the end.

In the "counterclaim" the government not only sought the censorship injunction. They also wanted the court to require me to repay all income from the *Dirty Work* series through establishment of a "constructive trust," the same maneuver they had successfully used to seize $140,000 from Frank Snepp. That was the income from *Decent Interval*, his book about the Agency's last days in Vietnam, which he hadn't submitted for censorship.

My lawyers and I found this strange because the CIA must have known that I took no fees for those books. Like all participants I ceded income to help finance the *Bulletin*. Stranger still was the total absence of any mention of *Inside the Company*, which, the Agency surely knew, had produced substantial income. Both McMahon and Turner had submitted affidavits with the "counterclaim," but they passed over *Inside the Company* as though it didn't exist. It seemed pretty clear that they had something to hide and wanted to avoid any probing by the court into the period when I was writing my first book.

Still more, in the "counterclaim" the Agency asked the court to prevent publication of *Dirty Work II: The CIA in Africa*, which they claimed was "imminent." That showed how utterly incompetent they were. A pre-publication paperback edition had been distributed by Lyle Stuart and the *Bulletin* staff to delegations at the Non-Aligned Summit Conference in Havana six months before. Then editorial changes delayed formal U.S. hardcover publication. But at that moment, as the government sought to prevent its "imminent" publication, over 4000 copies were on sale in U.S. bookshops including several in Washington, D.C. "You mean it's already on sale?", the Agency's lawyer asked. "I didn't know that." Humiliated, they withdrew this provision of the "counterclaim" but continued the others.

I now had to make a decision. The only way I could avoid the censorship injunction was to attempt to withdraw the FOIA suit. Was it worth more to avoid submission to the CIA's censors than to recover documentation about me under FOIA? I decided it was, but the judge disagreed. He ruled that I was trapped in his court and that both the injunction and the FOIA cases would proceed.

Mel and the ACLU lawyers decided to fight the injunction under the ancient equity doctrine of "clean hands," since the government's case alleged that I had violated my contractual and fiduciary obligations undertaken on signing the perpetual "secrecy agreement" when I entered the CIA in 1957. We would argue that the government had forfeited its right to injunctive relief because of the numerous illegal actions taken against me in violation of my civil and constitutional rights. The government, in other words, was seeking enforcement of the "secrecy agreement" with "dirty hands."

In order to substantiate my argument I prepared a thirty-page affidavit with an equal number of attachments. It was a chronological account of the Agency's actions against me beginning with the Paris visit by Keith Gardiner in 1971 and continuing through the episodes of Sal and Leslie/Janet, surveillances and harassment in different countries, attempts to prevent me seeing my children, harassment of my father by tax authorities, the "drunk/despondent" *New York Times* article, the Welch case, the Pawlowski canard, the various arrests and deportations, and the passport revocation.

For submission to the court I had to take the document to the U.S. Consulate in Hamburg for notarization of my signature. An especially unpleasant German woman, a local employee, had the job of clamping the pages together, placing a seal and stamps, and wrapping it all with red ribbon. When she finished, she said, "I'll be back in a moment."

Immediately I thought: No, no. They're not going to copy it. "You can't take it out of my sight, and nobody in this Consulate may read or copy it." Puffing and fuming she left the document with me and said she had to speak with the Consul. About ten minutes later a man appeared and introduced himself as James Walsh.

"Mr. Agee," he said, "I have to read the affidavit before I can notarize it. If you don't mind. . ."

I interrupted. "Just why do you think you have to read it?"

"Because I have to see that it's the truth before I notarize it."

With that I lost my temper. "The truth? Mr. Walsh you don't have one word to say about the truth of this document. It's my case against the government and the court will read it, not you. Your notarization is simply confirmation that I signed it in your presence. If you don't want to notarize my signature only, and if you insist on reading it, I will speak to the Consul General and inform the District Court in Washington."

He left to consult someone, and after twenty minutes or so he returned sheepishly to notarize my signature. Therese was visiting from Paris at the time and had accompanied me to the Consulate. As we walked out, she heaved a sigh of relief and said she feared I was either going to punch Walsh or have a stroke on the spot.

The affidavit went in, and the legal arguments continued. Decisions in both my passport case and the injunction were months away. In fact, with these two cases plus my FOIA suit, I would be embroiled in litigation for the better part of two years. But other things were also happening. Various journalists returned from Tehran with copies of secret CIA and State Department documents distributed by the militants still occupying the Embassy. Loss of the documents was nothing less than catastrophic for the Agency. I began organizing this material, which described dozens of extremely sensitive cases, for a *Dirty Work III* on the CIA in Iran. But it was a project I never finished, partly because the Iranians eventually published almost fifty volumes of the documents, and partly because I gave precedence to other matters.

About the time the FOIA, passport and injunction cases got going, Allan Francovich finished the documentary film on the CIA that he had begun, with my help, five years earlier. Since my last interviews with him when I was deported from Britain, I hadn't had much participation. But I knew he was busy interviewing other former CIA officers who were talking, including John Stockwell, Victor Marchetti and former Director William Colby. Now he came to Hamburg with an edited print, fresh from winning an International Critics Award at the West Berlin Film Festival. He had named it *On Company Business*.

I arranged for a projection room and sat there in quiet astonishment. Francovich had put the three-hour film together without a word of narration, just archive footage and interviews. It surveyed the CIA's history, from its founding as an instrument for secret intervention in 1947; its role in the Italian elections a few months later; 1950's propaganda and trade union operations in Europe; the coups in Iran and Guatemala; the Bay of Pigs invasion of Cuba; assassination attempts against foreign leaders like Patrice Lumumba; the coups, torture and murder in Brazil and Chile; and paramilitary operations in Angola in the mid-70's.

Dramatic scenes from Congressional hearings showed Senators fingering the CIA's poison dart gun and former Director Richard Helms blowing his top in argument with Senators over the semantics of assassination. Nobody could see this film, I thought, without understanding the hypocrisy and behind-the-scenes violence that pervaded U.S. foreign policy.

Francovich left me cassettes of the film, and I set out to get it on television in as many European countries as possible. He returned to the States, meanwhile, to make final arrangements for nationwide screening on the Public Broadcasting System. When the film was shown, it couldn't be ignored by the U.S. establishment press which by and large gave strong praise: ". . . fills you with a sense of rage and shame . . . a probing, often shocking study of covert operations . . . one of the most important American documentaries ever made . . .

full of painful revelations . . . should be seen by everyone who is concerned about this country's past mistakes and worried about its future." Conservatives, who couldn't contest the film on fact, based
their attack on my credit as "Special Consultant."

In late June, six months after my passport revocation, the Court of
Appeals announced their decision. The three-judge panel, in a
straightforward, 14-page opinion, upheld Gesell's January ruling in
the District Court. But the vote was two-to-one. The dissenting
judge, a man named MacKinnon, wrote a 68-page opinion in which
he set himself up as accuser, judge and jury and found me guilty of
various crimes in connection with my telephone conversations with
Mehdi at the Tehran Embassy. He even wrote the texts of suggested
Grand Jury indictments for: 1) unlawful intercourse with a foreign
government; 2) treason; 3) kidnapping; and 4) seditious conspiracy to
commit extortion.

MacKinnon set his case against me with a profound political analysis of the Iranian situation:

> Early in 1979 the Shah of Iran was forced to leave his country. The
> country soon passed into the hands of a self-styled Islamic Republic
> which termed itself "revolutionary." The person who became the prin-
> cipal figure in the government was a prominent Moslem cleric, and
> there were a great many quick executions of persons who held top po-
> sitions in the Shah's government. As frequently happens with revolu-
> tions, the government that replaced the Shah did not quickly reach
> maturity and dangerous unrest continues throughout the country,
> principally in the capital city, Tehran.

MacKinnon then dwelt momentarily on the Shah's cancer, bile
duct obstruction and hospitalization in New York. He went on to describe my activities as contained in the CIA and State Department
affidavits, and he cited the bogus *New York Post* article about the supposed "tribunal" in Tehran. Then, with reference to me, he quoted
from Sir Walter Scott's *Lay of the Last Minstrel* in allowing that the
government was well advised to "mark him well."

> Breathes there the man, with soul so dead, Who never to himself
> hath said,
> This is my own, my native land! . . . If such there breathe, go, mark
> him well. . .

I didn't exactly choke up with homesickness as I read MacKinnon's outrageous opinion, but the more I read the more I wondered if the man was sane. After attributing to me "a renegade character," he wrote:

> There are relatively few United States citizens who have the same capability and vicious intent to damage our national security as has Mr. Agee. And his particular brand of hate, i.e., alleged CIA activities, is presently at the very core of the Iranian "problem" with the terrorists' demand that the Embassy staff be tried as "spies."

With petulance and mourning, as if germane to any legal arguments, he added:

> Our foreign policy cannot stand much further damage, particularly since Agee is presently directing his attention in Iran and the Near East where the interests of our nation are most seriously hazarded.

In summary he concluded:

> It is an unreasonable interpretation of congressional intent to hold that a passport cannot be revoked for one with Agee's propensities to cause serious damage to this nation. No United States Congress would ever intend to require a President to issue a passport to one with Agee's record and intentions.

MacKinnon, of course, was only speaking for himself, and the fact was we had won. The majority opinion ended: "The judgment of the District Court . . . ordering the restoration of Agee's passport is affirmed . . . and the stay pending appeal is vacated. So ordered." The Friday night Mel Wulf called to give me that news Giselle and I celebrated with friends and began planning a summer vacation trip to Greece.

On Monday I called the Consulate for an appointment to get a new passport. The same James Walsh who had wanted to read my "dirty hands" affidavit told me that the Consulate had no message from Washington authorizing the passport. I asked him to send a cable asking for authorization. The next day when I called again he still had no message from the Department. Days later it was still the same. In an outburst of contempt I called him a "fucking clown" and hung up. Then I called Mel who had bad news. The Justice Department had gone to Chief Justice Burger of the Supreme Court, and he had agreed to an indefinite stay of the order to restore my passport pending decision by the Supreme Court on whether they would accept an appeal from the Court of Appeals decision.

"Goddamit," I said to Mel, "We've won twice and have three out of four judges on our side. Why in Christ don't I get the passport back while Burger makes up his idiot mind?"

"That's the way it is here, Phil. Look, you're free, aren't you? Over here they keep people in prison without trial for less than you're accused of. You're safe for now. Why don't you relax, take some time off, see some castles in Germany."

Later I learned that MacKinnon had held back his opinion until the Supreme Court's summer recess began. They wouldn't reconvene for three months, which meant it would be October before we would know if they would take the appeal. When the Supreme Court finally announced their acceptance, I knew we were going to lose. One way or another they would find a way to modify the Court's earlier decisions.

The Supreme Court also extended the stay on restoration of the passport, but by then it didn't matter. In order to deny the Court a chance to uphold the "national security" regulation for denial of passports, a decision that could affect many people besides me, I asked Mel to withdraw the case. I would get along without a passport for the foreseeable future. That wasn't possible, Mel said, because it was the government, not us, that was appealing. And when to expect a decision? Perhaps May but not later than June of next year.

At the Hamburg Consulate I asked to be put on Giselle's passport, but they said spouses could no longer be on one another's passports. So we postponed the trip to Greece and spent the summer at home. In Washington my "dirty hands" affidavit had gone to the court along with a request under the "discovery rules" for all the CIA's documents on each of the events listed in the affidavit. Our second defense against the injunction was "discriminatory enforcement." The Agency had only gone to court against strong critics—Marchetti, Snepp, Stockwell and me—and not against others who had violated the "secrecy agreement" by publishing without prior CIA approval.

The Agency and Justice Department responded that the "clean hands" equity doctrine did not apply because of lack of connection between my writings, i.e., my violation of the "secrecy agreement," and the actions I attributed to them in my affidavit. That argument was ridiculous because the chain of events began when I told Keith Gardiner in Paris that I was writing a book. Moreover, since the Supreme Court had upheld the perpetual nature of the "secrecy agreement," the binding nature of that agreement persisted throughout the period of my writings and their actions.

Mel telephoned in mid-September after the oral arguments. Judge Gesell had suggested that I "wipe the slate clean" by accepting the injunction and by dropping my FOIA suit. Twice during the hearing he expressed concern over the time he would have to spend in *in camera* review of documents. "Gesell must think we're fools," I said. "Hell no, I won't drop the FOIA. Somewhere in those documents is proof that the Agency committed crimes against me. That judge is paid to try cases, and if he has to review a lot of documents, too damned bad for him."

A couple of weeks later Gesell announced his decision. He rejected my "dirty hands" argument and request for discovery, dismissing my affidavit as "a litany of supposed wrongs." With reasoning worthy of a Jesuit, he wrote that there was insufficient connection between the Agency's actions against me and my writings. "Plaintiff had long since left the Agency when these incidents occurred and the alleged wrong-doing by the Agency since 1971 is not sufficiently related to Agee's failure to comply with the Secrecy Agreement." He issued the injunction requiring me to submit to pre-publication censorship, but he accepted our "discriminatory enforcement" argument and refused to require me to repay money from the two *Dirty Work* books—money I had never received in any case.

Just as Gesell issued the injunction, I was finishing a long article on the CIA's role in destabilizing the government of Michael Manley in Jamaica. It was for a Finnish publisher, who was bringing out a book on politics and reggae in that country. The article highlighted not only the Agency's operations leading to the 1976 elections, but also similar support for violence and turmoil this year, 1980, with new elections set for the end of October.

I had to decide whether to ignore the injunction or submit the article to the CIA. Since my original decision to write a book about the Agency I had been careful to stay within the law, even though mostly on the fringes. Should I now place myself in criminal contempt of the very court that was in charge of my FOIA case? I thought not. I sent the article to Mel Wulf who sent it to the Agency. They had no objections to the article, but they insisted that I submit future writings directly, not via Mel, because he had no security clearance. The possibility existed that he might read something classified in something I wrote. Mel and I rejected such a stupid demand, and after several exchanges of letters the Agency relented.

Jamaica was also the background of the CIA's continuing efforts to get a law passed in Congress making it a crime to name their undercover people. In June the *Covert Action Bulletin* staff had been in Jamaica denouncing Agency intervention during the run-up to the elections. At a Kingston press conference they named fifteen people from the CIA stationed in the U.S. Embassy. A few days later the U.S. press, the Congress, and the whole CIA support network were in a hysterical uproar over the "attempted assassination" of Richard Kinsman, the Kingston CIA Chief, who was one of those named.

Two nights after the press conference someone had fired shots at Kinsman's house. Some versions of the "attack" had bullets whizzing through Kinsman's bedroom and those of his daughters, along with a crater in the garden caused by an exploded grenade. The truth was that bullets were fired at a concrete wall near the garage, and the hole in the garden looked like a spot where a dog had buried a bone. No grenade fragments were found, Kinsman's wife and daughters had been out of town, and Kinsman himself hadn't even awakened. In the morning he reported the "attack" to the *Daily Gleaner* newspaper rather than the police.

The "assassination attempt" was a hoax, but it worked. The Welch case came back into the news, and Congressional committees of both Houses got back to work on "identities protection" bills as they unloaded fresh invective against me and the *Bulletin* staff. Of Lou Wolf one Senator said: "I want him put away." Still, the drive for a new law brought explicit recognition of the success of our campaign. As the Senate Intelligence Committee reported:

> In recent years members of the House and Senate Intelligence Committees . . . have become increasingly concerned about the systematic effort by a small group of Americans . . . to disclose the names of covert intelligence agents. . . . Foremost among them has been Philip Agee. . . . The destructive effects of these disclosures have been varied and wide-ranging. . . .
>
> The professional effectiveness of officers who have been compromised is substantially and sometimes irreparably damaged. They must reduce or break contact with sensitive covert sources and continued contact must be coupled with increased defensive measures that are inevitably more costly and time-consuming. Some officers must be removed from their assignments and returned from overseas at substantial cost, and years of irreplaceable area experience and linguistic skill are lost.
>
> Since the ability to reassign the compromised officer is impaired,

the pool of experienced CIA officers who can serve abroad is being reduced. Replacement of officers thus compromised is difficult and, in
some cases, impossible. Such disclosures also sensitize hostile security
services to CIA presence and influence foreign populations, making
operations more difficult.

In addition to pushing for the law to forbid "naming names," the
Agency was also lobbying hard for exclusion of the files of the Directorate of Operations from public access under the Freedom of Information Act. And they were falsely using my FOIA case as justification.
Time and again the Agency complained that my case was costing
them hundreds of thousands of dollars, that they had set up a task
force with as many as twenty-five officers reviewing the documents,
and that these people had worked some 25,000 hours.

In one report to Congress the Deputy Director for Administration
said that (Agee) "is not only succeeding in tying up the time of Agency
experts, but, in addition, [he] can be expected to use whatever information is ultimately released in his efforts to discredit the Agency and
destroy its operations." Senator Malcolm Wallop, among others,
agreed: "Congress never intended that the American taxpayers
should pay to provide Philip Agee with full-time research assistants
within the CIA, but that is exactly what happened under the
law. . . ."

The proposed changes, though, wouldn't in the least affect a case
like mine. The exclusion of operational files would only affect researchers, historians and other scholars who asked for information on
specific subjects. Any request from an individual for information on
himself or herself would still require a search of files in the Directorate of Operations. Nevertheless, in normal manipulative style the
CIA and its supporters used my case, with its emotive and provocative content, to push for new limitations to the FOIA.

Congress adjourned for the closing weeks of the 1980 electoral
campaign before taking final action on either "identities protection"
legislation or on changing the FOIA. But they were getting closer.
With the election of Ronald Reagan, who had strongly denounced
Lou Wolf and me during the campaign, it seemed pretty clear that
new legislation in both areas was only a matter of time. Reagan and
those around him had also denounced the supposed "emasculation" of
the Agency since the scandals of the mid-70's, and every sign indicated that the CIA would be strengthened and used aggressively by the

new administration. Central America and the Caribbean were at the top of the list, with Cuba, Nicaragua and Grenada as principal targets.

The Supreme Court set the oral arguments on my passport case for mid-January 1981. During the final days of December I called Mel Wulf about an idea I'd been mulling over for weeks. I wanted to attend the hearing. Not that my presence would affect the outcome; rather, I wanted to participate in the proceeding even if only in silence. Besides, I hadn't been back to the States in ten years, and the hearing seemed like an ideal moment to visit—maybe even to begin occasional travel back for political and solidarity work.

I asked Mel if he would file a request with the Supreme Court asking them to lift their stay against restoration of my passport for a ten-day period in January. He didn't like the idea. With the hostages in Iran now more than a year in captivity and the Carter administration in its final days desperately seeking a solution, the political climate was too unfavorable. Press comment on me for over a year had been virulent, particularly each time a new *Bulletin* came out with the "Naming Names" column. They were all Lou Wolf's work, but press dispatches always attributed the exposures to me, recalling Welch, Kinsman and the hostages.

For a couple of days I wavered. Giselle agreed with Mel and told me, without mincing words, that my going back for the hearing was nothing but an ego trip, foolish and dangerous. But I insisted, and Mel made the formal request to the Supreme Court. It seemed they didn't want me back there either because they refused to decide. Instead they passed my request to the Justice Department which, with State, said I could not have a passport. I could only have a "travel document" valid for a Hamburg-New York flight, and another one, to be issued there, for the return flight. Those conditions were impossible because the West Germans might not let me back in without a passport.

More dissuasive were several long conversations with Mel and Ramsey Clark. They outlined three dangers. The first, a possible criminal indictment, seemed remote enough to take the risk. The second, an order to appear for interrogation by Congressional committees, also seemed remote but something I could manage if necessary. The third danger was the one that convinced me not to go: subpoena by a Grand Jury which would give me immunity and ask me questions about other people which I would refuse to answer. Then imprisonment for contempt. Ramsey and Mel mentioned several political prisoners jailed indefinitely without trial through this maneuver. They both concluded that if I went to the States, the chances were good that I would not get back to Hamburg for a long time, if ever. In following years I've faced the same risk every time I considered returning.

The oral arguments were predictable with the Justice Department, relying heavily on MacKinnon's Court of Appeals opinion, asserting that historically Congress had given "implicit approval" for the Secretary of State to deny passports on national security grounds. Moreover, argued Wade McCree, the Solicitor General, my exercise of free speech went far beyond mere words. They were "activities" damaging to the national security. Mel followed the same line with which we won before, but when he called after the hearing he didn't seem so confident. At one point, he said, Justice Byron White remarked that if Mel had anyone but me as his client he would have no trouble winning the case.

Bill Schaap, who had attended the hearing, came on the telephone with a startling piece of news about the killing in El Salvador ten days before of two U.S. "land reform advisors" and their Salvadoran counterpart. The two were employed by the American Institute for Free Labor Development (AIFLD), which I had described in *Inside the Company* as a CIA front. I hadn't been the first to expose the AIFLD, which is an AFL-CIO "education and training institute" for Latin America, but press coverage of the killings mentioned my exposure as a possible contributing factor.

During the hearing, Justice William Rehnquist had asked McCree whether the Secretary of State could deny a passport to someone who wanted to go to El Salvador to criticize U.S. support for the junta. McCree answered affirmatively, and in trying to justify such action he became the first government official ever to confirm the CIA-AIFLD connection. "Recently," he said, "two Americans have been killed in Salvador. Apparently they were some kind of undercover persons working under the cover of a labor organization. . . ."

That was enough to send reporters scurrying to telephones. Next day the story circulated widely with McCree's lame comment that he had been misunderstood. The Agency, AIFLD and the AFL-CIO all issued their usual denials, but the damage was done. For me McCree's blunder made the passport case worth losing.

When I received a transcript of the hearing, the sophistry in the government's argument that my activities were different from exercise of free speech was clearer than ever. In answer to a question from

Justice Rehnquist, McCree said: "Agee was not punished for speech, but for his activities to disrupt and destroy the CIA."

Justice Brennan then asked: "Are these political activities?"

McCree: "Political and more. He identified undercover agents."

Justice Marshall: "But he did nothing more than words?"

McCree answered with the usual "lives-at-stake" argument: "That's right, but those words were deadlier than bullets. We're not claiming that he committed a crime, but that he engaged in activity that goes beyond mere speech."

McCree went on to admit that my "activities" were not punishable if undertaken in the U.S., but then had to concede that taking my passport away was punishment. "It's a form of punishment, but it's not criminal punishment. It's an implementation of the national security. . . ."

A week after the Supreme Court hearing the Reagan administration took office with all its initial bluster and arrogance about "drawing the line" and "going to the source" against revolutionary movements. The equation of armed struggle with international terrorism by the new Secretary of State, Alexander Haig, and the new primacy of anti-terrorism over human rights led to one sure conclusion: the CIA would be busier than ever.

I was finishing an article for *The Nation* on the proposed "identities protection" legislation, but my obsession at the moment was the events in El Salvador. Despite horrendous repression during the past year the Farabundo Martí National Liberation Front (FMLN) was seemingly stronger than ever. As their "final offensive" bogged down in the weeks after Reagan's inauguration, I decided to contact the FMLN and its solidarity organizations for whatever assistance I could provide.

The opportunity came quickly. One morning in early February I noticed a newspaper article entitled: "Russia, Cuba Agreed to Supply Captured U.S. Arms to Salvador Rebels, Papers Say." The article was by Juan de Onis of *The New York Times*, a man of many years' experience in Latin America. According to de Onis, "secret documents" captured from the FMLN and "considered authentic by U.S. intelligence agencies" revealed that in 1980 the Soviet Union and Cuba agreed to provide "tons" of U.S.-made weapons to the Salvadorans from stockpiles in Vietnam and Ethiopia.

One document, de Onis went on to describe, was apparently the report of a trip by the secretary-general of the Communist Party of El Salvador, Shafik Handal, to Cuba, Vietnam, Ethiopia, the Soviet Un-

ion and other Eastern European countries where he was promised
arms and supplies for up to 10,000 guerrillas. Another document reported a meeting in Havana between an FMLN leader and the President of Mexico's ruling political party.

As I read the article one thought came to mind. Was this another
Agency operation? Had they falsified the documents in order to
"prove" that the FMLN was sustained by communist countries? After
all, many allegations of FMLN support by Nicaragua, Cuba and the
Soviet Union had been made in Washington in recent months, but
until now without "proof."

I had a German class that afternoon, but I couldn't concentrate. My
mind kept wandering back to CIA operations in which I and others
had concocted and used false documents in Latin America. The same
happened while watching Giselle's performance that night. I had only
one thing on my mind. Next day I studied the article. De Onis hadn't
mentioned any of the circumstances surrounding the "capture" of the
documents, only "last month" by "government security forces."
There couldn't be any question that the CIA Station in San Salvador
was working daily with those security forces and had every opportunity for a "false document" operation.

During a tennis match a couple of days later I suddenly thought:
Why not try to speak to de Onis? I reached him by telephone at his
home near Washington D.C., and what he told me made me even
more suspicious. He had received the documents not through an unauthorized leak but officially—what we called in the CIA a "surfacing
operation." He was not authorized to show the documents or to give
copies to anyone, nor could he say who gave them to him. Twice in
his article he had mentioned "secret documents"—as if an archive
was captured—but then he admitted he had only seen the two he described. When were they captured? December. Why wouldn't the
government let others see them? He didn't know.

In coming days I telephoned de Onis two more times for details.
He had written that the documents were captured "last month," i.e.,
January, not December. He seemed confused. I asked if he knew
where they were captured, or from whom, or the date or place or battle, or whether they were in someone's knapsack. Apparently he
hadn't asked. He only said: "The people who gave me the documents
know."

My curiosity to see the documents kept growing. I called Congressman Ronald Dellums's office to see if I could get the documents
through him. They had already been on the case for a week, an aide
said, but the State Department wouldn't give them copies.

Ten days after de Onis's article came out the State Department sent several high level officials to Latin America and Western Europe to show the "captured documents" to government and political leaders. Vernon Walters, Ambassador-at-large and former CIA Deputy Director, went to Latin America while Lawrence Eagleberger, the Assistant Secretary of State for Western Europe, started his tour in Bonn. This diplomatic offensive reminded me of Averell Harriman's 1965 tour of Latin America to justify the U.S. invasion of the Dominican Republic. In each capital he pulled a list out of his pocket with the names of "58 trained communists" who supposedly were fighting against the invasion, "proof" that another Cuba was in the making. Was all this a prelude to another invasion, this time in Central America?

I talked to several people about my suspicions, including friends in the Bonn office of the JUSOS, the youth organization of the governing Social Democratic Party. They told me that Eagleberger's main purpose was to convince European social democrats to end their support for the FMLN and its political ally, the Revolutionary Democratic Front (FDR). Would I be willing, they asked, to have a press conference in Bonn to talk about my own experiences in "false document" operations and to discuss this possibility with respect to the Eagleberger "proof"?

I had to think. For the nearly three years I had been in the Federal Republic I had kept a purposely low profile for fear of "damaging diplomatic relations": no public meetings, few interviews, and no press conferences. Was this the time to take a risk? The FMLN-FDR had a representative in Bonn, Leandro Uzquiano, and I asked him if my speaking out could be of value. He checked and called back saying "yes." I decided to do the press conference, knowing it could get me into trouble again, but with no idea that it would be only the beginning of several years' intensive solidarity campaigning.

Before the press conference I discussed the materials I had prepared with Uzquiano and FMLN leaders from their Mexico City office. These included the de Onis article and others alleging Cuban, Nicaraguan and Soviet support of the FMLN; extracts from *Inside the Company* on cases in which the CIA falsified documents; extracts on the Agency's work through the AIFLD, its current use in the Salvadoran so-called agrarian reform, and the Solicitor General's confirmation of the CIA connection; and extracts on Agency operations with Latin American security services and connections with paramilitary death squads. I also had extracts from the transcript of *On Company Business*, Francovich's documentary, outlining assassination operations, and I had examples of false documentation from the Agency's files seized in the Tehran Embassy. The kit totaled more than fifty pages, and copies for journalists were run off in the JUSOS headquarters.

About fifty journalists turned out, including U.S. and European television networks. For over an hour I went through the documentation, section by section, one operation after another. In the end I urged skepticism toward Eagleberger's "captured" FMLN documents, said in the press to weigh sixteen pounds, until they could be carefully examined. Little did I know that the same day, in Washington, the State Department was distributing a 180-page White Paper entitled *Communist Interference in El Salvador* which included nineteen documents attributed to the FMLN.

As soon as I heard of the White Paper I called the *Bulletin* and asked for a copy. It took them nearly a week to get it, but in late February they sent a copy air mail express. Ten days later it still hadn't arrived. A journalist from Bonn called and said he'd seen the White Paper at the U.S. Embassy's Amerika Haus. He went back, persuaded them to let him have it for the weekend, then called to say he would bring it to Hamburg to copy. As if by magic my copy from the States came with the post the next morning, but with the envelope torn apart and the "Express" indicator marked out.

The White Paper consisted of State Department analyses, chronologies and conclusions, the principal of which was that "El Salvador had been progressively transformed into a textbook case of indirect armed aggression by communist powers through Cuba." Attached as "proof" were copies of the nineteen "captured documents," all in Spanish, with translations to English. I laid out the documents around my dining room table and began comparing the translations with the originals, and these with the White Paper analyses and conclusions.

I was astounded. I found errors in translations that changed the entire meaning of phrases; documents attributed in translation to certain people when no author's name was on the original; and unsupported suppositions, distortions and inventions in the State Department analyses. Moreover, I suspected more strongly than ever that several of the most important documents may have been falsified and added to authentic captured documents. But even if they all were authentic, they didn't prove that outside powers were arming the FMLN.

In order to check allegations in the White Paper and the contents of the documents I began several weeks of running back and forth to the Ibero-Amerika Institute, Hamburg's outstanding center for documentation on Latin America. Warner Poelchau, a Hamburg journalist who had brought copies of CIA documents back from Iran, offered to help. With Poelchau I put together a 48-page, line-by-line analysis of the White Paper that would completely destroy its credibility for anyone able to read. Warner edited the analysis for publication in Hamburg in book form, along with a transcript of my press conference and the kit I distributed there.

Establishment media in the U.S., meanwhile, had not a word of skepticism or criticism of the White Paper. I had sent copies of the book kit to publishers in fifteen countries, but with the Reagan administration's increasingly threatening stance and the possibility of military intervention in Central America, we couldn't wait for publication. Moreover, the Reagan administration had used the fraudulent White Paper to justify $65 million in emergency military and economic aid for the Salvadoran junta. I sent copies of the White Paper analysis to colleagues in Paris and London, and to the *Bulletin* in Washington. Through press conferences, interviews and solidarity meetings we were able to stimulate reporting on the White Paper's defects in much of the major European media.

The United States was different. Although the *Bulletin* staff distributed the analysis at a Washington press conference in early April, and publication of the whole kit in book form would follow in New York, the major media ignored us. Bill Schaap finally called in June to say that the *Washington Post* and the *Wall Street Journal* had published major criticisms of the White Paper. Both Robert Kaiser of the *Post* and Jonathan Kwitny of the *Journal*, he said, had received copies of my analysis and had used many items from it in their lengthy reporting.

"Did they mention that I'm bringing it out in book form?" I asked.

"They didn't mention you at all," Bill said.

How could they do that, I wondered, with anger and disgust. A few days later I got copies of the Kaiser and Kwitny articles, both of which received front-page position and continued inside. Kwitny had cited fifteen general and specific defects, all of which were in my analysis, and Kaiser cited twenty, seventeen of which were in my analysis. Some citations in both articles had wording quite similar to mine.

Kwitny, for example, wrote, "But nowhere in the documents is there any mention of 200 tons," while I had written, "Nowhere in the documents is it established that 200 tons actually arrived in El

Salvador." Elsewhere he wrote, "The notes, however, appear to be written in at least two different handwritings." My version was: "There are two very different handwritings involved in these notes." Kaiser wrote: "It is obvious that the document is written in two distinctly different handwritings." Kaiser also wrote "There is not a single word in the document about Arafat promising arms and aircraft," while I had written, "There is not a word about military equipment, arms or aircraft being promised by Arafat."

I called both Kwitny and Kaiser to ask why they had not given me credit in their reporting, but they were evasive. I thought of suing for plagiarism, but both Mel Wulf and Bill Schaap advised against it. After all, the political impact of the two articles was what counted, and other major U.S. media had echoed the *Post* and *Journal* stories. In the end the White Paper was discredited, and even its author, State Department officer Jon Glassman, admitted: "We completely screwed it up."

Later a friend in Washington told me that Kaiser had originally given me credit, but apparently Benjamin Bradlee, the *Post*'s Executive Editor, had ordered my name deleted. Almost immediately far-right writers and publications saw the similarities and began a fierce attack against the *Post* and *Journal* for not having acknowledged the contribution of such a disreputable person as me. *Human Events*, said to be Reagan's favorite reading, went so far as to juxtapose on two pages Kwitny's and my phrases to show the similarities. And *Accuracy in Media* headlined one of its attacks: "Disinformation Coup by Agee."

Another attack came in a *New York Times* article by Arnaud de Borchgrave who wrote that Agee's "material—supplied by his Cuban friends—was a primary source" for the *Post* and *Journal* articles. My material, of course, was nothing but the White Paper. Another writer, R. Emmett Tyrrell, wrote in the *Washington Post* of me: "Late last month this cryptic figure emerged from one of his vaporous foreign haunts to hold a press conference in Bonn. . . . For 90 minutes he held reporters in the grip of his hand. . . ." He went on to suggest, without a hint of irony, that at the CIA's direction I was trying to get recruited by the Soviets as a double agent.

In late June, in the midst of the White Paper controversy, the Supreme Court announced its decision on my passport case. As expected, they overturned the lower courts' decisions, ruling that the Secretary of State indeed had implicit Congressional approval for denying passports on national security grounds. It didn't matter that

Administrations as far back as Eisenhower had unsuccessfully sought such legislation from Congress. In its seven to two decision the Court ruled that the Secretary of State can deny a passport, with no justification required, to any citizen who the Secretary fears will damage U.S. foreign policy.

The Court overruled the *Kent v. Dulles* decision by drawing a false distinction between my "speech" and my "conduct." From then on any American who went abroad to protest U.S. policies at an international congress, a symposium or a political rally could have his or her passport lifted. Any journalist who reported news unfavorable to official policy faced the same fate. Prior doctrine that freedom to travel was a basic constitutional right disappeared.

Chief Justice Warren Burger wrote the majority opinion, straining through invention and innuendo to make me look bad. He said, for example: "To identify CIA personnel in a particular country, Agee goes to the target country and consults sources in local diplomatic circles whom he knows from his prior service in the United States Government." That was totally false and not even alleged by the CIA or State Department. He also wrote that I had endangered lives and suggested that I was in some way responsible for the Welch killing, the Kinsman "assassination attempt," which he erroneously put in 1974 rather than 1980, and the San Salvador killings of the AIFLD men.

Burger also cited allegations from the CIA and State Department affidavits that my activities had damaged the national security, he raised the spectre of the Iranian hostage crisis, and he mentioned the bogus *New York Post* article about the Tehran "tribunal" without my denial. Anyone reading his opinion would surely have agreed with former Chief Justice Charles Evans Hughes, who said, many years ago, that in the Supreme Court, "Ninety per cent of any decision is emotion. The rational part of us supplies the reasons for our predilections."

I used the flood of calls for statements and interviews on the Supreme Court decison to promote the book version of my analysis and other materials on El Salvador. They were about to come out in New York with the title *White Paper: White Wash.* The CIA had written demanding pre-publication censorship, but I insisted it was comment on public policy, not subject to review, and invited them to buy a copy of the German version already on the market.

Much of the establishment media and a number of constitutional scholars attacked the Burger decision as "overbroad" and a threat to "legitimate critics." In so doing most threw their ritual vitriol at me and called on Congress to pass a law that would distinguish between "Agee's kind" and "patriotic dissenters."

Just a week after the decision a new *Covert Action Bulletin* came out with names of fifteen CIA officers in Africa and Europe. As expected, it provoked a new wave of invective. "Renegade former CIA officer Philip Agee has struck again," wrote one columnist. Others saw me as the "gutless, traitorous rat . . . living in plump luxury," and "this Benedict Arnold . . . [who should be indicted for] . . . murder or treason." I hadn't named any CIA people for four years—it was all Lou's work—but the *Bulletin* was always "Agee's publication."

My father called from Tampa saying a lot of that trash had come out in the local press. He had seen all he could take and was going public about me for the first time. By then, at seventy-three, his views had come closer to mine, and he wrote several articles and gave interviews praising my work. "My son thinks every man in this world should have a proper shake," he said. "He is an intelligent, good American, the best kind of patriot."

The local papers contrasted my work with his role as a "city father," former president of civic organizations and charity drives who had built up a million-dollar business. But his support of me had its price. Old friends looked the other way, and hate mail began. A press photograph arrived with a target drawn over my face and "Dead Right!" scrawled underneath. People answered ads in his name for life insurance for children. Funeral homes "called back" in the middle of the night responding to "his call" for immediate service for his deceased son. He said those cranks didn't bother him, but I knew he worried.

Back in Washington my one remaining court case, the FOIA lawsuit under Gesell, was coming to a close. Of the 8,699 documents the CIA admitted to having, they only gave me about 500 and most of these were heavily censored. Their justifications for refusals and censorship were exemptions provided in the law to protect classified information and intelligence sources and methods. But they had to produce an index of the documents, and I was confident that by having dates and places of origin I could confirm that the Agency was behind certain events. Then I could ask the court to conduct an *in camera* review for evidence of illegal CIA actions against me.

The Agency resisted, arguing to Gesell that even including dates in the index would allow me to identify their operations and the agents working against me. Since the documents "provide a detailed account of . . . relatively private . . . developments or events in [his] life," and "he routinely used evasive intelligence techniques to keep very ordinary facts of his existence a secret," document dates and place of origin could reveal the Agency's sources and methods.

Gesell agreed and refused to order the Agency to include dates, point of origin or other details in the index. He did, however, make a "random *in camera* inspection" at CIA Headquarters. Afterwards he wrote of possible "marginal activity" with reference to their illegal work against me, but again he refused to order release of any more documents.

That seemed to be the end, but then the Justice Department released the remainder of their documents which, although censored, clearly showed that the Agency had committed "illegal acts" against me. They also revealed that in 1977 and 1978 Justice had done an investigation for possible prosecution of CIA officers for those crimes. We asked Gesell to order Justice to give us the censored portions containing details of the crimes. He read all the information *in camera* and again refused. But in his decision he no more wrote of a "a litany of supposed wrongs" or possible "marginal activity." Now he wrote that the documents "raise unanswered and in some respects serious questions as to the legality of the CIA's conduct." Yet, the documents were "properly classified," so we got none of the details.

Despite Gesell's rulings against me on the CIA and Justice Department documents, the materials I did get, especially those from the State Department, were extremely valuable. They showed the impact of my work in some forty countries around the world including places as remote (for me) as Fiji. In the end Gesell ruled that we had won our case, and under the law the government had to pay substantial fees to Mel and Bill.

In fact I had not won in the sense of getting details of the Agency's activities against me—just the vague confirmation of "illegal acts." I was also now under court order to submit everything I wrote about the Agency to the Agency for censorship. And without a passport, was I really a "man without a country"? Not quite. I had a secret.

Months before, when the Supreme Court accepted my case, I wrote to Maurice Bishop and said I would like to try the Grenadian passport again. He agreed. My plan was to go to Grenada and return to West Germany via, if necessary, East Germany. Since there was no document control for travellers from East to West Berlin, I would not need a visa and could fly from West Berlin back to Hamburg with my Card of Identity. But even that route wasn't necessary. I discussed it with Harmut Jacobi, which I had not done the year before, and he said I had every right to enter and leave the country, without visa, using the Grenadian passport. He obtained a letter from immigration authorities confirming my right to re-enter which I could use if I had any problem with the Border Police.

In my statements and interviews following the Supreme Court decision I decided not to mention the Grenadian passport. Rather, I thought I should speak to Bishop first. Grenada was under attack by Washington, and I didn't want to make matters any worse. Giselle was on tour in South America, and when she returned we would quietly fly to Madrid, from there to Havana, and from there to Grenada.

XV

"The Solidarity Circuit"

Giselle and I had both dozed off after our little Learjet flew high over Port-au-Prince and proceeded southeast toward Grenada. After two weeks' delay in Havana due to cancelled flights, and a mostly sleepless previous night in Santiago de Cuba, we were finally on the last leg of our trip to revolutionary Grenada. It was a Sunday morning in mid-August, nearly three weeks after leaving Hamburg on my first trip outside Germany in a year and a half. Waiting in Havana had been tiresome, but the elation I felt over being able to travel again hadn't abated in the least.

I awoke to a tug at my knee by our pilot. We were flying over clouds that covered the sea from one horizon to the other. The pilot shouted "Grenada" and pointed to the radar scope. I leaned forward and saw a perfect outline of the lemon-shaped island with fingers and tail jutting out at the bottom—a shape I'd seen many times in publications about Grenada. We began our descent, and the abrupt release from the clouds revealed jungle-covered mountains rising away from coves, sandy beaches and coconut palms.

353

We landed on a little airstrip by the sea about noon. Through the window I could read "Welcome to Grenada" and "Pearls Airport." As we stepped out into the heat, a handsome young man in military uniform approached. He introduced himself as Major Ian St. Bernard, Chief of Police for the Provisional Revolutionary Government (PRG). He said they had been expecting us for several days and had only learned a couple of hours before that we would be arriving with the Learjet charter. I explained the delays in Cuba, and St. Bernard presented us to a lad named Jonathan who said he was a member of Prime Minister Bishop's personal security detail. He would be our escort while we were there.

In the air-conditioning protocol room of the modest frame terminal building, St. Bernard told us that Jonathan would drive us to our hotel where we could have lunch. The afternoon and evening would be free, but the next morning "Ozoo" would come around to discuss the activities they had in mind for us.

"Who?" I hadn't caught the name.

" 'Ozoo.' That's Liam James, a political adviser to the Prime Minister. He is in charge of your trip but couldn't come to the airport just now. The Comrade Leader also wants to see you, but I don't know exactly when. 'Ozoo' will fill you in."

The Comrade Leader would be Bishop, I assumed, and soon I learned that most people referred to him informally as Maurice, which they produced like "Morris." Many people I met had nicknames. St. Bernard, for example, was known simply as "S.B.," and Unison Whiteman, the Foreign Minister, was known universally as "Uni."

With Jonathan at the wheel we started the drive from Pearls to our hotel. The slight bulge in the small of his back under a loose-hanging polo shirt was surely a pistol, I thought, but he leaned back against it with no apparent discomfort. He said the hotel was across the island at Lance-aux-Epines, a little less than an hour away if we took our time. That was fine with me, since I hated driving fast on narrow roads, but any concern over traffic disappeared with the wonders unfolding before us.

We drove along a valley filled with giant bamboo trees framed between towering mountains, then up and up around blind curves and sheer cliffs. Giselle and I were almost speechless. Neither of us had ever seen such breathtaking scenery, such lush vegetation.

Not far into the descent to the other side of the island we began getting distant glimpses of the red tile and rusted sheet metal roofs of

St. George's, the capital and main port. When we reached the first village Jonathan told us to keep the windows closed and the doors locked, and we quickly learned the reason. Several cars were stopped ahead, blocked by a mob of what looked like dancing teenage boys. As we got closer we could see that they were painted from head to toe: some with a greasy black substance that looked like old crankcase oil, others with something white that looked like flour.

Their chanting was unintelligible as they approached our car, jumping up and down in unison to a drum beat. Jonathan said it was just a summer carnival ceremony, but they looked anything but friendly to me. Suddenly Giselle yelled in fright, as we both noticed many of them twirling long black snakes which they pressed against the windows. Not to worry, Jonathan said, as they surrounded the car and held out tin cans for a contribution. He's got the gun, I thought, and he can open his window if he wants. But he kept it closed and inched the car forward behind the others. Soon we were through the village, but the fright from that surrealistic scene was still with us when we arrived at St. George's.

The travel folders had all described St. George's as "quaint" and "picturesque" and they were right. The town rose up steep hills from the Carenage or dock area which curved around the lovely natural harbor. Moored next to the road were several ancient wooden trading schooners with pigs, goats, chickens and assorted crates on deck. Across the bay on a bluff, Jonathan pointed out, was Butler House, a former hotel that was now the main government building.

We left St. George's, passed along several beaches including Grand Anse where the big hotels were located, then out a peninsula to the Horse Shoe Bay Hotel. It was set among luxury homes on the edge of an inlet and consisted of an administration building with restaurant and bar and six or eight multiple-unit cottages. All the buildings were white stucco with red tile roofs, and the gardens and walkways were lined with blooming hibiscus, trimmed almond trees and palms. Giselle and I agreed that a more beautiful setting was hardly imaginable.

Not that we hadn't noticed stark poverty all around during the drive from the airport. Most people, it seemed, lived in frame houses without water or electricity—in sharp contrast to the luxury tourism infrastructure. But the government was actively subsidizing home improvements just as it was struggling to improve the education and public health systems.

After a walk around the grounds we discovered the instant strength of Grenada's fabled rum punch, flavored with nutmeg, the island's main export and source of its fame as "The Isle of Spice." Then we had lunch with Jonathan, who beamed with pride as he described progress on the international airport under construction with Cuban assistance at Point Salines. He would drive us out to take a look whenever we wanted. Another obvious source of pride for Jonathan was the school system—this was the first year in Grenada's history that secondary education was tuition-free and available for everyone. At eighteen he was enrolled part-time in the tenth grade.

That afternoon as Giselle and I strolled along the beach I was filled with fascination to see and discuss first-hand the revolutionary programs I'd been reading about. Bishop and his comrades in the New Jewel Movement had led a popular insurrection against one of the ugliest and most bizarre dictatorships in the Western Hemisphere. They didn't call the revolution "socialist," but it had the essential elements: formation of a people's army and militia to defeat any counter-revolution, a literacy and adult education campaign, agrarian reform with emphasis on job creation and use of idle lands, improvement of public health services, establishment of mass organizations for peasants, small farmers, women and youth, and strengthening of trade unions.

The revolution also espoused a mixed economy and had introduced incentives for the private sector. In international relations Grenada had joined the Non-aligned Movement and established friendly relations with socialist countries including the Soviet Union and Cuba. The "Cuban connection" was the ostensible reason for the flow of hostile propaganda from Washington and through the major Caribbean press and broadcasting media.

Some of the stories were simply wild, like reports of a Soviet submarine base under construction in a bay not far from our hotel, or training in Grenada of "terrorists" from neighboring islands. But the main themes were clear: abuse of human rights because a modest number of political detainees had not been tried; no elections had been held; the opposition press had been shut down; and, by acquiring arms from Cuba, Grenada had become a military threat to its neighbors.

The new international airport, when it opened several years hence, would then provide Cuba or the Soviet Union with an airbase from which they could threaten shipping routes through which over half the U.S's petroleum imports and other essential resources passed. In fact, construction of the airport had been recommended by the World Bank even before the revolution as vital for developing tourism and reaching markets for fresh produce.

Grenada was indeed a threat, it seemed to me, but not in the military sense. The revolution had grown out of the Black Power movement of the 1960's. It was the first of its kind in an English-speaking country, the first in a practically all-black former slave colony. The New Jewel Movement's goals were to eliminate the squalor, unemployment and economic malaise that were the scourge of other Caribbean islands. But to do so they had to create hope, self assurance and initiative where little had existed.

In two and a half years the NJM had made real progress in reducing unemployment, somewhere around 50 percent when they took over, and in stimulating economic development—despite U.S. efforts to sabotage every Grenadian request for international grants and credits. Their success in mobilizing people from all social groups, but especially from among the workers and peasants, was an example that produced understandable fear among the elitist regimes of other island governments. The real threat in Grenada was its example, and the threat that this example would spread—perhaps eventually even among black people in the United States.

The U.S. government's fears about Grenada were immediate. Within days of his overthrow the deposed dictator, Eric Gairy, was trying to organize a mercenary invasion and counter-coup from Miami. Grenada's request to the U.S. for economic assistance was met with an insulting offer of $5000, a warning not to establish close relations with Cuba, and a reminder that tourism in Grenada, as in Jamaica under Michael Manley, was highly vulnerable to poor publicity. Bishop responded with a speech revealing this hostility and ending with the ringing phrase: "We are not in anybody's backyard, and we are definitely not for sale." Almost overnight a new calypso hit with these words spread across the island.

American hostility, of course, produced another version of an old game of psychological warfare. Under threat of U.S.-sponsored counter-revolution, Grenada turned to a friendly government, Cuba, for defensive arms. These were then portrayed as far beyond legitimate defense needs and therefore proof of hostile intentions towards neighbors. Propagandists placed the new airport project in this context.

The flight from Cuba and the initial excitement had left us pretty

tired, so Giselle and I went to bed about nine. I was just dozing off
when someone knocked at the cottage door.

"Yes," I yelled as I scrambled out of bed.

"This is Martin, from the bar. The Prime Minister is here to see
you. He's waiting on the veranda."

"Be right there."

We rushed to get dressed, hurried over to the main building, and
found Maurice Bishop and an aide sitting at a table. They stood up
and we shook hands all around. Bishop was tall, well over six feet, and
built like an athlete. He had a wide smile and clipped beard with several spots of grey—a handsome man by any standard. He welcomed
us, said he was happy we finally got there, and introduced the man
beside him as Liam James.

After we sat down, I noticed Bishop's left eye sometimes didn't
open quite as wide as the right one. Later someone told me that the
slight droop was a result of nerve damage from a near-fatal beating by
Gairy's goon squad, the "Mongoose Gang." Bishop began to talk in a
relaxed and informal manner but with a certain air of urgency.

"Phil, we have a fairly intensive program for you. We have militia-
recruiting rallies in different towns this coming week, and I'd like to
invite you to speak at as many as possible. Then next Sunday I'd like
you to speak at a big meeting planned for Market Square in St.
George's. It's Marcus Garvey Day, and other comrades from the Caribbean will be here. We're also working out meetings for you with our
youth and women's organizations, the cultural and media workers,
and some trade unions. In addition, I want to discuss the CIA with
you and how they would be operating here. Most of us read *Inside the
Company* a few years ago, but we've got some special problems. I also
want you to meet with some of our police and army officers. How long
can you stay?"

"Giselle has to be back at work in Hamburg in ten days, but I can
stay on until we finish. Let's see how it goes."

"Good, I think you can give us a lot of help."

"Prime Minister," I said, "I haven't said anything publicly about
the passport, but I want to thank you very much for letting me use it.
I don't want to cause you more problems with Washington, so if you
have any restrictions or instructions I'll be glad to follow them."

"Don't worry," Bishop replied without hesitation. "I don't think
there's anything you could do to make matters worse. Use the passport as you like."

Bishop went on to discuss the U.S. military exercises then underway on the Puerto Rican island of Vieques. They were war games involving the airdrop of Rangers flown from the U.S. and an amphibious assault against an "unfriendly, mythical" Caribbean island called Amber and the Amberines. Bishop noted that a stretch of coast not far from the hotel was called Amber and that Carriacou and Petit Martinique, two other islands belonging to Grenada, were the most southerly of the Grenadines.

The scenario announced for the exercises included "rescue of U.S. citizens taken hostage" and occupation until "democratic elections" could be held. Bishop said they took the exercises very seriously and considered them a dry run for an assault against Grenada. All Reagan needed was an incident like Johnson's Gulf of Tonkin attack, but Grenada was not going to give it to him.

Bishop then discussed the growing propaganda campaign against Grenada, and the importance of my emphasizing in my meetings the CIA's use of the media to discredit and isolate its enemies. As I was agreeing, Giselle flinched and ducked once again, as she had several times before, when small darting objects flew over our dimly lit table.

"Don't worry," I said, "they're only swallows."

"They're bats, bats," she said with her usual assertiveness.

"Swallows, that's all they are," I insisted.

Bishop broke in with a knowing smile. "I'm afraid Giselle is right. They're bats. You'll see a lot of them at night, but they're harmless."

We talked for another half-hour before they left. "Ozoo" would drop around in the morning with more details on my program, and Bishop would meet with me again in a few days. The next day I rented a car so that during our free time, when Jonathan wasn't around, we could see more of St. George's and the rest of the island.

During the next two weeks I spoke with other leaders of the NJM, activists in the mass organizations and others. With everyone I tried to imagine and articulate all the ways the CIA could be working to undermine, discredit and isolate the revolution. Since there was no U.S. Embassy in Grenada, where the Agency would normally have its principal office, they would have to work in part through residents and visitors.

The hundreds of American students at the St. George's Medical School formed one obvious pool of potential recruits and was an ideal mechanism for putting agents on the island. Another large group was the thousands of Grenadian citizens resident in Trinidad, the U.S.,

Canada and Great Britain. Surely efforts were underway, perhaps with the help of allied security services, to spot and recruit expatriates willing to return to the island.

Paramilitary operations would also have high priority in order to rekindle an armed opposition. Several bands of armed counter-revolutionaries had already been wiped out, but not before nearly killing Bishop and the entire NJM leadership in a bombing at a Queen's Park rally in 1980. Propaganda operations were already obvious through the same mechanisms used against the Michael Manley government: the Inter-American Press Association, the Caribbean Publishers and Broadcasters Association, the American Institute for Free Labor Development, and a wide variety of "private" research groups and "think tanks."

One night I was scheduled to speak at four rallies for militia recruitment—all in different towns some distance apart. A fifteen-year-old army recruit with a mini-Renault was assigned to get me to the meetings on time. Rain and hail falling on the tin roof of the first meeting hall interrupted us long enough to wreck my schedule, and for the rest of the night my determined driver sped around the island on one-lane roads like he was training for the Formula I championship.

I couldn't remember a darker night. With the driver's AK-47 jammed against my seat and munitions clips rattling on the floor, I sat in quiet panic watching the car lights blur against the jungle walls. We bounded from side to side, slid around corners, and slammed against one pothole after another. At the final meeting, where I spoke with Bishop, I was so done in I could hardly give my speech.

For the Marcus Garvey Day rally thousands of people jammed Market Square, and I got my first real taste of Grenadian revolutionary oratory. Kenrick Radix, the Minister of Legal Affairs, spoke first, concentrating on the Jamaican hero's work to raise black consciousness in the Caribbean and the U.S., and the hatred, harassment and imprisonment he got from the U.S. government in return.

Radix's energy and emotion brought an enthusiastic but curious reaction from the crowd. Besides cheering and applauding at appropriate intervals, people constantly responded with their own rambling expressions of agreement. Often they would interrupt him in midstream with long chants and political songs—rather like a time-out in a sports contest. Over and over I heard the main refrain: "No Backward Reaction Can Stop This Revolution."

Other speakers from progressive movements in Barbados,

Dominica, St. Lucia and Trinidad spoke in praise of Grenada, and I followed with the theme of Grenada's example as the real threat to U.S. hegemony in the Caribbean. At the end a somber Maurice Bishop described in detail the Ocean Venture war games and pledged that no amount of U.S. pressure would cause Grenada to stop its revolutionary programs to benefit the poor. His manner of speaking, in simple, reasoned and articulate expressions, brought huge ovations.

Before leaving I went to several mountain camps where militia and army units were on night maneuvers in response to the U.S. war games at Vieques. My talks were the same as at the recruiting rallies: to prevent a military attack the Grenadians had to demonstrate that the political, diplomatic and, above all, human costs were too high. That meant military preparedness and effective intelligence.

At my last meeting with Bishop he asked me to return at the first opportunity for more conversations on the danger posed by U.S.-supported counter-revolution. I did just that three or four more times during the coming two years, never catching a hint that dissension was growing within the NJM. My impression throughout was that they were united, making great progress in economic and social development, and successfully working out a new and unique form of popular, grassroots democracy.

As I followed events in Grenada and travelled back, I came to feel a special identification with the revolution. Partly this was due to their development projects and other revolutionary programs, but also to the passport, the friendliness of Bishop and others, and the incomparable beauty of the island.

From time to time Giselle and I discussed the possibility of moving to Grenada after she stopped dancing. She could start a ballet school, and I could continue writing and other activities from there. On one trip we mentioned this to Jacqueline Creft, the Minister of Education and Culture. Wonderful idea, she said. The ballet school could be a Ministry project in the old vacant hotel she planned to refurbish as a center for performing arts.

On that first trip my Grenadian passport had worked fine passing through Switzerland, Spain and Cuba, but I wanted to return to Hamburg via Trinidad where I could take a KLM flight non-stop to Amsterdam. Because of several recent cases of harassment of Grenadians at the Port of Spain airport, there was some doubt whether they would let me through. I flew over anyway and the passport control officer's look of recognition confirmed my fear. But instead of telling me I would have to return to Grenada, he smiled, gave me a friendly welcome, and said he was reading *Inside the Company*.

Back in Hamburg I found a pile of U.S. newspaper clippings with commentary on the Supreme Court's passport decision and my analysis of the White Paper on El Salvador. Depending on the columnist or editorial one read, I was "a villain for all seasons," "a loose cannon rolling around the world," "a terrorist in spirit," "a soiled bit of flotsam from the 1960's," or "an anti-American American whose actions have given aid and comfort to his country's enemies." And, of course, there were "full file" articles going back to the "kidnapping-his-children" and "Soviet-Cuban agent" scenarios.

Far-right publications were also continuing their attacks on the *Washington Post* and the *Wall Street Journal* for having used my White Paper material without naming me as a source. The *Journal's* Executive Editor even published a 1,400-word, three-column defense.

But there were many publications that asked for serious interviews about the CIA's probable operations against Grenada and Nicaragua, and their work in support of the Salvadoran death squads. Invitations to speak at solidarity rallies also came in abundance, as well as one to speak at the opening of the national conference of the West German Green Party. This one gave me special satisfaction because the Greens were growing by leaps and bounds and were subject to fierce red-baiting by right-wing parties and press. I had no trouble relating personal experiences of the same kind.

A couple of weeks after my return from Grenada the Nicaraguan Consul General in Hamburg, Alberto Evertz, called. He had received a message from the Nicaraguan Committee for Solidarity with Peoples (the Sandinista international solidarity organization) inviting me to visit Managua. They wanted me to come in early October, just three weeks hence. Sure, I said, whenever they want.

I reviewed my files and publications on Nicaragua, and by the time my flight touched down at the Managua airport I felt I had a reasonable knowledge of the main problems the revolution was facing. Most of these were economic difficulties relating to reconstruction following the war against Somoza and the determination of the Sandinista Front (FSLN) to bring immediate benefits to the country's majority, i.e., the poor. Only a few weeks before my arrival the government had declared a national emergency in order to curtail strikes, increase productivity, reduce decapitalization in the private sector, and reduce food subsidies and the fiscal deficit.

On the political front several important early supporters of the revolution had gone into opposition, including Alfonso Robelo, a leading industrialist, and Violeta Chamorro, widow of the former editor of *La Prensa*, the country's leading newspaper. This paper, in fact, had become the main organ in opposition to the revolution and was closely allied with the hostile Catholic hierarchy led by Archbishop Miguel Obando y Bravo.

On the Caribbean coast, which Nicaraguans called the Atlantic, early mistakes by the FSLN to incorporate the Miskito, Sumo and Rama indigenous communities to the revolutionary process had alienated large numbers. Several thousand had crossed the Coco River into Honduras where other communities of the same cultures existed, and they were a potentially fertile field for recruitment into counter-revolutionary activities.

Still more dangerous was the active and open recruitment of Nicaraguans in the U.S., Honduras and other countries for paramilitary training. Participation in this program by CIA-trained Cuban exiles and Argentine military officers suggested strongly that the Reagan administration had decided not just to expand the political, diplomatic and propaganda pressures begun under President Carter. Now, it seemed, the CIA would be called on to organize sabotage and irregular warfare against the revolution.

Why such open hostility from the U.S. government? After all, the revolution had broad support of the population, and the FSLN had fulfilled their promises of a mixed economy, political pluralism and a non-aligned foreign policy. True, thousands of Cuban volunteers were participating in the literacy crusade and hundreds of Cuban doctors and other medical personnel were serving in cities and countryside trying to eliminate polio, malaria and other endemic diseases. Both programs had received wide acclaim from international organizations that specialized in education and public health.

Nicaragua, it seemed to me, had the same problem with Washington as Grenada: it was a dangerous example. The FSLN and its supporters had overthrown Washington's most supine client, also one of its most repressive. In doing so they destroyed the National Guard, founded, funded and equipped by U.S. administrations stretching back to the 1930's. Real power was in the hands of the revolutionary army, and no Chile-style coup was imaginable. The dangerous example was that every revolutionary program was designed to help improve the lives of workers and peasants rather than the local version of America's ruling class.

Most important, the Nicaraguan revolutionary process had broad participation of organized Catholics in an overwhelmingly Catholic country. These were the "Christian base communities" that developed after 1968 when the Latin American church adopted its "preferential option for the poor." In Nicaragua these communities joined the war against Somoza under the principle that armed struggle for social justice was justified if no other means for relief were available. With the revolutionary potential of thousands of such communities all over Latin America, the Nicaraguan example was truly dangerous.

As Grenada had turned to Cuba for defensive assistance, so also had Nicaragua when the U.S. refused to help. The FSLN understood all too well that defense of the revolution, its first priority, would require arms, training and foreign assistance. This effort also duplicated the pretext used against Grenada: that Nicaragua's military buildup was far beyond its own defense needs and constituted a threat to its neighbors.

The "Cuban connection" and alleged arms transfers from Nicaragua to the FMLN in El Salvador were the Reagan administration's pretexts for hostility. And to make their case, they had to blame "outside interference," as in the White Paper on El Salvador, rather than internal poverty and repression as the cause of armed struggle in Latin America. In actual fact the revolutionary domestic programs and independence from U.S. tutelage were the real threat posed by the Nicaraguan example. For these reasons it had to be stopped.

Driving around Managua gave me a very strange feeling. Over half a million people lived there, but there was no city center. The 1972 earthquake had wiped out the "downtown" and it was never rebuilt. Shells of buildings stood here and there, and the grid system of city blocks was largely overgrown with weeds and bushes. There was no main shopping district or thoroughfare, just scattered small shopping centers.

Several residential districts in hills around Managua had beautiful homes, many abandoned by Nicaraguans now living in Miami, but most people lived in the poor "barrios" scattered around the city. These were villages with rows of rough frame houses of two or three rooms with sheet metal roofs hardly capable, it seemed, of withstanding a heavy downpour much less a tropical storm. Yet, along the unpaved streets, almost every house had its fruit trees and vegetable and flower gardens. When I visited the main market, the *Mercado Oriental*, I thought immediately of Mexico and the Andean countries:

stall after stall filled with produce, bustling with vendors and buyers, babies nursing and crying, stray dogs looking for a morsel.

For three days after arrival I spoke to people in the FSLN about counter-revolutionary activities from economic sabotage to propaganda to armed actions. These included members of the FSLN National Directorate such as Tomás Borge, the Minister of the Interior, and people working under him. Nearly every feature of my "CIA Blueprint for Nicaragua," written two years earlier, had by now occurred. But the pleasant surprise was seeing how advanced the Sandinistas were in anticipating the CIA's techniques for subversion and infiltration. In all these conversations, Portugal of 1974–75 was much on my mind because of the success counter-revolutionary forces had in splitting the Armed Forces Movement.

The only apparent effort to split the FSLN leadership was the resignation and voluntary exile of Eden Pastora. He had been a popular figure during the final years of the struggle against Somoza, but his defection was limited to himself and several secondary figures— nothing remotely like the Portuguese split. Still, unidentified people had begun painting "Eden" on traffic signs in Managua, and indications suggested that he was opening talks with the Department of State, doubtless with CIA participation.

I reviewed a stack of back issues of *La Prensa* and concluded, as had others, that the hand of the CIA was all too obvious. The paper was using the same techniques as the CIA-supported *El Mercurio* had during the Allende years in Chile, and as the *Daily Gleaner* had during the Manley period in Jamaica. These were designed to create a climate of fear and to discredit the revolution and its leadership. As for Obando y Bravo, his connection with the Agency was clear. In a private ceremony a few months earlier he had baptized the son of the CIA's Managua Station Chief.

Other obvious signs of probable CIA support to the counter-revolution were pirate radio stations operating from Honduras and Costa Rica. They attacked the Sandinistas as Marxists and atheists bent on suppressing religion. Another station broadcast to the Miskitos and was largely responsible for their migration to Honduras. The main grouping of private sector entrepreneurs known as COSEP was another obvious target for Agency support, as were the opposition political parties.

The American Institute for Free Labor Development (AIFLD) was trying with little success to strengthen two small "independent" unions opposed to the Sandinista confederation. More ominously, AIFLD was also working with rural cooperatives in the north, the area where Somoza's National Guard traditionally obtained recruits and where recruiting for paramilitary bands was already going on.

These bands in fact had already begun armed attacks in the north, singling out Cuban volunteers in the health and literacy programs. A few days after I arrived they murdered one, a teacher, as he slept on the floor of a peasant's hut. The Nicaraguan security forces were fully informed of the recruitment and training programs, knew they were sponsored by the U.S., and even knew the exact locations of "contra" camps in Honduras.

The Nicaraguan solidarity organization, CNSP, and the recently formed Central American Anti-Imperialist Tribunal, TACA, had organized an intensive program for me in Managua and several other cities. First was a press conference, then talks and speeches with trade unions, the women's organization, defense committees, media and cultural workers, the Sandinista youth organization, and military and security units. Additional interviews, including radio and television programs, were also scheduled.

To nobody's surprise the press conference itself started trouble with the U.S. Embassy—a controversy that continued even after I had left three weeks later. I planned in my remarks to describe the CIA's targets, the general techniques used to penetrate, divide and weaken progressive organizations, and to stress the need for unity and constant vigilance. But I also wanted to focus attention on the CIA's presence in the U.S. Embassy where they had as many as a dozen people, maybe more, under various covers. So I brought up the previous accusations that I had influenced the assaults on U.S. Embassies in Tehran, Islamabad and Tripoli.

"I denied it," I said, "but the people in those countries knew the CIA was hard at work every day in those Embassies, and they gave them a direct answer. People ought to prepare themselves, like the Moslems, so that the U.S. government knows the cost of aggression, that people will answer violence with violence, that the cost will be too high, that if the Reagan administration invades Nicaragua too many young Americans will be going home in nylon bags."

I was careful not to say anything that could be interpreted as inciting people to attack the Embassy or any Embassy personnel, but that people should be prepared to respond. I went on to emphasize that Nicaraguans should know exactly who the CIA people in the Embassy are: their names and home addresses. "They're not invulnerable, and they should know that they're in for the same fate as the people they attack."

Those remarks, I knew, would be seen as a provocation, but little did I anticipate the reaction. The next day they were carried in headline articles by *Barricada*, the FSLN newspaper, and by *El Nuevo Diario*, the other pro-government paper. Wire services reported immediately that the U.S. Embassy had gone on full alert against a possible assault, had implemented plans to evacuate families, and had started burning files.

That was fine, I thought. Let them worry a bit. As I expected, the wire services made their usual distortions with stories that I had called on people to take over the Embassy or burn it. They even quoted the Embassy Chargé d'Affaires as having told the Nicaraguan government that "this will not be another Tehran." Vice-President Bush, adding his two cents while on an official visit in Brazil, said he had nothing but "contempt" for me, said I was "totally irresponsible," and resurrected the "KGB-agent" canard.

The meetings that followed night and day were especially interesting for me because people were highly aware of the CIA's aims and methods. Copies of *Inside the Company* and other writings on the Agency had circulated widely, and recent showings of Allan Francovich's documentary, *On Company Business*, in theaters and on television also helped raise consciousness and understanding. All that made my goal of "demystifying" the Agency much less difficult than in most countries.

One meeting I really enjoyed was with religious workers and activists at the Antonio Valdivieso Ecumenical Center where I spoke of the CIA's penetration and manipulation of organized religion for political ends. This was a headquarters of sorts for the "popular" or "revolutionary" church. About a hundred people were at the meeting, including priests, nuns and lay workers from the United States who were working with the revolution. Some were my age and had gone through the same reactionary Catholic educational process as I, only to find new ideas and values as years passed.

I also spoke with people involved directly in the fight against the "contras." My impression after hours of conversations was that the Sandinistas had turned their rudimentary intelligence system of the guerrilla period into a first-rate intelligence and security organization. They were far more advanced than Cuba was at a comparable period, for I had learned in the Agency of some of the Cubans' blunders and oversights—mostly due to inexperience and lack of knowledge. But

Sandinista security was quite up to the job with notable successes in penetrating the "contras" as well as defending against the CIA's efforts inside the country.

At the end of my trip I had the strong impression that the Reagan administration's overall program against Nicaragua, especially the "contra" operation of terrorist forays in the countryside, was strengthening rather than weakening the revolution. With each death at the hands of the "contras," who everyone knew were mostly ex-National Guardsmen, thousands of mourners turned out chanting slogans against Yankee imperialism. And each program of U.S.-Honduran military maneuvers was answered in Managua by tens of thousands in mobilizations that swelled the voluntary militia, the defense committees, and the regular defense forces.

Perhaps the most impressive experience I had was watching the way members of the FSLN National Directorate spoke at rallies and on television. They were articulate, spoke the language of ordinary people, and made frequent references to Nicaraguan history. Knowledge of history, particularly of over 100 years of interventions and invasions by the U.S., was a pillar of strength of the FLSN and its supporters. I hadn't the slightest doubt that if Reagan invaded, the Nicaraguans would fight on indefinitely from the mountains and jungles—just as Sandino himself had done in the 1920's and 30's.

While in Managua I received several invitations for lectures in San José, Costa Rica, but I was refused a visa—at the request of the U.S. Embassy, I later learned. Apart from the lectures, I wanted to accompany a West German journalist, Gunter Neuberger, who was visiting Nicaragua and other Central American countries in preparation for a book on CIA operations and personnel in the region. In San José he released the names of several hundred CIA employees who were current or recent operatives in Central America and the Caribbean.

Among the names on Neuberger's lists were thirteen CIA people currently assigned to the U.S. Embassy in Managua. *El Nuevo Diario* picked up the story, publishing photographs and biographic information on them. This was followed by a "strong verbal protest" by the U.S. Chargé d'Affaires who called publication of the names a "provocation." Unidentified Embassy officials speculated that I had a hand in the exposures, complaining awkwardly that "the Nicaraguan government's support for Agee while he was here gives us grounds to protest to them that their willingness to countenance his activities led to this."

By that time I was in Havana and "unavailable for comment," although far from in retreat. For another week I did press, television and radio interviews and had many meetings to discuss CIA operations and the Reagan invasion threat—not just to Grenada and Nicaragua but to Cuba as well.

The whole country at that moment was mobilizing, taking very seriously the current U.S. naval maneuvers and bellicose language about a possible "quarantine" or "blockade" of Cuba, or a *cordon sanitaire* between Cuba and Central America. As in Grenada and Nicaragua, I discussed defensive measures with a variety of Cuban officials including Ramiro Valdés, the Interior Minister, but the Cubans were already well-prepared. An invasion there would have been met by as many as a million people in arms, but if Reagan was foolish enough to try, the Cubans were ready.

Back in Hamburg I found that the Reagan administration and its supporters in Congress were scrambling anew for the law to criminalize publishing the names of CIA undercover employees. The immediate reasons were my trip to Nicaragua, the Neuberger list published in San José and Managua, and the simultaneous publication in the *Covert Action Bulletin* of 69 more names of CIA people working in 45 countries.

The House of Representatives had already passed the law, but it had bogged down in the Senate Judiciary Committee. The Senate Intelligence Committee, in urging that the legislation be moved forward, wrote of the thirteen exposed in Managua: "Several of those named have already received death threats, and the families of a number of these American officials have been evacuated for their personal safety. U.S. officials in Managua believe the publication of these names is linked with the visit of Philip Agee to Nicaragua last month."

Naturally the Welch case came back in the news, as did the Kinsman "assassination attempt" hoax in Jamaica. President Reagan personally urged passage of the law in a letter to the Senate Judiciary Committee, wherein he wrote: "Nothing has been more damaging to our intelligence effort than the pernicious, unauthorized disclosures of the names of those officers whom we send on dangerous and difficult assignments abroad." Yeah, I thought, like the brave men training "contra" terrorists in Honduras to murder unarmed Cuban teachers and defenseless Nicaraguan peasants.

Establishment media pleaded for a version of the law that would "get the Philip Agees of this world" but not themselves—which also meant *not* getting "the Louis Wolfs of this world." For some editorial writers I was "a CIA agent turned CIA tormentor," for others "a swine."

Faced with the insoluble dilemma posed by Lou Wolf, Congress passed the law in June 1982, "getting" *The New York Times* as well as me and the *Covert Action Bulletin*. From then on any publication or journalist who published information identifying a "covert agent" would suffer criminal penalties including prison and substantial fines.

The offender would be guilty even if the information was unclassified and lawfully obtained, and even if the person exposed was engaged in crime. The law not only criminalized exposure of CIA officers but everyone around the world who was working with the Agency. As the *Village Voice* put it:

> This means thousands of CIA-bribed politicians and trade union officials; this encompasses the security police of dozens of countries; this includes kings, sheiks, presidents, party leaders, dictators and juntas from one end of the third world to the other.

The law even made it a crime for a U.S. religious organization, a university, or a political group to expose a CIA or FBI agent infiltrated for information, manipulation or disruption. In actual fact, as I said in interviews at the time, the law was written to protect secret *operations* as well as secret *agents* because exposures of "activities," including crimes, usually were impossible without including "participants."

The law was a close equivalent to a British-style Official Secrets Act. It only lacked the name. Its targets were indeed the "straight media" as well as our "guerrilla journalism," as Senator John Chafee, a sponsor of the law, confirmed. When asked if a reporter might be prosecuted for exposing a "covert agent" involved in crime, he answered: "I'm not sure that *The New York Times* or the *Washington Post* has the right to expose the names of agents any more than Mr. Wolf or Mr. Agee."

Proponents of secret operations were jubilant, and Reagan lost no time signing the law. Ronnie Dugger described the celebration in his chronicle *On Reagan: The Man and his Presidency:*

> On a warm and sunny day in June the press was invited to the CIA Headquarters in McLean, Virginia, near Washington. In the open, across a greensward, some hundreds of CIA people gathered. Reporters were served punch; the Army Band played patriotic music. Appar-

ently President Reagan first spoke secretly to about a thousand of the secret people inside. Then he came outside, and before those gathered on the grass he praised the CIA employees as "heroes in a grim twilight struggle" and signed the Intelligence Identities Protection Act into law.

Leading constitutional scholars in the U.S. said, as they had before, that the "Louis Wolf section" violated the free speech protections of the First Amendment. But nobody, not the American Civil Liberties Union or any other body, came forth to challenge the law in court. They all knew that the matter would end up in Warren Burger's Supreme Court where "national security" matters, as in my passport case, routinely took precedence over constitutional rights.

Reflecting on how crudely the CIA and other proponents of the law had used the emotive content of my "bad name," years after I had stopped publishing CIA names, I wondered if I should defy the law and resume research and publication of names. Lou Wolf, since he lived in Washington, was obviously silenced. The law applied to me, even though I was living abroad, but names could be published outside the U.S. where the law didn't apply to publications. Most extradition treaties, moreover, excluded "political crimes."

I consulted colleagues in the U.S. and other countries, and they all said not to defy the law. Some day I might want to return to the U.S., and some day I might be able to do useful political work there. I agreed, knowing that various foreign journalists already knew how to research CIA stations in U.S. Embassies, and there was no lack of foreign publications that would print the names.

So I obeyed the law and continued submitting all my writing to the CIA for censorship. And I travelled. For several years after returning from Nicaragua I travelled constantly to address solidarity meetings, political rallies, trade union conferences, and university seminars. On every trip I tried to generate support for Nicaragua, Cuba, Grenada, the Salvadoran FMLN, and other revolutionary movements.

Giselle took to calling it the "solidarity circuit," but she accepted my frequent absences with little complaint. So many invitations came that I started filming video talks for use at meetings I couldn't attend. Invitations from France and Britain were the only ones I couldn't accept, since those governments refused to let me in, even for a one-day university lecture or union meeting.

One trip I especially enjoyed was to Ireland. A friend and colleague, Jonathan Bloch, had co-authored in London the best historical survey yet published on British covert interventions. It was a tale of terror, murder, bribery, cheating, lying and torture which British intelligence had practiced in varying combinations from Malaya in the early 1950's to Ireland in the 1980's. It made the CIA look almost tame in comparison.

The book, *British Intelligence and Covert Action*, was published in London, and simultaneously in Ireland to preclude suppression by British authorities. I had written an introduction, pointing out that practically everything the CIA knew about covert action they had learned from the British during and after World War II. The publisher then asked me to come to promote both editions in Dublin.

There was doubt I could go to Ireland because that country and Britain have agreements allowing travel between the two countries without passport control. The conventions also provide that persons excluded from one country should not be allowed in the other—presumably including me. Nevertheless, the Irish let me in for the full press, radio and television blitz, some of which was carried in the British media.

Had my mother lived, I think she would have been proud. Her Irish lineage was pure, with parents named Hogan and O'Neill, and she never seemed to outgrow the buffets of growing up Irish Catholic in Protestant New England hinterland. Nor was she ever completely comfortable with the Deep South traditions in Tampa—more religious bigotry, more WASP status symbols.

She gave me my earliest political memory: her own indelible hatred of British repression in Ireland, something of a family tradition it seemed. So if I could get in a point or two against British imperialism, moribund though it was, it would have made her happy.

Eventually Giselle and I received unlimited residence permits in West Germany, and the constant fear of additional expulsions began to wane. My Grenadian passport enabled me to travel back to that country, to Cuba and Nicaragua from time to time, and in most of Western Europe. But the CIA and State Department never stopped intervening, as in Costa Rica, to persuade governments to deny me visas or prevent my entry. Embassies even wrote diplomatic notes saying that my presence for this or that activity, already publicly announced, would be considered a "hostile act."

During the spring of 1983 Giselle was in hospital recovering from an illness when she decided she wanted to finish her dancing career in Zurich. There she could dance many of the ballets she had learned earlier when working with George Balanchine in the New York City Ballet. She called her friend Patricia Neary, the Director of the

Zurich Opera Ballet, who said, sure, she had a contract for Giselle. Giselle resigned from the Hamburg company to be effective at season's end, and I went to Zurich and found an apartment. We would move in mid-summer.

One night in June, several months after Giselle's decision, Pat Neary called with bad news. That afternoon she had had a meeting with Helmut Drese, the Zurich Opera Director, and had asked why Giselle's contract was delayed. Drese replied the he would not issue a contract for Giselle Roberge because her husband was a "communist spy." The police, he said, had come to him and said they understood Giselle was to receive a contract. Because of her husband, they said, she would not receive a residence permit. Pat said she was powerless to do anything if Drese refused the contract.

I immediately called Gian Andrea Danuser, my lawyer in Zurich, and asked him to speak to the police. They told him that Drese had gone to them first asking about me. Moreover, they had not said that Giselle, or I, would be refused residence. Danuser informed Pat of Drese's duplicity, but Drese refused to change his decision.

All of us wondered how Drese learned of me. For all the notoriety I had gained, I was hardly a household word for an opera director. The decision was his, not the police's. Someone must have known his reactionary political views and decided to try to sabotage Giselle's contract and our move to Zurich by telling him about me.

The day after we learned of Drese's decision I flew to Madrid for a television program. Late at night I called Giselle, and she had more alarming news. Near midnight she had come home from a performance to find the fire brigade in front of our apartment house. Someone had entered the building, which was normally locked at night, poured gasoline down three flights of steps, then lit it from the bottom and disappeared.

Luckily a man visiting upstairs neighbors left as the fire started. He sounded the alarm and the fire brigade got the fire out. A few more minutes delay, the fire chief said, and the building would have been gutted. The arsonist was never discovered. Some neighbors suspected a derelict who had been sleeping around our building, but I wondered—maybe a free-lanced terrorist or one of the neo-Nazi groups?

Giselle lost the Zurich job because of me, then almost immediately received an offer from the Basel Opera Ballet. But the problems hadn't ended. She became ill again, had an operation that turned out unnecessary, then couldn't fulfill the Basel contract. So we had a relaxed vacation in Salzburg where friends were performing at the music festival, then returned to Hamburg where Giselle continued recuperating and eventually started a training program.

I went back to Managua in the fall for a solidarity conference organized by the Anti-Imperialist Tribunal of Our America (TANA), the same group that had helped organize my trip to Nicaragua two years before. They had changed "Central America" in the name to "Our America"—an expression taken from a famous essay by José Martí to distinguish Latin from Anglo America. The Tribunal had also expanded beyond Central America and now had chapters in many Caribbean and South American countries.

TANA published a quarterly magazine, *Soberanía*, which carried a "Naming Names" column identifying CIA people in Latin America and the Caribbean. I had written several articles for the magazine, which was now appearing in English-Spanish format. Among Tribunal members were Juan Bosch, former President of the Dominican Republic, and Guillermo Toriello, Foreign Minister in the 1950's Guatemalan goverment of Jacobo Arbenz. The CIA had a major role in the overthrow of both their governments, and many other conference delegates were victims of CIA operations in their countries. I joined the U.S. delegation which included John Stockwell and staff members of the *Covert Action Bulletin.*

By now the CIA's "contra" operation was completely public, with press reports carrying the details of Reagan's formal National Security Council decisions and the amounts of money approved. Nicaraguan intelligence estimated 4000 to 5000 "contras" of the so-called FDN (Nicaraguan Democratic Force—the former Somoza National Guardsmen) were operating along the Honduran border. These were organized in "task forces" that crossed the border for raids against rural towns and cooperatives, then crossed back to bases in Honduras. Another, much smaller "contra" force operated from bases in Costa Rica under the leadership of Eden Pastora.

The Reagan administration, in particular the CIA, had no illusions about the "contras" overthrowing the FSLN and the revolution. In two years of operations they had failed to take and hold even a small village. The strategy was to stop revolutionary development projects in all fields: economic development, education, health services, and political organization. Tactics adopted to achieve this end were destruction of cooperatives, state farms, schools and health clinics; terrorism in the countryside and kidnapping of peasants; and sabotage of the economic infrastructure.

By forcing the Sandinistas to divert resources from development projects to defense, and by disrupting the economy, the revolution could not deliver on promises of a better life for the poor. On the contrary, the beneficiaries of the revolution would be made to suffer in the hope that they would eventually tire of war and turn against the FSLN.

Another goal of Reagan's strategists was to force the FSLN to take action against counter-revolutionary institutions such as *La Prensa*, the AIFLD-sponsored trade unions, and sectors of the Catholic Church. Each restriction would then be used in the international propaganda campaign to "prove" that Nicaragua was becoming ever more "totalitarian." The desired result: weakening of progressive and liberal international support for the revolution, particularly of European Social Democrats.

Nicaragua had become a laboratory for Reagan's worldwide counter-revolutionary policy of "low intensity conflict," one of the most cynical euphemisms ever to come out of Washington. That city, in fact, was the only place where the war was "low intensity," from the luxury of the Oval Office to the panelled suites of the Senators and Congressmen who voted the money.

For the victims of Reagan's "contra" terrorists the war was anything but "low intensity"—pregnant women impaled with bayonets, children maimed, people of both sexes with genitals amputated, eyes gouged out, then summarily executed.

In the days before the TANA conference CIA paramilitary teams had blown up, for the second time, the Pacific coast offshore petroleum unloading facility at Puerto Sandino. It happened just after an Exxon tanker from Mexico had unloaded, and Exxon was considering suspending deliveries. Agency maritime teams had also destroyed several fuel storage tanks at the port of Corinto, also on the Pacific coast.

TANA arranged for delegates to visit Corinto just a week after the attack. Security officials told us the destroyed tanks contained diesel fuel and molasses, but the attackers had missed several tanks containing aviation fuel. Had these been hit, thousands of the city's population would probably have been trapped with no escape.

Nicaraguans did not believe these sophisticated attacks were carried out by the "contras" as the FDN had claimed. Rather, they thought they were special teams of CIA specialists operating from "mother ships" offshore. They were right. Press reports later revealed that these teams, known in the CIA as UCLAs (Unilaterally

Controlled Latin Assets), operated under direct CIA supervision carrying out operations for which the FDN would later claim credit. The
mining of Nicaraguan harbors in 1984 was another UCLA operation.

The three-day conference consisted of speeches by delegates, visits
to sites of "contra" raids, and briefings by Nicaraguans on the effect of
the war. Lenin Cerna, the National Security Chief, displayed various
U.S. arms captured from the "contras" along with unexploded mines
from the Puerto Sandino operation. He also brought to the conference a former pilot of Somoza's air force whose "contra" aircraft had
recently been shot down while on a re-supply mission. We questioned the captured pilot who admitted, among other things, that the
CIA paid him $2000 per month and that he flew from the Aguacate air
base in Honduras.

On the final day of the conference I gave a speech in which I called
for the launching of a continental front against CIA personnel wherever in Latin America they could be identified. It wasn't enough, I
said, to reveal their names and backgrounds in publications like
Soberania. Mass action was needed: at embassies, at their homes, at
rallies demanding their expulsion. In accusations against me the
Agency admitted how terrified they were of this prospect, and we
should make it a reality.

Every CIA officer and employee in Latin America, I said, was
working in one way or another, like the gears of a clock, to support
the war against Nicaragua, and the repression in El Salvador and
Guatemala. Every one of them was just as important to the war
against Nicaragua as those training the "contras" in Honduras. Solidarity groups in every Latin American and Caribbean country should
organize to return blow for blow against CIA people in response to
their aggression and support for repression. It's up to us, I said, to
show Reagan and his political police that aggression against Nicaragua
will have high costs elsewhere. The delegates gave me a standing ovation.

At the closing ceremony that night Carlos Nunez, President of the
Council of State and member of the FSLN National Directorate,
broke the news of the most recent "contra" atrocity. The day before, a
"task force" of 250 to 300 "contras" attacked the village of Pantasma in
the north, killing thirty-two people. Most were unarmed peasants,
and six of the dead were teachers. The health center, food storage
facilities, coffee collection station, adult education center, tractors
and domestic animals all were destroyed.

The other tragic news that night was confirmation that Maurice

Bishop, Jacqueline Creft, Unison Whiteman and others I had known in Grenada were dead. Reports were sketchy, without many details, but it looked like the NJM had split and that Bishop had been on the losing side. I couldn't believe it, didn't want to. A few days before, on a stopover in Havana en route to Managua, someone had told me of trouble in Grenada. But this? Bishop and the other leaders dead? That's the end, I thought, nobody can pick up the pieces after this. What a goddamned tragedy.

Many asked what role, if any, the CIA might have had in the NJM split and collapse of the revolution. From the news at the time, and from all the later revelations, I never thought they were involved. The problems were internal, it seemed to me, with no need for an outside hand.

Under a pall of gloom several of us in the U.S. delegation to the TANA conference began discussing additional solidarity work with Nicaragua. Someone mentioned the possibility of organizing volunteer production brigades—like the *Venceremos* brigades that for years had been going to Cuba to cut cane and work on construction projects. At that moment Nicaraguan schools were going on vacation, and nearly 30,000 students had already volunteered to pick coffee, tobacco and cotton. Would North Americans respond to a call for volunteers?

We thought the chances were good. Several hundred U.S. citizens were already working more or less permanently in the revolution, had their own loose organization, and picketed the U.S. Embassy every Thursday morning. Another group, sponsored by various U.S. churches and called Witness for Peace, kept a permanent vigil in towns near the Honduran border that were regularly under attack.

I was staying on a few days and I agreed to speak to the FSLN about the idea. Then came Reagan's invasion of Grenada and the certainty that my passport would soon be annulled. I spoke to Bayardo Arce, the FSLN National Secretary, and to Julio Lopez, the FSLN International Secretary, both of whom I knew from previous trips, about the volunteer brigades and my passport problems.

They both liked the idea of the brigades, and soon I was making arrangements with the solidarity organization, CNSP, which I relayed by telephone to my friend Dale Wiehoff in Minneapolis. Dale was well-connected with Nicaraguan solidarity in the U.S. and would get the first brigade going.

Within a couple of days I received a Nicaraguan passport. Once again I was the beneficiary of international solidarity. As in Grenada before, the Nicaraguans told me the passport was simply to help me keep working, which obviously required the ability to travel. It would be my travel document in the years ahead.

In Hamburg I mentioned the U.S. volunteer brigade at several solidarity rallies. Immediately the West German solidarity groups wanted to do the same, and they were followed by similar groups in other countries. I called CNSP and they agreed.

When we all arrived in Managua in mid-December, we numbered about 50 Americans and 150 Europeans. Giselle had stayed behind because she was dancing in France for several months, but my sons Christopher and Philip came. They were active in their university solidarity groups and with several friends had decided to spend the year-end vacation with the brigade.

The first day at our Managua assembly camp I saw a familiar face. It was Regina Fischer. Years before she had camped out on a hunger strike in front of the Home Office in London in protest against my deportation from Britain. Yes, in her seventies she was going to the mountains to pick coffee—in fact, she would be the doctor for the group of thirty to which I and my sons were assigned.

The Americans were a heterogeneous group from Vermont to California. We had bus drivers, a lawyer, a trade union official, community organizers, a self-taught Chinese linguist, Vietnam veterans, university professors, students and a former city mayor. The Nicaraguans assigned my group to *El Chaguitón*, a state farm taken over when the owner, a rich Somocista, fled to Miami. It was in the northern mountains about fifteen kilometers from the Honduran border, a region where 1500 to 2000 "contras" had recently infiltrated.

Before leaving Managua we all signed a telegram to Reagan informing him of our brigade. We added:

> We are aware that counter-revolutionary paramilitary forces organized, financed and directed by your administration have been carrying out terrorist operations that have cost the lives of over one thousand Nicaraguans during 1983. We are harvesting coffee precisely in the area where your forces have been operating.
>
> Our mission is one of peace and friendship between the people of the United States and Nicaragua. Your counter-revolutionary forces threaten this effort and our lives as well. We therefore demand that you withdraw all your forces operating in this country. Mr. President, just as you are responsible for the Nicaraguan lives being lost in terrorist attacks, you will be responsible for any injury or loss of life suffered by members of our group and other international volunteers.

We rode to the mountains in the backs of open dump trucks. Passing through Esteli, and all along the route, people waved and cheered, having already seen in the press and television that a "friendly" invasion from the U.S. and Europe was underway. As we began climbing the one-lane dirt mountain road, it was easy to see how hard it was for the Sandinistas to prevent infiltration by the "contras." The mountains were steep, rugged and covered with jungle.

Young militia escorts, AK-47's at the ready, rode with us, for it was perfect ambush country. The "contras" had attacked our farm a few months before, killing several workers and torching the warehouse. Now the area was supposed to be safe, but on arrival we found that our farm was an armed camp with a complete circular defense of trenches and foxholes.

The Sandinistas had converted *El Chaguitón* into a model farm. Where campesinos formerly slept on the ground, they now lived in frame barracks with two double-decker beds per room. Where no kitchen or dining room existed, the farm now had a large mess hall with kitchen. Showers and toilet facilities were also built, as was day-care center for children. The former owner's home was now a medical center.

We found about 800 people at the farm, roughly half campesinos and half secondary students. At the mess hall, which also served for assemblies, the FSLN representative and others gave us warm welcoming speeches. These were followed by a cultural program of folk and revolutionary songs, and a ballet with homemade costumes and choreography depicting the war against the "contras."

The war was close enough. The first few nights we could hear mortar and artillery fire in the distance, and from time to time our militia defenders, in trenches less than 100 meters from our barracks, fired bursts from their AK-47's. Each time we all jumped to the floor where we lay until it was over. Once, at about two in the morning, firing broke out from several different weapons with such intensity that I thought we were surely under attack. But it stopped, and as before one of the militia came around to say it was a false alarm.

Internationalists, students and campesinos: we slept, ate, worked and relaxed together, forming those short, intense friendships that will probably never be renewed, but never forgotten. Wake-up came at five, breakfast at six: beans and rice on a tortilla placed on the hand. No plates or forks—everybody ate with their fingers. Then the march to work with militia escort along paths with views over valleys and mountains as far as one could see.

The first day at work we realized where we'd come: spider city! Big ones, huge ones, ugly monsters with enormous, strong webs. You couldn't walk around them. They were everywhere. The first few days, before we got accustomed to bringing the spiders and webs down with sticks, every three or four minutes a piercing shriek would cross the jungle and everyone would know: somebody else had just turned a face against a web loaded with spiders four to five inches across.

There were snakes too, but the growth was so thick you could never see if you were going to step on one. And also lovely green caterpillars, from one to four inches long, hiding on leaves and branches. The slightest touch would create a welt and severe stinging, sometimes swelling and near paralysis of an arm. A woman in our brigade, not at all interested in politics, had come merely to collect the creepy crawlies.

Picking the coffee beans was easy, one just had to remember to pick only *el rojito,* the ripe and red one. The others on the branch, ranging from light green to pink and yellow, would be picked a few weeks later on the next pass through. One had only to fill up the basket tied around the waist, then dump the berries in the *quintal* sack, then fill up the basket again.

Each day about noon the pick-up truck brought lunch out to the jungle: more beans and rice on tortilla. Then back to work until three, then the walk with militia back to camp for an ice-cold shower. Afternoons we spent in conversation with militia, students and campesinos, or reading, washing clothes, and tending to that day's bites. Almost everyone got bites from fleas that infest the coffee bushes but are too small to see. Bites, welts and insane itching.

Supper came at seven: nobody had to guess—beans and rice on tortilla in the hand. After a few days of this some of us would have murdered for a Big Mac. It was a good place to lose weight though, because if you weren't a true beans-and-rice junkie you just lost your appetite. The students and campesinos were no more enchanted with the diet than we foreigners, but that was all there was. For variety I started eating only rice for breakfast, beans for lunch, and a tortilla for supper, then reversing the order the next day.

Far-sighted Dale had suggested in Managua that we take some rum to camp. We did—almost enough for the whole brigade. Our little room became the *cantina,* and on New Year's Eve we had the world's tiniest discotheque. We crowded more people in that room than any circus car that ever poured out clowns. Rum was our potion for the wooden slats we slept on. It made the barracks feel like home when at nine we blew out the candle and called it a day.

In January we returned to Managua where we had a press conference to describe the experience. Not one member of the brigade disagreed that it had been uniquely rewarding, especially the things we learned from the students and campesinos. My own feeling was that if only enough Americans could share this kind of experience, they would never let Reagan continue the war. One thing was certain: the Nicaraguan revolution had given us far more of lasting value than the value of the coffee we picked. On leaving my identification with the revolution was stronger than ever.

The brigades continued in following years, both from the U.S. and from Europe, and volunteer programs for technicians and specialized workers developed. Internationalists continued working in the war zones until, after several were killed and others kidnapped, the Nicaraguans moved them to safer areas.

A couple months after Reagan's invasion of Grenada we had in Hamburg a Europe-wide conference of Grenadian solidarity organizations. Kenrick Radix, Bishop's Minister for Legal Affairs, came. He had missed execution because, as a Bishop loyalist, he was imprisoned during the final days of confusion. From him we learned of the continuing harassment, intimidation and interrogations of practically everyone involved in the revolutionary government. The CIA, according to Radix, had taken over a building in St. George's from which they ran their anti-communist propaganda campaign and brought people in for questioning.

One such person at the conference was Regina Fuchs, a doctor from Berlin who had been working in the St. George's hospital for nearly two years. A West German government aid program paid part of her salary. At the Grenadians' request I had interviewed her when she applied for the job and had made a favorable recommendation.

During three weeks following the invasion she had been treating casualties in the main St. George's hospital. Without warning U.S. soldiers arrested her, ransacked her home, and took her to the CIA building. From there she was taken to a cell in Richmond Hill prison.

For four days and nights she was held incommunicado with nothing to read, no sheets, no towel, no toothbrush, no idea why she was there. Every request to see a lawyer, a West German representative, or to notify her family was refused. Several times she was interrogated by U.S. civilian officials, undoubtedly CIA officers, who revealed detailed knowledge of her background in Berlin.

They made her tell the story of her life. They frightened her with suggestions that she was connected with international terrorists. And they even asked questions about her feeling towards U.S. troops stationed in West Germany. Then they asked her about me and my visits to Grenada. In the end she was released and given forty-eight hours to leave the island.

Other former international volunteers in Grenada told the conference about their arrests, interrogations and summary expulsions. Radix appealed for support. He and other surviving Bishop loyalists had established a foundation in the name of Bishop and the others killed with him. The foundation would help families of people killed in the invasion and would try to carry on some of the revolution's political education and social programs—nearly all of which were stopped by the U.S. occupation forces.

It was then that I offered to tour for a month, collecting money for the foundation at solidarity meetings. The Grenadian solidarity groups were small, but they got organizing and other support from Nicaraguan, Cuban, Salvadoran and various African solidarity groups. While on that tour, at the end of a meeting at the Louvain University in Belgium, a young man approached me. He started asking questions about my experiences in the South Pacific and other exotic places I had never been. I said I didn't know what he was talking about.

He then showed me a book and said, "It's right here." The book was in Dutch with a title called *The Paper Pistol Contract*.

I said, "Look. The author's name is Philip Atlee, not Philip Agee. That's not my book."

"But see? Here on the back it says Philip Atlee is the pseudonym Philip Agee used for this and another novel, *The Silken Baroness*."

I offered to buy the book, but he gave it to me. Then I checked, thinking maybe I should get some royalties. It turned out that a company in The Hague had published the two books, supposedly under license from a British company, but had closed its office with no forwarding address. I took the book home, placed it next to *Inside the Company*, and added "Novelist" to my résumé.

Nicaragua and El Salvador were my main themes at European solidarity meetings in the period ahead. One such rally, at the Hofgarten in Bonn, drew 25-30,000 people. Other speakers were Heberto Incer, the Nicaraguan Ambassador; Ana Guadelupe Martinez of the FMLN: and Willy Brandt, former Chancellor and SPD Chairman. The right-wing press later speculated that the reason Reagan refused to see Brandt, on the visit when he laid a wreath at graves of Nazi S.S. troops, was that Brandt had spoken at a rally with me.

When news leaked out that the CIA was providing huge amounts of money for the Duarte electoral campaign in El Salvador. I spoke of the real reasons for those elections. Besides creating a facade of democracy, the whole population outside FMLN areas was being computerized thanks to a $1 million Wang contributed by U.S. taxpayers. Those voter registration lists, with addresses and other personal data, would be invaluable to the CIA, the Salvadoran security forces and the death squads.

Within ten days of Reagan's bombing of the civil population in Tripoli, at least 20,000 people turned out in Bonn to express solidarity with the Libyan people and with Nicaragua. At that meeting I pointed out that, as in the aftermath of the Grenada invasion, polls showed 60-70 percent of the American people approved the bombing. Reagan, I said, had done his job well. Over six years his telegenic optimism had restored the aggressive spirit, like a continuing nationwide injection of the latest mood elevator, to the point of making a widespread Rambo syndrome respectable.

When the comic book on sabotage and arson produced by the CIA for the "contras" surfaced, followed shortly by surfacing of the Agency's "selective assassination" manual, I put them together, wrote an introduction, and got the package published in five languages.

One morning the postman brought a surprise letter. The return address was Micro Associates, P.O. Box 5369, Arlington, Virginia 22205. It was from someone named Daniel Brandt. It began,

Dear Mr. Agee,
I remember reading around seven years ago that you wanted to computerize published data on the CIA. At that time it wasn't feasible without a major investment in hardware and software. But now, with a microcomputer and the programs I have written, the task has been accomplished.

I smiled, almost in disbelief, and read on. Daniel Brandt was a Vietnam war draft resister who had become a computer programmer and technician. For the past several years he had worked quietly to produce an index, or data base, on the CIA and other elements of the U.S. security establishment. His index had nearly 15,000 names gleaned from about 100 books and numerous periodicals including the *Covert Action Bulletin* and major newspapers and magazines. All

3000 or so names that Lou or I had published would be there, but many more. His project looked just like the one I had in mind which got me expelled from France and Holland.

We exchanged letters. His motivation was to adopt high technology to the anti-imperialist struggle, and his product, available on floppy disks, was accessible to anyone who wanted it. All they had to do was write and send a modest, nominal fee for a set of disks. He thought, and I agreed, that journalists, researchers, political activists, even governments, could find the information valuable.

Brandt's project renewed my curiosity about computers and word processing, and with his encouragement I started reading and looking for a machine. As soon as I had it, he came to Germany and in ten days taught me everything I needed to know for writing books, articles and all my correspondence. In a flash my productivity soared, and I joined all those who wondered how they had ever lived without computing.

I asked Brandt if the "Intelligence Identities Protection Act" didn't worry him. He had taken legal advice. His index was based on already published materials, not new exposures. But it was not static. He returned to Arlington and continued adding and updating in the years ahead.

In the mid-1980's most of my energies went into research and writing for another book. After ten years of public meetings and innumerable conversations about the CIA, I felt strongly that the Agency was still a mystery for too many people. Despite all the books and articles, the Francovich film, and an untold number of published interviews with former CIA people, the questions people asked showed a surprising lack of understanding.

Too few people, especially university students and young activists in the peace movement, seemed to understand the CIA's role in American foreign policy, its aims and methods. Chief among the problems was a lack of historical perspicetive.

I proposed to Lyle Stuart a book I would call *The CIA for Beginners*. Such a book, I thought, might also serve as a guide for another of the comics series by the Mexican artist Eduardo del Rio, "Rius," who had already done *Marx for Beginners* and *Cuba for Beginners*. I would try to do it in question-and-answer form, basing the questions on those I most often got in conversations and public meetings.

Lyle liked the idea but wanted to know what ever happened to *On the Run*, the political autobiography he asked for years before. "Okay," I said, "I'll do that one too," and we signed a contract for both books. I started *The CIA for Beginners* by reading diplomatic histories of the post-World War II era, re-reading the many books written by former CIA officers, and reading still other books written by journalists and political figures about the Agency. Then I tried to place the Agency operations in historical context.

From the Agency's first paramilitary operations against Eastern Europe and the Soviet Union, its multi-million dollar intervention in the Italian elections, and its union bashing operations in France—all started in the 1940's—I could see the same methodology repeated. Nothing was surprising, since I had worked in operations, but the sheer mass of information left practically nothing to speculation.

The research I did consumed my attention because the Reagan administration was repeating so many of the failed policies of the 1940's and 50's. The so-called Reagan Doctrine of subverting revolutionary governments and movements, which he announced in 1985, was little more than a restatement of the 1947 Truman Doctrine. The "new interventionism" of the Reagan team was hardly new at all. The United States was simply carrying on earlier efforts to "manage the world" for the benefit of corporate America, to achieve the illusive "American Century" advocated in 1941 by publisher Henry Luce. Counter-revolution through the CIA was still a principal means.

The CIA for Beginners soon became a mammoth history project, and I bogged down just collecting materials. Three years after I started I still had only one-third of the first draft written, and I could see the end was not getting closer. At the Frankfurt Book Fair, the one time each year that Lyle Stuart and I could meet, we discussed my problems and agreed that I would switch to *On the Run* and then return to the history.

"But Lyle," I said, "We have to recognize that the Agency and all its friends will do everything to sabotage this book, and if I submit it for censorship they'll have plenty of time to prepare their campaign. They'll get out word for reviewers to ignore it, or write that it's an old story, or that it's just Agee's diatribe against the press. You'll see."

"Phil," Lyle said, "You may be surprised. Why don't you write it and let me get it out. You want to come home to promote it? You want to talk directly to Americans?"

"That's what I've always wanted."

"I'll do everything I can to bring you home."

XVI

S. S. Bahía de Santiago de Cuba: 15 Years On

I was writing *On the Run* when the fifteenth anniversary of my trip to Cuba aboard that rusted old Liberty Ship passed. As I reviewed diaries and files during those months, reliving so many experiences, recalling so many friendships, and remembering all the people who helped me along the way, I kept wondering what my life would have been without that help.

When I got on that ship in Canada, I didn't realize it and would have denied it, but in fact I was burning a bridge to the past. I had no grand plan and really didn't know where I was going. I only wanted to write a book and would take whatever risks were required to get it done. Beyond that all was darkness, a future I couldn't see, a path that didn't exist.

I thought I was my own person, that I was going to do it all alone. It was self-delusion. At every step, every crisis, someone was there to help. Far from acting alone, I hardly took a step without support. I realized that literally thousands of people had helped me, from the moment I stepped on that ship to this very day. That "whole world out there" meant there wasn't a country or major city where I wouldn't find people interested and anxious to help, ready to contribute their efforts, determined to fight for shared ideals.

When that ship took me to Havana in 1971 I had only the vaguest notion of the problems of socialist development. Soon I realized that the struggle to take power was only a first step, and that the real revolution was the hard part: political, economic, social, agrarian and fiscal reforms; development of education, health and housing programs; and defense against counter-revolution and foreign intervention.

With each trip back to Cuba I saw their remarkable progress in all these areas as well as their continuing problems. On balance, though, the revolution was enormously successful and retained overwhelming support. International agencies of all kinds praised Cuban programs in education and public health and their generous foreign aid projects.

It doesn't take a clairvoyant to see that Reagan's policy of aggression against Nicaragua, Grenada, Angola, Ethiopia, Mozambique and other young revolutionary states is designed to prevent those countries from equaling the Cuban success.

My unknown path that started with a ship passage is a personal story, but relevant to every CIA employee today. I wrote it because I wanted to show that a CIA employee, or former employee, can reconsider, take a stand, and survive.

Others have done it. John Stockwell, for one, wrote a detailed history of the CIA's 1970's intervention in Angola, a book of extreme relevance today. He has toured the entire United States pleading for rejection of covert interventions and for solidarity with Nicaragua, Cuba and other revolutionary movements. Ralph McGehee, for another, also wrote memoirs of his Agency career, joined the solidarity movement, and lectured widely. David McMichael, still another, exposed the sham pretexts for Reagan's war against Nicaragua and testified for Nicaragua in the International Court of Justice.

One can resign from the CIA and start a new life helping rather than hurting human beings. It need not mean a life in exile, expulsions from country to country, or revocation of your passport. Nor does it mean opprobrium or isolation. Condemnation will come, of course, from people and institutions that benefit from imperial control—and these include the establishment media.

Their criticism in understandable. Those who condemn a CIA

officer, or former officer, for revealing the truth are people who feel
threatened by movements for a fairer world. They are part of, or allied with, the 2 percent of American families who control over half the
net assets in the United States. They are the people who benefit from
the widening gap between rich and poor, who tolerate and benefit
from a system in which 14 percent of Americans, 33 million people,
live in poverty.

These are the people carrying out the beliefs of John Jay, the
Founding Father, President of the Continental Congress, and first
Chief Justice of the Supreme Court. Jay held, as Noam Chomsky
wrote in *Turning the Tide*, that "the people who own the country
ought to govern it." CIA employees hardly own the country, but as a
secret political police they certainly help those who do.

And for what? By mid-1986, according to Nicaraguan President
Daniel Ortega, Reagan's dirty war had caused 14,000 casualties
among those defending the revolution. With a population eighty
times greater, the comparable number for the U.S. would be
1,120,000—more than all U.S. casualties in World War II, and more
than three times the total number of American casualties in Viet
Nam. Casualties on the "contra" side have been even greater than
those of the defenders, bringing the total on both sides to 31,000. The
comparable figure for the U.S. is nearly 2.5 million, far more than the
1.9 million total for American casualties in every war since the War
Between the States. That's the five-year toll of Reagan's "low intensity conflict."

CIA employees who reject this policy should know that there is a
"whole world out here" ready to give the help and support you if you
take a stand. You will find the same approval I did, the same acceptance, the same loyalty I found in the peace movement and among
progressives and revolutionaries everywhere I went. And if you take a
strong and principled position, you will never regret it.

For more effective resistance to the Reagan Doctrine, the cruelty
of "low intensity conflict," and the "new cold war," present and
former CIA employees are needed now more than ever.

I hope this book will encourage some of them to join the international solidarity movement and to speak out on Agency deception and
promotion of terrorism. Those who join will not find enemies of the
American people, but enemies of a system that appropriates natural
resources, imposes mass poverty, and relies on political repression for
social control.

International solidarity is one of the actual and potential threats

most feared at top levels in Washington no matter who sits in the
White House. In late 1986 at the General Assembly of the Organization of American States, Secretary of State George Schultz expressed
this fear once again:

> Foreign intervention in the form of alien ideologies and foreign
> cadres—from Cuba, the Soviet Union, East Germany, North Korea,
> Viet Nam and Libya—is at this very moment promoting instability and
> violence in Central America. The only road to peace and stability is to
> eliminate that intervention.

The Reagan war, of course, has nothing to do with "foreign intervention, violence and instability." International solidarity in *support*
of Nicaragua is the source. That hypocrisy reminds one of the
justification for the invasion of Grenada: a "rescue operation" to save
American students who weren't in the slightest danger. The "alien
ideology" of which Schultz speaks is alien only to those whose security rests on U.S. control and dominance in Central America. To Nicaraguans the struggle for self-determination, that "alien ideology," is
their history.

During the year I wrote this book Giselle and I lived in southern
Germany where she began a teaching career with a municipal opera
and ballet company. U.S. bases with Pershing II missiles were next
door, and G.I.'s in fatigues roamed the streets. That was unsettling
enough, but we also received Armed Forces television with all the
U.S. network news broadcasts (or what passed for news), the current
events programs, and public affairs discussion programs.

After twenty-five years of almost continuous living abroad I could
hardly wait to play the tapes I pre-recorded each twenty-four hours.
Most interesting for me were the almost total lack of historical context, and the things that were *not* said.

If it is true that more than 90 percent of Americans get their news
from television, there can be little wonder so few know the central
issues of Central America, the Near East or southern Africa. And little wonder the Reagan administration can wage evil war against
Nicaragua, a small, impoverished country struggling to build a new
society, when polls show a vast majority of Americans opposed. Television news is show business, designed to entertain and, intentionally
or not, programmed to keep people ignorant.

Nevertheless, the prevailing opinion in the U.S. against the war in
Central America, against direct invasion and another Vietnam, and

against Reagan's support for racist South Africa—all these are signs of hope, signs that the Reagan years have not really turned the United States into a nation of Rambos, rednecks and hate mongers.

Popular reaction to Reagan's hypocritical arms-for-hostages dealings with Iran, and diversion of the profits to the "contras," is another sign of hope—hope that in the wake of this scandal Reagan will lose Congressional support for his wars against Nicaragua and other countries. Of course, those wars have been crimes from the first year of Reagan's administration, but even after six years the recognition that this is a criminal administration is welcome.

Investigations by Congress and the "independent counsel" will spare Reagan the Nixon path to ignominy, in the "higher interest" of preserving the office of the President, but loss of public confidence should greatly impede his ability to wage "covert" war. What a fitting historical irony: Reagan's obsession with destroying the Nicaraguan revolution brought on the crippling, if not destruction, of his own presidency.

My 1983 call for a continent-wide action front against the CIA's people in Latin America went nowhere. People had other preoccupations and priorities. With this book I make that call again.

North Americans, Latin Americans and Caribbeans should organize to find and fight the secret political police that directs Reagan's war. Our own research and publishing, together with mass mobilizations, could cripple the CIA in the Western Hemisphere and raise dramatically the cost of war against Central America.

Those who question whether such a program is realistic simply don't realize how easy it is to identify CIA people and how vulnerable they are abroad. Their own admissions in the legal statements against me ought to be proof enough of how fearful they are of exposure and mass action. Failure to act gives them an open field with little opposition.

In 1987 the CIA will have its 40th birthday. After so many years of covert interventions in Latin America, decades of military dictatorships, untold numbers of tortured and "disappeared," and socioeconomic systems increasingly serving the rich, there ought to be enough interested people to ensure a successful campaign.

Why not also in Africa where the CIA works daily in support of the South African security services?

It only takes the decision and the will.

INDEX

Introductory Comment: The author has mentioned several persons in the text using pseudonyms rather than actual names. These are people with whom the author was unable to discuss their inclusion in the book and whose anonimity he wishes to preserve. Their names in this index are followed by (PS).